PARADE

Tributes To Remarkable Contemporaries

Hon. Jerry S. Grafstein. Q. C

mosaicPRESS

To my son Laurence Grafstein and my grandsons, Daniel Aaron, Edward Adam and Isaac Morgan, who I hope, at least once in their careers will experience the joy of a stint in public service as I have. And to my son Michael Kevin, whose boundless love of people, young and old alike, and innate generosity is a marvel to behold.

Table of Contents

2001-2010

Introduction

I have always loved parades.

My first vivid memory as a four year old was watching a wonderful parade. Dressed in short brown English wool pants and white starched shirt, long brown itchy woolen stockings and tight shiny brown oxfords, my father perched me on his broad shoulders to get a good view.

While we waited for the parade, my father handed me a big delicious apple to munch on. The sidewalks were swarming with a restless cheerful crowd expecting the soldiers led by pipers to smartly march along the parade route on the narrow street in front of us.

From this vantage point, I could get a clear look at King George VI in his regal uniform, and Queen Elizabeth, his beautiful radiant queen, wearing a stylish hat with white tulle that my mother always favored, pinned on the side of her dark silky hair.

It was 1939 in London, Ontario, my birth place and home town, just months before the outbreak of WWII. The Royals were there as part of their cross Canada visit. They drove past us slowly in a stately long black open shiny limousine and turned, waving at me! That picture remains alive in my memory.

So I came to love parades, all kinds of parades. Marching as a cadet officer in my high school army cadet brigade before the famed Major General Rockingham of the "Princess Patricia's" stationed in London, later to lead Canadian troops in Korea. Any Santa Claus parade, Caribana, the colorful parade in downtown Toronto; St. Patrick's Day parade in New York City; the parade of colorful scantily clad dancers at the Brazilian Ball where my wife and her friends were so actively engaged for decades; any military or police parade; especially with bagpipes. And, yes, the Labour Day and Gay Pride Day parades. I just love a parade, any parade.

As a parade aficionado, you observe, up close, a wide range of people from every walk of life having a grand time strutting their stuff in unison. All individuals turned into marchers, as do spectators, tend to act and react in waves and in unison, as trained, disciplined crowds, each moving together as if on an invisible cue!

What does the love of parades have to do with the Senate of Canada where I served over a quarter of a century?

The Senate, when in session, starts with a solemn traditional parade of Senate officers led by the Chief Usher carrying the mace, followed by the Speaker and Clerks clad in their tri-corner black hats and black robes. Once the gold embossed mace is placed on the table separating the Government Senators from the Opposition, the Speaker mounts the podium where the Speaker's tall red throne-like chair awaits and commences the daily proceedings.

The Senate of Canada, following the antique precedent of the House of Lords and the American Senate, provides in the Orders of the Day a short period, near the start of every sitting, for Senators to rise and pay concise tributes to their contemporaries, especially on their retirement or death, to note, for the record, a noteworthy achievement or anniversary of an outsider. Some take on the antique Latin form called "eloges" - tributes to commemorate "the illustrious dead".

When I came to the Senate, I found these tributes informative in both substance and style, offering a compelling insight into interesting public figures, both the speakers and their chosen subjects.

For me, it was history in the raw. A historic passing parade of famous and not-so-famous figures, most of who by their contributions large and small, left their imprint, light or heavy, via parliamentary history.

I took to reading old Senate Hansards to gain a deeper context and a deeper understanding of the interests of my predecessors. I found them fascinating, a fount of information and insight not otherwise available in our history books. History, like an onion, has different layers. If you suffer from curiosity, as I always have, you can peel away each layer. As you do, a clearer, vibrant, picture of players and events emerges as they occurred, or in reality as they are freshly remembered. Usually, personalities are ripped out of context so reading these snapshots gives one a rawer, closer view of history as it happened.

In the course of studying the history of Parliament and parliamentary democracy to better grasp my role as Senator, I was introduced to the works of the English historian, Sir Lewis Namier.

The late John Stewart, a senatorial colleague, a former Member of the Commons and a respected scholar of politics, was a recognized expert on David Hume. John Stewart became a fountain of political lore and intellectual history. He led me to this curious English historian, Sir Lewis Bernstein Namier, who immediately resonated with me and my roots.

Namier was the rare exception to British historians, especially those that dwelled on parliamentary history. Most histories focus on parliamentary leaders, like Gladstone or Peel or Disraeli or, of course, Churchill, or legislative landmarks, like the Reform Act of 1842, or external wars or domestic upheavals like the Cromwell era and the restoration, the American Revolution, the Conscription debates or technological progress like railways or shipping or telegraph, or manufacturing innovations like the cotton mill, or steel fabricating, or military modernization, all of which Parliament served as a pale backdrop. Not often is Parliament explored as the cockpit of pivotal events or the centre stage of great events. Rarely mined, Parliament is made up of a diverse class of interesting men and women from all aspects of civil society.

Namier dug deep into the personal histories of Members of Parliament. He uncovered this unexplored aspect of the intricate interpersonal networks, the inner workings of daily political life. In his laborious painstaking work, like an archeologist, he dug down deep. In this process he excavated, and exposed the heart, the unwritten sinews and origins of factions that then morphed slowly into modern political parties as we see them today.

Political parties are constantly forming and reforming, even in their present configurations. Personalities tether these disparate individuals together in an almost invisible way, all seething with ambitions. Cabals, cliques, always shifting, transform into factions, then caucuses emerge, parties are formed and lie at the core of modern party politics. Loyalty to the leader and the caucus became and remains the mainsail of our responsible government. Lewis demonstrates how "confidence" the often used but scarcely understood word, played and still plays such a crucial role in parliamentary democracy today.

The leader needs the confidence of his caucus to sustain his party vote for his government's legislation in Parliament. Without his party's support on major measures, the leader loses his legitimacy to govern.

Namier painstakingly mapped out how leaders gained and maintained the "confidence" of their ever restive, ambitious, followers.

He uncovered the vanities, the rivalries within party factions and how these personal squabbles and contests played out against parliamentary and legislative outcomes. Namier's protégé was the more famous historian, A.J.P. Taylor , a self-defined "progressive" whose works on history are based on the "great man theory" rather than the grass roots, bottom up, approach instigated by Namier. In 1953, Taylor wondered, "What is it that such individual authors as, say, Sir Lewis Namier, E.H. Carr and Hugh Trevor-Roper, have in common? Great scholarship, of course; but also literary mastery, insight and clearer convictions. A work of history, like any other book that is good, must bear its author's stamp. The reader should feel that no one else could have written this particular book in this particular way."

In reviewing another book by Namier, *Diplomatic Prelude 1948*, a historic depiction of diplomacy leading to WWII, Taylor wrote this about his mentor and now rival colleague: "you can find in Namier the more humdrum truth, discreditable no doubt to both sides in the negotiations - not discreditable from wickedness or sinister intention [but] discreditable from shortsightedness, vanity and ignorance."

Sir Lewis was considered an eccentric and a contrarian by his peers. Both these attributes attracted him to me. He questioned conventional wisdom. He chose to go against the grain, perhaps because that was the only way to gain recognition from his peers. Fiercely independent in his personality and opinions, he wrote with precision and always surprising insight.

Born Ludwig Nemorowski in 1888 in southern Poland, then a part of the Czarist Russian Empire, he immigrated to England in 1908. He became a British subject and, in the process, reinvented himself, changing his name to Lewis Bernstein Namier. He studied at Balliol College at Oxford (as did my older son, Laurence) whose alumni became storied leaders in Parliament. In due time, Namier, while often disliked for his brittle personality, became one of Britain's acknowledged historians. For the first time, a historian delved deeply into the infrastructure and workings of Parliament through the detailed biographies and interests of its members. Its practices became precedents and, hence, the traces of the unwritten constitution of the mother Parliament and England.

Parliament cannot be separated from its membership. Parliament is its membership. Parliamentarians are so often criticized but rarely studied and less understood. So the Lords in England and Senate in Canada are lacerated and scarred by the appointment process and lapses in probity, yet rarely measured by the essential careful work they do since the cash strapped and tweeting media focuses on only scandals or crises in the Upper Chamber and rely on sound bites rather than analyses.

Rarely is the fastidious inglorious painstaking review of the minutiae of flawed Commons legislation considered. Legislation, unread and unnoticed, is usually whipped through the Commons or, worse, understood. This scandalous practice has been exacerbated of late in Parliament by numerous bills attached to Budgets pushed for a swift up or down vote with little or no oversight. Responsible government absconds in this shoddy process.

The Senate, like the Lords, remains a Blackstonian check and balance on the amorphous popular will. The Senate's detailed painstaking review of piles of obtrusive legislation is overlooked, except "in extremis" where flaws or controversy in legislation, and hurriedly passed in law by the Commons, rarely reach or attract public attention. The making of the "rule of law" the backbone of parliamentary democracy is most often ignored. The minutiae of law making suffers from benign neglect in the cyber world. Respect for the "rule of law" and respect for the authority of the "rule of law" is the linchpin of civic society. Pull that linchpin and civic society descends to chaos.

The constitutional role Senate plays as one of the three essential legs to parliamentary legislation is rarely fully comprehended or even considered. The Commons, the Senate, each divided by Party, and the Executive as represented by the Cabinet, are the three essential players in our parliamentary democracy.

Of course, the fourth most neglected player is the Crown. the Queen in Canada, represented by the Governor General who, by Royal Assent , transforms legislation, passed by the two Houses of Parliament, into the law of the land, when sitting in the Senate by written assent of each piece of legislation. Assent remains an unexplored core foundation of Canadian responsible government.

Namier focused on Members of the English Commons. He demonstrated how the English Parliament interacts with the Upper Chamber and the Executive, an engine of democracy that works remarkable well and corrects itself by its internal mechanisms. When any check is demonstrably abused, maligned or flawed, the common law of Parliament somehow repairs the damage and grinds on, slowly to be sure, but inevitably. Reform never stops in a functioning parliamentary democracy. The Rules Committees' work never ceases. Explicit rules or precedents, like the common law, are in a constant state of reform. The human condition given to errant conduct needs rules and constant modernization and renovation to curb excesses.

Namier's leading work on *The Structure of Politics in the Accession of George III* diligently researched each Member of Parliament, then drew the threads of their collective actions into groups, then factions, then parties.

Namier strung together from these many human stories a coherent history of the workings of Parliament. Later he wrote the majestic *The History of Parliament* in series starting in 1940 when Parliament was in peril under the Nazi threat.

Namier himself had a most fascinating career. After a brief stint in the British army during WWI, where he was let go because of poor eyesight, he joined the Foreign Office as an expert on Eastern Europe, especially Poland. As a result of this expertise, he served on the British Delegation to the Versailles Treaty in 1919.

When I read more about Namier, my curiosity in him became even more aroused. My late father, Solomon Grafstein, who also was born in Southern Poland, served as a volunteer in the Polish Army in WWI and later returned to serve in the Pilsudski Brigades that gave birth to Polish independence, especially in the Battle of Warsaw in 1920 after defeating the invading Red Bolshevik Army led the infamous Leon Trotsky. The Bolshevik forces suffered their first defeat with superior forces on their side on the outskirts of Warsaw in 1920, considered one of the great battles of modern times. Namier was an opponent of that fledgling independent Polish state.

As a diplomat, Namier was instrumental in redrawing the Curzon line called by detaching Lwow, known in Yiddish as Liviv, from Poland. But his career took another interesting turn. He had been an ardent Zionist for years, another trait that endeared him to me but did not endear him to his teaching colleagues. Having met Chaim, the leading Zionist of his era, then a research scientist at University of Manchester where Namier had begun to teach history, he worked for a period for the Jewish Agency, the bureaucrat organism of the nascent Jewish state, from 1929 to 1931.

Weizmann was Head of the Zionist Congress that mandated the Jewish Agency as the organizing seed of the State of Israel. It was Chaim Weizmann, now discarded as Head of the Zionist Congress but a mesmerizing, symbolic figure who later convinced Truman in 1947 to recognize the Jewish state despite State Department and General George Marshall's deep-seated antagonism and objections and yes, anti-Semitism. Weizmann became the first President of the nascent State of Israel.

Namier and Weizmann, once intimate friends, had a falling out after Namier's first wife died. Namier married a gentile woman and converted to Anglicanism. From 1931 to 1953, he taught history at Manchester University. He remained an ardent Zionist throughout his life. Churchill admired Namier's work. Namier lobbied Churchill actively to establish a fighting Jewish force within the British Army in mandated Palestine. This built on the earlier work of Churchill in WWI where a small Jewish cadre was formed into a mule company. It was these links that formed the fighting spirit of the Israel Defense Forces and led to the creation of the Haganah, first underground then, after the state was proclaimed in 1947 as Israel's First Armed Service, the Israel Defense Force. Churchill, from the start of his legendary career, became and remained a lifelong Zionist.

Namier, although considered a conservative, was the mentor of A.P.J. Taylor, considered one of Britain's most brilliant historians and a confessed liberal.

Isaiah Berlin, a leading liberal thinker and writer, a colleague at Oxford, described Namier as "one of the most remarkable men I have ever known: his immediate intellectual ... and (his) moral impact was such that even those who, like myself, met him infrequently, are unlikely to forget it."

Namier's original work, rooted in the turbulent politics of the 1760s in England and focused on the origins of party politics, remains unsurpassed as a teaching tool of politics. He magnified the fluidity of party politics, less motivated by the myth of common principle than the practice of personal ambition and the individual quest for power which remain the heartbeat of the political pulse today. The human condition has not changed. Politics does not change. These influences remain, intact, though distorted by today's 24 x 7 news cycles, and continue to attract and mystify.

Politicians do not change, inspired as they are primarily by self-interest and careerism. The dualism in politics, the bipolarism is seen as politicians resonate between ambition and rationalization, rooted in party principle practiced more by the expediency of the exception rather than adherence to a pristine belief structure or principles. That belief structure, loosely embodied by party, colors each parliamentarian's world view and perceptions. Facts give way to desire and wishful thinking. My eldest grandson, Daniel Aaron Grafstein, in his Honor Thesis at Harvard College in 2015 wrote an excellent paper on this topic "Wishful Thinking and the Belief in a Just World - An Exploration". Rationalization and loyalty give the practicing politician comfort food for his besotted conscience.

In recent times, the amorphous word "values" that can mean anything and everything has replaced the word "principles", less opaque and less subject to manipulation. Arguing "values" is the last refuge of wishful muddy rationalization. "Values", using Orwellian argumentation, is a political word, like all political words is so elastic it can mean whatever the speaker desires it to mean. It fits any amorphous argument. Shared "values" are so narrow. Yet conflicted "values" are used to paint over contradictory or opaque meaning. Whenever a politician proclaims that a policy or program meets "values", it means he cannot define his polemic. I prefer the politics of principles. It seems that "principles" and "convictions" and "character", formerly the essence of politics, has dissipated into the maw of cyberspace and "sound bites". Perception has become "reality."

David Hume in his various books explored the nature of human conduct and held curbing self interest lies at the heart of virtue in public service.

John Stewart convinced me that Hume's works were primus for all politicians to separate vice from virtue in all choices.

Namier pruned then knitted together these common threads that resonate, issue by issue, and influence the twists and turns of all questions in political life. Namier was a vitriolic opponent of appeasement, a view I came to understand and share. It was his contrarianism, however, that attracted me. I commend his writings to those who have the patience with the intricacies and complexity of politics, and for those who maintain an interest in the underpinnings of democracy and how it actually works.

To those with greater forbearance, I recommend a companion book written by Elias Canetti, a Nobel Prize winner in Literature, who, in the throes of Nazism, wrote *Crowds and Power*, how individuals irrationally yet rationally unite and, in this union of individuals within groups, move in common if at times with irrational but common purpose. One can only appreciate this if one becomes aware as a member of such crowds, is liberated of its restraints and is then able to dissect this phenomenon.

Once free of these binding links, it is easier to understand how an individual is transformed, and transforms the crowd, and is swept in to become a functioning member of a crowd, or a party. The need to belong and the thirst for upward mobility with the group becomes overwhelming, obtrusive yet comforting. To become a member of the inner sanctum of the caucus gives one a strange feeling of empowerment.

Parties may best be described as tribes with a definite hierarchical structure, laced with dissension and tension within the ranks of each tribe, as individuals and groups vie for upward mobility, position, notoriety and power. Are parties "movements"? Hardly. But a "movement" can be evoked in whatever form, but, it too, is a passing parade.

The passing parade never stays still, and is always on the move.

This modest offering of short tributes are reprinted as a reflection on Parliamentarians and others whom I encountered and who influenced politics and me in my time. These thumbnail sketches are reprinted from the original in the Senate Hansard and elsewhere without deletion or editing. The weary reader may find the repetition of phrases exhausting or, worse, boring. But it is the best source of remembrance. Most were written and delivered hastily because of the exegesis of time. All fault for repetition and errors lies with the author. Done, as they were, usually on short notice with little research.

Caveat lector. I urge the patient reader's forgiveness. I have added a speech on David Croll, whom I articled as a law student and whom I came to serve with in the Senate. As well, a eulogy of Fernand Cadieux printed in Le Devoir, written by me and translated from English into French by Claude Ryan, and an essay by Roy Fabish on Ferdinand Cadieux, all three indelible influences on me and my politics. I have added a paper I prepared and delivered to the Allan J. MacEachen Annual Lecture on politics at St. Xavier University in New Brunswick that I helped to establish. This paper will provide a wider context towards my understanding of the central role of members and party caucuses.

I was privileged to attend Federal Liberal Caucuses from the '60s until 2010, first as a guest under Mr. Pearson, and then as a serving Senator under Prime Ministers

Trudeau, Turner, Chrétien, Martin and under two Liberal leaders, Stephan Dion and Michael lgnatieff, as well as interim leaders, Herb Gray and Bill Graham. "Caucus" remains the unsung core of power in Parliament.

The master Member of all Liberal caucuses in both Houses of Parliament was, in my view, The Hon. Allan J. MacEachen. For this reason, I have added for the reader's edification an introduction to Allan MacEachen at a dinner to commemorate his retirement from the Senate, his last membership in Parliament after a half century in public service

For me, the debate about the driver of history between Namier and Taylor collides. Taylor, in an essay entitled *The Historian as a Biographer* wrote: "Not long ago: Namier and others set out to compile brief biographies of Members of Parliament." Taylor, a believer in the great man theory of history, having written an astounding biography of Bismarck went on:

> "This": Namier claimed, "would be a history of Parliament." I asked him whether this history should not rather be sought in the parliamentary debates and the resolutions and bills which Parliament passed. Namier brushed me aside. "History," he insisted, "is to be found the biographies of innumerable ordinary men."

Allan J. MacEachen was no ordinary man. Born of humble origins in Inverness, Cape Breton, Nova Scotia, he was a brilliant scholar. He became superbly educated, first at St. Francis Xavier University in Nova Scotia, then at University of Toronto in Economics. He went on to continue his studies after teaching economics to University of Chicago and M.I.T. (Massachusetts Institute of Tenchology). A storied political career as adviser first to Mr. Pearson and then Minister, he held numerous cabinet posts. A highlight was his tenure as Minister of National Health and Welfare when Medicare was created in Canada in the 1960s.

MacEachen was a superb master of the arcane rules of Parliament. A gifted legislator with a storied record of liberal legislation and amongst the most gifted parliamentary debaters of his and perhaps anytime in Canada's parliamentary history. A good strong speaker, he was mesmerizing in the confines of Parliament.

He was a marvel to listen to in caucus, whether the national weekly National Liberal caucus or the Senate caucus. After his retirement from the Commons, I served in the Senate under Allan's skillful leadership. When he slowly rose to speak, whether in caucus or in Parliament, Allan started quietly, softly, almost in a soft feminine voice, waiting for the audience to pause and listen. Then, as he caught the attention of caucus, as he built his case, his voice moved down to deeper masculine octaves and held his audience in thrall as they became convinced of his arguments, sometimes despite themselves. Slightly bending to face those in his audiences who responded, his hands and arm moving in gentle graceful circles for emphasis as he drew the listener closer ever into his oratorical orbit. Dressed in a dark suit, white shirt and dark tie, it was his dark thick hair and eyes and brooding sincere Celtic face that attracted his listeners and held them with his enveloping voice. As his argument was built, step by step, he would smack a backhand against an open palm for greater emphasis. And sometimes, his pauses, his silences, had even greater impact than his words. He waited until his words sunk in.

I was always amazed how Allan could weave a consensus out of the disparate views in the Senate caucus. Yet, out of the confines of the parliamentary precincts, he was "an ordinary man." This is a crucial element to understanding Parliament. There might have been some merit to Pierre Trudeau's outburst for the most part that Members of Parliament are "nobodies" outside of Parliament "when they are 50 yards from Parliament Hill, they are no longer honourable members, they are just nobodies." Within the confines of Parliament, each and every member is a "somebody." Perhaps current parliamentary history is changing, but it is still too early to opine. For it's not what members did before, it's how they make their individual contributions in Parliament.

For my tributes delivered in the Senate and elsewhere during my 26 year tenure in Parliament, composed of those in both the Commons and the Senate and other figures, I offer my appreciation to those who have served as the unwitting subject of my observations on their lives. History is fabricated by many coats of verbiage, some bright and glistening, others dull and colorless. The reader will decide. Any and all faults lie with the author.

I disagree with John Galbraith, a self-professed "true grit" born in southwestern Ontario, not far from my home town, whom I knew and admired, and who once wrote "politics is the art of choosing between the disastrous and the unpalatable." I hope you will too!

If the reader sense these tributes or "eloges" reek with too much praise, I follow the advice of my two rabbinic masters, the "Sfas Emes, A.H.L.," the "Mouth of Truth," and the seventh Lubavitch Rebbi, M.M. Schneerson, A.H.L., both of whom taught to accentuate the positive impressions of others. So I have painted these subjects with light impressionist, at times, primary colours, coating over the darker or grayer character or record of the subject matter.

I have added three speeches that demonstrate two historical and intellectual interests that might attract the reader's curiosity: *Winston Churchill as a Liberal,* and *Winston Churchill as a Zionist.*

Winston Churchill, the most remarkable Parliamentarian of this or any age, remains the object of my admiration and study.

Having twice met with lengthy encounters the Seventh Lubavitch Rebbe, the late M.M. Schneerson, I retell the little known story of the Rebbe's key role in the Soviet dissident movement. The Rebbe A.H.L. was another major influence on my thoughts and actions.

Penultimate additions are: my first speech in the Senate called the Maiden Speech, and The Farewell Address, my final speech in the Senate in response to speeches by my Senate colleagues on my retirement after over a quarter of a century. Modesty does not prevent me from including these generous speeches. These also provide an aggregation of tributes to those in the Senate and elsewhere that so informed my political life.

I have included my contribution to the Debate in the Senate on Meech Lake to illustrate the interplay of Parliamentarians and Policy. I was involved in organizing Pierre Trudeau's last appearance in Parliament for the Meech Lake debate in the Senate when he came out of retirement for only one time. His speech, questions and answers, were my most moving experience in Parliament. Curious readers should read of that speech and the ensuing debate. It was an example of the Senate as a House of Parliament at its finest.

Two essays on citizen events which I co-organized as a volunteer: Canada Loves New York in New York City and Romancing the Stones in Toronto, are included to demonstrate the crowding spirit of volunteerism deep in the Canadian DNA that I discovered always to my surprise and delight.

I have added a eulogy to an old friend, David Nugent, a decorated British soldier, and a tribute to the late Jim Coutts who played a signal role in the Liberal Party from 1961 when we first became friends until his recent untimely departure.

To conclude, I have added two final addenda:

My contribution to a book called *"Pierre"* edited by Nancy Southam, *"Reflections by Those Who Knew or Worked by Pierre Trudeau"*; and my take on *"Elusive Destiny: The Political Vocation of John Napier Turner"*, a remarkable biography by Paul Litt. I had the privilege of working closely with these two outstanding political leaders and Parliamentarians, both of whom formed essential aspects of my political career.

I remain indebted to Mary de Toro, my last Assistant in Ottawa and Larraine Chong, my Assistant in Toronto, for their patience in preparing on the fly these tributes, and to Selma Davidson, the most capable Librarian at Minden Gross LLP, who assembled the bulk of these tributes from her laborious research of Senate Hansards, by no means a congenial task. Naaznin Pastakia, my current assistant, has provided remarkable help in assembling this book.

I want to thank my friend, Ed Cowan, who urged me to complete this miscellany of Tributes, Eulogies, Introductions, Speeches and Essays of remarkable men and women.

My appreciation to Mosaic Press, Howard Aster and Matt Goody for their infinite patience and creative ideas without which this book would not have been possible.

And, finally, words to those who encouraged me to publish this book and bare no responsibility whatsoever for its reception. "Print is indelible," a wise and good friend once opined; I alone should be the receptacle of Gutenberg's chagrin.

Jerry Grafstein
February, 2016

FERNAND CADIEUX: EULOGY IN *LE DEVOIR* (IN THE ORIGINAL ENGLISH) WAS THIS COUNTRY TOO SMALL FOR HIM?

BY JERRY S. GRAFSTEIN
March 8, 1976

How many great minds can we count in Canada or for that matter in the world?

How many great minds, without leaving important or imposing works, have been capable of such an instantaneous and profound influence on the people around them that upon just being in their presence, one is transformed in a manner that is inalterable and forever. Socrates, perhaps Plato, were such minds. Fernand Cadieux was another.

On the 21st of February 1976, at the Saint Charles de Vanier church, a large circle of friends, including Pierre Trudeau, met to say a quiet, peaceful adieu to Fernand Cadieux. Following the simple ceremony with relatively little pomp and speeches, I reflected on how little I actually knew about his history, the roots which shaped his amazing personality, his life. But I also realised how little that mattered. It was enough for me to recall the memories and recollections of the time I spent in his company.

One or two hours spent with Fernand Cadieux was like a month's worth of intellectual challenges. Each time I left a session, I felt completely physically drained, but at the same time strangely invigorated and replenished intellectually.

His method was quite simple. With enormous modesty, he gently managed to take an idea, a thought, a concept and amplify it, develop it, turn it inside out and upside down in all directions until it became stronger, more resilient or subject to his unique method of intellectual discernment, it would fall apart, to be abandoned quickly and thrown out. There was no room for easy answers, emotional reactions, obtuse rhetoric. The scintillating speech and quick-silver brain would quite accurately and cleanly cut through these cumbersome attitudes as a breath of fresh air. He knew how to remove all excess in one's thought process to reveal the simple basic solid foundation or the lack thereof in many cases.

Thanks to an insatiable interest and curiosity, he developed and nurtured a vast knowledge of literature and cultural history which he mined continuously to inform his decisions.

Everything that he read, everything that he thought about, was directed and mastered to be of service to his intellectual and practical needs. Far from becoming prisoner to his research, his studies were à source of liberation. As in the example of Buber, Gluek or Freud, he could make use of the Bible as an instrument of psychological analysis or understanding. When it came to finding a synthesis between two diverse ideas, he could as readily call upon the classics as well as the modern sources.

Whether it was Russian romantic literature, military strategy, sociology, languages, technology, the vast array of current political thought from socialist revisionism to Goldwater conservatism, all disciplines were within his intellectual universe. He could as easily pass from a Jesuit dialectic to that of the Talmud or Marx. He could even make sense of some of the weaker or poorly conceived arguments of the person with whom he was speaking. He succeeded in often taking up or reformulating your own propositions with more clarity than you yourself could. Aron, Illich, Von Neumann, Kahn, Buddha, Tolstoy, Cervantes, Kafka: the ideas of all of these authors were sifted through Cadieux's own reflections.

Fernand Cadieux never ceased to study, explore and discover the fissures and weaknesses of the modern world. He could acutely identify the sources of erosion in our modern institutions, and show how the imminence of a collapse could unblock a potentially beneficial reconstruction if only there was a will to act, a will to lead, at the right moment with the required measure of commitment.

He understood the weakness, but also the incredible power of the media. His every thought, his every commitment was for the betterment of the 'human condition'. With the precision of a computer, but using the more gentle traits of passion, and emotion, he was able to literally captivate your absolute attention with a volcanic flood of ideas emanating from his brain which could completely overpower you. He could reduce your arguments to the barest skeleton that you yourself begin to see how thinly veiled they were in the first place.

"You must write, Fernand!", many would often suggest to give more value to his work.

"Oh I have no time. There is far too much to think about!", he would reply.

He behaved as if we were all beings on reprieve, never taking care of himself but rather totally preoccupied with our future and our society. As much as his analyses were often engraved with pessimism, he continued to speak about the future and his children with great optimism. He worried deeply about whether his children and every one of us were prepared enough to confront the reality of this modern world. Reality! As he understood it, it was a terrible truth!

Few of us give the impression that we really understand the reality of what hides behind the words such as power, change, hope, virtue, evil.

With a gentleness, bathed in the omnipresence of his eternal cigarette smoke, with his lively eyes like coals which glowed from his pale face, deep and sombre, Fernand

Cadieux would literally conquer you your mind as would a lover. He would not stop until he succeeded by the sheer force of his words and his perceptions, to transmit into your lesser spirit a fraction of his visions and his energy.

In Canada, we do not give enough value to a Frye, a McLuhan, a Klein or a Selye. But Fernand Cadieux, incarnates in an even rarer fashion, this family of minds. He had a catholic mind in the sense that he conceived all as much in action as in analysis. In the eyes of some, Canada was too small for him given the unique fullness of his mind. Perhaps Cadieux was too big for our times. In the end, the brilliance and keenness of his own visions probably overcharged the circuits of his human system which remained rather fragile.

The simple fact of having been able to travel in his company, even once, to the extreme limits of his mind, has been a great and unforgettable and transformative experience. A light has gone out in this country where much of our days pass in the shadows of the Northern gloom. The death of Fernand Cadieux has diminished this frail light which shines within all of us. Because he helped us to be more honest with ourselves and more engaged intellectually, his brief time in this life has been of indispensible worth.

For him, the supreme joy was to feel that he made us think, really think, if even just once. Whenever that "keg was detonated", he would laugh, lean back in his chair, lift a glass to his lips, inhale deeply the smoke from his cigarette and smile again, beaming with satisfaction. Those of us who have had the privilege of having known Fernand Cadieux, will never again be the same.

WELCOMING SPEECH TO THE SENATE BY HON. ROBERT MUIR TO SENATOR JERRY S. GRAFSTEIN

February 2, 1984

Hon. Robert Muir: Honourable senators, in commencing my remarks in this debate in reply to the Speech from the Throne, I should like to be among the first to welcome those of you who have recently been summoned to the Senate of Canada. I have already congratulated some of you in person, but now, formally, I should like to extend my sincere congratulations en bloc. Those new senators who are not here will read my pearls of wisdom in the Debates of the Senate when they receive their copies.

I wish for all of you good health and every success. Now that you are here I should warn you that you will be the target of all the slings and arrows of the media - as if I had to tell you that. I am sure you are aware that this is the institution that so many criticize and condemn - until they are summoned to it, to use the usual term.

It has been said, "Where but in the Senate of Canada will you find men and women with strength of character enough to lead a life of idleness?" Someone else once said that the motto of this place is, "If anyone said it cannot be done, the hell with it." You will also hear that this is one of the few places on earth where sound travels faster than light, that among people who own windmills we are much in demand as neighbours, and that the air in this place is always full of speeches, and vice versa. To quote another wit, and I am only half correct in referring to him as that, "A man or woman gets up to speak, says nothing, no one listens and then everybody disagrees like crazy with what he or she has said." It's been said that a great many of us have more on our minds than there is room for and that we should have our mouths taped instead of our speeches.

Honourable senators, I spent some 22 years in the House of Commons or, as we refer to it, "the other place", before coming here. During that length of time I used to hear all these things said about members of the Commons - and I still do.

My dear, newly arrived colleagues, you will have to get yourselves a back like a turtle to withstand the attacks of some members of the media - not all, of course. I am happy to say that there are still some who do investigative reporting; then there

14

are others who are a few months out of a school of journalism who are assigned here to the Hill. When you read their articles you will find that they pontificate from the stratosphere. Indeed, they would have you believe that they have forgotten more than any member of this place or the other place ever knew. It would be nice if, on occasion, we would see them in the press gallery in this chamber or at Senate committee hearings.

Yes, my dear friends, you will be accused of being senile, especially those of you in your early forties. You will be accused of being lazy no matter how active you are. You will probably be told that you are as busy as a Swiss admiral. Someone may even say that your insomnia is so bad that you cannot even sleep in the chamber any more.

Of course, I have read these comments before, but they were written about members of the House of Commons.

I mentioned being active, and to those of you who have just arrived, there is plenty of activity here - if you want to indulge in it. There are plenty of committee meetings to attend. You can represent your regions well and to the best of your ability. Frankly, there is plenty to do if you want to do it. The Senate, like the other chamber, is somewhat similar to our churches, fraternal organizations and service clubs: a number of people do a great deal of work and others really do not do an awful lot, human nature being what it is.

I must mention some of the fringe benefits available to you and your guests, such as subsidized meals in the parliamentary restaurant and the parliamentary cafeterias, subsidized haircuts and shoeshines. These privileges are also available to the members of the press gallery and their guests. If you look around - oh boy! - do they have guests. But in their critiques about the members of the Senate, or the Commons, for some strange reason they do not mention that they also participate in these fringe benefits.

In your short time here some of you new senators have already come under the tongue, or pen, of the scribes - and some of it not too flattering. As the old song goes, "You'll get used to it!"

Incidentally, some of you, especially from the Toronto area, should get a copy of the script used by that all-wise, all-knowing soothsayer and seer by the name of Stephen Lewis on station CKO. Yesterday, the same gentleman, and I use the term loosely, indicated on the air that Senator Molgat and his committee on the reform of the Senate had more or less lost their marbles. But, my dear colleagues, is it not great that we live in a country where there is still freedom of the press and freedom of speech and other freedoms? Long may it continue.

I have been in countries, as many of you here have, where no person in the media would dare go on the radio or television and say some of the things that are said in Canada. They would not dare to congregate in groups on corners; they would not dare to protest. The media would not be allowed to write some of the things that are written in Canada. However, I am truly glad that they can do it in Canada and I hope that they will continue to criticize us. In fact, I hope they will continue to do all that they wish any time they want to criticize us. It is a great form of government that we have here in Canada - of course, not the present government. It is a great system and long may it continue in this country.

Let me draw your attention, honourable senators, to an article written by Hugh Segal in the *Toronto Star* dated January 25. This is an article a wee bit different from the comments of Lewis. It is headed *A Good 10 Days for the Senate.*

By and large, the past 10 days were good days for Canada's Upper House. In the context both of policy matters laid before the Parliament of Canada and one or two appointments made by the Prime Minister to the Senate, the relevance and potential usefulness of the Senate has been underlined significantly.

The redraft of the government's security legislation incorporates in it almost all of the significant recommendations made by a Senate committee in order to moderate a bill which had been poorly drafted in many respects. Now before Parliament, this is a piece of legislation that can serve to create an appropriate civilian security agency which can serve the interests of the country without in any way subverting the basic elements of our democracy.

I am not quite sure that I agree with all that he has said, but in any event he is making the point and I quote him again:

The original legislation that was put before the Parliament was ham-handed and would have caused far more difficulty than the problems it sought to remedy. The new legislation is a triumph of moderation and, while there may be significant changes yet to be made at the committee stage, it is a far better piece of legislation for the solemn, sober and careful assessment which the Senate committee provided.

Then he goes on to talk about Senator Grafstein, one of the new members summoned to the Senate. He says:

Two of the appointments made to the Senate are also particularly uplifting. Torontonians will know that the appointment of Jerry Grafstein constitutes the appointment of a loyal Liberal who, despite that one fundamental flaw in his reasoning, is an accomplished lawyer in communications, broadcast and entertainment law, and a significant spokesman for different policy and political concerns. He will be an ornament to the Senate and a strong voice for Metropolitan Toronto and, in that sense, the Prime Minister chose well.

The article concludes by saying:

Hugh Segal is a former senior aide to Premier William Davis.

This type of comment coming from someone with his background is important, I think.

He then goes on:

For those who had the opportunity of being part of the constitutional development, the appointment of Michael Kirby from Nova Scotia is of particular significance.

And he then relates all of the attributes of Senator Kirby. Further down, he says:

Moreover, in the case of both Grafstein and Kirby, the Senate was by no means the only option that they had before them in what have been significantly successful and dynamic careers. But because it is an option that they did choose to accept when offered, they have made a commitment to public service and to an enrichment of the legislative and political process from which all Canadians will benefit.

He finishes by saying:

The courage to take a political stand should by no means disqualify those of genuine competence …I would like to talk a little more about some of our new appointees. I have here an article from the *Toronto Sun* of January 17, 1984 by Barbara Amiel, and she says:

> "In describing Toronto's new Senator Jerry Grafstein, one paper summed up his career with the terse line 'Toronto Liberal communications strategist.' The wire story described him as an advertising executive. The mind boggles."

Jerry Grafstein, in spite of the bizarre fact that he is a Liberal, is the kind of man who sums up the best qualities North America can bring out in a man. To dismiss a life that has been devoted to public service, is to devalue not only the man but the tradition that helped create him.

Barbara Amiel then goes on in great detail with respect to Senator Grafstein, outlining a great many things that I never knew about him. I have one little quotation here I would like to read:

> "There is a quality in Grafstein to which no one who has met him can remain oblivious: He is a deeply moral man, a man of genuine conviction - and a man with that rarest of qualities: Generosity. He came up the hard way and has not forgotten."

Further on, she says:

> "Even Pierre Elliott Trudeau ought to be allowed to appoint his friends and supporters to appointed positions - like the Senate. Most people when in a position to hire or reward someone, would prefer to give the benefit to a friend. This is not for bad reasons. Friends are usually people with whom one shares certain values and philosophy."

In any event, honourable senators, from what is said here, if I were Senator Grafstein, I would be a little worried. I had ten years in municipal politics and now I have been in the federal end of politics for almost 27 years. If I had as many nice things written about me as have been written about him here, I would be a little concerned as to whether I was going to survive in this dear old world much longer. However, I say to Senator Grafstein that he should enjoy it, because he will have a lot of other things written about him.

The new arrivals will soon notice, from listening to their colleagues on the government side, that there are two sides to every question, and the thing for you Grits to do is to defend both. It is good, however, that you are here. With only 55 Liberals and 23 Conservatives, things were getting dangerously out of balance.

It would also appear that there is now absolutely no danger that anyone will take the subject of Senate reform seriously. I know what a blow this will be to some of my colleagues, especially Senator Roblin and Senator Frith who are champing at the bit to get out on the hustings. Just a day or two ago, Senator Molgat tabled in the Senate his interim report of the Special Joint Committee on the Reform of the Senate; I have a gut feeling that they will not be able to run for this house for some period of time yet. In that event, I presume Senator Roblin and Senator Frith have given great thought and serious consideration to the choice of constituency in which they will seek a nomination so that they will be able to run for election to the House of Commons, which election, I hope, is not too far in the future.

With regard to Senator Sinclair, if he is not interested in running for election, I am sure he could always go back to the Canadian Pacific and his honest job as brakeman.

Senator Roblin: Brakeman he was not; anything else but that.

Senator Muir: I am sure Senator Sinclair understands what I am saying. He needs no defence. He can take care of himself, I am sure.

MAIDEN SPEECH IN THE SENATE ON COMPENSATION AND APOLOGY TO JAPANESE CANADIANS

May 8, 1984

Hon. Jerahmiel S. Grafstein, pursuant to notice of April 10, 1984, moved:

That the Senate of Canada endorses, on behalf of all Canadians, the position that a formal apology be extended by the Government of Canada to those living Canadians of Japanese descent for the acts of incarceration of such individuals and the confiscation of their businesses and properties made during the Second World War; and recommends that:

(1) the Government should consider the advisability of appointing a Special Claims Commissioner to adjudicate partial compensation for claims made by living Canadians of Japanese descent for the loss of their businesses or properties as a result thereof; and

   (a) that such claims for partial compensation be received by the Claims Commissioner for a period of one year from the date of proclamation of the Act establishing the same;

   (b) that $50 million be allocated by the Government in the aggregate for all such claims;

   (c) that the balance of any such $50 million be returned to the Government when the Commission completes its responsibilities; and

(2) the Government take the necessary steps to ensure that any personal records or fingerprints of Canadians of Japanese descent obtained and kept by police officials, if any, during the Second World War be destroyed forthwith.

He said: Honourable senators, before addressing the substance of the motion, with your leave perhaps I might address some personal perambulatory remarks of self-introduction.

Honourable senators, I come from a "proud and stiff-necked" people and have been brought to this place, not by my efforts alone but by the contributions of many who sit in this chamber and elsewhere. Early in my life, my late father, a gentle man, taught me almost daily four lessons which still, to this moment, are as difficult for me to practice as I should: The joy of learning, the importance of tradition and family and the pursuit of humility. As we studied together, he would gently ask me, "And why do you say that?" Now, honourable senators, my wife and sons act as my daily professors in that illusive quest for happiness.

From the late Cecil Augustus Wright, one of Canada's great law teachers, I learned of:

> The importance of law as a vehicle of reform, and that, fragile as reason is, and limited as the law is as the expression of the institutionalized medium of reason, that is all we have standing between us and the tyranny of mere will and the cruelty of unbridled, undisciplined feeling.

These words by Mr. Justice Frankfurter, repeated by Dean Wright at the opening of the University of Toronto Faculty of Law in 1962, were stamped on the minds of all law students who were privileged to be taught by the great "Caesar" Wright, that great man with an original mind.

When I turn to Prime Minister Trudeau, who brought me to this place, I must express my debt for his oscillating intellectual inspiration. My admiration escalates daily as I watch him close at hand, now from a vantage point here in Ottawa, wrestling with the demanding burdens of governance. In his enigmatic way, the Prime Minister defines for all of us the issues of the day. Through the exercise of his extraordinary political will, our Constitution was repatriated and our Charter of Rights entrenched. We are now free in law from the last vestiges of colonialism that stultified our minds and stunted our spirit. By this political act, he forced us, as Canadians, to face up and grow up to the tasks of political maturity. "British" justice has finally been transplanted by our own brand of home-made Canadian justice.

As for others in this chamber, I am greatly indebted to Senator Keith Davey, a grand friend who taught me the joy of politics and the excitement of participatory democracy. I am grateful to Senator Daniel Lang, who taught me the importance of graceful precision of political planning and execution; to Senator Charles McElman, who teaches us all that liberalism grows with age rather than diminishes; to Senator Croll, with whose firm I articled as a green student of law and who continues to carry the torch, if flickering from time to time, of the underprivileged; to Senator Paul Lafond who, at a critical juncture, assisted me in the promotion of the Journal of Liberal Thought which, in the 1960s, was crucial to my own intellectual and political development.

I am grateful to Senator Andrew Thompson whose geniality, wit and commitment served as a vanguard for all young men first embarking upon the sea of public life; to Senator Lorna Marsden, who taught me to fight against my traditional biases respecting the role of women in politics and the necessity, indeed the importance, of first reforming one's own mind set and then semantics in seeking their equal rights and their treatment; to Senator Richard Stanbury who, as President of the York Centre Liberal Association, where I first started my serious political activity in Metro Toronto and who, later, as the President of the Liberal Party of Canada, was, for me, the personification of liberal fairness.

I am grateful to Senator Lowell Murray, an honourable, self-effacing political opponent whom I have always respected for his skill and commitment both to the political process and to Canada. More recently, I am grateful to Senator Robert Muir for his gracious words of wisdom and welcome to this chamber; to Senator Royce Frith, who stands out always for me as the exemplar of sartorial and linguistic elegance; to Senator Austin for his political encouragement and comradeship and to Senators Godfrey, Bosa and Cools who personify for me, each in his or her own wonderful way, the best and diverse qualities, the exciting faces and the voices that make up the boisterous cacophony and vibrant collage known as Metropolitan Toronto, the metropolis I so proudly now represent. Metropolitan Toronto, where the majority of the heads of households speak a first language other than English and French, has become a new, free-form model, a unique, resonating, harmonious city of the world which relishes and respects individual expression and human dignity.

I would like to point out other senators in this chamber for whom I have had a distant yet deep respect: Senator David Steuart, one of the great political orators of the west; Senator Robichaud, who at an earlier time and in a different place, expressed with fire and eloquence a passion for equality that has yet to be matched in Canadian public life.

Among today's senators, I would like to pay tribute to Senator Roblin who, by his fairness and grace, personifies for me the best qualities of character and intelligence that I see so evident and at such surplus in this chamber.

To you and to other senators, I owe a debt, but today I should like to turn to the question of a larger debt that we, as a nation, owe to a group of Canadians who, by the awful arm of government and by reason only of their race, were uprooted and deprived of their freedom, their businesses, their homes, and separated from their families and from their dignity. That is a debt that we should repay and it is to that debt that I wish to address my first full remarks to this chamber.

The following are only certain of the salient facts giving rise to this grievance. Let me take you back, if I can, for a moment to 1941. In 1941, 95 per cent of Canada's Japanese population, 22,000 people, lived in British Columbia. Of these, 60 per cent, or 13,600, were Canadians by birth. Another 14 per cent, or 3,650, were naturalized citizens, most of very long standing.

While more than half resided in urban areas of British Columbia, the rest were spread along the coast and the interior. Yet these were different Canadian citizens. They could not vote in British Columbia by reason of a restriction in the British Columbian and federal statutes prohibiting citizens of Japanese origin or Asian origin from voting. Excepted only from those restrictions were war veterans who had been allowed the vote. Canadian citizens of Japanese descent suffered from silent restrictions in businesses, all occupations, trades and professions. There were expressed restrictions against them so that they could not work as federal or provincial civil servants, lawyers or teachers, and the list goes on. They were limited as to their landholdings and were given quotas on logging and fishing rights based purely on race. Labour unions shared the prevailing bigotry of the day by excluding them from union membership. Of course, as Canadian citizens, they were not restricted from paying their taxes.

British Columbia and other parts of Canada were simply not congenial to those of Japanese ancestry by restrictive practices, bylaws, land covenants, regulations, business permits and attitude. Racism was alive in Canada in 1941, fertilized by government, politicians and the press.

Early that year, on January 8, 1941, Prime Minister King announced to the House of Commons that Canadians of Japanese ancestry were exempted from military service, thereby further foreclosing their opportunity to get the vote.

On Sunday, December 7, 1941 - that infamous Sunday - the Japanese attacked Pearl Harbour. Within hours the Canadian war cabinet declared war on Japan, and immediately issued a statement expressing confidence in the loyalty of Canadians of Japanese descent. Within hours officials of the United States government and officials from the Canadian government met and agreed to "concert their efforts" on what they called the "Japanese problem" in both countries.

Early on December 8 - the day after Pearl Harbour - 1,200 fishing vessels owned by Canadians and others of Japanese descent were impounded by the Royal Canadian Navy. The owners fully co-operated. The CPR Railway - which had been built with the help of cheap oriental labour - followed by other leading businesses began to discharge Canadians of Japanese origin. Second generation Canadian-Japanese, called Nisei, wrote Prime Minister King affirming their loyalty. They repeated the requests they had made since war had broken out in 1939 to volunteer for active military service. Those requests went unanswered.

By order in council dated December 16, 1941, all persons of Japanese origin, whether Canadian citizens or not, were required to register with the Registrar of Enemy Aliens. No such steps were taken against Canadians of German or Italian descent, despite the fact that we had declared war on Germany and Italy two years earlier.

On December 25, Hong Kong fell and almost 2,000 Canadians were captured. Vitriolic opposition to all of Japanese origin was ignited and fanned by municipal, provincial and federal politicians, who urged the removal of all of Japanese origin from British Columbia.

On January 8, 1942, a conference was convened in Ottawa composed of federal, provincial and municipal politicians, together with public servants, including the RCMP, officials from the Department of External Affairs and members of the military general staff in Ottawa. All public servants, including members of the military, concurred in the RCMP's strong assessment that those of Japanese origin were loyal and represented no military or strategic threat to Canada. This strong recommendation cut no ice with the politicians. Ultimately, after a bitter debate, a recommendation was made that Japanese male aliens aged 18 to 45 be evacuated from designated areas, those areas being approximately 100 miles along the British Columbia coast, that fishing vessels owned by those of Japanese ancestry, whether Canadian citizens or not, be sold to non-Japanese, and that there be a prohibition from holding fishing licences.

Escott Reid, a distinguished public servant, who was an official in attendance, later wrote in his memoirs of that conference that he felt "evil" in the room because of the patent racism and the racist decisions taken despite the clear facts.

From that conference followed a chain reaction of events fanned by the winds of war. Based on the conference recommendation and heated strong representations from B.C. politicians at all levels of government, an order in council dated January 16, 1942, was issued under the War Measures Act authorizing the Minister of Defence to evacuate from protected areas residents who were enemy aliens, restricting them only to their possessions of personal property and articles approved by the RCMP. Two thousand alien Japanese men were evacuated to road camps in the interior of British Columbia. That order in council also authorized the sale of the fishing vessels owned by the Japanese aliens. The first order referred only to aliens and did not designate others such as Canadians of Japanese origin. But no difference, all vessels owned by Japanese, whether Canadian citizens or not, were impounded and sold. However, this action still did not satisfy local B.C. politicians who continued to lobby actively for more drastic measures against all those of Japanese origin. No distinction was made as to whether they were aliens or citizens; all those of Japanese origin were included.

In February, Singapore fell. On February 19, 1942, the American government ordered the removal of 110,000 men, women and children of Japanese ancestry from American Pacific coastal areas, increasing the pressure on the federal cabinet to take sterner steps. Rumours of enemy attacks and enemy sittings, which were dispelled by the military, further inflamed public opinion, always egged on by B.C. political leaders at all levels of government.

At that time Prime Minister King and the cabinet were concerned about another emotional issue which was dividing the entire country, the conscription question. Subsequent analysis suggests that King considered further steps against Canadians of Japanese ancestry as just another tactical weapon to help him in his political strategy to diffuse the hot conscription issue and gain public support wherever and whenever he could.

He was down in the polls and he knew it. Be that as it may, by order in council dated February 24, 1942, the Minister of Justice was given the power to require any person to leave the restricted or protected areas. That general order was followed by a specific order of the Minister of Justice, then the Honourable Louis St. Laurent, ordering "every person of Japanese race" to evacuate the protected areas.

That was followed by yet another order in council, dated March 4, 1942, evacuating all persons of Japanese descent. Included in that order was section 12, which stated that "as a protective measure only" all property owned in such protected areas, except the fishing vessels and the cash and securities, was to be vested in the Custodian of Alien Property and kept under his management and control - again, I repeat, "as a protective measure."

The British Columbia Securities Commission - a great name - was created by Order in Council dated March 14, 1942, to supervise the evacuation and place all the property that could not be carried by the evacuees into the trust and custody of the custodian. Thus, a group of Canadian citizens were dispossessed and their property confiscated without due process purely on the grounds of racial discrimination. No one, not even the members of the CCF Party, at that time raised a voice of objection. The political opposition was silent. The press was silent. The churches were silent as the dispersal and dispossession of Canadians and the confiscation of their property took place.

By the middle of 1942, after the battle of Midway on June 6, 1942, it was clear that Japan could not win the war. The Japanese advances had been stopped in the Pacific. The Japanese war threat was ended in the middle of 1942. Yet by the end of 1942 virtually the bulk of the population of those of Japanese ancestry was moved. Many families were separated, except those families which were moved to sugar beet farms on the prairies and elsewhere in the east. Others were sent to six camps located in the interior of British Columbia. Provincial authorities did not provide educational facilities. Makeshift educational facilities had to be set up in the camps by the evacuees themselves. Universities throughout Canada, for all practical purposes, were closed to those Canadians eligible to enroll in courses. Sustenance remuneration was given, from which room and board was deducted.

By order in council dated January 19, 1943, the government changed its mind. Now the Custodian was empowered to liquidate or otherwise dispose of the property that had been originally vested in him as "a protective measure" only under the order in council dated March 14, 1942, issued almost a year earlier.

This finally alerted public opinion and the opposition now pleaded unfairness. These pleas were unheeded by the government. The property was liquidated by various methods, admittedly on unfavourable terms and conditions that minimized rather than maximized the return. On the average, not more than 10 per cent of the replacement value was obtained. By order in council of February 5, 1943, the Minister of Labour was empowered to relocate those of Japanese origin. Some of the able-bodied males of these families began to disperse to the east when they recognized that their homes and businesses would never be returned nor would they be fully compensated.

As the war drew to a close in August 1944, Prime Minister King addressed the House of Commons, declaring in these words: "It is a fact that no person of Japanese race or born in Canada has been charged with any act of sabotage or any act of disloyalty during the years of the war."

Now, suddenly, due to urgent requests received from the British military, 150 Nisei

Canadians were finally allowed to enter active service in the spring of 1945. They did so primarily as members in the intelligence and as interpreters, and they served with distinction in the Far East.

But what to do with those left in the camps? Four thousand had by now relocated throughout the east. But the young, the elderly, young women and others without work skills, who had not already dispersed - the great majority - were still left in the camps. Prime Minister King had a plan. To allow them to return to the protected areas along the coast might cause some political problems. Again the federal government acted. First, a resolution of Parliament to prevent Canadian citizens of Japanese descent in the east from voting in federal elections. Then an order of the Minister of Labour dated March 12, 1944, in which Canadians of Japanese descent were given two choices - either to be deported at their request or to be relocated east of the Rockies. Free transit and allowances were to be granted for those who chose relocation east. These Canadians were given six weeks to make up their minds. Then an order in council dated December 15, 1944, stipulated that persons of Japanese origin who so requested were to be deported to Japan. Now the opposition in Parliament finally raised full alarms. The public knew the threat of war had passed. Cries were heard in Parliament that the deportation order was contrary to the will of Parliament. Nevertheless, deportations commenced and continued. It should be noted that these decisions took place after the end of the war in the Pacific.

Even the formal end of the war in 1945 was not the end of injustices against these Canadians of Japanese origin. Only after battles through the courts up to the Privy Council, which supported the government's powers to deport, and public outcry heard in Parliament and elsewhere, did the government cave in in January 1947 and agree to discontinue the deportation policy. Deportation orders, however, continued until they were formally revoked in April 1947, some two years after the formal end of the war.

The other orders in council which lapsed under the War Measures Act in 1945 were continued under the National Emergencies Transitional Powers Act of 1945. It was not until 1949 that the orders in Council prohibiting Canadians of Japanese descent - Canadian citizens - from re-entering the protective areas of British Columbia lapsed. Thus, Canadian citizens had been restricted in their own country for seven years, four years of which were after the end of World War II.

It now became evident, based on the hearings held by the Public Accounts Committee of the House of Commons in 1947, and active representation by the Japanese community in Canada and others, that the enforced liquidation by the Custodian of alien properties originally ordered to be held under protective custody, was unfair as to the timing, the method and the quantum of certain property sales.

The House of Commons committee focused on certain transactions.

Specifically, they examined sales of farmlands to the Veterans Land Act authorities in 1943, which were to be purchased for use by returning war veterans. The best farmland in Canada, located in the Fraser Valley, sold for $64 per acre. Even then, that was a pittance. What delicious British justice! Some of these farms were confiscated from Canadian citizens of Japanese origin who were World War I veterans, to be turned over to returning Canadian war veterans of World War II. The House of Commons committee came to the conclusion that the compensation was unfair and grossly undervalued. It recommended that a royal commission be established to investigate alleged losses. When proceeds were forwarded from time to time by the Custodian to those in the camps, their living allowances were deducted from such proceeds. In the end, in many, many instances only paltry sums finally reached the property owners.

A court attempt in 1947 to make the Custodian, a Crown agent, and therefore accountable to the Exchequer Court Act, failed. The court decided that the Custodian was not a servant of the Crown and was therefore not accountable, if you can believe it, before the Exchequer Court. Representations continued; which, added to the recommendations of the House of Commons committee, led to the appointment of a royal commission in 1947 under Mr. Justice Bird of British Columbia to review the compensation question. His terms of reference were so restricted as to be unfair. Compensation terms were broadened ever so slightly raising expectations of the National Japanese Canadian Citizens Committee and the Co-operative Committee to participate. They did so in the belief that the evidence they gathered would lead to a full and fair compensation based on fair terms of reference. However, value was determined at the date of sales regardless of market and other depressing conditions, and nothing at all was ever allowed for goodwill and business. Finally, to expedite the lengthy hearings that went on until 1950, settlement was based on arbitrary percentages allotted to certain categories of property. The decision of the royal commission was finally handed down in 1950. The community committees that collaborated never felt that the Bird Commission would be an end to their claims to just compensation.

Subsequent analysis determined that not more than a range of between 11 to 16 per cent of the market value of only certain property claims were granted in the aggregate by proceeds received both from the Custodian and from the Bird Commission. Settlements were made - by the way, without any interest - for the intervening years, because they were desperately in need of funds after eight years and it was their belief that further fuller claims would be granted. Of course, the sustenance allowances were deducted from even these partial proceeds. No further steps were ever taken by the government to remedy the situation despite repeated claims by community groups to remedy injustices suffered by these citizens.

Four categories of claims of property still exist to this date. First, those receiving partial compensation ranging from 11 to 16 per cent who accepted funds from the Custodian and the Bird Commission in the honest belief that further and fuller compensation would be authorized; second, no compensation whatsoever for personal property and family heirlooms entrusted to the Custodian "as a protective measure" which just disappeared; third, marginal or no compensation for the 1,200 fishing vessels impounded by the Royal Canadian Navy; and, fourth, no compensation whatsoever for numerous claims still lodged and unsettled with the government by those

Canadians who refused to agree with the Custodian or the Bird Commission and whose files are still open and with the federal government to this day. No claims were ever awarded for incarceration or anything that ever approached replacement value for the property taken.

Honourable senators, I am indebted to three excellent and fair accounts of this period entitled *The Politics of Racism* by Ann Gomer Sunahara, *The Enemy That Never Was* by Ken Adachi, and *Fragile Freedoms* by Thomas R. Berger.

The Prime Minister has said that he is open to arguments on this question. He has assisted public debate by fairly and fully defining concerns shared by many Canadians. The Prime Minister argues forcefully and logically that this generation cannot and, indeed, should not, seek to redress past injustices. He argues that we must change the law and our practices today to correct the unjust practices of the past and to enable us to live in a better and fairer society now and in the future. Hence, he implies that our Constitution is properly prospective and not retrospective in its application. He argues that any other application would be costly and time consuming to the nation's agenda, bedevilled as it is by the overwhelming economic and social problems of today. He takes Bentham's utilitarian position that the costs to the majority by dredging up the evils of the past outweigh any benefits to the minority. What good would it do to stir up ancient animosities? We cannot repay the sins of our grandfathers, else we will be flooded with a widening cycle of demands. If we are to give financial compensation, where would it stop? he argues. Where do you draw the line? What about the Acadians? What about the Chinese head tax, and what about the imprisonment of Canadians of German and Italian origin during that same world war?

This is a perfectly legitimate and pragmatic, philosophical position for the Prime Minister and many other Canadians, who have argued that position, to take. Indeed, I share the same underlying pragmatism. We both share a concern for past injustices. We both share a concern that the law and society must be forward-looking. We both share a concern that the present generation cannot bear the undue financial burdens of the past. We are all worried about crowding the public agenda and draining the public purse with matters of little present importance.

But, honourable senators, this case is different. It stands alone. There are material, significant considerations and, I hopefully believe, persuasive principles alive in this case that simply make this a different, unique precedent. Not to differentiate cases of injustice by legal and philosophic tests is to plunge the law and politics into an abyss. To do so would be to condemn all definition of the public interest and all legal analysis to the gross balancing of interests and quantification. We shunt aside the ideal of justice - its means and its end - on to a rusty track of non-use and abuse. This is not a case of *de minimis non curat lex*.

Why then does this grievance so compel our attention and redress? Let me bring a decalogue of differences - ten different facts - to your attention:

First, these were acts done to Canadian citizens when they were Canadian citizens. This differs from the Chinese head tax question. We are dealing with living Canadians, living Canadian citizens. Of the approximately 22,000 Canadians of Japanese descent who were damaged by these acts, approximately 12,000 are still living in Canada.

Second, no evidence, no scintilla of evidence, was ever adduced of their disloyalty to king or country. Even Prime Minister King thrice repeated this. This differs from the Acadian affair and the FLQ crisis. We are told that of the 196 Canadians of Japanese descent who volunteered for military service in Canada during World War I, over 50 were wounded, 96 were killed, and 49 returned safely to Canada. Those 49 veterans who survived to World War II were treated equally: They were interned, dispossessed and dispersed with the others.

Third, there was no evidence of violence or threat of violence to the state ever demonstrated during or after the war.

Fourth, despite actions taken against them, positive acts of loyalty to Canada and the war effort permeated this community by their exemplary conduct, full co-operation and repeated attempts to volunteer for active service. Indeed, we are told that they invested over $300,000 of their meagre savings in Canada Savings Bonds.

Fifth, there was no notice, no public forewarning, given to enable them to voluntarily sell their property or rearrange their personal affairs.

Sixth, there was no recourse to the law. No "due process" to the courts was made available to them. This differs from the Riel affair, the Manitoba language rights question, the Acadian outrage, and even those who were incarcerated during the FLQ crisis. These Canadian citizens had simply no way to object through the courts.

Seventh, admittedly there was no full, fair compensation given for property or incarceration. Indeed, we are told that, despite the moneys received from the Custodian and later from the Bird Commission, not more than a range of 11 per cent to 16 per cent on the average was ever allotted for those property claims that were made. Many major claims sit in the government's file - yet to be settled - made by Canadians who refused the Custodian and the Bird Commission offers as being totally unjust. No final settlement was made for the Royal Canadian Navy's impounding of 1,200 fishing vessels.

Eighth, their initial trust in "British justice" and the government's express order in council that the property be "protected" by the Custodian led these Canadian citizens to leave their most cherished possessions and irreplaceable family heirlooms behind in their homes. These were never returned or never traced. No compensation at all was ever allotted.

Ninth, after the war, when no semblance of war threat could even be sustained, these Canadian citizens were still prevented, until 1949, from being able to return to the protected areas of British Columbia and their old neighbourhoods.

Tenth, and finally, most damning of all - no vote. These Canadian citizens were deprived of our most precious franchise - the right to vote, the right to choose. It was only on June 15, 1948, some six years after the 1942 order in council and four years after the end of World War II, that Parliament finally passed Bill 198 amending the Dominion Elections Act. This bill deleted the section which had disenfranchised all

Canadians of the Japanese race except war veterans and those few resident outside British Columbia since 1902. The offending section of the Dominion Elections Act had specified that persons denied a provincial franchise were also to be denied a federal franchise. Those who make a claim for greater respect for provincial rights should review our history on this question. British Columbia had passed legislation in 1895 excluding all citizens of Asian origin. With the evacuation, the Japanese who moved outside British Columbia borders would have automatically gained the right to vote in federal elections, but the disqualification was continued in the notorious clause 5 of Bill 135 passed in 1944 by Parliament under the leadership of Mr. King. No vote. No choice. No vote until 1949. Reason: racism.

Returning to Prime Minister Trudeau's utilitarian argument, my concern is equally pragmatic. I believe, as I have said in the defeated preamble to this motion, that the Constitution, the Charter of Rights, reflects certain natural rights. These rights are not of recent origin, but were rights that were scorched into common law, in our statutes, in our conventions and in our practices. These rights, now made explicit in the charter, were basic rights which were and are inalienable. Certain new charter rights were added, but the rights here infringed predate the entrenchment of the charter. These rights are to be found expressed in Magna Carta. These rights deal with respect for the person and his property. These rights ultimately deal with the question of human dignity.

Respect for human dignity is the foundation of our legal system. Respect precedes rights. Duties and obligations come before rights. As Simone Weil has so eloquently written in her book, *The Need for Roots,* and obligation to respect human dignity precedes and is a precondition to the entertainment or enjoyment of human rights. Therefore, is it not appropriate, when an injustice appears, particularly this injustice that was done to these citizens by a Liberal government, that a Liberal government should act to redress these injustices?

If we do not have a collective conscience, if we do not have a sense of remorse, and if we do not look backward, how then can we justify supporting the present amendments to Manitoba laws which seek, in the name of a distinct numerical minority in Manitoba, to redress a historic and unjust grievance? In the 1940s, Canadians of Japanese origin represented just under 3 per cent of the British Columbia populace. Today, francophones in Manitoba represent 3 per cent of that province's populace. Both, then, are distinct numerical minorities. How do we support allocation of precious taxpayers' dollars for services to benefit that small minority today? Because this was a past injustice to that francophone group. Is it not a recognition that there was a disproportionate and unfair treatment before the law, that the democratic majority repressed their minority rights? Is not bilingualism in this country and the amendments to the Manitoba laws, which are a reflection of that bilingualism, an attempt by this generation of Canadians to correct injustices of the past, even though there is still only a very small francophone minority in Manitoba? Restitution by compensation is an essential element giving substance to theory - beef to the bone - in the same way that amendments to the Manitoba laws and the investment of taxpayers' dollars in francophone services is a manifestation of justice in action. Is this not the essence of distributive justice?

Would William Lyon Mackenzie King have led the Canadian government to do what it did had those Canadians of Japanese origin held the vote? Without the vote, they were disarmed; they were naked in politics. No vote, no franchise, was critical in the opinion of Jack Pickersgill who was at that time in 1942 Mr. King's executive assistant. Mr. Pickersgill said:

> I have always felt that if the Japanese had had the vote it would not have happened the way it did... I don't think any Liberal government in the 1940s would have dared take the vote away from anyone.

By depriving those Canadians of our most cherished possession, the right to choose by vote, Canada deprived them of their implied consent, necessary in a democratic society to restrict their rights - take away the fruits of a subject's labour, or even isolate them - all in the interest of the greater good; all in the interest of the majority. There was no full democratic social contract entered into with these Canadians, these citizens. Yet they kept up their end of the social contract by their loyal actions. Deprivation of the vote places this case on a higher plane. Those Canadians had no opportunity to influence the majority with their vote. This is not the case now, in Manitoba, nor was it the case in the other instances given as a rationale - given as historic analogies - to curb redress.

In pressing for the principle of equality for French Canadians, Prime Minister Pierre Trudeau, then Minister of Justice, made a speech entitled, "Quebec and the Constitutional Problem," which he presented to the Canadian Bar Association in Quebec City on September 4, 1967. I would like to quote his words:

> If French Canadians are able to claim equal partnership with English Canadians, and if their culture is established on a coast- to-coast basis, it is mainly because of the balance of linguistic forces within the country. Historical origins are less important than people generally think, the proof being that neither Eskimo nor Indian dialects have any kind of privileged position. On the other hand, if there were six million people living in Canada whose mother tongue was Ukrainian, it is likely that this language would establish itself as forcefully as French. In terms of *realpolitik*, French and English are equal in Canada because each of these linguistic groups has the power to break the country. And this power cannot yet be claimed by the Iroquois, the Eskimos, or the Ukrainians.

The Prime Minister, in that passage, was describing the classic case of the power of a strong minority backed by substantial numbers. Now we have a Charter of Rights that expressly offers protection to the individuals or to minority groups - a charter based not on *realpolitik*, not on the power of the majority, but on the basis of justice to all before the law. This was the idea of "British" justice that these loyal Canadians clung to in the hope that justice would correct injustice.

Earlier, an insightful political observer wrote these words, arguing conclusively about the delusion of national motivation that fuelled democratic majorities to trample over the rights of the minorities. I quote again:

> At Ottawa and in provinces other than ours, this nationalism could wear the pious mask of democracy. Because, as English-speaking Canadians became proportionately more numerous, they took to hiding their intolerance behind acts of majority rule; that was how they quashed bilingualism in the Manitoba Legislature, violated rights acquired by separate schools in various provinces, savagely imposed conscription in 1917, and broke a solemn promise in 1942.

As a footnote, this author added these explanatory words:

> Andre Laurendeau has just written with great clarity an account of how, with the plebiscite of 1942, the state became the tool of Anglo-Canadian nationalism, and of how that state look advantage of French-Canadian numerical weakness to divest itself of pledges it had made (La Crise de la Conscription, Montreal, 1962). A tale even more shameful could be told of how, during the same war and with similar inspiration, the vengeful powers of the state were turned against the Japanese-Canadian minority.

These were the words written in a brilliant article entitled *New Treason of the Intellectuals*, published in 1962 in a little-known magazine called *Citi Libre* by a little-known law professor called Pierre Elliott Trudeau. And these words lead me back to my original argument. The infringement of basic rights should indeed be examined on a cost benefit analysis. If the Prime Minister takes Jeremy Bentham's utilitarian view, I take Immanuel Kant's view that the benefit of restitution today transcends the costs. To use Bentham, and even Mill, without Kant is like playing hockey without a puck. How the players play is just as important as the score to Canadians. Kant argued, in *Critique of Pure Reason,* that rights are "natural" precisely for this reason. Kant foresaw that natural rights could not be removed without the consent - at least, the implied legitimate consent - of the citizen victim in the interests of the majority. Kant laid the groundwork for a pluralistic society that could not be tyrannized by the majority. Today we should not swallow concepts of general welfare at the expense of minority rights which fail to respect the plurality of our democracy and its distinctiveness. John Rawls, in his book *A Theory of Justice*, wrote:

Each person possesses an inviolability founded on justice that even the welfare of society as a whole cannot override - the rights secured by justice not subject to political bargaining or to be the calculus are of social interests.

Now, if certain rights are inalienable - which I believe they are - can we not agree, honourable senators, that what we are really dealing with is the question of human dignity? Any destruction of human dignity not yet restored, as was done to the Canadians of Japanese descent, cannot now be fully restored. The Prime Minister and other Canadians are right - compensation now can never restore them fully. Hence, my argument that we seek partial compensation from the many in our society to the few. Cannot this act of partial restoration demonstrate a real respect for the sanctity of human dignity? Can we not agree that government has a duty to redistribute taxpayers' dollars to adjust this present grievance, this unfinished business left smouldering and moulding in open government files?

Is this not the basic philosophy behind the liberal idea of affirmative action? Why is it that secretaries and others in the federal public service still rail against seemingly unjust treatment by affirmative action that bonuses those who have French as an additional language? Is not affirmative action a method to induce affirmative equality before the law? Affirmative action is a method to increase respect for human dignity. Is not this the engine driving affirmative action for women? Does not the charter recognize the principle of affirmative action in section 15(2) as a legitimate means to pay the cost now for past injustices? This is a cost, a true cost, a fair cost that we, as individuals in society, must pay and continue to pay for injustices in the past, for compensation is a product of the past. Thus is the rationale of affirmative action for French Canadians embedded in our principles of bilingualism which I, for one, freely accept and gladly applaud.

Let us approach the concept of compensation from the point of view of the common law. Let us examine the viewpoint, as well, that it was necessary in time of war to do what was done!

The common law has always recognized the principle of compensation as a fundamental principle of restitution and equity between individuals, even in cases of necessity. It was pointed out to me by my friend, Professor Martin Friedland, that this principle was hotly debated in our first year class at the U. of T. law school. We were taught this idea from a leading case in "Caesar" Wright's famed case book on torts. In *Vincent v. Lake Erie Transportation Company,* a decision of the Supreme Court of Minnesota, 1910, we were asked whether the defence of necessity could withstand a claim for compensation for damage. A wharf had been severely damaged by a ship owner keeping his vessel tied to the wharf in a storm. The ship owner alleged that, after discharging the cargo, the wind had attained such a great velocity that the master and the crew were powerless to move the vessel. Necessity was the defence. Damages were granted to the wharf owner by the ship owner. The ship owner argued that his captain and his crew had no control over the conditions which caused the damage. The court, however, found that compensation must be made.

Honourable senators, let me quote from that case:

> Theologians hold that a starving man may, without moral guilt, take what is necessary to sustain life; but it could hardly be said that the obligation would not be upon such person to pay the value of the property so taken when he became able to do so. And so public necessity, in times of war or peace, may require the taking of private property for public purposes; but under our system of jurisprudence compensation must be made.

What would the common law courts have said, honourable senators, had a ship of state intentionally continued the damage after the velocity of war had disappeared for over four years? What kind of additional damages, what kind of punitive damages would have been awarded here in our case?

The essence of the argument at common law is the same as our present argument in favour of affirmative action. Affirmative action restores equality before the law. We are redressing past injustices at a cost to society today. Therefore what we are treating here is the very foundation of the Constitution, the very basis, the intrinsic nature of our legal system - and that is how our law treats our people. Our Constitution demands that all people be treated equally before the law. This is the cornerstone of our legal system, the cornerstone of the legitimate authority in this chamber. Here in the Senate this is no mean national ethic that holds the national idea supreme. Parmountcy of the Charter means placing people before parliamentary supremacy. Primacy of Parliament has been transplanted by sovereignty of the individual in a democratic state. British justice has been replaced by Canadian justice. To undermine now this principle is to violate the first principle of democracy, which is equality before the law. If we consider, in the deepest part of our heart, that a group of Canadians are treated unequally or unjustly on the facts here argued, not to restore them in law and dignity to their full place is to deny the very essence of the Constitution. This is a functional solution to a pragmatic problem.

Therefore, honourable senators, we are not here to debate an injustice. This we can agree upon. We are not here to moralize. We are not here to reconstruct the past. We are not here to expiate the sins of our fathers or grandfathers. We are here to give pragmatic support to the law's pragmatic principle, namely, respect for our laws and our institutions; to breathe life into the first principle of equality before the law.

Once we choose not to confront historical cases, we open up the possibility of arbitrariness in obeying the law. If, in the Senate, we refuse, when we are all satisfied that there was a grave injustice, to remonstrate with government and Parliament, are we not on the slippery side of a slope? Think of the message we are sending if we turn our backs on this transgression. Are we saying that in certain cases, for certain reasons, the government can break fundamental laws and then disavow the consequences after the event? What reason remains for individuals to feel guilty when they break the law? By what rights in a democratic society can a government distance itself from the principle of equality before the law when its constituents cannot? Just as important, how can we argue that it is prudent to do so when it is the first step down the slippery slope to arbitrary authority?

The message that we in the Senate should send out is that we cherish legal rationality as a necessary precondition to legitimate government; that no government or its successors can get away with singling out individuals or groups for unfair persecution; and that human dignity comes prior to considerations of convenience. This is not some radical argument. It is as old as the Bible itself. It asserts that cost/benefit calculations must give way to profound principles on which utilitarian considerations rest. As usual, principles and pragmatism stand side by side, and they stand best when they stand together.

I argue that this case for compensation is a practical one, that requires this government to uphold equality before the law for its citizens. With compensation, the task of politicians is to show why this case stands apart. A Committee of Parliament, representing all parties, in its report entitled *Equality Now*, unanimously called for an apology and compensation. If we concede that violations of basic rights or equality before the law have been made, and we do not recompense or seek to make whole those citizen's rights, have we not therefore eroded our own authority and that of the government in the eyes and minds of our citizenry? Take a step down that slippery slope, let violations or infringements of law go unanswered or unpaid, then do we not join the conspiracy that undermines both the legitimacy and the rule of law?

Can we avert our glance and say "I cannot burden my mind with acts of the past. I have to go forward. I cannot deal with the past"? Is this not itself a step to lawlessness? If we dilute the glue, which is equality before the law, we undermine the very bricks upon which our legal, parliamentary institutions, and indeed this very chamber, is constructed. What is the cost to Canadians if we do not compensate? What is the deterrent to future acts of injustice? Will it be an invitation to lawlessness if society has no memory? We are now told that Mr. Justice Ilsley in 1948 warned his cabinet colleagues: "History would denounce the party for having continued those orders"; but they were continued nonetheless; and today there is still no haste to make amends.

What kind of precedent do we establish if we approve a scheme of partial compensation? We would set a tariff barrier against future misconduct? We would endorse a precedent that reduces respect for those leaders of that day and relegates them to figures of disrepute in history - as they should be. Is this not important in itself? Do we not set a practical set of values for this generation to follow? Do we not, by our action, now suggest a different standard of national and international conduct that the Prime Minister himself has so actively pursued in his quest for peace? Do not norms of international conduct start with the treatment of individuals at home rather than the treatment of nations abroad? What would the growing Third World, composed as it is of visible majorities, make of this? Would they not applaud our courage and generosity to one of our visible minorities?

In Canada we now have an opportunity to make history by rewriting it. What will people of other nations say about this? That Canada placed restoration of human dignity before *realpolitik*, that Canada placed respect before pride. That human rights live in our foreign policy precisely because of our domestic policy. Justice was done and seen to be done. That racism, alive in Canada in 1941, is dead in 1984.

Racism is rooted in our minds. Hannah Arendt in her book *The Origins of Totalitarianism* defined extreme racism as "radical evil". She wrote:

> When the impossible was made possible, it became unpunishable, unforgivable ... evil which could no longer be understood and explained by evil motives or self interest, greed, ... resentment, thirst for power, and cowardice and therefore which anger could not avenge, love could not endure, friendship could not forgive ...

The 1981 Nobel prize winner Elias Canetti in his book *Crowds and Power* analyzed the origins of racism by showing the actual pleasure one group gets by pronouncing an unfavourable verdict against another group in society. He said:

> At the root of the process lies the urge to form hostile packs, which, in the end, leads inevitably to actual war packs. Through being applied to many different spheres the process becomes diluted, but even if this means that it operates peacefully, apparently resulting only in verbal judgments, the urge to push it to its conclusion, to the active and bloody hostility of two packs, is always there in an embryonic form.

Honourable senators, is not our task here in the Senate to be vigilant? We can stamp out this pernicious embryo of racism whenever it rears its ugly head. And we can create conditions that suffocate its growth!

And after all, is not justice defined by history and restitution? In Deuteronomy XVIII, 20 we are told "Justice, justice shall you follow". One interpretation given for the repetition of the word justice is that justice means justice both in goals and ends. The Hebrew word for "justice" is the same as the word for "giving" and "victory". Giving is a duty that precedes a right or a privilege. "Giving" in this biblical sense is deemed necessary to correct injustice. Only by an act of "giving" can we start a fresh clean page in history. Only in "giving" do we get "victory."

The Bible is instructive on the laws governing the governors. In 2 Samuel VII, 7 we are told that when the prophet Nathan asked King David what is proper compensation when a rich and powerful man takes a poor man's only precious possession, King David, infuriated, responded that the poor man should be compensated four times over. Nathan then told King David he was the culprit because he had abused his powers as king for personal reasons. David immediately acknowledged his error thereby concurring in the concept of compensation. Maimonides, the twelfth century philosopher, explained this passage and the words used by saying that if a king discriminates against his subjects, this is not law, this is robbery. We are also told by other teachers that King David by publicly acknowledging guilt and restitution allowed his kingdom to flourish while King Saul, who under similar circumstances refused to publicly apologize for errors of government, saw his kingdom, his legacy and his dynasty quickly disappear.

Hence, I argue, honourable senators, that our responsibility here is clear to ourselves, the government and this institution of Parliament we have sworn to uphold. Pay today. Calculate a fair formula for these living Canadians - perhaps an annuity. Pay we must. Pay we should! We are told that the Japanese community is divided on this question. Some demand an apology and compensation; others think an apology will suffice. Still others wish to forget the whole painful episode. However, this is not a question for that small minority of Canadian citizens of Japanese origin who were injured to remonstrate - this is a question for the majority of Canadians to answer.

For those who have argued against the entrenchment of the Charter of Rights in our Constitution, the American experience during the same World War II period is instructive. While Japanese were incarcerated and dispersed, their property was not taken and measures were terminated in 1944. In the interim, as American citizens, they were allowed into active service and they volunteered in great numbers serving with great distinction, as honourable senators know. Their government was restrained by their constitution. Now a Commission of Congress has reviewed this history thereby reopening the question of compensation in America. In Seattle, Washington just last week, on April 27, the Seattle School Board authorized $5,000 reparation payments to each of 27 Japanese-American clerks forced to resign after Japan's attack on Pearl Harbour. Honourable senators, it is still not too late to change history.

I would like to leave with honourable senators three ideas - three thoughts to galvanize your support. First, this injury to our citizens was different and unique. Second, pragmatism dictates that by fostering respect for human dignity we gain respect for the Senate and ourselves. Third, good old Canadian common sense knows it is never too late to correct a wrong. Canadians believe in affirmative action!

For me, honourable senators, the question of reform of the Senate is tied up in this issue. My reading of voluminous comments made about Senate reform in the last decade shows me an almost total preoccupation by critics with the "ethics of process" - John Stuart Mill's idea that the method of the appointment of representatives is a key element, a precondition, to the actual acceptance of a democratic institution. To address this question is for another time and, perhaps, for other voices.

In the interim, by the passage of the Charter, has not the Senate in fact been reformed? Has not the Senate been reborn again and given a new mandate by the repatriation of the Constitution and the entrenchment of the Charter of Rights? Has not this vital new fact been virtually unnoticed and unheralded? If we have been granted a new role then this is a chance for us to prove it.

As for calls for more regional representation, I simply do not understand the call for greater regionalism in the Senate unless it is in terms of seeking to reduce inequalities between regions and reduce inequalities between groups as best we can. One wonders whether representatives of the region necessarily are the best spokesmen for injustices against minorities within a region. However, that argument is also for another day.

In closing, let me repeat my belief that there is a new, exciting and paramount role for this chamber. That is to say, we act as a surety - a protector of rights for those groups in society which require affiaction, those groups which require the long and strong equal arm of the law. In this imperfect world, as best we can, we must endeavour to build a platform equally open to all upon which Canadians of whatever origin, colour, race, gender or disability can be launched into a Canadian society of growing and equal opportunities. On this platform all of us in this chamber now proudly stand. Is it not our turn to bend and help the rest of Canada to stand with us? Can we not hammer two strong planks in that platform by apology and compensation to finally close the compelling case of Canadians of Japanese origin?

We have heard in recent days much about the need to redress structural deficits in our economy and move towards balancing our budget. In this way, so we are told, future generations will not be burdened with increasing costs of today so our economy can continue to grow. Equally, honourable senators, our conscience demands we redress this government - created deficit of human dignity so that we can finally balance our books of justice - so that we can free our conscience and allow our spirit to flourish and grow. We were not brought here to dilute the quality of justice. Let us give a new definition to Canadian justice.

Respectfully, honourable senators, I request your support for this motion.

Hon. Senators: Hear, Hear.

On motion of Senator Frith, debate adjourned.

The Senate adjourned until tomorrow at 2 p.m

DON JAMIESON: EULOGY

November 25, 1986

Hon. Jerahmiel S. Grafstein: Honourable senators, I would like to add my words of tribute to the late Don Jamieson. The magic of public speaking is a lost art. The ability to elevate and transform public audiences by the spoken word may soon be forgotten. When we think of this changing state of public affairs, we remember with kindness and great respect Don Jamieson who was a living bridge between the oral tradition of public speaking and the new electronic state of broadcasting, both radio and television.

I was first introduced to the late Don Jamieson under very exciting circumstances. I was introduced to the magic of Don Jamieson in Hamilton by our colleague, Senator Dan Lang, who was then the Ontario campaign Chairman of the Liberal Party in the 1965 general election. Don Jamieson was asked to be the announcer of a very historic event - the last political rally not only of that campaign but what was to be the last political rally of the late Lester Pearson. It was Don Jamieson's great broadcasting presence serving as the over-the-air and behind-the-scenes speaker who transformed a rather difficult and what might have been otherwise a disastrous political event into a compelling and exciting piece of electronic history. So when I think of Don Jamieson, I think of how, by the magic of his words and his voice, he could take an ordinary event and transform it into a memorable electric moment of political history. Recently - just over two years ago - I had the occasion to listen to Don speak under very different yet equally impressive circumstances. He was one of the guest speakers at the Oxford Union where he had been invited to debate the issue of the future of the Commonwealth. Even there in that greatest of oratorical forums, once again, Don's flights of oratory lifted the audience. Not only did he transform the audience but, more important than that, he carried the debate and his side won.

Don Jamieson exemplified the Canadian dream to many other young Canadians. He demonstrated how a man could rise above adverse circumstances by sheer ability and the force of his personality. He was a great public speaker, a historic broad-caster, an outstanding political figure and a great diplomat. Above all, he was a great Canadian. For me he will always remain alive. What greater tribute could one pay to a friend than to say to his family and legion of admirers that Don Jamieson lives on; the lilt of his voice and the grace of his words will remain alive forever in our hearts and in the pages of Canadian history. We will miss you, Don.

Hon. Senators: Hear, hear!

DAVIDSON DUNTON: EULOGY

February 11, 1987

Hon. Jerahmiel S. Grafstein: Honourable senators, when one of our nation's wise men passes, it is appropriate to pause and mark the nation's loss.

The late Davidson Dunton, writer, journalist, academic, public servant par excellence, and visionary, served Canada with distinction. In his multi-faceted career, he was editor of the Montreal Star, Co-Chairman of the Royal Commission on Bilingualism and Biculturalism, head of the CBC, and President of Carleton University. Schooled in the depression, leavened by war, Davidson Dunton was one of Canada's transitional leaders who, by their collective wisdom and commitment to the public service, guided Canada's transition from an economy dependent as a colony into a vibrant, independent post-industrial power.

The nation generally deserves the leadership it gets. Canada deserved and gratefully accepted the wise, sound leadership of Davidson Dunton who was noted for his internationalism, his grace, his culture, and by his efforts he helped the fragile bloom of Canadian culture blossom and grow.

At a time when our cultural institutions are once again under massive attack, it is important to remind ourselves of the work of our great men, quiet Canadians like Davidson Dunton who were proud to stand for Canada and who were proud to give identity and definition to our independence.

It is no small consolation to his wife and daughters that their loss is shared by thousands and thousands of grateful Canadians.

Hon. Senators: Hear, hear!

WALTER GORDON: EULOGY

March 24, 1987

Hon. Jerahmiel S. Grafstein: Honourable senators, one test of political greatness is the ability to change conventional wisdom and to transform political values. Walter Gordon changed Canadian values and, in the process, became the political conscience to a generation of Canadians.

I first met Walter Gordon in 1961. At that time my belief in Pearsonian internationalism collided with Walter Gordon's belief in nationalism. I feared nationalism. I failed to see how one could ignite nationalism for Canada and yet deny the nationalist impulses of Québec, a nationalism, I believed, that would divide rather than unite. Yet, I came to see that Walter Gordon's brand of nationalism was different; it was a self respecting nationalism; a caring nationalism; a humane nationalism; a nationalism that could unite.

Sometimes leaders contribute less than their followers. History has yet to measure fully Walter Gordon's contribution to what we and historians now refer to as "Pearsonian Liberalism." Yet, for me, Walter Gordon was a quintessential Toronto liberal, engaging, enraging, envied, even reviled, but never ignored.

Walter Gordon was a Toronto Liberal, a true believer who, in turn, gave birth to an entire generation of true believers. He was a Toronto Liberal who believed in regional equality - ask Maurice Sauvé or my leader in this place, Allan MacEachen. He was a Toronto Liberal who believed in Medicare - ask Mitchell Sharp; a Toronto Liberal who believed in bilingualism - remember, kindly, Senator Maurice Lamotagne, his true friend.

Walter Gordon was a Toronto Liberal who believed in closing the gap between the rich and the poor - ask the Toronto business establishment. He was a Toronto Liberal who believed in enlightened state enterprise - remember the Canada Development Corporation. He was a Toronto Liberal who believed in nationalism - ask Pierre Trudeau; a Toronto Liberal who believed in an independent Canada - ask Mel Hurtig today; and a Toronto Liberal who hid his personal generosity behind a self-deprecating mask - ask his legion of friends.

Walter Gordon was a gentle man who did not go gently into the night. He raged against the coming of the night and, in turn, became a source of light for all Canada. We shall mourn him and we shall never forget him.

AN INTRODUCTION TO SENATOR ALLAN J. MacEACHEN ON THE OCCASION OF A DINNER OF LIBERAL SENATORS

June 22, 1988

Your honours:

While pausing between grand national debate on the constitution and trade, I have been quietly debating with my good friend Senator Gigantes about the appropriate English translation for a key phrase from the works of Heraclitus - the great Greek philosopher - whose philosophy was based on the theory of a constant change. Heraclitus wrote in Greek: "ethos anthropou daimon." Now, I say the quote means "man's character is his fate." Philippe Gigantes says "man's character is his guide." In any event, Heraclitus preached that "character" is the motor of politics.

Tonight we can agree. We're here to talk about one man and how one man's character has influenced the national perception of the Senate. And indeed all senators.

Allan MacEachen! Allan MacEachen! Allan MacEachen! Just repeating those two names, side by side, sends ripples through the media, tremors through Tory ranks and waves through Tory leadership. And if those two names were not enough, you all bear witness at each session of the Senate to what happens when Allan MacEachen himself, in the raw, appears in the Senate and slowly rises in his place on the Senate front benches to face the leader of the government in the Senate, another maritimer, that very honourable Lowell Murray. Watching from the rear one can see an almost invisible shudder as Murray's back stiffens and his shoulders hunch up and he cringes deep in his seat. And from the front, one can always detect on Senator Murray's grim face a slight tremor of the lower lip and a quiver of the left eyebrow as Allan MacEachen softly, almost aimlessly at first, commences to address the chamber . Even from the perspective of my seat in the Senate I note that the otherwise, almost perfect roman profile of avuncular Senator Finlay MacDonald, a fellow Nova Scotian, quickly becomes distorted as his wistful smile is drained, his florid face pales and he moves forward to the edge of his seat to hear what new blows emanate from the lips of one

Allan MacEachen to bruise and batter yet again the Tory body politic!

It is not, honourable senators, our duty as members of this chamber of second sober thought, to explore carefully, in the national interest, the sources of this awesome power. A power that can so readily transform mighty men into shivering mice! Let us do so this evening - frankly and fully. One can only imagine in one's most erotic fantasy what impact those two names, Allan MacEachen, make on the Committee of Priorities and Planning that plots the government's daily public agenda in the Langevin block or in grandeur of his intellect that allowed him to escape the narrow confines of his modest origins and move to St. Francis Xavier University, in Antigonish, where he started what was to become a singularly distinguished academic career. However he was determined to better himself. So, he spent what in retrospective was probably his most useful early period to broaden his perspective, in studies at the very heart of the Canadian soul itself, my alma mater, the University of Toronto which obviously then propelled him onto greater intellectual heights at the University of Chicago and finally to highest grove of academa in North America, MIT in Cambridge, Massachusetts, before he returned to St. Fx to teach.

More than 30 years ago, it was in the 1950s, he joined the right Honourable Lester Pearson in opposition as an advisor and in the early '60s was elected and served in the House of Commons until he was summoned to this highest and holiest of all places, the Senate, in 1984. We have watched in amazement as Allan MacEachen waves his semantic wizardry and performs his intellectual gymnastics in the Senate and, as if by magic, to our delight, can elevate a minor point of procedure into a grand indictment of national malfeasance. You can tell he has drawn blood when some senators opposite turn an ever flaming ruby red or even better begin to whine.

Our rabbis tell us that such a man with such an intellect is so gifted by God that he can demonstrate how two angels can dance on the head of a pin.

Your honours, Balzac, the great French author, once wrote that the world was divided between the deceivers and the deceived. And we, honourable senators have been deceived. Have been deceived by the conventional wisdom in the media. First we were told that Allan MacEachen was a radical, a destroyer of Canadian values, a small "L" Liberal and worst yet, a reformer. Then we were told he was a large "L" Liberal, a reactionary. A dinosaur. First we were told he was a Pearson Liberal and then we have been reminded that no, he is truly a Trudeau Liberal. All this, honourable senators, is deception. All is deceit. For if the truth be known, Allan MacEachen is not a Pearson Liberal. Never was a Pearson Liberal! Allan Maceachen is not and never was a Trudeau Liberal! Allan MacEachen is a MacEachen Liberal.

Now pray tell you may ask, just what precisely is a MacEachen liberal. A MacEachen Liberal is one who has never given up his belief in reform at a time when reform was not fashionable. Never gave up his belief in the Liberal party as a vehicle of social justice when both the Liberal party and social justice were not fashionable. Never gave his belief in reversing the fortunes of the Liberal party. You'll recall in 1979 when he single-handed set the stage for Mr. Trudeau' s triumphant return he was merely repeating history. Earlier, in the '60s even Liberals had written and read off the Liberal party, Allan's ideas and actions paved the Liberal return to power in 1962. In the '60s, Allan MacEachen was instrumental in radically reforming the labour code as Minister of Labour and established a new standard for minimum wage. And Allan MacEachen was the architect of the Liberal Social Agenda of the '60s through the Health Resources Fund, the Assistance Plan, the Old Age and Security Act all of which were introduced and amended during his period as Minister of National Health and Welfare. He piloted Medicare through the tumultuous debate in the house where Medicare was almost derailed. That greatest of modern political reforms, the Election Expenses Act was introduced when he served as House Leader and President of the Privy Council. Finally during his tenure as Foreign Minister in the '80s when he almost single-handed transformed the global dialogue between east and west into a dialogue between north and south. Truly a Liberal dialogue. All these were steps, grand Liberal steps, taken by Allan MacEachen, made the liberal party synonymous with social justice.

Honourable senators, apparent failure in politics is cyclical. Just a matter of timing! Being ahead of one's times sometimes creates a strong reaction that ultimately leads the way to greater social justice. It was in Allan MacEachen's measures as Minister of Finance in 1981, measures on tax reform that again showed he was ahead of his time. If one goes back and examines carefully the contours of MacEachen's tax reforms - reduced tax rates, elimination of preferential tax shelters, while closing the gap between rich and poor in this country - his measures, still stand out as a model of equity and fairness.

And so, honourable senators, we come this evening to praise Allan J. MacEachen. He has transformed the Senate into a body of conviction and activity. Late in 1984, I was asked to attend a meeting to consider the Senate's image. At that meeting, he stoutly argued that no legislative body, no national body, can maintain any legitimacy, any credibility, unless it has a public presence. A public profile. Indeed by eradicating prestudy and slowly stimulating, a reformist attitude Allan MacEachen has, for better or worse, heightened the Senate's presence and promoted the Senate's public profile.

So honourable senators, the secret source of the power, that awesome power that emanates from Allan MacEachen is not the man himself but his Liberal ideas. In this time of Liberal travail let us say what was said recently of the late Robert Kennedy: we know that Allan MacEachen is not a myth but a man. We know that Allan MacEachen is not a hero but a hope. What better accolade can one Liberal render to another in times of Liberal dislocation than to say that he is a Liberal, he is a man, and he is a hope! Ladies and gentlemen, your honours, it is with pride and without prejudice that I introduce to you the honourable Allan Joseph MacEachen, privy councillor, master of arts, doctor of laws and doctor of letters, our leader, and the leader of the opposition in the Senate.

JAMES E. WALKER: EULOGY

May 2, 1989

Hon. Jerahmiel S. Grafstein: Honourable senators, James E. Walker, a former Member of Parliament for the riding of York Centre, former Chairman of the Liberal Caucus, former Assistant Whip of the Liberal Caucus, former Whip of the Liberal Caucus, former Parliamentary Secretary to Prime Minister Trudeau, is dead.

As Northrop Frye wrote in his book *Fools of Time:*

Tragedy revolves around the contract between man and nature. That contract is fulfilled by man's death, death being the debt man owes to nature. What makes Tragedy tragic is the presence,

Frye teaches:

of a counter-movement of being that we call heroic... the capacity for action or passion that is above the ordinary and beyond the everyday human experience.

Well, Jimmy Walker was not heroic in that tragic sense. He was not that kind of hero, but Jimmy Walker was a hero nonetheless. His heroism was based on his quiet service to ordinary, average, hard-working Canadians in North York, part of Metro Toronto, who raise a family, buy a small house, pay off a mortgage, or rent an apartment, pay their taxes, put their kids through school, go to church or synagogue every week, and believe that helping one's neighbour is a daily duty.

Jimmy represented that type of heroism - heroism that does not grab the daily headlines or titillate the media - yet Jimmy represented for me and for many of his friends the essence of political democracy, because his character exemplified the very base upon which our parliamentary democracy rests.

He was every man; the "average guy", as he called himself. He worked hard as a volunteer in his community, got elected to the Board of Education and then to the local council. Then, when the opportunity arose, Jimmy sought and obtained election to the House of Commons, which he felt was the highest honour his neighbours and friends could bestow upon him.

Nobody believed at the time that Jimmy could win the riding. Most Liberal bigwigs felt that a big name candidate was needed, someone who could grab public attention. But Jimmy waited and was patient. He sought the nomination, he won the nomination and won the election. That is not the stuff of classic leadership, because Jimmy did not aspire to leadership. He believed in traditional values of service, loyalty, party, and hard work. No one disliked Jimmy, because he could not bring himself to say a bad word about anyone, including his political opponents.

Race or religion was simply irrelevant to Jimmy. People, people, he would say, even when people disappointed him. He was a natural. The average Canadian, at a time when the media were looking for the quirky, the photogenic, that "something different" - well, Jimmy just was not different. He remained the same type of average guy from the time he first started in politics.

I admired Jimmy. He gave me my real start in politics. He was the one who invited me to join the Young Liberals as part of his organization when he first ran for Parliament back in the early 1960s. I became his Young Liberals President, served on his riding executive, and helped him in all his elections by knocking on doors, setting up coffee parties, travelling around with him, and helping to arrange his schedule.

I remember when he was asked to attend a meeting of union workers to represent the Liberal cause. David Lewis, who was then running in the adjacent riding of York South, was to debate the issues of the day on behalf of the then CCF, and the Liberals sought a spokesperson to represent the Liberal cause, but no one would dare face David Lewis. No one was prepared to debate with David Lewis, who was then considered the greatest public speaker in Canada. Finally, Jimmy was persuaded to go because no one else would go. My job was to help Jimmy prepare for that meeting.

Jimmy was frightened because he felt he would be buried, simply buried in David Lewis's superb rhetoric. But Jimmy won the hearts and the votes of that meeting. At the end of a most magnificient speech by David Lewis, Jimmy stood up, applauded wildly, like all the other labour supporters in the hall. Then, quietly, he opened his remarks by saying, "Well, that is the greatest speech I have ever had the privilege to listen to." Then he went on in his own quiet, conversational way, saying that although he could not match the oratorical power or intellectual brilliance of David Lewis he just wanted to tell his friends and neighbours why it was important to vote for the Liberal Party.

Jimmy was Jimmy - he was always himself; he was a natural. For me he was the personification of everything good, sincere and decent in politics and in public life. Our hearts go out to Lillian, his wife, who first met him in his election campaign and who worked by his side in each and every one of his elections and helped him in his recent illness.

Now, Jimmy, you have earned your rest. We will never forget the pleasure of your company. God bless your soul and give you peace.

Hon. Senators: Hear, hear!

CHARLES McELMAN: ON RETIREMENT

March 28, 1990

.Hon. Jerahmiel S. Grafstein: Honourable senators, over 25 years ago I first met and became aware of the awesome political talents and fearsome character of one Charles McElman, who I was warned was a triple threat. He was a master of the art of party politics, public policy and public administration. Since that time his sterling reputation has not diminished but has only been enhanced.

To consider him a friend or, may I say, even a mentor has its rewards but also its risks. If Charles McElman disagreed with an argument, he could, like a crocodile aroused, snap off the leg of an argument, making it impossible, if not uncomfortable, to continue. Sometimes his silence could be more powerful than his words.

I, for one, will miss his wisdom and wit, his capacious memory, his rock hard honesty, his love of country and, above all, the pleasure of his company. We can only wish Charles, his wife Jessie and his family all the very best in the years ahead.

Hon. Senators: Hear, hear!

JOE GUAY: ON RETIREMENT

October 3, 1990

Hon. Jerahmiel S. Grafstein: Honourable senators, Joe Guay, Joe Guay, Joe Guay, Joe Guay. What a pleasant musical name to match an even more pleasant and musical personality.

Each senator brings many qualities to this house, but usually one singular quality emerges from his many to separate that senator from his peers. In Joe's case, for me at least, it must be his voice, his magical, wonderful voice.

One can debate, as one should, who has the greatest voice in this house. Was it the Hon. Senator from Quebec who nagged us with his gnawing voice from time to time, a senator who has since departed? Is it the roaring thunder of Senator Ray Perrault? Is it the decent, quiet, persuasive down-east dialect of Senator Doody? Is it the dulcet tones of Senator Royce Frith? Is it the graceful francophone rhythms of my friend Jacques Hébert? Is it the broad Celtic range of Heath Macquarrie? Is it the Celtic rage of our leader, Senator MacEachen? Is it the elegant depths of Finlay MacDonald? Is it the staccato voice of Senator "Staf" Barootes?

No, senators, it is none of these. The greatest voice in this chamber belongs to Joe Guay.

Some Hon. Senators: Hear, hear!

Senator Grafstein: Splendid, golden, soft, gentle, sweet, harsh - that great voice and acclaim belongs to our friend, Joe Guay. Honourable senators, we will miss Joe. We will miss his courtesy, his wise counsel, his most pleasant personality and, above all, that golden voice that has spoken up so eloquently for his province of Manitoba and for all Canadians. We will miss you, Joe.

HUGH MACLENNAN AND MORLEY CALLAGHAN: EULOGIES

November 13, 1990

Hon. Jacques Hébert: Honourable senators, I simply want to say that I too knew Hugh MacLennan. Senator Chaput-Roland, I can assure you that had he been in this chamber the other day he would have voted against the GST, something which you did not do.

Some Hon. Senators: Shame!

Hon. Jerahmiel S. Grafstein: Honourable senators, I appreciated the comments of Senator Chaput-Rolland.

Senator Simard: What about the last comment of Senator Hébert?

Senator Grafstein: — about Mr. MacLennan. Perhaps because this is an oversight on the part of all of us, we should also note the untimely passing of Morley Callaghan, who was an equally great Canadian author. Is it not tragic that two such great authors have passed away at a time when we need their voices, minds and hearts to tell us what Canada is all about? So I share in the condolences to both those families. When we read their eloquent works, we are reminded how small we are and how great they are with respect to their visions of Canada.

CHARLES ANDRE JOSEPH DE GAULLE: 100th ANNIVERSARY OF HIS BIRTH

November 22, 1990

Hon. Jerahmiel S. Grafstein: Honourable senators, today marks the One-hundredth anniversary of the birth of one of the twentieth century's greatest statesman Charles André Joseph Marie de Gaulle, who was born on November 22, 1890, in Lille, France. Charles de Gaulle was a great strong leader who stood for freedom when others refused to take a stand. He stood for friendship after the Second World War. He joined in the grand alliance with Germany in 1963, with another great statesman of Europe, Konrad Adenauer. That agreement in 1963 in turn led to the new Europe which we celebrate this week.

Finally, probably one of his greatest achievements was his ability to understand the constitutional malaise of the country in which he resided. He was able, in a peaceful way, to transform the constitutional makeup of France in peacetime.

As we know, honourable senators, great leaders are not perfect. Charles de Gaulle had many faults and made errors in judgment, but he is still entitled to an honoured place in the pages of history, and we should so respect that.

Some Hon. Senators: Hear, hear!

DAVID CROLL: EULOGY

June 13, 1991

Hon. Jerahmiel S. Grafstein: Honourable senators, how many politicians can aspire to become legends? Rarer still, how many politicians become legends in their own time? David Croll transformed himself, by dint of his own efforts, into a legend in our time. Jew, immigrant, lawyer, politician, soldier, hero, partisan, liberal, Zionist, fighter, visionary David Croll was all of these. Yet David Croll was essentially a loner. He fought his way from the bottom to the pinnacle of each career he chose: from immigrant to boy mayor of Windsor, from Member of the Ontario legislature to Ontario Cabinet Minister, from volunteer private to lieutenant colonel of his regiment in wartime, from Member of Parliament to Senator to Privy Councillor. Only one goal, one public office eluded him: it was his dream to be a member of the federal cabinet.

David Croll was a politician of conviction. His conviction was based on choice. He chose between competing ideas of Canada, competing visions of Canada, that haunt us to this day. We have heard echoes of these competing ideas in this very chamber this week. David Croll made choices: he chose between "Everyman" and the elites, between the poor and the rich, between the dispossessed and the possessors, between the powerless and the powerful, between the disabled and the capable, between immigrants and the establishment. He always took the side of the weak against the strong.

During a vitriolic, now-celebrated, strike in Ontario in the late 1930s, when he was a cabinet minister, he again made a choice. In the midst of that strike, which was deeply dividing a province still suffering from the dregs of depression, he resigned, declaring that he would "rather march with the workers than ride with General Motors". Those words became the battle cry for workers across Canada, and they still resonate across the land over a half a century later.

He chose. He always chose. He refused to go along with conventional wisdom. Perhaps because he was a prickly performer, but certainly because he was a Jew, he was denied admission to the federal cabinet. At that time in 1945, David Croll had just returned from overseas, a war hero. He was the only elected Liberal in Toronto in the Spadina riding. Yet he was refused admission to the federal cabinet by Mr. King.. Mr. King, that great racist in the old Canadian tradition, simply refused to appoint him. King is reported to have said words to the effect that Croll "would not be a compatible companion". One was too many for King. So, too, for Mr. Saint-Laurent. Later in 1955, Saint-Laurent appointed David to the Senate. All his life Croll fought against racism. Yet he was the victim of racism, foreclosed from achieving the one great goal of his life.

In Toronto, in the Spadina riding, that microcosm of modern Canadian society, every race and every ideology flourished. David Croll fought the left. He fought the right. He fought communists. He fought fascists and socialists alike. He fought for the people. He fought against radical solutions, for the Liberal way, the consensus way, the middle way. He was a reformist who believed he had to bring people along.

He became an architect of our modern social welfare system, and when he came to the Senate, he piloted benchmark studies on aging and the poor that replenished the national pillars of our modern social welfare system. He fought against racist ideas. He fought for reform. He was a Lloyd George Liberal, and the fires of reform burned in him brightly to the very end. He never gave way.

I first heard of David Croll as a young boy in my home town of London, Ontario. He was then, for many of us, a great exemplar. He was to become for me an early role model. Later, when I came to Toronto to attend law school, I met him for the first time. I had admired him from afar for his public reputation and especially for his performance as a stump political speaker. I had heard him speak many times in smokey basements, crowded restaurants, and in halls packed with veterans. He could on occasion be electrifying.

I joined his law office as an articling student and learned then never to refer to David Croll as a Senator. He was called simply "the Colonel". He was the great simplifier. He was practical. He taught me, and taught many of us, that common sense was the best way to promote one's causes.

David Croll all his life was a record setter: youngest mayor at age 30, first Jewish Ontario Cabinet Minister, first Jewish Senator. From 1930 to 1991, for over 60 years, spanning most of this country, he served Queen, cojuntry and party without pause. Therefore, he became a living legend. David Croll became the quintessential Liberal and the quintessential Canadian.

David, bearer of that royal name, passed away this week doing what he liked to do best: working, arguing, speaking. His spirit lives on: restless, dissatisfied, seeking change, seeking reform, seeking betterment for the little people. David Croll was a man small in stature and he always identified with little people, but he had a grand spirit and a giant will.

In the Jewish tradition, we do not mourn the dead. We celebrate life. For me, and for most of us, David Croll, the man and his ideas, is alive and well. In the words of David the great psalmist, "May his soul be bound up in the bonds of life ... in thy light do we too see the light".

"WINSTON CHURCHILL AS A ZIONIST!"
TO THE CHURCHILL SOCIETY, TORONTO, CANADA

October 24, 1991

The year is 1952. Winston Spencer Churchill has once again become Prime Minister of England. And, as Prime Minister, Churchill wrote his old friend and wartime comrade, General Eisenhower, now President of the United States:

"...As you know"

Churchill reflected,

"I have been a Zionist <u>since</u> the Balfour Declaration..."

Churchill was 78 years old at the time. His memory was not accurate. In fact, Churchill had labelled himself a Zionist years before the Balfour Declaration, which first proclaimed in 1917 the British Government's promise of a Jewish home in Palestine.

In 1955 Churchill himself corrected the public record. In a spontaneous interjection whilst addressing the Lord Mayor of London's annual banquet, when he was passed the news of the sudden death of Chaim Weizmann, a founder of modern Zionism and Israel's first President, Churchill departed from his prepared remarks and said:

"Those of us who have been Zionists in the days before the Balfour Declaration know what a loss Israel has sustained in his death..., respected... throughout the free world and whose son was killed fighting for us. Weizmann led his people back to the Promised Land where we have seen them invincibly installed as a sovereign state...."

Earlier Churchill corrected the private record. Britain had finally recognized Israel nearly two years after its establishment. When Churchill met the first Israeli Ambassador to the Court of St. James, Eliahu Elath, Elath recounted:

> "that he (Churchill) had said he had been a Zionist <u>all his life</u>, that the creation of Israel was a great event in the history of mankind... he was proud of his contributions towards it... he believed that Jews had the moral and physical qualities to lead in The Middle East and that save for Abdullah of Trans-Jordon, he did not care for the reliability or stability of any Arab Sheik.

But the mystery to me is what led Winston Churchill to tell Elath that he:

> *"had been a Zionist <u>all of his life</u>..."*

A study reveals that Churchill professed to be a supporter of a Jewish National Home as early as 1904 - more than a decade before the The Balfour Declaration. Churchill, it seems, became a Zionist supporter even before Zionism was popular amongst English Jews. In 1904, Churchill left the Conservatives and joined the liberals. Now, as a Liberal candidate running in Manchester, Churchill took up the plight of the Jewish refugees which had become a matter of heated public debate in Britain, triggered by the Conservative Government's introduction of a highly restrictive "Alien Immigration Bill." The year before the Government had suggested East Africa as a site for a colonial haven for Jewish refugees. In the run up to the 1904 election, Churchill wrote to members of the Jewish community in Manchester that,

> *"The proposal to form a colony of refugees in some part of British East Africa deserves fair and patient consideration."*

In 1906 Churchill, now safely elected as a Liberal member for Manchester, which was at that time a hot-bed of Zionism, wrote to a Dr. Dulberg, a community leader, that he recognized:

> *"... the supreme attraction to a scattered and persecuted people of a safe and settled home under the flag of tolerance and freedom ... that the noble vision... ought (not) be allowed to fade ...."*

Churchill continued:

> *"...There should be room... within... the British Empire...."*

An early Zionist leader in Manchester, Nathan Laski (father of the famous socialist thinker Harold Laski) said at a public meeting during the 1905 election campaign:

"Anyone who votes against Winston Churchill is a traitor to the cause."

Laski's admonishment to the Manchester Jewish Community was based on Churchill's dual advocacy of a less restrictive Alien Immigration Bill and the idea of a Jewish national home - the Zionist ideal.

Churchill at first supported a Zionist splinter group led by Israel Zangwill, the famous novelist who advocated an asylum in Africa for Jewish refugees as an interim step. A site, if found suitable, had been offered in 1903 by the British Government as a:

"colony or settlement for Jews... to observe their national customs..."

Herzl himself, the founder of modern Zionism, was at first excited by the prospect. Meanwhile, Churchill had travelled to Africa in 1907 and recognized the folly and the limitations of this scheme due to local colonist opposition and the unsuitability of the geography.

So by 1908, Churchill had dismissed the option still being debated of establishing a Jewish settlement, first in East Africa and moved to join the Zionist mainstream in their efforts for a national home in Palestine. In a draft letter found in his files which Churchill never sent, he affirmed:

"... of course,"

Churchill declared:

"Jerusalem must be the ultimate goal. "When it will be achieved, it is vain to prophesize. But that it will some day be achieved is one of the few certainties of the future ... and the establishment of a strong free Jewish state... as... the bridge between Europe... and... Africa, flanking the roads to the East... would not only be an immense advantage to the British Empire but a notable step towards the harmonious disposition of the world amongst its peoples."

So Churchill was not merely a passive Zionist. He actively investigated, considered and explored the options. He promoted the cause of Zionism, as a Member of Parliament, Minister, leader, writer and journalist from the onset of his legendary public and literary career.

In 1921 when, as Colonial Secretary, Churchill spoke in Jerusalem at the founding of the Hebrew University, he said that:

"Personally, my heart is full of sympathy for Zionism...since 12 years ago, when I made the acquaintance of Manchester Jewry."

The origins of Churchill's robust attachment to the cause of Zionism are rather mysterious. Was he a Zionist "all his life"? Churchill's motivations and enthusiasms were more complex and elusive than most and, because of the capacious range of his interests, are equally difficult to unravel.

Perhaps the most interesting insight into Churchill's thought processes was the famous philosopher, Isaiah Berlin who knew Churchill. Berlin wrote during the Second World War that Churchill,

> "saw history and life as a great renaissance pageant. He was inflexibly attached to first principles."

Berlin went on to say that:

> "Biographers and historians... describe... and analyse his views... on Palestine... they will find his opinions... are set... and fixed patterns set early in life and later only reinforced... He always believed in great states and civilization in historical order... The Jews' (search) for self determination in Palestine engaged this intervention... He believed in the permanent character of races... and of types of individuals."

To support Berlin's thesis, Churchill himself was to write in his war memoirs a lengthy passage praising the gifts of the Jews and Greeks to civilization. Churchill wrote:

> "No two races have made such an impact on the world.... No two cultures have counted more for history than Jerusalem and Athens. Their messages of religion and philosophy and art have been the guiding lights... of modern freedom and civilization."

But why this very early identification with Zionism? Was it founded on Churchill's religious beliefs? Churchill was not particularly religious. He was not a churchgoer yet he believed in Christian principles and the pageantry of the Church. Was it based on his spontaneous sympathy for underdogs? Or was it due to his admiration for the Jewish people as historic survivors of an ancient era? Was it because of Churchill's visceral abhorrence of anti-Semitism? Was it based on his romantic sense of history? Was it related to Churchill's fascination with ancient dynasties and imperialism? Was it rooted in the mythic connection that some British historians had made between the origins of early Britain and the Biblical lost tribes of Judea and Israel? Was it connected to his identification with the myth of King Arthur and the sword of Excalibur reputed to be the biblical sword of King David himself? Did it spring from Churchill's rather fundamentalist belief in the words, in the cadences of the Old Testament? Or was it due to the influence of his tragically deceased father, Lord Randolph Churchill, whom he revered, and who is said to have enjoyed and preferred the friendly values and ideas of his Jewish friends (as was reputed to be the case of Edward VII) to others in English society.

Perhaps this is the firmest platform on which to delve into the tangle of influences that shaped the idiosyncratic mind and actions of Winston Churchill. Nothing was stronger in his life than the career and memory of his father. Churchill carefully researched his father's career and wrote a monumental biography about Lord Randolph which was published in 1904. Virtually one of the first letters Randolph Churchill wrote to his bride-to-be, Churchill's mother, Jenny Jerome, was noted in her memoirs. Lord Randolph wrote to her of his admiration for Disraeli whose early novels, *Alroy* and *Tancred,* read by both Lord Randolph and Winston Churchill projected the idea of the restoration of a Jewish State. Indeed, Churchill's only novel, *Savrola*, was modelled on the romantic Disraeli notion that a novel could captivate public attention, enhancing the author's path to public acclaim and onto high public office. Lord Randolph's greatest friend and supporter was Lord Rosebery, Foreign Secretary and briefly Prime Minister of England. Lord Rosebery's wife was Hannah. Hannah was a devout practising Jewess and the leading heiress of the English Rothschild clan. Her granddaughter, Lady Crewe, became an active Zionist and was a great friend of both Winston and Clementine. Indeed, Winston first met Clementine at Lady Crewe's home. Rosebery was to write, as did Churchill, a shorter, no less perceptive biography of Lord Randolph. After Rosebery died in 1929, Churchill wrote a brilliant biographical eulogy to Rosebery. Rosebery was the English politician who first coined the phrase "the British Commonwealth."

Rosebery's tenure as Liberal Prime Minister was brief and Churchill described his flaw as the inability to mix effectively in "caucus politics." Yet Churchill went on to describe Rosebery in a curious way and I quote that he:

> *"was not only a prophet but a judge in Israel."*

Rosebery was Churchill's early model for standing against the tide of conventional wisdom:

> *"one voice against public opinion."*

Rosebery, virtually alone, predicted that the Anglo-French Agreement of 1904 would lead to "war not peace." Churchill consciously or unconsciously later emulated Rosebery's solitary stand against overwhelming public opinion in his own 'wilderness years' in the 1930s.

It is fascinating to note that in 1885, Lord Randolph wrote a blistering essay entitled *Elijah's Mantle* using an unusual biblical metaphor to describe the mishaps of Tory succession to the Disraeli heritage of "Tory Democracy." Three years later, in 1888, at the precocious age of 14, one month after he first commenced attendance at Harrow, Winston Churchill wrote his very first essay entitled *Palestine at the Time of John The Baptist.* In this amazingly mature essay, the young Churchill described, in sweeping terms, the geography of Palestine. Then he went on to describe the division of the population in that early era and took the side of the Zealots, who in biblical times were the leaders struggling to restore the sovereignty of the Jewish State from Roman domination. So Churchill, from the tender age of 14, read and wrote with astonishing maturity about the precursors of the Zionist idea. You'll recall that his days at Harrow lingered with Churchill with great clarity until his dotage.

An even more intriguing influence on both Randolph Churchill and Winston Churchill was Lord Shaftesbury, Lord Randolph's cousin. In the first half of the 18th century, Shaftesbury was the foremost social reformer of the Industrial era. Shaftebury railed against such evils of the early industrial revolution as child labour. Shaftesbury's marauding reform spirit was broader. Shaftesbury was also propelled by strong messianic religious ideas into a fervent belief in Zionism. More than half a century before the first Zionist Congress was held, he organised and animated a society for the Jewish return to Zion. In 1847, Shaftesbury directly lobbied Lord Palmerston, Foreign Secretary and later Prime Minister, to intervene against the Ottoman Empire to protect Jews who were then being persecuted in Syria and Turkish provinces. Shaftesbury was related to Palmerston by marriage. He inspired Palmerston to extend British protection to Jews then living in Palestine. Palmerston mistrusted the reliability of the Ottoman Empire as did Churchill a century later. Palmerston himself went on to advocate the restoration of the Jews to 'The Promised Land.' Shaftesbury's fervour lay in his evangelical belief in the Jewish return to Zion. Shaftesbury no doubt helped shape Lord Randolph's ideas about Tory democracy as did Disraeli's ideas of social reform, which all in turn deeply influenced Winston Churchill's ideas of social justice. Recent psychological studies of the tormented inner life of Winston Churchill all pay special attention to the far-reaching influence of Lord Randolph's meteoric rise and fall that played on Churchill's psyche. Many have suggested that Churchill spent his entire career seeking to emulate and vindicate his father. Many of Randolph's close Jewish friends became Churchill's confidantes and advisers. Baron de Hirsch, Sir Ernest Cassels and Lord Rothschild were early advocates and financial supporters of Jewish settlements in Palestine.

Yet a more intriguing source of Churchill's interest in Zionism may be found in two of Churchill's trilogy of personal heroes, Oliver Cromwell and Napoleon Bonaparte. Churchill had planned early in his career to do a definitive biography of Napoleon and to that end he had read over a hundred books in preparation. As for Cromwell, Churchill had spent an inordinate amount of time studying him and later in his *History of the English-Speaking Peoples* dwelling at great length on the Cromwellian period of British history. Churchill's unvarnished admiration for Cromwell even conflicted with his love of the monarchy. Some observers have noted that Churchill was able to resolve this ambiguity by focusing on Cromwell, not as a regicide, but as a promoter and protector of Parliament. In fact, Churchill almost came to verbal blows with King George, when, as First Lord of the Admiralty, Churchill wished to name a Warship after Oliver Cromwell who the King detested as a regicide. After a flurry of debate, Churchill finally, reluctantly, demurred to the King's wishes.

Both Cromwell and Napoleon were out of step with their times in their support for Zionist aspirations.

Both believed in the restoration of Israel. Cromwell's belief flowed from his deeper religious convictions that the ingathering of Jewish exiles was a precondition to the Messianic Era. In 1655, Cromwell restored Jewish rights of settlement and domicile during his Commonwealth. Literary critics had detected a strong similarity in Cromwell's cadences and Churchill's famous speeches, particularly during World War II. It seems clear from his rhetorical style that Churchill modelled many of his ideas on his hero, Cromwell.

As for Napoleon, the germ of many of Churchill's strategic and tactical ideas originated with Napoleon Bonaparte whose bust adorned Churchill's work desk at Chartwell and who was closely studied and admired by Churchill.

In 1799, almost a hundred years before the advent of modern Zionism, Napoleon proclaimed his support for the restoration of a Jewish State in Palestine, the first Western leader of the modern era to do so. Napoleon followed this proclamation by restoring, during his reign, full rights of citizenship to the Jews of France and elsewhere throughout his Empire. He convoked, for the first time since the destruction of the Temple in Jerusalem, the Sanhedrin, a college of learned Jewish scholars and teachers, who in ancient days had settled issues of law.

Churchill shared Napoleon's strategic belief that a Jewish State rising in Palestine would form a bulwark of western civilization in the Middle East against the unpredictable, unstable, vagaries of Eastern influences. Both sought support from the Jewish masses for their strategic plans and both understood the centrality of the Zionist idea in the Jewish experience and world history. Both identified with "greatness" and the chosen few as instruments of "greatness." Lord Fisher knowing of Churchill's lively affinity for his heroes once described him as

"Napoleonic in audacity (and) Cromwellian in thoroughness."

Yet another source of Winston Churchill's affinity to Zionism may be based on the remarkable exploits of Colonel Charles Henry Churchill. Charles Henry Churchill was a grandson of the Duke of Marlborough and thus a cousin of Lord Randolph, Churchill's father. Colonel Churchill, as an Officer in the British army was sent to serve in the Middle East in 1838. Then in 1840, Colonel Churchill was assigned the responsibility to protect the Jewish community of Damascus in the Turkish Province of Syria from Muslim massacre. In numerous speeches and letters, Colonel Churchill predicted to the Damascus Jewish community that their hour of liberation was approaching when the Jewish Nation would once again take up its place among the powers of the world. So Colonel Churchill was an early enthusiastic adherent to Zionism. In 1841 he wrote to the most prominent Jewish leader in England of the day, Moses Montefiore,

"First it is up to Jews to make a commencement towards a Jewish State."

and then Colonel Churchill argued:

"European powers will follow."

Colonel Churchill urged colonization and:

"the glorious struggle for national existence under British auspices and sanction."

Colonel Churchill later advocated a Jewish State in Palestine in 1843 in a book he wrote called *Mount Lebanon* which was based on his 15 years experience in the Middle East. Colonel Churchill believed that the restoration of Israel as a nation would be a strategic element in Britain's Imperial progress and mastery eastward. Colonel Churchill anticipated his famous descendant when he argued that propping up the Turkish hold on Palestine was useless. The Turks, he felt, were unreliable. Palestine must become part of the English Empire as an independent Jewish State. Consider to this early example of Churchill's cousin's eloquence published in 1853:

"Land of Jacob's might and Israel's wandering power, David's lyre and Isaiah's strain, of Abraham's faith and Immanuel's love - where God's mysterious ways with man began and where in the fullness of time they were to be accomplished... it also has a claim on England's watchful vigilance and her sympathising case..."

So Winston Churchill shared his antecedent's and earlier British travellers' beliefs that English strategic interests in Palestine, concided with a Jewish State that would balance the intimate grip of the Ottoman Empire, Syria, and Egypt. Such eastern influences, if unchecked, could thwart English ambitions, not only in Palestine but beyond in her vital possessions and interests in India.

Another strange and potent influence on Churchill was Lord Fisher, whom Churchill deeply admired. Churchill and Fisher shared a tempestuous relationship before and during Churchill's famous stint as First Lord of the Admiralty at the outset of World War I. You will recall, Churchill's appointment of Fisher had been controversial. He had brought Fisher back as First Sea Lord. Later, Fisher repaid this kindness by failing to support Churchill's Dardanelles strategy, even though he first encouraged it. In any event, Churchill adored and respected Fisher, at times to his wife's Clementine's consternation. Fisher believed that the Royal Navy was under divine protection. He told Churchill repeatedly that the English were the ten lost tribes of Israel and that Churchill would be succeed in his naval ventures because of this divine connection. Fisher exhorted Churchill on the eve of a naval engagement:

"You are wrong to worry and excite yourself. Do try to remember that we are the lost ten tribes of Israel. We are sure to win!!!"

Strange but true.

Winston Churchill's strategic sense of Empire, merged with his romantic sense of history when Churchill served as Colonial Secretary in 1921-1922 following World War I. Then Churchill became directly involved in the evolution of Palestine into a Jewish State. The plan, which he crafted, was for Trans-Jordan, Iraq and Saudi Arabia to be created and joined by a Jewish State. Under his tutelage, Trans-Jordan was established as an independent Arab state in Palestine East of Jordan. Churchill's plan was to establish first an Arab State East of Jordan and later a Jewish State West of Jordan when the Jewish population evolved.

Trans-Jordan occupied 80% of the land of historical Palestine which seemed a wholly reasonable amount to set aside for the local Arab population.

And, it was as Colonial Secretary that Churchill finessed the anti-Zionist tactics of the Vatican designed to thwart the British mandate and Churchill's policy for laying the foundation for a Zionist homeland by his White Paper which reaffirmed the Balfour Declaration and the Zionist idea "as of right and not of sufferance".

No matter what the precise origins and potent influences, Churchill was not alone in his early profession of Zionism. The roots of Zionism were planted deep in the British Christian Establishment since the days of Cromwell. During Churchill's lifetime Prime Ministers such as Gladstone, Rosebery, Balfour, Lloyd George and political figures such as Joseph Chamberlain, Leopold Amery, Lord Robert Cecil, Lord Milner, Brendan Bracken, Lord Cherwell, the fabled Lawrence of Arabia, and earlier political and social leaders such as Lords Melbourne, Palmerston and Shaftesbury, all shared Churchill's convictions about establishment of a Jewish State in Palestine that was the raison d'etre of the Zionist movement. Ironically, early opposition to a Jewish State came from established English Jews including a Jewish member of the British Cabinet during the World War I debate about the Balfour Declaration, who believed their loyalty to the Crown would be questioned.

Churchill had another strong reason for promoting Zionism in the aftermath of World War I. In 1920 Churchill wrote that Zionism was a much more attractive and preferable ideology to attract the Jewish masses than Bolshevism which he abhorred. Zionism, he felt, would present a greater benefit to civilization than Bolshevism.

So Churchill, aside from his repeated profession as a Zionist, played a little noted and unheralded role as a Zionist while an MP, Junior Cabinet Minister, particularly as Colonial Secretary in the early 1920s and later as Prime Minister and Leader of the Opposition.

Churchill played a significant role in four crucial areas affecting the creation of Jewish State.

First, Jewish immigration to Palestine. Second, on the creation of Jewish military formations that form vital links in the creation of the Hagganah, the Israeli National Defence Force. Third, on formulating concrete ideas of partition of Palestine that were drafted by Churchill after World War I in 1921-22 and then were revisited and revised by the Cabinet during World War II. It was this last plan that ultimately formed the basis of the creation of the State of Israel in the United Nations. Finally, the formal recognition and legitimacy of Israel, beleaguered as she was, from the very moment of her birth in 1947.

Churchill was deeply disappointed in the Atlee Government's mishandling of the birth of Israel. Churchill had envisaged the creation of Israel as a Jewish Dominion within the family of the British Empire. The Atlee Government and Bevin's actions, including those of the Foreign Office and the Prime Minister's Office, were seen as acts of militancy against the Zionist cause that made this impossible.

Martin Gilbert's majestic volumes on the life of Winston Churchill touch on Churchill's crucial interventions on behalf of the cause of Zionism. After World War I, the Jewish Brigade, (the "First Jewish" battalion) which had been created in the latter part of that War, would demobilise much later at Churchill's insistence in his position as Minister of War. Churchill countermanded orders to disarm Jews in 1921 and in 1940 in Palestine. In the Second World War, Churchill promised to establish a Jewish fighting element despite repeated attempts by the military and the Foreign Office from 1941 to 1944 to thwart Churchill's directives. Independent Jewish fighting units were finally established as the 48th, 49th and 50th and 51st Fusiliers. These military formations were manned by Jewish volunteers led by non-Jewish officers. These military formations, combined with the settlement defence establishment forged by the singular efforts of Colonel Wingate, were the roots of the Haganah - the Israel Defence Force and its fighting philosophy.

On the question of Jewish immigration, Churchill was instrumental in crafting a policy leading to building the foundations of the Jewish State. For the best display of Churchill's mindset on this question, let us turn to the Spring of 1939. Churchill was still an outcast in his Party and in the country. He had few followers. Even as late as the spring of 1939, the idea of war was not imminent nor had it permeated the minds of the English public. The awesome plight of the Jews in Europe, particularly in Germany, was evident. Yet, the British Government issued a White Paper effectively restricting Jewish immigration to Palestine. That 1939 White Paper broke repeated promises of previous British Governments that pledged to allow Jewish immigration to Palestine based on the:

"principle of economic absorptive capacity."

In fact, Churchill had been the author of that very principle when he was Colonial Secretary in the early '20s. Now the Secretary of State for the Colonies, Malcolm Mac-Donald, on February 22, 1939 vigorously defended his White Paper in Parliament. The Chamberlain Government had accepted his restrictive policy.

MacDonald's limited interpretation of the Balfour Declaration meant that a Jewish national home in Palestine would only be established with the consent of the Arab population. Of course, the Arabs opposed any change, including any increase in Jewish immigration. MacDonald argued that the authors of the 1917 Balfour Declaration, including Churchill, later envisaged the Jewish national home would be "something less than a National State."

This less ambitious concept, he claimed, set in motion an earlier White Paper of 1922 authored by Winston Churchill himself. MacDonald blamed Churchill, pointing out that when Churchill was in office:

> *"That master of beautiful and powerful English"*

watered down the original promise:

> *"declaring that it is no part of Her Majesty's policy that Palestine should become a Jewish State."*

Still MacDonald agreed that economic absorptive capacity principle after 1931 was the sole criterion for measuring immigration and was so noted by the Council of the League of Nations. MacDonald went on to say that his government, the Chamberlain Government:

> *"... cannot now be bound for all time in all circumstances to maintain the strict economic principle without qualifications."*

MacDonald concluded that the next five years would be highly restricted immigration. Thereafter, expansion of immigration would depend on the consent of the Arabs. MacDonald then sketched out the various options the Chamberlain Government envisaged which included a unitary state controlled by the Arabs, a federal State where there would be a Jewish Province, but never offered a Jewish unitary state. What was Churchill's response, when challenged as he was and charged with complicity in this reversal in government policy? Churchill recalled that he was not even a member of the War Cabinet when the Balfour Declaration was promised in 1917. Yet Churchill said:

> *"I found myself in entire agreement with those sentiments as well as those expressed by the Prime Minister and his friends."*

Churchill then traced his own involvement with the policy. In 1922 as Colonial Secretary, the first paragraph of Churchill's own dispatch read:

> *"His Majesty's Government has no intention of repudiating obligations into which they have entered into towards the Jewish People."*

He repeated that the British Government's pledge was preceded by the covenant of the League of Nations. The British Government went on to say:

> *"could not undertake a mandate that would make impractical fulfillment of this solemn promise made not only by the British Government but their allies as well....."*

Churchill said:

> *"this pledge was to create a home of refuge"*

or as he said:

> *"of an asylum."*

It was not made after World War I but during World War I in 1917 and then repeated in 1922. Churchill condemned the White Paper of 1939 as immigration would now only be allowed with the consent of the Arabs in Palestine. Churchill roared in Parliament:

> *"this was a breach. A violation. A violation, of repeated pledges. Jews would be forever outnumbered by Arabs. Their future would be subject to Arab determinism."*

So on May 23, 1939 Churchill repeated to Parliament:

> *"that the Jewish people ... have through centuries of dispersion and persecution patiently awaited the hour of its restoration of its ancestral home."*

Well before the Holocaust was even imagined and before the Second World War had started, Churchill repeated the pledge given by the government in 1917 of which he was then a junior member. On the question of Arabs and justice, listen carefully what Churchill told Parliament in 1939:

> *I cannot feel that we have accorded to the Arab race unfair treatment after the support they gave us in the late war. The Palestinian Arabs, of course, were for the most part, fighting against us. But elsewhere over vast regions inhabited by Arabs independent Arab Kingdoms and principalities have come into being such as has never before been known in Arab history before. Some have been established by Great Britain and others by France. When I wrote this despatch in 1922, I was advised, amongst others, by Colonel Lawrence, the truest champion of Arab rights modern times has known. He has recorded his opinion that the settlement is fair and just - his definite settled opinion that we place the Emir Abdullah in Trans-Jordania where he remains faithful and prosperous to this day. The other under the responsibility of the Prime Minister of those days, King Feisal, was placed on the Throne of Iraq where his descendants now rule. We also showed ourselves to*

continually resolve to close no door upon the ultimate development of a Jewish national homefed by continuing Jewish immigration into Palestine. Colonel Lawrence thought this was fair then, why should it would be pretended that it is unfair now."

In that speech, Winston Churchill Prime Minister reminded Neville Chamberlain of Chamberlain's own words 20 years before:

"A great responsibility will rest upon Zionists who, before long, will be proceeding to join their hearts to the ancient seat of their people. Theirs will be the task to build up a new prosperity in a new civilization in an old Palestine so long neglected in this rule."

As for the Arabs being persecuted in Palestine in 1939 and Arab population flows, here's what Churchill had to say:

"So far from being persecuted, the Arabs have crowded into the country, multiplied until their populations increased more than all the world Jewry could lift up the Jewish population."

This then was Churchill early in 1939 on the eve of World War II, speaking against the odious White Paper which was the direct cause of so many deaths in Europe that could have been saved if Jews had been allowed to emigrate to Palestine.

In 1949 when the question of recognition of the State of Israel was debated in the House of Commons, Britain had still not recognized Israel almost a year after its establishment. Here's what Churchill had to say to the House of Commons in 1949 urging the Socialist Government led by Clement Atlee to recognize Israel:

"Whether the Rt. Hon. Gentleman likes it or not and whether we like it or not, the coming into being of a Jewish state in Palestine is an event in world history to be viewed in the perspective, not of a generation or century, but in the perspective of a thousand, two thousand and even three thousand years. This is an event of world history. Now that Israel has come into being, it is England that refuses to recognise it and by our actions we find ourselves regarded as its most bitter enemies. All this is due, not to mental inertia or lack of grip on the part of the ministers concerned, but I am also afraid to the very strong and direct streak of bias and prejudice on the part of the Foreign Secretary."

Then he went on to say that:

"I am sure that he thought the Arab League was stronger and that it would win fighting broke out.... and the course he took led directly to a trial of strength and the result was the opposite to what I believe he expected it to be.... ...it turned out in the opposite way to that which he, acting on the advice of his military advisers, and against the recorded opinion of Lord Wavell as to which side was the stronger, expected."

"I certainly felt that the spectacle of Jewish settlements being invaded from all sides - from Syria, Transjordan and Egypt and with a lot of our tanks and modern tackle, was, on the face of it, most formidable, but I believed that the combination would fall to pieces at the first check, and I adhered to the estimate I had formed in the war of the measure of the fighting qualities and the tough fibre of the Zionist community, and the support which it would receive from Zionists all over the world. But the Foreign Secretary was wrong, wrong in his facts, wrong in the mood, wrong in the method and wrong in the result, and we are very sorry about it for his sake and still more sorry about it for our own.... ....This is a poor and undeserved result of all that we have created and built up in Palestine by the good will and solid work of 25 years. We have lost the friendship of the Palestine Jews for the time being. I was glad to read a statement from Dr. Weizmann the other day pleading for friendship between the new Israeli state and the Western world. I believe that will be its destiny. He was an old friend of mine for many years. His son was killed in the war fighting with us. I trust his influence may grow and that we shall do what we can.... I hope that later on, a truer comprehension of the Zionist debt to this country will revive. ...Moreover, as I mentioned just now, the Foreign Secretary's policy has been the worst possible for the Arabs. I am sure we could have agreed immediately after the war upon a partition scheme which would have been more favourable to the Arabs."

In a telling exchange, Atlee interfered and said:

"May I ask the Rt. Hon. Gentleman if he thought that could have been done, why he did not do it after the war? He was in power."

Churchill responded:

"No. The world and the nation had the inestifable blessing of the Right Hon. Gentleman's guidance,"

drawing attention to the fact that the Atlee government had been elected immediately prior to the end of World War II:

"I am sure that we could have agreed immediately after the war upon a partition scheme which would have been more favourable to the Arabs than that which will now follow their unsuccessful recourse to arms."

Churchill went on to say:

"I do not pretend or propose to enter tonight upon the drawing of frontier lines... I will, however, say that we ought not to grudge a fair share of the deserts of the Negeb(sic) to the Jews.... The Jews by the gift they have and by the means which they do not lack, have a way

of making the desert bloom."

And he pointed out that the desert lands did not bloom under Arab control then. Churchill turned to the Arabs pointing out that Feisal had been placed on the throne of Iraq and Emir Abdullah with the advice and guidance of Lawrence in Amman. He further pointed out that when Syria was liberated, Syrian Arabs were ensured their full rights and independence although it meant a bitter controversy with General de Gaulle. Churchill then explained:

> *"I will not have it said that we have not behaved with loyalty to the Arabs or that what has been asked for the Jews. ... Hon. Gentlemen do not seem to realise that Jew and Arab have always been there."*

He talked of:

> *"a hope of affording refuge to the survivors of the Jewish community who have been massacred in so many parts of Europe and letting them try their best and their efforts are amazing to bring back into economic usefulness lands which the world cannot afford to leave lying idle."*

Churchill went on to criticize the Government for flying reconnaisance missions with Arab-Egyptian planes. He criticized the government for using RAF as opposed to the United Nations planes. Then he criticized Bevin of being unfair even to King Abdullah of Jordan.

Here's what Churchill said in 1949:

> *"I am sure Abdullah would have done everything in his power to work for a peaceful solution with the Jews. I believe that the Government of Transjordan would have been glad to see His Majesty's Government having an affective representative in Tel-Aviv during these difficult times. I am sure that Abdullah has done everything to work for a peaceful solution, which is in his interests, and to maintain his loyalty to the British who placed him in his seat at Amman and his brother on the throne of Iraq."*

As to Zionist Settlement policy, again let's listen to Churchill as over and over again he supported Zionists for their settlement policy:

> *"The whole point of our settlement was that immigration was to be free, but not beyond the limits of economic absorptive power. But the newcomers who were coming in brought work and employment with them, and the means of sustaining a much larger population than had lived in. Palestine and Transjordan. They brought the hope with them of a far larger population than existed in Palestine at the time of Our Lord. One has only to look up to*

the hills that once were cultivated and then were defaced by centuries of medieval barbarism, to see what has been accomplished."

He finally concluded with these words:

"When the British Government quitted the scene and the Arab Armies from Syria, Transjordania and finally in considerable strength from Egypt rolled forward to extinguish the Jewish National Home, all this Arab population fled in terror and took refuge behind the advancing forces of their own religion. Their condition is most grievous and I agree that it should certainly not be neglected by the Government. The one great remedial measure is peace and a lasting settlement. I make this prediction once the fighting stops in the great bulk of the present refugees will return to do work essential to the growing prosperity and development of the Jewish settlement in Palestine. I thank the House very much for allowing me to speak ....
I feel so very strongly and have always tried to form my own opinions. All this Debate is, of course, on a small scale compared with the sombre march of events throughout the world. But it is a disquieting thought that the mismanagement we notice here in the working model, may perhaps be typical of what is proceeding over much wider spheres under the present Government.... We must take this opportunity of severing ourselves beyond all doubt or question from these latest acts of mismanagement on the Palestine question. ....we must tonight make our protest against the course of action ....which has deprived Britain of the credit she had earned, and of the rights and interests she had acquired , and made her at once the mockery and scapegoat of so many States who have never made any positive contribution of their own.."

In summary, Churchill 'all his life', or at least, almost from the very outset of his political career was devoted to each crucial turning in the evolution of the Ztonist idea into the State of Israel

Harold Wilson, former Labour Prime Minister, wrote after his retirement, a remarkable book called *Chariot of Israel* dealing with the American/British experience with Israel. I quote Harold Wilson:

"That Churchill should stand with Harry Truman as two of the greatest friends of Israel when peace comes to the Middle East as it should come (and) Churchill will emerge as a giant in the Zionist cause."

Some modern scholars disagree. They argue that Churchill had ulterior motives. He was, they charge, merely a political opportunist. He first used Zionism, they argue to gain political support in Manchester. He wavered after World War I when he had the power as Colonial Secretary and then, during World War II when he was Prime Minister. He used Zionism as a leverage for U.S. support for his own interests as he perceived British interests when he was in power and needed an American alliance. As Prime Minister during World War II, he would not override entrenched anti-Semitic and pro-Arab support in the British bureaucracy and military establishment to promote the creation of the State of Israel as he could have. His words, his critics say, never matched his actions. Worse, he is now condemned by revisionists for his failure during World War II to act on saving the Jewish victims of the Holocaust including bombing the Death Camps when he could have ordered such raids even though Zionist leaders such as Ben Gurion, at the time in England, did not recognize the paramountcy of the problem.

So these modern scholars have found Churchill wanting. As for me, I prefer to believe Churchill stood against the tide in his early support of Zionism, and thus, that Churchill earned an honourable place in history as an architect of the Zionist state. When Britain sought to disengage her promised support of a Jewish State, in the '20s, '30s and '40s, Churchill spoke out! Politicians waver, change and compromise. They vacillate between hot and cold on even their most passionate principles. Yet Churchill remained resistant to the anti-Zionist voices of his countrymen and of his times.

Let me conclude on a Churchillian literary note. In 1932, while out of office, Churchill wrote a most remarkable essay on Moses, the first and greatest Zionist who led his people back to the Promised Land.

> *"There is no doubt about one miracle. This wandering tribe undistinguishable from numberless nomadic communities, grasped and proclaimed an idea of which all the genius of Greece and all the power of Rome was incapable.*
>
> *Moses was the greatest of the prophets. ... the supreme lawgiver... he was one of the world 'greatest human beings who led one of the most decisive leaps forward in the human story."*

Winston Churchill believed in history and he believed in Zionism. Now we will see in our time whether history will prove him right or wrong.

* * * * * * *

*These untutored thoughts and conjectures reflect a pastiche of my random and episodic excursions over three decades into the life and times of Winston Spencer Churchill, gleaned from it's own words, countless biographies, memoirs, histories and essays on the majestic pageant of British history and the cauldron of the Middle East. Churchill, like a blazing comet, illuminated the political landscape where he, his antecedents and contemporaries acted out such energetic and fascinating roles. Even the brilliant light and dark shadows cast by Churchill's singular career could not camouflage the startling recurrence of trends and cycles in history and human conduct, where the past swerves into the present with eerie regularity.

TOAST TO THE UNIVERSITY CLUB OF TORONTO
CHURCHILL AS A LIBERAL
ADDRESS TO THE UNIVERSITY CLUB ANNUAL DINNER, TORONTO

OCTOBER 27, 1993

My topic for the toast to the club is Churchill, Winston Churchill - as a Liberal! A strange topic for a club toast, some might suggest, since Churchill himself was considered by some as not exactly "clubbable" - though he was a member of a number of clubs. Since we, in the Senate, particularly these days, get the feeling in the country that we are not exactly "clubbable" ourselves, Churchill as the classic irreverent outsider seems a rather kindred spirit.

In 1910, Churchill jointly founded, together with the great F.E. Smith, Q.C. - one of the greatest speakers of his day (later Lord Birkenhead L.C. of England) yet another kind of club - a speaking club for politicians of all stripes and outstanding non-politicians interested in ideas, served up with superb cuisine, laced with fine wine and shrouded by mellow smoke of aged cigars. The purpose of the club was designed to cut across party lines and create friendships to minimize political differences and partisanship. This, they grandly named the "other club" and Churchill rarely missed one of its regular fortnightly dinners. "Great tact will be necessary in the avoiding of bad moments," so Churchill wrote to Bonar Law - about the "other club's" organizing idea. Churchill always believed that personal friendship and civility were more important for those in public life than personalized political partisanship.

It seems that your convenor hopes to establish, within the boundaries of the University Club, a similar enterprise and courageously concluded that he could think of no other outsiders, so, sensing my unnatural lust to hold any audience captive on any topic, asked me to launch this year's toast to the Club. I sensed my topic - Churchill as Liberal - might both be diverting and timely in light of recent events though coupled with the stern admonishment by your President that I was not to speak about politics.

So enticed, I intend to give you a taste of one embattled senator's revisionist view of history, rather than current politics any semblance in my remarks between today's politics and yesterday's history is therefore purely coincidental .

The year is 1903. The place is England. England stands at the very height of her imperial power. Germany plots to outstrip England's superior seapower by secretly laying plans for the construction of massive dreadnoughts. Military strategists in england respond that Britain's control of the seas should be accelerated by enlarging her already awesome fleet to safeguard the Empire in all her majesty and maintain the balance of power in Europe.

Meanwhile, on the domestic front, a number of young sparkling political stars are emerging. Winston Spencer Churchill, first elected to parliament as a Tory in the 1900 election in the constituency of Oldham is bent on following in the illustrious, if ill-fated steps of his late father, Lord Randolph Churchill, who was a Leading member of the Tory establishment. Lord Randolph was a friend of the Prince of Wales and inheritor, so young Churchill believed, of the great social policies of Benjamin Disraeli called by all - "Tory Democracy".

Unfortunately, Lord Randolph Churchill's meteoric career, aimed right at the Prime Minister's office, was cut down by a contagious social disease, upsetting his rationality, causing him to resign suddenly as Chancellor of the Exchequer and slowly slide into a tormented and deranged death.

After his father's unhappy demise, young Churchill, aalready a soldier, became a notorious columnist and respected author, whose sensational escape from a Boer jail in South Africa was widely publicized in all the London papers. He returned to England to pursue his fame and fortune in print and in politics.

England finds herself embroiled in a divisive national debate, splitting the coalition government led by the Conservative party and its alliance with Liberals and others who call themselves Unionists. Suddenly, the Tory Prime Minister, Arthur Balfour, reverses 50 years of traditional Tory free trade policy and supports higher tariffs for the first time.

Churchill, an unabashed 'free trader,' uncomfortable with this sudden departure from the traditional policies of the Tory party, seeks new friends and alliances to maintain his principled philosophy as a 'free trader.' At the same time, Churchill was also becoming increasingly disenchanted with the elitism of Tory social policies that protected the prerogatives of the upper classes at the numbing disadvantage to the poor .

Churchill meets and quickly becomes enamoured by another rising political star, Lloyd George destined to become the greatest Liberal of his age. They seem to share more things in common than set them apart. Lloyd George, a Welsh lawyer rising from humble origins by his lyrical gift of tongue, is a mesmerizing and charming personality. Churchill is both mesmerized and charmed.

Churchill writes and speaks in favour of 'free trade' in the run-up to the 1905 election antagonizing Tory loyalists on all sides, including Prime Minister Balfour himself and Churchill's own Tory riding association in Oldham. Conspiring with the Tory whips in London, in his absence, his Tory association passes a resolution. Suggesting that Mr. Churchill seek another constituency, since Churchill disagrees with party trade policy .

So it is in spring of 1904, Churchill rises to speak in parliament after Lloyd George in yet another turbulent debate on 'free trade.' Churchill is a Tory still!

Churchill is insulted when the Tory front bench and almost all the Tory backbench (except a few hecklers) immediately leave the House and repair to the smoking rooms while he is speaking - as a deliberate snub. Weeks later, Churchill rises in the House of Commons and in mid-speech, loses his train of thought and retires embarrassed. Members murmur that he may be suffering from the same defect that doomed his father decades before.

Shortly thereafter - on May 31st, Winston Churchill, revived, re-enters the House of Commons, pauses, bows to the Speaker and crosses the floor to sit beside Lloyd George in the same seat occupied by his revered father, Lord Randolph, when in opposition. Churchill realized he must make the move, even though his riding association deferred taking further punitive action against him. As a newly minted Liberal, he assays opportunities and chooses a Liberal Riding, a seat in northwest Manchester, the home of Cobden and Bright - the bastion 'free trade.'

Now he finds himself not only comfortable as a promoter of free trade in this new welcoming environment, but takes up the cudgel for alien minorities - the immigrant society - that make up Manchester's polyglot population. Churchill quickly becomes a leading champion against the proposed conservative alien bill which gives greater discretion to the Home Ssecretary to keep out so called "undesireables" - mostly impoverished Eastern European refugees - and captures the liberal conscience and a Liberal seat.

When asked why he left the Conservative party, he retorts that he did not leave the Conservative Party or his principles. Rather, the Conservative Party deserted its principles and left him. Churchill warms to the task carrying his Liberal colours and in June 1905 at the Cobden Club held within the auspices of the Midland Club in Manchester, the home of 'free trade,' Churchill launches a scathing attack on his former conservative colleagues.

> The words today sound familiar. "We know perfectly well what to expect. It (the Tory Party) has become the party of great vested interest; corruption at home - aggression to cover it up abroad; trickery of tariff juggles, tyranny of party machine; sentiment by the bucketful, patronage by the pint; openhand at the public exchequer; open door at the public house; dear food for the millions and cheap labour by the millions..."

Does not this diatribe, friends, sound faintly familiar?

After the 1905 election, a new government forms. This time it is a Liberal - Unionist coalition and is led by Sir Henry Campbell Bannerman, (a relative of a distinguished member of this club and my great friend, the Honourable David Smith, Q.C.).

Winston Churchill becomes a youthful member of the Outer Cabinet as Under

Secretary of the Colonies under Lord Elgin who sits in the Lords. It was at this time that Eddie Marsh, soon to become Churchill's lifelong assistant, reluctantly agreed to join Churchill as his private secretary . He was told by Lady Lytton, to assuage his fears about the mercurial Churchill that, "the first time you meet Winston you see all of his faults and the rest of your life too spend discovering his virtues". This remains for me a most perceptive insight into the Churchill psyche.

May I digress by saying I am obviously a lifelong fan of Winston Churchill. My fascination with Churchill started, early in high school, when I first read his autobiography entitled *My Early Years*. I learned then that he was slow to speak, slow to write and considered slow of thought by his teachers and his peers. For a person who had flunked kindergarten because I was considered slow, these traits allowed me to identify strongly with the young Winston.

But my admiration for Churchill deepened even further after I happened across a speech he gave in his successful bi-election in 1908 at Dundee following his defeat in Northwest Manchester. The speech was made during Churchill's most enlightened period when he ran flat out under Liberal colours. The speech made by Winston Churchill also clarified for me my youthful confusion when I was first attracted to the siren song of socialism. Churchill, with powerful clarity, boldly contrasted liberalism and socialism with these words which have echoed down through the decades, with even greater resonance.

> *"Liberalism is not socialism, and never will be. There is a great gulf fixed. It is not a gulf of method, it is a gulf of principle. Socialism seeks to pull down wealth, liberalism seeks to raise up poverty. Socialism would destroy private interests; liberalism would preserve private interests in the only way in which they can be safely and justly preserved, namely by reconciling them with public right. Socialism would kill enterprise; liberalism would rescue enterprise from the trammels of privilege and preference socialism exalts the rule; liberalism exalts the man. Socialism attacks capital, liberalism attacks monopoly."*

And so, in the next two decades, from 1905 to 1923, Churchill held a dizzying array of portfolios as a Liberal Minister, President of the Board of Trade, Home Secretary, First Lord of the Admiralty, Minister of Munitions, Secretary of State for War and Secretary of State for the Colonies.

His vibrating fortunes matching his ideas, raced up and down, in public opinion, like a roller coaster.. In each ministry, he brought a volcanic energy and a visionary stream of ideas. He was, in turn, the father of the "submarine", the father of the "tank", father of "oil driven warships". He created the first Anglo/Arab oil consortium to fuel and secure British naval might.

As President of the Board of Trade, he organized labour exchanges to prevent sweat labour. He first established unemployment insurance in England.

He led attacks against the House of Lords when it defeated a Liberal budget - the famous people's budget - which led to the first reform of the Lords.

He wrote articulate tracts - radical in their time - entitled *Liberalism and the Social Problem* and *The People's Rights* defining a sweeping social agenda of reform that only became accepted public policy decades later.

He railed against property speculation and contrasted wealth built on real estate as "plunder" compared to "production" of goods as being in the public interest. He advocated public works in times of unemployment (public jobs in reforestation and road building). He promoted legislation restricting 8 hour work days for coal miners and restrictions on child labour. He repeatedly advocated a social net to protect the victims from the ravages of competition.

While he believed in the 'free trade' and competition, he also believed in offering some protection to those who simply could not compete.

He declaimed on public platforms that the biggest threat to the cause of peace came not from abroad but the crisis at home - the gap between rich and poor - obsolete laws protecting inherited property and the vested interests and he argued repeatedly for "minimum standards of life and work" to attain domestic civility.

As Colonial Secretary, he personally drafted in 1922, the first partition plan for Palestine, establishing in the process Trans-Jordan, Iraq, and set out their boundaries - leaving room for the development of a Jewish state - all ideas still haunting the public agenda today. He considered himself a early Zionist who envisioned, west of Jordan, a Jewish state in the form of a dominion as part of the British Empire.

Viscount Simon, a close and lifelong contemporary, wrote after Churchill became leader of the Conservative party in 1952...

> *"At the root of his many sided nature... remains the essence of liberalism. His tolerance, his sympathy with the oppressed and the underdog, his courage in withstanding clamour, his belief...in the individual... all derive from a heart... a head... made him a Liberal statesman.... his Liberal views were not a mere pose, so that he has carried his Liberal temper with him throughout his life..."*

Other colleagues noted that a major theme of his life was individual rights and his unswerving belief in the liberty to work out - as one civil servant wrote - one's own salvation, to follow one's own star - so Churchill wished to afford equal freedom to others to do likewise "*I stand for liberty,*" he proudly proclaimed more than once. This was his lifelong Liberal theme. He vehemently opposed bolshevism and communism because he believed bolshevism and communism was, at its very roots, opposed to individual liberty. He carried over this belief in the essence of liberty as the foundation for relations between states that so informed all his foreign policy principles.

In 1921-1922, Churchill was a player in Cabinet that led to the Irish settlement. This sudden reversal in the Liberal policy turned out to be a key to the fall of Lloyd George and the Liberal party. The Irish treaty was fatal to both Lloyd George and the Liberal coalition government as it led not to peace but continuing civil unrest. This sudden reversal in liberal policy was the beginning of the end for the Liberal party in

England.

In 1923 Churchill fell ill during an election. Churchill, wrote looking back on this period, a decade later:

> *"in a twinkling of an eye, I found myself without an office, without a seat, without a party, and without an appendix."*

Later in 1923, Churchill ran two more times, as a Liberal, and was defeated. He finally reverted to conservatism again, after making his peace with Baldwin, the leader of the Conservative party, who, after the 1924 election immediately appointed Churchill to the Exchequer. Churchill never would return to the Liberal fold and the Liberal Party, never regained its lustre. Again, Churchill believed that he had not left the Liberal Party, but the Liberal Party had deserted its own principles and lost its way .

One of the most fascinating insights into Churchill's attraction to the Liberal party was his lifelong helpmate, companion and wife, Clementine Churchill, born and bred a Scottish Liberal. Churchill was once asked why his marriage was so successful and he responded by saying that he had never had breakfast with his wife. Of the volumes written of Churchill about his relationship with Clementine, awkward, complex and difficult at times, one note endeared me most to Clementine. Throughout their loving and illustrious relationship spanning six decades together, she always voted Liberal .

When Churchill looked back on his long and exciting journey of life he wrote, "t*he journey has been enjoyable and well worth making - once."*

Friends, on that note, may I conclude by asking you to rise, liberally charge your glasses and raise a fulsome and Liberal toast to the Club - The University Club.

RABBI MENACHEM MENDEL SCHNEERSON A.H.L.: ON HIS PASSING

June 14, 1994

Hon. Jerahmiel S. Grafstein: Honourable senators, I should like to call the attention of the Senate to the passing of Rabbi Menachem Mendel Schneerson, of blessed memory, teacher and leader of the Lubavitch Movement, whose countless deeds speak for themselves.

I had the privilege of personally meeting with "the Rebbe", as he was called, on two memorable occasions in New York City.

May his life be bound up with the living and serve as a blessing for all.

ROYCE FRITH: ON HIS APPOINTMENT AS HIGH COMMISSIONER TO THE UNITED KINGDOM

October 4, 1994

Hon. Jerahmiel S. Grafstein: I, too, honourable senators, should like to add my comments on the resignation of the Honourable Royce Frith.

"Royce Frith" - what a graceful name to match such a graceful man. Royce Frith - barrister, solicitor, Queen's Counsel, senator, actor, author, athlete, orator, singer, musicologist, broadcaster, bibliophile, linguist, raconteur par excellence, strategist, Beau Brummel, connoisseur of rules and protocol, gourmet, chess player - indeed, a man of many excellent parts. Now, he has become a diplomat, and soon to be statesman.

Royce is a Renaissance man. He would have been a star in any career he chose for himself. Royce chose politics, because politics was his passion. I first met Royce in 1960 in Toronto, where he was a leading political activist. I was immediately struck by the timbre of his voice; his energy, his elegance, his eloquence, his wit, his scintillating repartee and his engaging personality. We became friends, and I became an admirer and remain so to this day. I was amazed to discover back then that his Yiddish expressions, all with the appropriate local dialect, rivalled my own.

When I was appointed to the Senate, I asked Royce to act as one of the two customary sponsors to usher me into this chamber. He not only ushered me in, but acted as a guide to help me navigate through the tortuous rules and unwritten customs of this place.

If there is one characteristic, to my mind, that illuminates Royce, it is his loyalty - loyalty to his convictions, loyalty to his friends, loyalty to his colleagues and, above all, loyalty to his country.

Royce revelled in the Senate. He obviously adored this place, and so the Senate suffers a deep and wide loss in his leaving. We can only be consoled by the fact that our loss is Canada's gain. He will be a superb representative of Canada's interests in the United Kingdom and beyond.

Truly, Royce is a man for all seasons, and now our man goes to the United Kingdom for all the right reasons. We can only wish him God speed.

ROMÉO LeBLANC: ON HIS APPOINTMENT AS GOVERNOR-GENERAL

November 23, 1994

Hon. Jerahmiel S. Grafstein: Honourable senators, I wish to add my words of congratulation to those paid to Roméo LeBlanc on his appointment to the highest office of the land. I also congratulate the Prime Minister for his brilliant choice.

I have known Roméo LeBlanc for 30 years. To me, Roméo LeBlanc is a person of the people. In his new position, I am sure that he will remain that same person. He is a person without pretensions, a person of great common sense and deep wisdom, a person who will never forget his roots while touching the stars.

May I extend to him, his wife and his family best wishes and God speed. In the days and years ahead, he will need it, and Canada will need it more.

JOAN NIEMAN: ON RETIREMENT
ON THE OCCASION OF A DINNER OF LIBERAL SENATORS
July 13, 1995

Hon. Jerahmiel S. Grafstein: Honourable senators, Senator Joan Neiman seems so young, so vibrant, so energetic, so intellectually engaged, that I was surprised today to find that her retirement was quickly approaching. I just simply cannot believe it.

I have had the privilege of sitting with Senator Neiman on a number of committees and in caucuses. At all times, Joan's was a voice of moderation, a voice of reason, a voice of great tactical skill, a voice of intelligence and, above all, she was always courteous, even to those with whom I know she violently disagreed, including me.

Having said that, honourable senators, Joan is no angel. My roots in the Liberal Party go back to the early sixties when Joan and her husband Clem were considerable and aggressive political forces. While we shared many views about the Liberal Party and the importance of it, on many occasions we found ourselves on different sides and supporting different personalities. However, throughout that whole period, our personal relationship was good and sound, and always pleasant.

The Neimans were - and are - considerable political activists, deeply committed to the public affairs of Canada at each level of political activity. Theirs is one of those great stories which, as alluded to by Senator Stanbury, is rarely told about the political life of our country and the life of our party.

Joan goes on to a well-deserved retirement, but I do not think it will be a rest. I think it will be the start of yet another, equally new, exciting and energetic career. I want to thank both Senator Neiman and her husband Clem for the pleasure of their company.

YITZHAK RABIN: ON HIS ASSASSINATION

November 6, 1995

Hon. Jerahmiel S. Grafstein: Honourable senators, for over 3,000 years, not far from the blood-drenched stones of Jerusalem, another great warrior leader, striving to unite his people and to provide them with security and peace with their neighbours, wrote these words, which are now customarily recited at a house of bereavement. It is the 23rd Psalm:

The Lord is my shepherd; I shall not want.

He maketh me to lie down in green pastures: he leadeth me beside the still waters.

He restoreth my soul: he leadeth me in the paths of righteousness for his name's sake.

Yea, though I walk through the valley of the shadow of death, I will fear no evil: for thou art with me; thy rod and thy staff they comfort me.

Thou preparest to table before me in the presence of mine enemies: thou anointed my head with oil; my cup runneth over.

Surely goodness and mercy shall follow me all the days of my life: and I will dwell in the house of the Lord forever.

Honourable senators, we are told that King David was the greatest of God's beloved because David never lost faith. David was humble. He never blamed God for the failures of man or himself.

Yitzhak Rabin, may he rest in peace, was born in Jerusalem, the City of David. Farmer, soldier, general, strategist, politician, diplomat, statesman, peacemaker - he played a pivotal and leading role in each of the many wars that have engulfed Israel since the founding of that state in 1948. He became its youngest Prime Minister, the eighth Prime Minister, and the first to be born in Israel. As Senator Cohen said, Yitzhak Rabin was a "sabra", and the word "sabra", as she pointed out, is a desert cactus, tough and prickly on the outside and soft on the inside. This symbol personified Yitzhak Rabin's life and personality and, indeed, reflects the personalities of many of the citizens in Israel.

Honourable senators, I first met Yitzhak Rabin over 20 years ago, just after he became Minister of Defence. We met in his small office located in a temporary wooden building in the Defence compound in Tel Aviv for what was scheduled to be a very brief introductory exchange. At his insistence, this brief exchange turned into a dialogue lasting longer than two hours. Almost as if he was thinking out loud, he insisted on painstakingly reviewing the difficult options and the painful choices facing Israel in its search for security. I simply became enthralled by his precise grasp of the myriad issues, the minute detail and the knowledge that he had at his fingertips, ranging from the strategic to the tactical, from the public psychology to the private anxieties. I learned then what a meticulous thinker and a brilliant planner he was.

We know that God, like genius, lies hidden in detail. In that sense, Rabin was a genius, for he understood, as few other politicians did, that behind every public pronouncement, behind every public policy, a sure grip of detail was essential for public comprehension and ultimately for public consensus and acceptance. He seemed motivated at that time by an obsession, since he emphasized that there was a zero-sum margin for error confronting Israel's security. "Simply no room," he said, "for ill-considered ideas or shallow policies."

Honourable senators, Israel, at its widest point, covers a shorter distance than the boundaries that separate Greater Metropolitan Toronto. A hair's breadth separates Israel from its neighbours without, and a blink of an eye from its neighbours within. Yitzhak Rabin understood and lived this reality, and so he painstakingly and patiently analyzed each brick necessary to support and ensure the security and ultimately the peace for his people.

As time went on, I glanced at my watch, not wishing to intrude further on his tight schedule. Yet, he seemed to have all the time in the world. I was puzzled, quite frankly, why he spent so much of his precious time on me, for though interested in Israel and its security, I held no public office or influential position at the time. Yet, he seemed anxious for me, and I assumed countless others he encountered, to understand the complexity of the issues and the need for careful navigation through the minefields of problems. When we talked then of the "Palestinian problem," he shocked me by saying that the difficulties with the Palestinians will certainly be resolved, but only with great care and great patience. "Solutions would come," he said, "but it would take time." This was certainly not the conventional thinking at that time "Palestinians," he declared, "were not the strategic problem".

The real strategic problem of security confronting Israel, he quietly argued, was Syria. Syria had the military strength; Syria had the military power; Syria had the military support and the political support to undermine and destroy Israel's security. Yet, when referring to Syria, he was optimistic. Again, he shocked me when he said that when Syria moves towards peace, Syria could be relied upon because Syrians, unlike any other group or state in the region, had always kept their word. This was new information to me. They had kept their word, he said, from the time they signed the first disengagement agreement on the Golan. He was convinced that they would keep their word once they signed an agreement for peace - a written agreement for peace.

That conversation, honourable senators, took place over 20 years ago in Israel. Many times since then, when I have watched Yitzhak Rabin or listened to his carefully crafted words, I remember that dialogue, and still I marvel at his perception, his precision and his vision.

The last time I saw Yitzhak Rabin was in his office in Jerusalem, just this last August, on the Wednesday morning following the signing of the agreement between Arafat and himself, which had taken place the night before in Tuba. I arrived mid-morning just as a meeting of the Israeli cabinet responsible for security was breaking up. This committee was chaired by Rabin as Prime Minister and Minister of Defence, and the generals continued to noisily debate the issues as they moved outside the cabinet door. Some sat down beside me on a sofa to review detailed maps and schedules spread out on a coffee table in front of the sofa. I watched with some amusement as some of the military leaders would leave the discussion from time to time, walk into the cabinet room, fetch a piece of honey cake or a piece of fruit, and return to the coffee table to continue the debate.

Yitzhak Rabin emerged after hearing the commotion from his office, which was right next door, and glanced at me as the only stranger in the anteroom observing the scene. He was dishevelled, smoking heavily, looking for all the world as if he had just slept in his clothes or, worse, as if a tank had just rolled over him. We glanced at each other, and he returned to his office with a quizzical look on his face wondering who this alien was, who this stranger was, and what I was doing there at this critical time. He emerged a few minutes later talking to an assistant and a military aide, and again he glanced at me. Finally, there was a flicker of recognition. He quickly approached me, apologized for not being able to spend some time but, as I could see, he was quite busy. I reminded him that I was there primarily not to meet with him, but to meet with Mr. Eitan Haber, his chief of staff, whom I had met several times in Canada. A few minutes later, after Rabin had returned to his office, Haber came out, apologized for the delay, and ushered me into his office connected to Rabin's office next door.

Honourable senators, for those of you who watched Rabin's funeral early this morning, you will recall that Eitan Haber was the last speaker who spoke so eloquently, reading from the blood-stained words of the song sheet dedicated to peace that Rabin sang from and stuck in his pocket just before he was so cruelly struck down.

On that August morning in Israel, Haber and I discussed the deep divisions that both of us recognized within Israel. I had not been there for some time and I mentioned to him that I had never seen the divisions so deep and so vitriolic. Yet, Haber said that both Rabin and he were optimistic. Movements, manoeuvres and tactics were under way to unravel the polarization, to change the very dialectics of division, to alter the public dialogue.

We discussed at length the role of the Orthodox community. We discussed certain leadership personalities within that Orthodox community. We reviewed our respective roots that lie deep within that Orthodox community and Mr. Rabin's relationship to that group. Mr. Haber reviewed for me the complexities and difficulties necessary to gain political momentum to overcome the internal objections to peace and to the peace process. He covered the ground, as Rabin would, with a lucid, optimistic and penetrating analysis stressing, not minimizing, the day-to-day difficulties facing the Rabin government - making peace with both its neighbours on the outside and seeking to reconcile the deep and passionate divisions splitting Israeli society on the inside. His voice echoed the wear and tear, the stress lines, that I saw deeply etched on Rabin's face that morning.

Honourable senators, those in Israel now face a double tragedy - the death of a great leader and caused by the hand, of all things, of a fellow Israeli and co-religionist, unheard of since the founding of the state and so contrary to the basic tenets of Judaism, so inimical of the precious value system of Israel itself. This cowardly, vicious act will compel those within and without Israel to probe the foundations of their inner beliefs, to question how Israel could have fallen from a state of grace. This introspection and soul-searching will continue in every corner of Israel and amongst its supporters throughout the world, until a moral equilibrium is regained, until a collective sense of human dignity and respect for human life is at least partially, if only partially, recaptured.

Honourable senators, watch now. Watch carefully how this vile act will convulse the very core of that democratic society, constructed as it is on the very first principles of civilization.

Even at this early stage, is there a parallel lesson one can learn from this tragedy? The Hebrew sages remind us that we must train ourselves to seek to repair every disaster to the human condition. These sages tell us that words can kill, that ideas can kill. At the end of each service, at least three times daily, Jews the world over conclude their prayers with this phrase: "Oh, my God! Guard my tongue from evil and my lips from speaking guile." This self-restraint from speaking and spreading evil lies deep at the heart of Jewish morality.

Those in Israel and beyond who are deeply religious, orthodox in their beliefs, as well as others, have forgotten their prayers, forgotten the tenets of their faith. The uncivil discourse, the crude analogies, the obscene name-calling acted as a catalyst for this vile and venal act. Guarding one's tongue is a lesson that all of us must learn in our daily political discourse if we are not to incite others to acts of violence. Words have always been important to Israel. Now those words must be carefully chosen to continue the endless search for peace.

Jews, honourable senators, do not mourn death. The Kaddish, the blessing commemorating the passage of a human soul, contains words that celebrate life. We celebrate the words, the deeds and the life of Yitzhak Rabin. The final words when reciting the Kaddish are these:

> "He who maketh peace in his high places may he make peace for us and for Israel and let us say, amen."

To Yitzhak Rabin, for all of his public works, for all of his acts of humanity, for all of his public dedication and personal sacrifice, for all of his deeds of greatness, for all of his mitzvot, let us say amen.

VINCENT PETER PAUL: EULOGY
GIVEN AT THE BLESSED SACRAMENT PARISH, TORONTO

February 3, 1996

"Non viribus, ullis vincere posse ramum. Vincere noctem flammis."

Vincent Peter Paul conquered life and his life was a light against the darkness.

"I walked a mile with Pleasure.
She talked to me all the way;
but left me none the wiser,
For all she had to say.

I walked a mile with Sorrow,
And ne'er a word said she;
But, oh! the things, I learned from her,
When Sorrow walked with me."

Oh what loss in Vince Paul! Dear Vincenzo! Dear Vincenzo! Oh what sorrow!

"His life was gentle and the elements
So mixed in him that,
Nature might stand up,
And say to all the world, This Was A Man."

Still, we cannot comprehend the passing of this man. For you see, Vince Paul was my friend and we loved him dearly and he was a best friend to so many who mourn him today. Who was this rarest of men, this sweet, elegant, graceful man.

For Vince had the gift of many talents, yet he most modest of demeanours. There was no side to Vince, yet he was a private person. Vince was a gentle man, a gentleman, an elegant man, elegant in dress and word. He had taste in his home, a superb taste he shared with his beloved Nancy - and he took a great delight from fine wine and food. He was a great cook and an even greater lover of fine music. He believed in the simple virtues: God, family, friends and fairness. He never took the name of the Lord or of any person in vain.

When disappointed in others that did not meet his own standard of fairness, he would kindly, never critically, quietly, despair - by lowering his voice to a whisper, shrug his shoulders or roll his dark sparkling eyes and then smile - that sweet smile.

He was the most magnificent of charitable men - for he gave fully (more than his fair share to all the charities so ably led by Nancy, and beyond and always quietly without fanfare. If you called Vince on behalf of any charity, he never questioned! He only asked how much and where he should send the cheque. One never got a no.

He was involved in every Italian charity, as a leader, from Columbus Centre to the Italian Flood Relief Fund. He simply loved all things Italian, from his birthplace in Reggio Calabria to Italian opera.

He found it hard to believe that anyone could not be as charitable or as fair as himself. Things were so clear to him! Why not others? In this frenzied world of high tech and high finance where he performed so brilliantly, he never lost sight that life had a good purpose, to maintain good standards and communicate good values. He always kept his promise. He always kept his word. You confided in him because you could trust him.

I first met Vince over 30 years ago when he was already an established star and still rising in Toronto business and accounting circles. He was quick, fair and astute. And we became fast friends.

His reputation then and now was always honest and fair - he was a good man to be a partner. We became co-venturers in several creative businesses - with his calmness and skill we persevered - we did well together. We would talk regularly in those days for mutual updates and I valued his insights and brevity.

At times I could not understand why he failed to get upset when others took advantage of his fairness or failed to understand his ideas. Only now, when I look back, do I begin to understand he always demanded the most from himself and only hoped for the best in others. This was his good talent, this irreplaceable talent with people. He never gave an order. He always promoted others ahead of himself.

His genius was putting complicated business ideas simply. He had one of the quickest business minds of any man I've ever met yet - to grasp the essence of a complicated business problem and, he was patient with others, allowing them to slowly catch up to his ideas.

Vince always gave his personal best. His mind was always cooking. He could do more in a few hours than others could do in days. In business and in life, Vince was a strong competitor. He had a heroic heart, yet he never cut corners or took unfair advantage. He often paid dearly to lean over. He never acted in private what he was unwilling to defend in public. He never asked you to do what he was unwilling to do himself.

And there is nothing in this world that Vince could not do ably himself. He was adored by all because he thought of others first, never of himself.

He had status, but he did not believe in status. He had power, but he did not believe in power.

He treated people the same - whether clerks, waitresses, secretaries, captains in industry, public figures or politicians. Vince treated everyone the same.

He was always curious, searching for answers. We travelled together and always Vince's curiosity and intelligence became a wonderful travelling asset.

Vince was a dreamer. He saw things others could not see. He dreamed dreams others could not dream. Still, he was a small town boy who never forgot his humble origins.

He was a great citizen of Canada who loved and worked for his country and feared for its future. He served his country with distinction in WWII, first in the army and then in the air force. That experience left him with an indelible love of country .

So Lord, what I am to do, what are we to do now, without our dear Vince. We so enjoyed the pleasure of his company. What are we to do?

Stories, several personal stories, stand out from a barrel of memories which exemplify Vincent's love of life. Vince invited Carole and I to join him when he was inducted as a Knight of Malta. After the magnificent ceremony, Vince tried to convince me that I could become an auxiliary Knight of Malta and he was serious. Sometimes his friendship had the better of his judgment.

And, just before Christmas, we met Vince and Nancy as we often did, our small circle of friends, Catherine and David, Cathy and Rudy, Anna-Marie and Ivan and Carole and I at Cathy Bratty's wonderful restaurant for good food and good fellowship. In the holiday spirit, we sang carols and old songs and Vince sang in his marvellous baritone voice small segments of famous opera arias and Italian love songs.

After dinner, as we customarily do, each in turn, stood and toasted each other. When it came to Vince's turn, we all realized then he was soon to confront his maker. He spoke eloquently of his love for Nancy and his children and how much his love of Nancy had increased because of her special affection and resonance for his children. So he concluded he was doubly blessed - because of his love for Nancy and their mutual love for their large family.

The poet Aeschylus once wrote:

"Even in our sleep, pain which cannot forget,
falls drop by drop upon the heart
until, in our own despair, against our will,
comes wisdom, through the awful grace of God"

When illness attacked his body, he never complained. In his distress, he only worried about Nancy and his growing family. I remembered vividly last summer when we travelled to Rome together. I had arranged for Vince to meet the Holy Father, the Pope John Paul II, in Rome. Nancy and I sat holding hands, with Rudy sitting next to us, and watched as Vince and Cathy Bratty mounted the steps to greet the Pope. When Vince turned to walk down the stairs, you could see from afar the aura, the radiance and glow on his face. We both cried softly because we could see how happy and content he was! He was at peace with himself.

His family adored him. He raved about his children. He lived a beautiful live and taught his children to live a beautiful life. And, if his children had any criticis, Deborah told me, it was that he was sometimes too much of a mother!

And so to his dear family, his children Deborah and Philip, Marina, Vincent, Jr. And Cathy and Sara. Lovely Sara. His grandchildren, Dora, Andrea, John Paolo, his brothers, Frank and Sam; and sister Jean. And to his beloved wife Nancy who fought like a tiger for his health. Vince's friends watched as Nancy struggled for his life, found him the best doctors possible, watched over his treatments, caressed him, eased his pain, bolstered his courage and gave him days and added hours of pleasure - all while Vince fought to the end to retain his most precious possession, the clarity of thoughts, what special words of consolation to Nancy and his family. Perhaps these words from *Romeo and Juliet* may comfort her and his family:

> "When he shall die,
> Take him and cut him out into little stars,
> And he shall make the face of heaven so fine,
> That all the world will be in love with night."

So, dear Vincent, your search is done, your race is run, your battle won, now . . . Come to rest. Vincent, you did not die! You live on in the hearts and the minds of all who love you and respect you. Your memory burns brightly because you were larger than life - when you lived - and so you shall remain.

And Vincent, you live on in our dreams. Can we hear you! I know Vince that you will be singing your favourite aria "Nessa dorma." Vincere, vincere, vincere! Vincenzo, vincere.

So we say . . .

Then shalt dust return to the earth, as it was, and the spirit shall return unto God who gave it.

ALLAN JOSEPH MACEACHEN: ON RETIREMENT

June 19, 1996

Hon. Jerahmiel S. Grafstein: Wherein, honourable senators, lie the roots of our national disunity? Failure of memory: failure of historic memory and, worse, disrespect for public figures and public institutions that were precisely and politically constructed to bind Canada together.

If those in public life must bear their share of culpability for the falling esteem of public service, the national media in the Press Gallery must be considered amongst the most pedestrian, if not the most vitriolic, collaborationists of this unhappy trend. Few in the media today display even a passing knowledge of Canadian history or any historic memory whatsoever beyond this year's headline or even, if I might say it, last week's headlines.

Youth, inexperience, revolving chairs in the national media, combined with the distortion brought about by electronic sound bites; grounded in the new world of virtual reality, in the era of musical clips - all of these so distort and fragment our memories that the history lessons that we transmit to this and the next generation become almost surreal. The uses of history require reiteration of history, and the repetition of historic facts. The absence of historic fact, and the displacement of context relegates the authenticity of history to the electronic trash bins of limited recall, and in the process, demeans public service.

The Senate can keep the historic record straight; that's what I believe we are doing today. I am sure you will forgive me if I take a few moments to deal with this subject while focusing on our friend and colleague, Allan J. MacEachen.

A telling example is a rather dyspeptic newspaper column, published last week, on the retirement of Allan Joseph MacEachen, penned by one of Canada's leading journalists who perhaps was still suffering from jet lag. Weeks before, this same journalist described his chagrin at the provincialism and parochialism which he found in media coverage of events since his return to Canada after a brief sojourn covering events in the Middle East.

This column caused me to review more acutely the legendary record of public service of Allan Joseph MacEachen. What I found was both astonishing and refreshing. I thought I knew everything about Allan J. MacEachen but I had actually forgotten most of it. Out of my study emerged a diamond record of service, dazzling in all its many aspects. Senators on both sides today have spoken of the many brilliant sides of Allan MacEachen's career. I hope not to detract from the essential, for amongst Allan's most endearing traits is his modesty, while the hallmark of his leadership has always been the avoidance of hyperbole and exaggeration.

Yet from any fair retrospective of Allan J. MacEachen's career, as one traces the highlights of a legendary parliamentary career, what emerges, without exaggeration, is the profile of the greatest Canadian parliamentarian of this or any century.

On a comparative basis with British parliamentary history, Allan J. MacEachen might be compared with such greats as Edmund Burke, James Fox, Richard Cobden or John Bright. While Allan's Canadian canvas was smaller, he looms all the larger in comparison.

Can there be any question? Is there any member in this chamber who, having witnessed Allan's craftsmanship, cannot say that he is simply Canada's outstanding parliamentarian? Allan has spawned, as others have said, a generation of parliamentary protégés who have kept the tradition of Parliament alive and well both here and in the other place. He has served in public life with great distinction both as a member of cabinet and as a parliamentary leader. He has served in more ministerial portfolios and in a more striking fashion than any other Canadian since Confederation, perhaps save one. He has held more different cabinet posts than any other Canadian spanning nine Prime Ministers from St. Laurent to Chrétien, except perhaps for Mr. Chrétien himself who, I believe, held nine portfolios before assuming the Prime Ministership.

Time allows me only to brush-stroke a few of Allan's unique contributions to Canadian life which, from my vantage point, I have had observed firsthand.

As others have said, Allan MacEachen is the father of Medicare, now cherished by Canadians from coast to coast as the distinguishing social feature of our Canadian profile and of our national cohesiveness.

I recall very well the crushing policy battles within the Liberal Party culminating at the 1966 Liberal convention that parallelled similar battles that went on in the Pearson cabinet. On one side there was Allan MacEachen, supported by young Liberal activists including Lloyd Axworthy, David Smith and myself. If Senator Prud'homme were here at this moment he might confirm his presence there too. If my memory serves me correctly, the resolution on Medicare did not pass by an overwhelming margin. The cabinet was deeply divided with Allan, Walter Gordon and John Munro and others on one side facing opposition from the likes of that other great Nova Scotian, Robert Winters, and Mitchell Sharpe and his protege, Jean Chrétien.

Opportunity remains for historians, perhaps Senator MacEachen himself, to more deeply probe this split which ultimately ended in victory for Medicare proponents.

Many of those who were opposed to Medicare have since become avid supporters, both within our party and across the way. Medicare transformed the Liberal Party; it transformed Parliament, and it transformed our national identity. Allan led and won that fight. Medicare forever changed our public dialogue.

In 1979, as House Leader and Deputy Prime Minister, Allan's parliamentary brilliance and his tactical finesse, which many scorned and scoffed at then, brought down the Clarke government, ushering the return of Pierre Trudeau which, in turn, led to the passage of the Charter of Rights which is now ensconced in the Constitution. The Charter of Rights has become inseparable from our daily political lexicon. We hear the demand for and the respect for rights virtually every day here in this chamber and in the other place and beyond, across the country, whenever any touchy issue of public concern is debated. The Charter is now a part of our language, our common parlance.

Political genius is the ability to transform radical ideas into conventional wisdom. In 1981, one apparent political disaster at the time became part of the conventional dialogue just a few years later. When Allan MacEachen, as Minister of Finance, introduced his first budget in 1981, it was replete with measures to close tax loopholes and redress the imbalance in our national finances. Vested interests clobbered that budget. The press clobbered it as well. Allan and the Trudeau government were forced to retreat under attack.

Today, honourable senators, virtually every one of those tax reforms has become law. Had that budget been implemented at the time, the sorry state of public accounts would have been transformed sooner and with less distress to the public good. Again, Allan led the way.

Honourable senators, no one today has touched on the fact that as Minister of Foreign Affairs in the Trudeau government, Allan's global strategy led to a transformation in our public preoccupation from the east-west dialogue to the north-south dialogue. Again, it was radical thinking at the time. Allan's radical thinking transformed itself into conventional wisdom, into conventional thinking.

Allan also led with his belief that Canada's future security as a trading nation required the philosophy and the practice of balanced trade to counter our heavy dependence on trade with the United States. Look towards Europe and other markets, he argued, convinced it was in Canada's interest to secure more balance in our trade, and a greater security in our trade patterns through diversity.

He moved towards closer bilateral relations in Europe. In his quest, he believed stronger relations with Germany - that giant of Europe - were essential. The work he did then, and the bridges he has built more recently through the Atlantischer Brücke brought Canadian-German relations to their highest level of bilateral cooperation. It is clear to those of us who attended with Allan in Europe with the Foreign Affairs Committee, while pursuing our study of Canada and its relations with the EU, that Germany is now Canada's best advocate in Europe, surpassing our traditional relations with both the United States and France, and again Allan has led the way.

Hon. Jerry S. Grafstein. Q. C

Honourable senators, all in this chamber have watched Allan, first as Leader of the Government and then as Leader of the opposition, bring radical reform to the Senate. By discarding the practice of pre-study and insisting that every bill, with rare exception, be referred to committee, he brought about a slow return to the original principles of this chamber of second sober thought, allowing the Senate to re-emerge, to regain some of its legislative legitimacy, if not credibility. His choice of issues slowly moved the Senate's public opinion to a greater acceptance of the Senate's exercise of its legislative powers.

Indeed, if our recent distress on this side with the opposition aggravates us, it is precisely because it was consistent with the principles of reform introduced by Allan into the Senate. It is a most appropriate legacy of his Senate leadership.

Last week, we held a dinner for Allan MacEachen, at which he made a marvellous speech. In that speech, he reminded us that politics was not a game; it was serious public business. Probably, we can reduce his career to three words: people, party, and Parliament. Possibly, Allan, a fourth word can be added: partisanship - a fitting tribute to an outstanding Canadian for this or any generation.

Allan MacEachen leaves public life much as he entered it over four decades ago, with his lively mind, his passion for reform, his concern for people, his modesty, his wit, his love of country, his patriotism, his honour - above all, his honour - and his principles intact. Therefore, honourable senators, let us praise him, let us adorn him with a garnet of accolades, for in doing so we add lustre to Parliament and the Senate.

When I look back on this wonderful career, I think Allan made one mistake - one small mistake - which we could have corrected. Allan chose never to seek election in the Province of Ontario. Had he done so, who knows, he might have achieved the one political prize that eluded him: the leadership of the Liberal Party and finally the Prime Ministership of Canada.

I must end, Allan, on a personal note. I will miss the pleasure of your company, and we will all miss your gentle leadership and your irreplaceable wisdom.

DOUGLAS KEITH DAVEY: ON RETIREMENT

JUNE 20, 1996

Hon. Jerahmiel S. Grafstein: Honourable senators, this has been a rather long week for Liberals - first, Allan Joseph MacEachen and now Douglas Keith Davey.

Keith Davey, Keith Davey. Those two wonderful, almost musical, interchangeable names, spoken together or sung apart, have been a magical rallying cry for Liberal activists in every corner of Canada, while they have served as a dire warning to Liberal opponents for four decades.

A dashing presence, an ebullient voice, dazzling speeches, wonderful wit, sagacious strategist, practical joker, perceptive reader of public opinion, a passion for people and party, a reverence for Toronto, and a love of country - these are just a few of the delectable, unmatchable trademarks of the Davey charisma that I have been privileged to witness at close hand.

Keith believes - and, he has practised and preached it - that any person, any Canadian, regardless of gender, age, religion or race, can make a difference. All he asked for was energy, skill, dedication, loyalty, liberalism. These would be the criteria that would allow them to enter into his charmed circle.

Keith radically reformed party politics in Canada. He created and adopted modern election techniques and tactics which are now part of our accepted practice. He injected "grassroots" and "bottom up" as the organizing principle of the Liberal Party, as my friend Senator Stanbury said so eloquently just a few moments ago.

Door-knocking, riding associations, riding elections, canvassing, riding policy meetings, polling, campaign colleges, advertising, magnificent rallies and campaign slogans were just a few of the rudimentary elements that he perfected and were copied by others. Politics in the master hands of Keith Davey became and were transformed into the politics of joy. There was never a moment in politics with Keith that was not a joyous moment. He inspired, enlisted and led three generations of party activists, as Senator Bryden said, and persuaded numerous political leaders to take the political plunge. He was, at various times, a confidante and a powerful advisor of Mike Pearson, Pierre Trudeau, John Turner, Jean Chrétien, and a host of other political leaders across the country, municipal and provincial. The Liberal Party, since his arrival in the late 1950s, has never been the same.

If he had one small failing, it was that he offered so much to so many, but that was part of his charm, for Keith believed every promise that he made would be kept. He never held a grudge. He was almost too modest about his own abilities. He does not have a mean bone in his body. He remains sensitive and sympathetic to the feelings of others, even in the bruising, political battles that he led. He always promoted others ahead of himself. He was, and is, the consummate loyalist, always there when trouble struck. He is, in his own words, a pro - perhaps the ultimate pro.

On a personal note, I will miss Keith dearly. Since 1961, when I first joined the Liberal Party in Toronto, barely a week has passed when I have not called or been called by Keith. He has become an extended member of my family, present at each event in our family life from the birth of my sons to the arrival of my grandsons. We must ask ourselves what we will do without the irrepressible, irresistible, irreverent, irreplaceable Keith Davey, for we are all on this side Keith Davey Liberals.

"THE REBBES & THE RUSSIAN COUNTER REVOLUTION" AT 18TH ANNUAL DINNER OF THE CHABAD LUBAVITCH OF TORONTO

December 5, 1996

When Rabbi Zalman Grossbaum first approached me to be the honouree for the 18th Annual Chabad Dinner, I declined. My wife agreed. We had never accepted such an invitation in the past and felt that there were others, many others, in this community, who were not only much more worthy of this honour, but would provide a greater magnet of attraction.

But Rabbi Grossbaum persisted. As we all know, Rabbi Grossbaum has great powers of persuasion. After several months and calls from many friends, I reluctantly agreed. What finally convinced me was when Rabbi Grossbaum called to say he was about to visit the Lubavitch Rebbe's "matzevah" in Crown Heights on the Rebbe's Yahrzeit and needed to know what he should put in his "kwittel," his message to the Rebbe. So here I am. Still unworthy of this singular honour.

And, who cannot be made humble when approaching the shiny gates of "the Chabad." Humility seizes and paralyses one just to have one's name associated with the grand and mysterious history of Lubavitch and their extraordinary leaders..

In the Torah and Talmud, seven is a mystical number. We are told ... 'all those who are seventh are cherished and all those who are seventh are most beloved.' Just as there was seven prophets from Abraham to Moses, so there have been seven great rebbes who transformed the Chassidic movement and created a living force within that movement called "Chabad Lubavitch."

The founder of "Chabad", Schneur Zalman, was born in 1745 in white Russia. The 'Alter Rebbe' wrote that each man is like the burning bush seen by Moses. Each man burns with desire to do good deeds and have good thoughts, but Schneur Zalman, the first Lubavitch Rebbe - the 'Alter' Rebbe did much more as the most conspicuous, second generation successor to the 'Baal Shem Tov', - the acknowledged founder of the Chassidic movement (who died in 1760) - Reb Schneur Zalman created, through his personal leadership, by his humane ability to attract followers, and by his high standards of intellectual excellence, a precise and detailed and coherent formula for living a good life. 'Chabad', He wrote in his major Canon - *the Tanya* - Chabad stands for wisdom, understanding and knowledge.

Three words, yet each word, expressed within the mystical context of the Kabbala, is replete with complexity and pierces the inner heart and awakens the soul of man. Awake, awake, he taught, as has each Rebbe since him, awake to the possibilities of a fuller, better life by good thought and deed.

This year, by the way, we celebrate the 200th anniversary of the first publication of the 'Tanya' - ('It is taught') the great platform and masterpiece of Lubavitch and Chassidic thought.

The last Rebbe, the 7th Rebbe, our Rebbe, may he rest in peace, said that each chassid, each faithful man, is a leader. To lead, one must lead his own mind. He must lead his own soul. Only by actions and deeds. Only by his own conduct can he hope to have others follow him.

The Rebbe said to lead means leadership in issues large and small. To lead oneself is a daily, hourly, even a minute by minute struggle. So leadership starts and ends with oneself. The world can be changed by one man. To repair the world, one must not neglect to repair himself. This idea lies at the base of Lubavitch Chassidism.

My own family roots are deeply rooted in Chassidism. My late father, Simcha Shlomo, as his father before him, was a Chassid, a Shomer Shabos and a lifelong student of Talmud and Torah - especially the 'Shas.' He was a Talmid Chacham. Mother's father, my grandfather, of blessed memory, Israel Isaac Bleeman was a Chasid, a student of the "Sfas Emes" (the Mouth of Truth), the first gerer Rebbe in Poland.

He studied there with the Gerer Rebbe's son and successor, the "Imre Emes" (the Lip of Truth) and through the good offices of my cousin and his nephew, Avrum Bleeman, my grandfather's notes on "tillum", on the Psalms, was recently published. Until his death in 1962, though blind for most of his life, he studied regularly with the great rabbis and leaders of Toronto Chassidism, Rabbis Price and Gordon and Ox, of blessed memory and was consulted by them!

But my grandmother, my mother's mother, had more illustrious antecedence. Engraved on her tombstone on Roselawn Avenue, where she was buried in 1942, my grandfather wrote, she was a granddaughter of the "Solicer Rav," who in turn was a direct descendant of the "Sheloh" ("the Sheloh Hakodesh"), one of the greatest Rabbinic writers and sages of the 16th century.

The 'Sheloh' was born near Prague in 1570. His meteoric chassidic career, across Europe, led from Chief Rabbi of Dubnow, to Ostraha, to Prague and then to Frankfurt and finally, after the death of his wife, he left Europe for the Holy Land in 1621. He started yeshiva in Jerusalem and he was elected Chief Rabbi of Jerusalem, where he completed his masterpiece - *'The Two Tablets of the Covenant.'* On his death in 1627, the "Sheloh" was buried next to the Rambam - the great Maimonides, in a small cemetery in Tiberias. My wife and son were privileged to visit his metzevah last year, in 1995. Now you ask, why is this relevant to Chabad Lubavitch?

Amongst the first discourses, the Rebbe gave when succeeding the previous Rebbe in 1950 as the head of Lubavitch movement, the Rebbe described the founder of Chabad, the first Rebbe, Schneur Zalman of Liadi, as a "Sheloh Yid", a Sheloh Jew!

He explained Schneur Zalman's reliance on Sheloh's written masterpieces, the Two Tablets the Covenant, "shnei Luchos Habris" and his siddur called the "Shar Hashomayim" - the Gates of Heaven. These two principle texts, were used by both the first Rebbe and his son and successor, "Dovber" as instruments of devotion and teaching. That's the good news.

The bad news is when the second Rebbe Dovber (called the Nittler Rebbe) was in the process of consolidating his post as the head of the Lubavitch movement as a son and successor of Schneur Zalman in 1814, he was challenged by his closest friend and co-student, Reb Aharon Halevi. A fierce struggle for leadership broke out between their supporters based on differing principles of prayer and practise.

Reb Aharon Halevi almost succeeded in splitting Lubavitch in two camps. Rebbe Dovber met this challenge and succeeded in capturing the leadership of the Lubavitch movement and the vast majority of its followers with his superior cerebral erudition, devotion and ideas. The conflict was resolved when Reb Aharon left Lubavitch and set up a splinter group in Starosselye.

That same Rebbe Aharon, Halevi of Starosselye, was also a direct descendant of my ancestor, the 'Sheloh.' So friends, my family roots predate and yet are deeply entwined in the history of Chabad and stretches from the 16th century to the present day.

Why, my current fascination with Chabad? I was privileged to meet with the Rebbe on two occasions. Each time, I came away with the overwhelming belief that he was an extraordinary man destined to be recorded as one of the great leaders in the 20th century and not just within the context of Judaism. Let me explain!

I started to study the lives of each of the seven leaders of the Chabad and their voluminous works. One could only scratch the surface. Each Rebbe lived a blindingly splendid life of devotion and prodigious intellectualism. Each Rebbe, through his writings and by his actions are considered Tzaddikim, the holiest of men. Yet all were not perfect. All made mistakes like the prophets of old.

Several were imprisoned for their beliefs. Many were detained and interrogated by authorities for their practises including the previous Rebbe. All, all risked their lives for their faithful. In the Tanya, the first Rebbe divided the Jewish community into two parts. The holiest men - tzaddikim - he wrote could achieve perfection in word and deed. While others in the wider community could only strive for perfection. Every man had his place in repairing himself and the world. On even a cursory glance at the works written by the first Rebbe or the mystical and majestic works of Rebbe Dovber, the second Rebbe who wrote magnificent discourses on ecstasy and on meditation, we find all the Rebbes' never lost sight of the importance of the ordinary Jew.

In fact, Dovber's books contained brilliant ideas on pain and pleasure. Precise definitions of emotions and mind, on human psychology, that preceded Freud and

Jung by over 100 years. Only by a broken spirit, - only by 'tzubrochenkeit' - he wrote, could one hope to rebuild oneself from within with greater truth or stronger vision or reach a higher state of self awareness. Freud and Jung argued from the same premise. But the Rebbes taught that preoccupation with one's thoughts, one's own concerns, are not enough. Thoughts must be matched by deeds to others to achieve a better life.

The 3rd (Rebbe Tzemach Tzedek), 4th (Rebbe Maharash) and 5th (Rebbe Rashab), each wrote equally impressive and voluminous works. Words are precious. They taught. Each word is essential. Words can teach or maim or kill. Care, great care, therefore, must be taken with daily speech, with each spoken word.

Nothing is unimportant. The last Rebbe taught that each letter, each word, each combination of words or letters, even pronunciation of each word is crucial. Even the humblest letter 'Yud', the smallest letter was used in the word that created the world. So all letters, all words, any words spoken or written, whether in private or public, whether in gossip or politics, must be used with great care. All Rebbes stressed repeatedly the importance and care to be given to each written and spoken word!

Reading the two volume autobiography of the previous Rebbe, ("Rayatz") Rebbe Yosef Yitzchak, one is awestruck by the simplicity yet depth of his thought and the humility of his deeds. So scholarship is a tradition in the Chabad. Here in Toronto, we are blessed with the Schoichet family, outstanding scholars on Rabbinics & "Kabbala", in the Lubavitch tradition. Rabbi Immanuel Schoichet's books allow one to begin to lift the veil and penetrate the pathways of Kabbala and Chassidism.

To even have a cursory knowledge or sure grasp, requires not only an understanding in English but in the ancient languages of Hebrew and Aramaic. So much is beyond my reach without greater scholarship.

So tonight, I thought I would talk about the work of the last two Rebbes and the still hidden impact that they had to capture the hearts, souls, minds of the millions of Jews trapped in Russia before Perestroika. They perform the greatest of 'mitzvot' - they saved lives. They did more. They helped ignite the first sparks in the second Russian Revolution, the counter Russian Revolution, that led to the collapse of Soviet Empire seven decades later.

I came upon the hidden work of Lubavitch in Russia in a strange, almost accidental way. Carole and I, together with some friends here tonight, joined George Cohon and travelled to the U.S.S.R for the opening of MacDonalds in Moscow in 1990. We were so busy, crowded with public events, dinners and meetings that we didn't have time to visit Jewish synagogues in Moscow. When we arrived in Leningrad (now St. Petersburg), we decided to make it our business to visit the large Leningrad Synagogue before we left. It was Friday afternoon. I insisted that our Russian guide take us there before sunset.

After much persuasion, our guide, who first insisted it was impossible to visit since the synagogue was closed made the necessary arrangements. We arrived by bus at 3 o'clock with more than twenty friends. The synagogue was unlocked by a 'shamus.' He spoke in Yiddish. I asked if we could hold a 'Minucha' service before 'shabbos.'

The Russian guide said it was impossible. The synagogue could not be used for services. I insisted. The shamus asked who would lead the service. I said I would. So I counted a minyan and we recited 'minucha' service in the large delapidated beautiful synagogue. As we finished, the shamus beckoned me to follow through a different exit. Attached to the synagogue was a small 'shtebel.'

There, several boys were studying Torah with a young bearded teacher. On the wall, as I left, I noticed a poster of the Rebbe. Surprised, I asked the "shamus," "When did Lubavitch get here?" He said, "Lubavitch was always here. They never left". This statement aroused my curiosity. It turned out to be almost a mystery story.

We all are familiar with the recent history in Russia. We have all witnessed the rise of dissident movement, both Jew and gentile. The plight of Sakharov and Sharansky are well documented. What is less documented and less known is the deadly struggle for religious freedom that started after the Russian Revolution in 1917 and continued until the collapse of the U.S.S.R just a few years ago. We discover that faith can move mountains!!

When the Bolsehviks took control in Russia in 1917, one of their immediate aims was to, in practical terms, to wipe out religious freedom. While the Russian constitution allowed for freedom of religion, in practice, Bibles were forbidden. Prayer books were effectively outlawed. Particular attention was paid to the powerful Jewish community. Russia had millions of Russian Jews, most of whom were religious in orientation. The object of the revolution was to change all that and to transform each person into a 'new' Soviet man or a 'new' woman, free of religious training, free of religious cant!

This was a strange and turbulent time. Jewish families were divided. The last Rebbe's own brother, became, for a time, a Marxist, a Trotskyite. A short time later, he became an early dissident. Jews, at that period, were haunted by pogroms. Communists believed that Utopia could be achieved by "the rejection...of all notions of religiously and ethnicity." The last Rebbe, in 1919, as a 17 year old youth, even joined the local Jewish defense force to physically defend Jews who were under threat and attack. Departments of the Soviet government were established, staffed by Jews, including former chassidic Jews, who chose to become Communist in their politics and secular, atheistic in their beliefs. Special sections of the government staffed with these Jews, aimed to dismantle Jewish institutions, specifically Jewish religious institutions. This branch of government was called "Yevseksia". A primary target was the Lubavitch movement which had spread to virtually from its origins in western 'White' Russia to practically all parts of Russia.

The previous Rebbe was living in Leningrad at the time. He was under surveillance yet he recognized that to keep Chassidism alive in Russia, an underground movement must be immediately established. As each synagogue was closed or each yeshiva was dismantled, an underground version was immediately established.

In 1924, the previous Rebbe secretly called together the nine leaders of the underground and they swore to continue to build Judaism, even at the risk of their lives. This was highly dangerous work. Indeed, the previous Rebbe was imprisoned seven times, the last in 1927. Then and only through the efforts of followers and representations by political leaders in the west was he released from prison. This date is still celebrated in Lubavitch movement.

The previous Rebbe moved from place to place across Europe until, in 1940, he secretly escaped from Europe and was brought to Crown Heights in Brooklyn, where the Lubavitch movement was recreated. The Lubavitch headquarters became firmly established in America.

The last Rebbe and his wife followed and joined his father-in-law, the previous Rebbe, months later in 1941. Throughout all that period to the end, the previous rebbe and the last rebbe kept in close contact with each community in Russia - with the underground. Indeed if one were to trace the dissident movement, a direct link can be made to the sparks that were lit by these efforts starting in 1917. The efforts were not sporadic. They were comprehensive. They were detailed. They were community oriented, street by street, synagogue by synagogue, yeshiva by yeshiva - one Jew at a time.

Regularly Chabad messengers were secretly sent to live covert lives behind the Iron Curtain, to teach and keep the flame of faith alive. The Jewish flame, the flame of religious freedom, was kept glowing at great personal cost and many times at the risk of death or imprisonment.

It is my hope that in the fullness of time, this remarkable, still hidden, history of the 20th century can be told. Historians will conclude as I did, that first cracks in the Soviet Empire were started by Lubavitch and widened by their silent, covert, yet relentless efforts. There is one story that is known because it is published.

Many stories have been slowly published, but the story of Herman Branover, one of the world's leading scientists who was educated in Russia, I found most instructive. Branover came from an assimilated Jewish family in Russia. His father was an atheist and was killed in World War II. His grandfather would take him occasionally to synagogue but he was educated in the Soviet system and was an atheist. He began his search for a better life when he has roughed up in the streets. This was during the anti-Semitic policies of Stalin in the late '40s and early '50s. While he swiftly moved up the academic ladder and was involved in the highest levels of strategic research in the U.S.S.R, he became increasingly curious about Judaism. In the '60s, he decided to attend a small basement "shtebel" in Moscow for Saturday services, to avoid detection. There he met his first Chabad Chasid. He was invited to the Chabadnik's home and they began discussions about physics and space.

They discussed the kabbalistic ideas of creation, questions of time, space and even Einstein's theory of relativity. He was persuaded to put on tephillim for the first time. Soon he learned about the Rebbe himself. He began to receive handwritten 'sichot' of the Rebbe's in the mail because they could not be transmitted otherwise.

At the end of the '80s, he decided to emigrate from Russia to Israel. He applied for a visa and was immediately kicked out of his high position in the Soviet Academy of

Sciences and imprisoned. After being released from jail, he decided to telephone the Rebbe directly. He got through, but one of the Rebbe's assistants intervened. Finally he heard a second voice on the line saying, "Tell him he already has all the blessings, he must be sure that he will immediately go out." After persistent protests, he was advised three weeks after the Rebbe's blessings that he had received his papers to emigrate.

He emigrated to Israel and soon after travelled to the United States to meet the Rebbe for the first time. Initially he could not figure out what the Rebbe was saying as he spoke to him in Yiddish. The Rebbe then in Russian asked him minute questions about dozens, indeed hundreds of families, everywhere in Russia including Siberia. The Rebbe wanted details, details, and Branover did not have the information. He merely recognized some of the names. The Rebbe wound up telling him what each husband was doing, the wife, the ages of the children, the interests of the children, the family problems. Branover could not understand how so much precise information with such specific detail could come from one man.

And now let me quote from Branover, directly, "then I started paying attention to how the Rebbe was speaking. When he speaks about a certain Jew, a certain woman, a certain child, a certain man, the whole world doesn't exist. The only thing that exists is the Jew about whom the Rebbe is concerned at the moment." He goes on to say that "if the Rebbe is speaking about a Jew somewhere in Siberia, the whole world is non-existent."

In 1985, one week before Gorbachev took office in Moscow as Secretary-General of the Communist party and later President, Branover got a call from the Rebbe. He told him to call all of his contacts in Moscow, Leningrad and other cities and tell them they should be assured that from now on the situation in Russia will improve. "Not immediately", he said, "it will take time. The whole thing will fall apart and Communism will come to an end and that whoever wishes to leave will be allowed. Everyone who wishes to stay will be able to practice Judaism". This was unbelievable. No one, no one in 1985, predicted the U.S.S.R. collapse was at hand, but the Rebbe's prediction came true. Genius, like god, lives in the detail. The Rebbe kept the light of faith alive by herculean detailed efforts, by patient attention to the details of the life of each Jew, one at a time! Much of this story is still hidden from the public. This is what the Rebbe desired. The work was more important than the credit. The recognition, the attention might detract from the work at hand, the work of saving lives. Lubavitch had a different approach from others. At all times, both Rebbes insisted the Soviet Constitution be upheld.

The Soviet Constitution provided for freedom of religious instruction. Yet the Soviet government failed to uphold its own rule of law - its own constitution. Still, the Rebbes insisted. They always believed in the 'rule of law.'

So the Lubavitch's work, this particular work, origins of the Refusnik Movement, transcended saving Jewish souls and became a universal message of hope for mankind. Before concluding, let me answer a question I am always asked by non-Jewish friends. My gentile friends have asked. What do Jews believe about gentiles'? Do Jews consider themselves as 'Chosen People?' Why? Well, the Rebbe echoed the answer about gentiles, repeated by the great Rambam - the great Moses Maimonides.

In the 11th century if non-Jews obey the seven simple laws of Noah - called the 'Noahide laws' - prohibitions against idol worship, blasphemy, murder, adultery and robbery, eating flesh from living animals and establishing courts of justice - establishing the 'rule of law', they are assured an equal place in the world to come. Thirty-six times in the Torah, Jews are repeatedly admonished to treat strangers better than themselves. The Jews chose and were chosen to place greater, heavier burdens of law and practice on themselves, to gain and sustain their place in the world (613 commandments in all).

It can best be summed up in the eloquent words of Rabbi Hillel over twenty centuries ago - do not do unto others what you would not have done unto yourself!

So the message of Judaism, the message of Lubavitch is Universal. My friends, belief ends where we started - with oneself!

DENG XIAOPING: ON HIS DEATH

February 20, 1997

Hon. Jerahmiel S. Grafstein: Honourable senators, yesterday marked the death of Deng Xiaoping, the unchallenged leader of China for the last two decades.

Canada is an "old friend" of China's. Yet, in 1989, the Tiananmen incident triggered undulating tremors within China's leadership cadre which have yet to be fully detonated. As China emerges as the fastest growing economic power in the world, changes in China's leadership are becoming more vital to Canada's economic stability and well-being.

China has the largest standing army in the world, the second largest navy, air force and nuclear force and, early in the next millennium, will have the world's third largest gross national product.

The remarkable career of Mr. Deng matches the turbulent history of China in this century. He was a brilliant political organizer, hero of the Long March, unparalleled military leader and, finally, a pragmatic, if rather harsh, visionary who led first in agricultural reforms and, ultimately, in the wide economic reforms that have fueled China's unbelievable engine of growth.

A protégé, first of Mao and then of Zhou En Lai, he was thrice toppled from power, only to be resuscitated, twice by Zhou, after his clashes over policy and personality with Mao and his acolytes. Deng's colourful quip about socialism, that "...it did not matter whether the cat was black or white as long as it caught the mouse..." clearly antagonized Mao, the ultimate ideologue.

Mao wrote that being "Red" was more important to the continuing revolutionary struggle than being "expert" in technology and economics. In 1967, Mao declared that China "loved struggles." Deng retorted, "In real life not everything is a class struggle!" Yet in the periodic purges in China between 1957 and 1959, Deng joined the chorus of criticism against "rightists" and "capitalist roaders" that resulted in the brutal purging of over 500,000 bureaucrats, including 100,000 teachers.

During the uncertainty of the Tiananmen incident, Deng chose the hard-line leaders led by the current premier Li Peng over the more liberal group led by the then premier Zhao Ziyang who, since Tiananmen, has been living under close guard, and I believe house arrest, in Beijing. Apparently, Deng feared the spectre of civil disorder more than repression.

Still, Deng Xiaoping will be remembered as one of the most remarkable figures of the 20th century for his monumental achievements. We can only hope that the pragmatic, liberal side of his contradictory nature will re-emerge as the organizing consensus within the Chinese leadership that succeeds him. Before Tiananmen, Deng told party leaders, "Democracy has to be institutionalized and written into law." If the cycles of Chinese history are to be heeded, look to the re-emergence and rehabilitation of Zhao Ziyang to the Chinese leadership élite.

China has never separated the state from its people. China will change, but in its own way. Lu Xun, China's leading revolutionary writer, preached that China's progress depends on growth inward, not outward. Will China's next leadership heed the advice of its revered revolutionary thinker and activist, Lu Xun, who wrote these words in 1925:

> When the Chinese are confronted with power, they dare not resist, but use the words "taking the middle course" to put a good face on their real behaviour so they can feel consoled.

Canada must help create circumstances to allow China to take "a middle course," a moderate course that will help China to take up its rightful role as a promoter of civilization's greatest humanistic values. Our only hope is that, in the leadership struggles that will no doubt follow Deng's passing, China will adopt a humane, "middle" liberal course, continuing the "open door" policy so firmly fixed by Mr. Deng.

MAURICE RIEL: ON RETIREMENT

March 11, 1997

Hon. Jerahmiel S. Grafstein: Honourable senators, I, too, was surprised today to learn our colleague and distinguished friend, Maurice Riel, will be leaving us.

I was called to this place when Maurice, a legendary figure, was occupying your Chair, Your Honour, and I found him in person to be greater than his legend. He was quiet, at all times expert, always sound, always wise and blessed with a capacious mind that was both subtle and supple.

We share a love of books. Rarely was there an occasion when Senator Riel would not be seen in this chamber reading a book. Indeed, we share the love of French novels, he, obviously reading the original French, and I, a bad English translation.

I recall one occasion here in the Senate when I was preparing to give a speech and intended to quote a famous French author. Before making that speech, I decided to be careful, since my French is less than satisfactory. I therefore consulted my great friend Senator Riel and asked him how one would pronounce the name of this great French author Albert Camus, in particular, whether or not the "s" was pronounced. Senator Riel thought for a moment and said, "I believe his name came from a certain part of France. In that part of France, the word "Camus" was enunciated with the "s" sound; therefore, his name should be pronounced Albert Camus" - sounding the "s." I therefore followed Senator Riel's advice when making my speech, but I was soundly attacked by my colleagues, both opposite and on this side, for my ignorance and illiteracy, and my disrespect for la belle langue.

After completing my remarks, I sat down and was silent. I did not defend myself. My friend Senator Riel approached me and said, "You know, we will have to seek higher counsel on this matter." He decided, with my consent, to send a letter to a mutual colleague of ours in France who is the Secretaire Perpetuel de l'Academie Francaise in Paris. After a lengthy exchange of correspondence, Senator Riel stood in his place in this chamber and advised honourable senators that his advice had been incorrect and, indeed, Albert Camus's name should be pronounced without the "s" - and in the process, defended my honour. I tell this story because it touches only the tip of the iceberg, of the fastidiousness of this cultural man who is leaving us. He was always graceful and scholarly. He has a bold, sagacious mind.

We share a love of precision in language and a love of Canada, and we shall miss him. I wish Senator Riel and his wonderful and beautiful wife - Godspeed.

Honourable senators, the word "honourable" is a word that, at times, we throw around loosely in this chamber. We are called honourable, and call each other honourable, but somehow we slide over the articulation of that phrase. When I think of the word "honourable" and when I think of the words 'the honourable senator,' there is no better exemplar of those words than our dear friend, the Honourable Senator Maurice Riel.

OPENING REMARKS TO THE 1ST ANNUAL ALLAN J. MacEACHEN LECTURESHIP ON PARTY POLITICS AT ST. FRANCIS XAVIER UNIVERSITY

April 1, 1997

Your honours:

Some time ago between debates in the Senate, I was quietly debating with my good friend Senator Gigantes about the appropriate English translation for a key phrase from the works of Heraclitus the great Greek philosopher - whose philosophy was based on the theory of a constant change. Heraclitus wrote in Greek: "ethos anthropou daimon." Now, I say the quote means "man's character is his fate." Philippe Gigantes says "man's character is his guide." In any event, Heraclitus preached that "character" - a politician's character - is the motor of politics.

Today we can agree. We're here to celebrate the career of one man and how one man's character has so influenced the nation, the federal government and party politics.

The Canadian constitution. The heart of our governance, that piece of paper that has so preoccupied, and continues to preoccupy, so many in this room - and in so many ways - is silent. Absolutely silent about two words that animate our public life - two words that form the sinews and life blood of our constitution - "party politics".

Just as St. Francis spent his life exploring and celebrating the mysterious canons and hidden patterns within man's soul, so this lecture celebrates the life, the work and the genius Allan J. MacEachen.

Allan J. MacEachen! Allan J. MacEachen! Allan J. MacEachen! Just repeating those two names, side by side, would send ripples through the media, tremors through Tory ranks and waves through Tory leadership.

And if those two names were not enough, I could bear witness at each session of the Senate to what happened when Allan J. Himself, in the raw, would appear in the Senate and slowly rise in his place on the Senate front benches to face the then leader of the government in the Senate, an other distinguished Maritimer, that very honourable Lowell Murray. Watching from the rear, one can see an almost invisible shudder as Murray's back stiffens and his shoulders hunch up and he cringed deep in his seat. And from the front, one can always detect on Senator Murray's grim face a slight tremor of the lower lip and a quiver of the left eyebrow as Allan J. MacEachen softly, almost aimlessly at first, commenced to address the chamber.

Even from the perspective of my seat in the Senate I note that the otherwise, almost perfect roman profile of avuncular Senator Finlay Macdonald, a fellow Nova Scotian, quickly become distorted as his wistful smile is drained, his florid face paled and he moved forward to the edge of his seat to hear what new blows would emanate from the lips of one Allan J. to bruise and batter yet again the Tory body politic!

Obviously, the Tories learned to their regret Allan J. MacEachen's secret. This awesome secret triggers fear and trembling. Allan's middle name is Joseph, a good biblical name which translated from Hebrew means to multiply or to add to or to increase. Clearly every Member of Parliament who sat opposite Allan Joseph MacEachen can add to their miseries and increase their misfortunes, hence their obsession with Allan J. MacEachen.

Why this angst and anguish in the highest circles of the political landscape. Can we find a clue, in his origins? Let us cast our minds back six decades to his background. It has been recounted many times and in many places!

The rise of Allan MacEachen from his most humble beginnings in Inverness, Nova Scotia, propelled solely by the power of his personality and the grandeur of his intellect that allowed him to escape the narrow confines of his modest origins and move to St. Francis Xavier University here, in Antigonish, where he started what was to become a singularly distinguished academic career.

However he was determined to better himself. So, he spent what in retrospective was probably his most useful early period to broaden his perspective, in studies at the very heart of the Canadian soul itself, my alma mater, the University of Toronto which obviously then propelled him onto greater intellectual heights at the University of Chicago and finally to highest grove of academe in North America, MIT in Cambridge, Massachusetts, before he returned to St. Fx to teach.

More than 40 years ago, in the 1950s, he joined the right honourable Lester Pearson in opposition as an advisor. And in the early '60s was elected and served in the House of Commons until he was summoned to the highest and holiest of all places, the Senate, in 1984.

We watched in amazement as Allan MacEachen waved his semantic wizardry and performed his intellectual gymnastics in the Senate - as if by magic, to our delight, he could elevate a minor point of procedure into a grand indictment of national malfeasance. You can tell he has drawn blood when some Senators opposite turn an ever flaming ruby red or even better, begin to whine.

Our Rabbis tell us that such a man with such an intellect is so gifted by God that he can demonstrate how two angels can dance on the head of a pin.

Balzac, the great French author, once wrote that the world was divided between the deceivers and the deceived. And we, honourable senators have been deceived. Have been deceived by the conventional wisdom in the media. First we were told that Allan MacEachen was a radical, a destroyer of Canadian values, a small "L" Liberal and worst yet, a reformer. Then we were told he was a large "L" Liberal, a reactionary. A dinosaur. First we were told he was a Pearson Liberal and then we have been reminded that no, he is truly a Trudeau Liberal. All this, honourable senators, is deception. All is deceit. For if the truth be known, Allan MacEachen is not a Pearson Liberal. Never was a Pearson Liberal! Allan MacEachen is not and never was a Trudeau Liberal! Allan MacEachen is a MacEachen Liberal.

Now pray tell you may ask, just what precisely is a MacEachen Liberal. A MacEachen Liberal is one who has never given up his belief in reform at a time when reform was not fashionable. Never gave up his belief in the Liberal Party as a vehicle of social justice when both the liberal party and social justice were not fashionable. Never gave his belief in reversing the fortunes of the Liberal Party. You'll recall in 1979 when he single-handed set the stage for Mr. Trudeau's triumphant return, he was merely repeating history.

Earlier, in the '60s even Liberals had written and read off the Liberal Party, Allan's ideas and actions paved the Liberal return to power in 1962. In the '60s, Allan MacEachen was instrumental in radically reforming the labour code as Minister of Labour and established a new standard for the minimum wage. And Allan MacEachen was the architect of the Liberal Social Agenda of the '60s, through the Health Resources Fund, the Assistance Plan, the Old Age and Security Act, all of which were introduced and amended during his period as Minister of National Health and Welfare. He piloted Medicare through the tumultuous debate in the house where Medicare was almost derailed. That greatest of modern political reforms, the Election Expenses Act was introduced when he served as House Leader and President of the Privy Council.

Finally during his tenure as Foreign Minister in the '80s when he almost single-handed transformed the global dialogue between east and west into a dialogue between north and south. Truly a Liberal dialogue. All these were steps, grand Liberal steps, taken by Allan MacEachen, made the Liberal Party synonymous with social justice.

Apparent failure in politics is cyclical. Just a matter of timing! Being ahead of one's times sometimes creates a strong reaction that ultimately leads the way to greater social justice. It was in Allan MacEachen's measures as Minister of Finance in 1981, measures on tax reform that again showed he was ahead of his time. If one goes back and examines carefully the contours of MacEachen's tax reforms - reduced tax rates, elimination of preferential tax shelters, while closing the gap between rich and poor in this country - his measures, still stand out as a model of equity and fairness.

Allan J. MacEachen transformed the Senate into a body of conviction and activity. Late in 1984, I was asked to attend a meeting to consider the Senate's image. At that meeting, Allan stoutly argued that no legislative body, no national body, can maintain any legitimacy, any credibility, unless it has a public presence. A public profile. Indeed by eradicating prestudy and slowly stimulating a reformist attitude Allan MacEachen has, for better or worse, heightened the Senate's presence and promoted the Senate's public profile. If imitaiton is sincerest test of flattery, the conversative oppositon in the Senate has followed the MacEachen thesis and made the Senate lively and so friendly, the secret source of the power, that awesome power that emanated from Allan MacEachen is not the man himself, but his Liberal ideas. In this time of Liberal travail, let us say what was said of the late Robert Kennedy: we know that Allan MacEachen is not a myth but a man. We know that Allan MacEachen is not a hero but a hope. What better accolade can one Liberal render to another in times of Liberal dislocation than to say that he is a Liberal, he is a man, and he is a hope!

So when time came for Allan J. MacEachen to be retired from public life, he made it emphatically clear that he was not leaving party politics qr the political party of his choice.

And then, as I look on Allan's record of almost four decades of unblemished and honourable participation in the public life of our country, it became abundantly clear to me, that there could be no more fitting or lively honour to bestow on Allan and his passion for politics than to create the Allan J. MacEachen Annual Lecture on Party Politics - so that we could continue to share his enthusiasm for party and for politics with the next generation, especially here in his beloved academic environment of St. Francis Xavier where he first launched that astonishing political career.

Last June, hundreds of friends, allies and adversaries alike, gathered in Ottawa to hold a memorable dinner in Allan's honour, together with one of his great party cohorts, the honourable Keith Davey who was retiring from the Senate at the same time.

We had assembled a tribute committee from coast to coast, who quickly and joyfully pledged funds to establish this annual lectureship here at St. Francis Xavier University in Allan's honour, and a similar annual lectureship at Victoria College at the University of Toronto in Keith Davey's honour.

When I was told by President Riley that Bob Rae was to be the first guest lecturer, I could have not been more delighted. Bob Rae throughout his astonishing and prolific career has never failed but to give Liberalism a good name. I attribute this particular quirk in his professed philosophy to the breeding place of his birth, Ontario, where. I must tell you 'true grits' continue to be discovered, and in some numbers.

I must confess, I too, was born in London, Ontario, to be exact. There must be something in the air in Ontario that determines that once a Liberal, always a Liberal.

Before concluding, may I take this opportunity to thank all the generous contributors of this lectureship, many of whom are here with us today, and to President Riley and his colleagues without whose creative assistance and encouragement this remarkable event would not have been possible.

One final indulgence. A personal word to Allan. Allan, when I recently returned to Canada from vacation and I read the newspapers, I thought to myself that the party needs you again as never before. So keep alert, and keep your phone lines open. You may be in high demand yet again.

Thank you St. Francis of Xavier, thank you ladies and gentlemen and thank you Allan J.

PIETRO RIZZUTO: EULOGY

September 30, 1997

Hon. Jerahmiel S. Grafstein: Honourable senators, I sat next to Pietro Rizzuto in this chamber close to a decade, and at practically every session we exchanged our views. In his quiet and gentle manner, I came to appreciate his artfulness and his astuteness in all things political, particularly with respect to Quebec. I came to understand that he was a passionate Canadian who loved his community, his province, and he was a living link to all the rich, varied, unique and distinct societies that make up Quebec.

Pietro, most of all, believed in loyalty. He was loyal to his friends; he was loyal to his leader; he was loyal to our party. He was, for me, the ultimate loyalist. At his moving and magnificent memorial service in Laval-sur-le-Lac this summer, five languages were spoken and sung - Latin, English, French, Italian and Spanish - for he was so closely and so strongly rooted in each of those cultures. As we listened to the beautiful operatic voices and music that Pietro loved so much, we could see and feel his presence among us. It was, honourable senators, a most fitting conclusion and tribute to an outstanding career of public and community service.

To his wife, Pina, and his family, we offer our condolences and our memories.

Pietro will be sorely missed for his strength, his sensibility, his sagacity and, above all, for his service to Canada, which he loved so very much. Pietro, *pax vobiscum.*

Ciao, Pietro.

JOHN SOPINKA, Q.C.: EULOGY

November 25, 1997

Hon. Jerahmiel S. Grafstein: Honourable senators, it is with the deepest regret that I rise to bring to the Senate's attention the tragic passing of Mr. Justice John Sopinka.

John Sopinka was first a classmate and then a friend of mine for over four decades. We met first in Toronto in September of 1955 at Baldwin House, a tiny brick building on St. George Street, the historic home of Robert Baldwin, which was then the house and home of the University of Toronto Law School.

John and I were both members of the class of 1958. The law school was small, populated by a circle of brilliant teachers - some say the greatest collection of legal teaching talent in Canada - led by Cecil Augustus Wright, known as "Caesar" Wright, who was a great Canadian law reformer and who taught torts. Bora Laskin taught labour law, real property and constitutional law. J. B. Milner taught contracts. Others included a part-time lecturer known as John J. Robinette.

Caesar Wright had introduced the case method of law teaching to Canada from Harvard, polishing and perfecting this method on the raw, ungainly minds of his students. It was an awesome intellectual experience to review a case in his class, and then have your logic dissected point by point by Caesar, all to the delight and consternation of the next victims, your classmates.

John Sopinka had a quick body and a quicker mind. He had a direct, pungent, concise style that quickly cut to the core of the most complex legal facts. He showed his talents early, and soon rose to near the head of the class, where he stayed for the balance of the three years that we laboured there.

Many in the press have already extolled John's virtues, and his superb legal and juridical talents that clearly guaranteed him a very bright and lasting place in the firmament of our public life and the history of our country. John came from a minority group. He understood more than most what it took to move from a minority to the mainstream in Canadian life. He was instinctively and spontaneously on the side of the underdog. He was such a great competitor. He lived and embellished the Charter, and played a leading role in making Charter values inseparable from the values of our civil society. History will better judge the consequences.

John also had a wicked sense of humour. Let me illustrate. Naturally, everyone approached Caesar Wright's classes with great fear and trepidation, I more than most. I was the second youngest in our class, and had a very slender academic preparation that did not really prepare me for the greater group of talents and experiences of my older classmates, including John.

Dean Wright would go through the class list one by one and ask each student, in turn, to analyze the case assigned for the week. Then he would dismember that student's response with his critical exegesis. John took his turn bravely and weathered the storm. When my turn came, crouching at the back of the class, I said, when my name was called, "Not here, Sir" to the muffled discomfort of the rest of the class. Several weeks later, the same scene was repeated. When my name was called, I whispered, "Not here, Sir" and Dean Wright moved on to the next victim.

This angered John Sopinka and, at the very next class, John and another classmate took all my books and precious notes and papers and locked them in the Dean's car, which was parked at the side of the law school, forcing me to finally confront the Dean in his classroom. That day, gingerly, I stood at the front of the class for the very first time and said, "Mr. Dean, may I have the keys to your car?" He looked at me, looked at Sopinka and glanced at the class over the top of his glasses with bemused delight and said, "Here, Grafstein. Nice to see you for the first time. Take the keys, take my car, and take the rest of the afternoon off." John absolutely roared with the rest of the class because he had a fabulous sense of humour.

The loss of John Sopinka is a tragedy. He was cut down in the prime of a brilliant judicial career. This is a terrible loss to his friends, to his colleagues, to the country, and an irreconcilable loss to Marie and his family. There are but two solaces that remain. Thence, in time, we shall go by the awful grace of God. The smaller solace is that John will not be forgotten. His memory will burn brightly in the hearts and minds of all who came to know him.

DAN LANG: ON RETIREMENT

December 2, 1997

Hon. Jerahmiel S. Grafstein: Honourable senators, Canada is a blessed by often unheralded personalities who daily work as volunteers, diligently and selflessly, to make our political system work. This week Canada lost such a remarkable personality.

Dan Lang was a friend and one of my first mentors in the Liberal Party. Dan's career instructs and informs all of those who seek public life. In more than a footnote to political history, Dan's public life serves as a lesson in civics and citizenship.

At the end of the fifties, the once mighty Liberal Party was in ruins, moribund, facing a deficit of ideas, and devastated by the Diefenbaker sweeps of 1957 and 1958. Dan, then a municipal counsellor for Forest Hill Village and a respected lawyer, joined a small circle of spirited volunteers, including our colleague Dick Stanbury and former colleagues Keith Davey, Royce Frith and the late John Aird. Together, they made a difference. Collectively, they became the engines of reform and revival that led to the radical transformation of the Liberal Party and then on to successive Liberal minority governments of 1962, 1963, and 1965 led by our hero, Mr. Pearson - not Lester Pearson but Mr. Pearson.

It was a bottoms-up, grass-roots volunteer movement, and Dan Lang was one of the key spark plugs in that movement. The spirit that they embodied was the catalyst that led to electoral reforms and reforms of campaign spending that transformed the practise of party politics in Canada. That same spirit led to the passage of Medicare in 1966. Together, they stood for Liberal principles, Liberal ideas and Liberal policies.

Dan was then - and remained throughout his life - a gentlemen and a man of honour. Although Dan loved the Liberal Party almost as much as his family, he believed that commitment to country, as he perceived it, was above loyalty to party. This, he repeated often, was one's highest duty.

Sometime after his appointment to the Senate by Mr. Pearson, Dan became dissatisfied and frustrated with what he concluded was the increasing party polarization in the Senate. He left the Liberal caucus and sat for the remainder of his term as an independent. He felt that the Senate was the supreme source of sober second thought and that he could better serve the country by being free of party restraints, although he never ceased to consider himself other than a member of the Liberal Party.

When he spoke, as he did infrequently, he spoke shortly and concisely; and when he spoke, he adhered to William of Occam's principle, known as Occam's Razor, which dictates that, in any rhetorical explication of any issue, no matter how complex, better less said than more - a practice I too often fail to emulate.

Over the years, I came to disagree with Dan at times over personalities, processes and policies. Yet I never despaired of his commitment, integrity, friendship and self-lessness. He was always a man of honour, always the consummate gentleman, and always a delight.

Dan was my first political boss in Ontario. He served as Federal Campaign Chairman in 1962 and 1963. His hard work, honesty, cool analysis, tactical skills and humour made him a model machine politician. You followed what he asked because you trusted his motives and his judgments. He remained beyond personal reproach.

Now, honourable senators, as we approach the autumn of our years, disagreements fade, and what remains are glowing embers of a remarkable personality. I will always recall Dan's dapper fedora, perched on the side of his head, the intensity of his gaze and manner, the deep yet quiet authority of his voice and words, and his deeper commitment and pride in party and in country.

What I will miss most will be the pleasure of his company, his wonderful chuckles, and his ability to bring a fresh, almost clinical perspective to complex political problems .

To the ever lovely Frances and his family, we can only grieve, remember, and - if even in a small way console them in their loss, which diminishes all who knew and respected him.

FAMOUS FIVE (EMILY MURPHY, NELLIE McCLUNG, IRENE PARBLY, LOUISE McKINNEY, HENRIETTE MUIR EDWARDS ON A RESOLUTION TO ERECT THEIR STATUES ON PARLIMENT HILL

December 16, 1997

Hon. Jerahmiel S. Grafstein: Honourable senators, I too, am an enthusiastic supporter of this resolution to erect a statue on Parliament Hill commemorating the five women who were instrumental in provoking the 1929 change in Canadian law so that women could be considered "persons," equal under the Canadian Constitution, the British North America Act of 1867 - hence, eligible to serve in the Senate. It is long overdue.

As students of history, we should also take note that, back in 1938, a plaque was erected in the Senate lobby commemorating that event by the then Prime Minister Mackenzie King. Honourable senators, sometimes the Senate is slightly ahead of our times.

Honourable senators, while we commemorate the political work of the Famous Five that enabled women to join the ranks of parliamentarians and public officials, we should not neglect to praise at the same time the unsung work of millions of women who toiled and continue to toil to make Canada the great country it has become today. This news is not new. All senators know about it from their own personal experience.

As for me, my maternal grandmother came to Canada in 1907 with her family and worked all of her adult life to support her blind husband and her two young daughters until her premature death over 50 years ago - some say because of overwork. In turn, my mother - born in 1900 and now 97 years old, alive and lively, worked all her adult life throughout this century to sustain first her parents and her younger sister and then our family. When my late aunt, my mother's younger sister, came of age, she worked all of her adult life to help her parents and then her own family. She worked until her death some years ago when she was in her '80s. My late sister worked all of her adult life to support her family, culminating in the establishment of her own business, which started in her kitchen and became a food company with global reach.

The women in my life have always been graceful, critical and forceful partners in all aspects of my life. They taught me and my family that the greatest dignity was the dignity of hard work.

It would be remiss of me if I did not comment on one aspect of Senator Fairbain's passionate and informative speech yesterday. She reminded us that she would not have become a member of the Senate without the efforts of Emily Murphy, Nellie McClung, Irene Parlby, Louise McKinney and Henriette Muir Edwards, known as the Famous Five, the women who are the subject of this resolution that we support.

For those who know me and also know of my career, by the same token, I could not have become a Senator without the efforts of those strong women in my family whom I mentioned, as well as my wife and my mother-in-law, who continue to be equal and active partners in all phases of my life.

I am confident, honourable senators, that I speak for the millions of other men in our country who would say no less about the women who have shared their lives.

In conclusion, may I note the special efforts of an old friend, Frances Wright, whose drive and single mindedness brought the contents of this resolution to its fruition. By her focus and strength of purpose, she reminds me of all the strong women - both family and friends alike, and more in number than the Famous Five - who have contributed so much to me in my public and private careers.

To you Frances I say, "Well done!" I hope that the statue that we will erect will serve as a living symbol to all Canadian women in every walk of life. To them, I say: "Well done. The best is yet to come!"

SENATOR BILL PETTEN AND SENATOR AND DR. LORNE BONNELL: ON THEIR RETIREMENT

December 16, 1997

Hon. Jerahmiel S. Grafstein: Honourable senators, on this bittersweet occasion when our colleagues Senator Bill Petten and Senator and Dr. Lorne Bonnell take leave of this place, I did not intend to speak until I heard the lyrical comments of the Maritime senators: Senators Graham, Phillips and Rompkey. I did not want Bill and Lorne to leave this place believing that we in Ontario are without some culture.

To Lorne and to Bill, may I take the liberty of saying these words from perhaps the greatest of all Irish playwrights , Sean O'Casey, in his wonderful play, *Juno and the Paycock:*

> Come in the evening,
> Come in the morning,
> Come when you're asked,
> Come without warning.
> You are both darling, darling men,
> and you will both be missed.

JOE B. SALSBERG: EULOGY

February 10, 1998

Hon. Jerahmiel S. Grafstein: Honourable senators, last Sunday The *Toronto Star* reported that one J.B. Salsberg, Joe Salsberg, aged 95, died peacefully at his home in Toronto. Yet J.B.'s life was anything but peaceful. His compelling career mirrored the turbulence and tribulations of Canada in the 20th century. His life serves as a kind of mixed metaphor for the anguish and honour, the travesties and the triumphs, the paradoxes and the passions, the disasters and the dreams of our era.

Born in impoverished circumstances in Poland, Salsberg came to Canada with his immigrant parents just before World War I, settling in the heart of Canada, the Spadina and College working district.

Following his father's wishes, as a youth he studied to become a rabbi. His penurious parents were observant and early leaders of the parochial school system in Toronto. Then his life took an abrupt turn.

At 13, he went to work in a sweat-shop in the garment district, earning $3 a week as a purse maker. With hard work, he earned quick salary increases to $5 a week. Suddenly, the rules changed and he was told that he would now have to work on commission. The first day he made $5. The following day, his boss changed the work rules again.

This experience transformed Salsberg into a tribune of the working classes. He lifted a torch for labour which he carried from that time until he drew his last breath. He always carried the torch with humour and honour. While searching for political answers, he joined a Zionist workers' group and quickly rose to leadership, including the editorship of a newspaper in New York City, speaking to groups across North America.

This canvas was still not broad enough for Joe; not broad enough for his ideas or his energy. While post-World War I in the 1920s was booming, the working conditions in Toronto were simply appalling. By 1926, Joe came to believe that communism as a means of eradicating discrimination, eradicating anti-Semitism, encouraging Jewish culture, but above all alleviating the working conditions, was the answer.

He began to work as a union organizer, rising to Vice-President of the International Hatters' Union, and within a short period J.B. was a key organizer behind just about every industrial union in Canada. Meanwhile, he became a member of the Central Committee of the Communist Party of Canada. As a speaker, he would address mass rallies from coast to coast. He revelled in the idea that a Jewish immigrant boy from Spadina could be at home organizing miners in Sydney or dock workers in Vancouver.

Salsberg was invited to secret workers' meetings across Canada. Union organizers would conceal him in their homes and churches while his speeches and ideas ignited the passion of key organizers and small worker groups. who spearheaded the creation of a Jewish Family and Child Services in Toronto, which became a leader in its field in Canada.

The Hon. the Speaker: Honourable Senator Grafstein, I am sorry to interrupt you, but your three minute period has expired.

Senator Grafstein: Honourable senators, may I have leave to continue?

The Hon. the Speaker: Is leave granted?

Hon. Senators: Agreed.

Senator Grafstein: Thank you, senators.

About this time, he married Dora Wilensky, the love of his life. She was a pioneer social worker who spearheaded the creation of the Jewish Family and Child Services in Toronto which became a leader in its field in social work in Canada. In 1959, Dora died prematurely of cancer. They had no children, and J.B. never remarried.

Union organizing naturally led to politics, and politics was never the same once J.B. was elected to the Toronto City Council in 1938. He became a tribune of the working classes, and he was re-elected. He became Toronto's most effective alderman, changing Toronto's living and social environment and, in the process, even the values of his staunchest adversaries.

In 1943, he was elected to Queen's Park, becoming the lone Communist in the legislature. He became an eloquent advocate against discrimination of any kind, and he led the passage of the first bill outlawing discrimination in public places in Canada.

An inspiring orator, he was usually drowned in a sea of heckling in the legislature.

He could not afford rent for an office on College Street. My Uncle Morris, who owned a dry goods store, gave Joe an office without rent and on condition that no one would know. My uncle was first a scholar and then a business man who never forgot his political roots.

Once, Salsberg, fed up, threatened to stop asking questions in Question Period, and the Premier of the day, Leslie Frost, banned heckling from Question Period. Frost so admired J.B.'s eloquence, his wit, his commitment to his ideas and his integrity that he named a township in Northern Ontario after him. J.B. held the seat for the St. Andrew's riding until 1955, when he lost in one of the most bitter electoral campaigns in Canada.

At the height of the Cold War, J.B. was accused of complacency, if not complicity, towards Soviet persecution of Jews in Russia. When rumour about purges and prosecutions emanated from Stalin's Soviet Russia, J.B. remained mute, neither opposing nor defending the horrendous stories seeping out from behind the Iron Curtain. J.B. was a true believer. After he lost the provincial election, he travelled to Moscow in 1956 to learn firsthand the fate of Jews and others at the hand of the Soviet state. This included an angry confrontation with Nikita Khruschev himself in the Kremlin.

In 1957, returning to Toronto disillusioned, he denounced Communism. As the number two person in the Communist Party in Canada, he left the party and took half the national executive with him. This effectively destroyed the Communist Party in Canada forever. Supporters of all parties then wanted J.B. to run for them, but Joe had had enough of politics. Joe's heart was broken and became a leading figure of local Jewish culture and worker's causes, writing a regular column for the Canadian Jewish News.

Joe knew each member of my family intimately. It was in this latter capacity that I came to know and admire him when I came to Toronto to study law in the late 1950s. Joe had an encyclopaedic knowledge about politics and people. He knew each member of my family - my paternal uncles, my maternal grandfather. He could place each in various shades of politics or culture or learning from left to right, from observant to secular. He was familiar with my father's own military record, fighting against Bolsheviks in Poland after World War I, yet he never criticized him or his memory. "Each man," he said, "must do what he must do."

The very first day after I was appointed to the Senate, I received a call, well after midnight, at the Chateau Laurier. It was J.B. on the line, whispering to me in Yiddish. In hushed tones, he told me that he had decided to write a story about me, my family, and my appointment to the Senate for the Canadian Jewish News. I asked him, "J.B., why so late, why in Yiddish, and why were you whispering?" J.B.'s response in Yiddish was, "Because...they are still listening in Ottawa." We continued to whisper our interview in Yiddish for an hour or so in the darkness of that cold, dark January night.

As I said earlier, J.B. was a true believer. He learned the harsh way that radical ideology first separates, then crushes, and eventually eradicates the dreams and the hopes of those very people who promote any harsh or radical ideology.

When he was about to turn 90, he was asked to look back on his career. About his convictions, he said this: "Despite my age, I'm still filled with faith in man's rise to ever higher and higher levels. I am still hurt when I see, or hear of people being cruel to one another."

Then he was asked, if he were to write his epitaph, what it would read. He said, "Here lies a man who tried to do the right thing." J.B. did.

JOHN G.H. HALSTEAD: EULOGY

February 23, 1998

Hon. Jerahmiel S. Grafstein: Honourable senators, sometimes there comes a moment to pause and reflect on the origins of Canada's foreign policy that is so active and so respected in all corners of the globe.

Over 70 years ago, a small circle of scholarly, brilliant young bureaucrats, under the tutelage of O.D. Skelton, were gathered by Mr. King as an adjunct to the Privy Council Office in the East Block, just a few steps away from this chamber, to create an independent foreign service. They were chosen because they were bright, young, vital, well-travelled, brilliant scholars and athletes who shared common values as sons of the manse or sons of missionaries. To themselves and others, they were simply "the brightest and the best." All were imbued with the social purpose gained by their faith. All sought to put their values of private morality into public practice in politics and diplomacy, as their parents had in their church. Notions of morality lay at the heart of their principles and policies. The standards of excellence and honesty they set for themselves and others made them exemplars of the public service culminating in the rise and career of one of their own, Lester B. Pearson, public servant, diplomat, Nobel laureate and Prime Minister.

Such was the life of John Halstead, who died in Ottawa last Monday at age 76. John was born in Vancouver, educated at UBC and the London School of Economics. During the war, he served as a naval officer in naval intelligence in the North Atlantic, Britain and Germany. His skills in German led him to the interrogation of U-boat prisoners and, after the war, naval elements of the German high command, tracking down suspected war criminals.

On his return to Canada, he joined the Foreign Service. In his 36-year career as a public servant, which spanned most of the Cold War, he rose rapidly in the Department of External Affairs from Assistant Undersecretary, to Ambassador to Germany, and then to NATO.

John was a superb writer and a strategic thinker. His duties included advising Mr. Pearson on the Canadian flag and writing the speech for Mr. Pearson's famous riposte to Charles de Gaulle's infamous intervention in Canadian affairs via his "Vive le Quebec libre" speech given in Quebec.

John's career included stints as visiting professor and lecturer at Georgetown, Carleton, Queen's, Dalhousie, Windsor, think tanks in the United States and universities in Germany. He was an active member of the Institute of Strategic Studies.

However, John's great love was Europe, NATO and Germany. John and I shared a deep interest in German literature and history. It was in this latter capacity that I came to know him as a member of the Atlantik Brucke. For over a decade, we met annually in Canada or Germany to discuss Canada, German and European relations. As always, John was a superb presenter, essayist and writer who, while perceptive, revelled in precision.

When he was awarded the Order of Canada in 1996, he said the following: "I have a very strong conviction that people should not be in the foreign service unless they have a strong commitment to serving their country and its people ....Government serves the people who elected it." John lived every word of his lietmotif.

Last fall when we met, tragically for the last time, John handed me a superb essay on the dangers of expanding NATO, concerns which he knew I shared. John would always think ahead with clarity and conclusion

I offer my condolences to his wife, Jean, and his son, Christopher. Canada and the foreign service will be diminished by his death, as we are all by his loss. He will be sorely missed by his many friends throughout North America and across Europe.

Godspeed, John.

STANLEY HAIDASZ: EULOGY

February 26, 1998

Hon. Jerahmiel S. Grafstein: Honourable senators, I should like to add words of tribute to Stanley Haidasz. I first met him in 1961 in his riding in the heart of Toronto, which was really a Central European enclave. He was a doctor and had a large family practice and loyal patients. As President of the Young Liberals at that time, I organized the Young Liberal organization in his riding. It was in that process that I came to know him, his riding organization and members of his family.

Shortly thereafter, the Toronto and District Liberal Association established what we called the Ethnic Committee, which was really a multicultural committee, to focus on multicultural issues. I think that was the first time within the bosom of a national party that a microcosm organization of this type was established. The thrust of that organization really came from Stanley's riding and from Senator Haidasz himself. It is interesting how ideas filter up from a riding association, from the grass roots to the senior echelons, and finally become part of the fabric of the country. It was from those early days and that experience of various groups working in a concerted area, from various ethnic and multicultural groups led by Senator Haidasz and his colleagues, that those ideas ultimately filtered up into the federal government, and then into national policy.

Senator Haidasz was a pioneer at the grass-roots level, and one of the originators of our multicultural policy. In that sense, when we talk about the bilingual and multicultural essence of the country, Senator Haidasz is one of the leaders in that formulation.

We also shared another interest. He and I have deep but different roots in Poland. We share a common hero, Jozef Pilsudski, who was the first leader after the First World War in Europe, and at that time in Poland, who believed in the idea of European federalism. Therefore from time to time, Stanley and I have talked about our interests in the culture, the history, if not the different pasts that we share with respect to Poland, and in that sense I shall miss him.

To you, Stanley, I say you are a great gentleman, a great scholar, a man of strong principles and stronger beliefs, and you will be sorely missed.

LEONARD MARCHAND: ON RETIREMENT

March 19, 1998

Hon. Jerahmiel S. Grafstein: Honourable senators, Canadians are often exhorted by leaders to ponder, and ponder yet again, two adjectives, 'unique' or 'distinct,' that form such a tantalizing part of our current political lexicon, and which have now become embedded in the hieroglyphics of Canada. One could certainly apply those adjectives to our retiring senator and great friend, the Honourable Leonard Marchand.

Think, honourable senators, of his last name, Marchand, and of his roots as a member of that creative aboriginal community, the Okanagan tribe of British Columbia. Think of his storybook climb to public prominence and power from a one-room school house in Six Mile Creek, up through the Indian reserve school system, to the public high school system, to the University of British Columbia as a Bachelor of Science in agriculture, and then on to the University of Idaho for a Masters degree in forestry.

Think of Len as the first status Indian to graduate from his public high school, and the first status Indian to serve as a Ministerial Assistant in Ottawa. He was the first status Indian to become a Member of Parliament, a Parliamentary Secretary and a Minister of the Crown. Think of Len rising from those modest origins to become the Honorary Chief of the Okanagan tribe. Think what a unique and distinct blend of concentration, capability and courage it took to make that astonishing rise upwards.

I first met Len when I became a member of a small group in Ottawa I like to call the "Class of 1965." I joined other young Canadians who flocked to Ottawa to serve in the Pearson government as Ministerial Assistants. In fact, as I look around the chamber, I reflect on the fact that Senators Austin, Pitfield, Joyal, De Bane, Bosa and our recently appointed Senator from British Columbia, Ross Fitzpatrick, all served in that so-called Class of 1965. We came from all parts of Canada, all walks of life, from different backgrounds, all bound by one common cause: to serve as proficiently and proudly as we could under Mr. Pearson's banner.

Len was a distinct and unique member of that unique and distinct class. Len worked first for the Honourable J.R. Nicholson and then the Honourable Arthur Laing, both Ministers of Indian Affairs. Both ministers were powerful and shrewd political regional barons from British Columbia in the Pearson government.

Len came to Ottawa and quickly gained a reputation as a fast study in the corridors of power. As young ministerial assistants, we met often to discuss public and partisan business. Len was always quick, quiet, ambitious, articulate, incisive and judicious in all questions of political and policy matters and, most important, the political plans necessary to execute those ideas. He was also a great and calculated wit, as Senator Hays pointed out.

Though small in stature, Len possessed a quality rare in politicians: a vast storehouse of common sense that he would summon to each and every question that he addressed. Few of us could appreciate or understand then the incredible hurdles - both physical and personal - that Len overcame to climb the political ladder.

In Parliament, Len led on all issues related to the aboriginal community, where he remains a recognized and respected leader. As with the Okanagan tribe, he was always peaceful and productive. He spoke rarely in Parliament or the caucuses, but when he did, he cut to the quick of the problem with authority and precision.

We watched Len rise above his modest origins and his tribal community to serve a higher loyalty, the sometimes unfashionable loyalty to Queen and country. For Len was - and is - first and foremost a Canadian.

Honourable senators, may this not then be Len's lasting lesson to his tribal community and to his country. Let his career in Parliament, in the other place and in the Senate, serve both as a dream lodge to his community, and an admonition to those who wish to separate and bifurcate their loyalties and identities by dividing, fragmenting and so parsing the essence of Canada that the parts become particles. In turn, those particles form less than the whole. Beware, senators, for the Okanagan shaman can be a potent adversary against those who would divide the spirit and the body.

For me, Len's life serves as a living idea of Canada. Canada, like poetry, so organizes the fragments of ideas into a provoking, if imperfect, work in progress that we would know not what we have until there is a danger in the losing of it.

Len, as you return to private life and what we all hope will take you along the path to a healthier and happier hunting ground, may wind and water, fire and earth, sun and stars always be with you and yours.

THE HOLOCAUST: VIEWS ON STATEMENT ISSUED BY THE VATICAN AS TEACHING DOCUMENT

March 31, 1998

Hon. Jerahmiel S. Grafstein rose pursuant to notice of March 25, 1998:

> That he will call the attention of the Senate to the Statement of the Vatican on the Holocaust as a teaching document.

He said: Honourable senators, at the outset of this inquiry, let me say that I approach this subject with some trepidation, and a deep feeling of inadequacy. More than 50 Passover and Easter seasons have passed since the furnaces of the Holocaust cooled and closed down. Two weeks ago, in Rome, the Vatican issued a document assaying the role of the Roman Catholic Church, the papacy, the Vatican and its followers, titled, "We Remember: A Reflection on the Shoah." In a way, one could read the document as a collective mea culpa. In a covering letter, His Holiness Pope John Paul II hoped that the document "will help to heal the wounds of misunderstanding and injustices." Some leading Catholic observers and others have noted that the document now leaves room for the Pope to make an even stronger statement in the future. Other Catholic observers expect that the document will serve as a teaching document for the church in all its aspects.

Why, honourable senators will ask, should one senator bring this document to the Senate's attention? Well, in the last six months we have heard much of the centrality of Roman Catholic education in the lives of most Canadians. We have studied, debated and passed two constitutional amendments respecting religious education and the school systems in Newfoundland and Quebec. Thus, in a way, Roman Catholic education has been a preoccupation of this Parliament and, hence, any educational documents sanctified by the Vatican and gleaned for a wider audience should be carefully examined and placed on the public agenda, if not the teaching agendas of schools and, in particular, the Roman Catholic school systems. I hope those in the church hierarchy - from whom we heard in abundance in the Senate respecting the importance of Catholic religious education - will advise us in the Senate what concrete steps by the Canadian Conference of Bishops and other professors of the faith will be taken to use this important historic document as a teaching tool in the schools, churches and beyond into the public arena across Canada.

Other observers have noted that the document falls short in its historical analysis of the responsibility or role of the church with respect to the root causes and the implementation of the Holocaust.

Before I turn to that aspect of this inquiry, let me remind honourable senators that I had previously drawn the Senate's attention to the consequences of nationalism as a source of 20th century malaise. Indeed, as if to support my contention, the Vatican document makes two telling references to the invidious role that nationalism played in the larger history that led to the Holocaust. First, the document notes that:

...in the 19th century a false and extremist nationalism took hold.

Later the document notes:

...that an extremist form of nationalism was heightened in Germany ....

In that clear sense, the church reminds us all of the dangers inherent in nationalism . Nationalist ideology was a political engine that propelled a horrific state agenda of preference, then discrimination, followed by exclusion, segregation and, ultimately, extinction. The "Final Solution" was seen as a considered, logical extension of a nationalist agenda.

The concerns about extreme nationalism in the Vatican document echoed one of Pope John Paul II's most passionate speeches condemning worship of the nation when he declared to the diplomatic corps at the Holy See earlier in this decade:

This is not a question of legitimate love for one's homeland or respect for its identify but rejecting the "Other" in his diversity so as to impose himself upon him....For this kind of chauvinism, all means are fair: exalting race, overvaluing the state, imposing a uniform economic model, levelling specific cultural differences.

For me, the first lesson of the Holocaust is the intrinsic danger of temporal nationalism encouraged or accommodated by a non-secular acquiescence if not acceptance.

Pope John Paul II has espoused the primacy of individuality over collectivity. In his encyclical *Centesimus Annus,* he wrote:

Something is owed to human beings because they are human beings.

Honourable senators, the church militant has always been a source of intense historic interest to me, in particular the nature of leadership. I belong to the school which believes that trends in history can be altered by individual leadership. Let me take this opportunity to share some of my thoughts with you respecting the role of leadership and, in this case, the papacy through the ages. What should we remember?

Let us start with the example of gregory vII, the sixth-century Pope who supported laws preventing Jews from holding public office or building synagogues or practising trades. Promulgated as a papal bull, a successor, Pope Stephen IV, continued to promote these restrictions.

With the advent and the birth of the first idea of Europe, Christian Europe, the first European Holy Roman Emperor, Charlemagne the Great, showed leadership by ignoring and strongly objecting to a litany of papal edicts and restrictions against Jews at that time. Later, Clement III even tried to prevent newly baptized Jews from joining the church. This conduct contrasted with Bernard de Clairvaux, a founder of a Cistercian monastery, who warned:

> Whoever makes an attempt on a life of a Jew, sins as if he attacked Jesus himself.

Bernard de Clairvaux earned his sainthood in that Dark and Medieval age.

Of course, we have Pope Urban V, who praised the death of Pedro I of Spain because that Spanish monarch established a liberal regime of privileges and sanctuary for Jews in his time. On the other hand, we discover the words of St. Thomas Aquinas, author of *Summa Theologica*, who harshly criticized the murder of Jews, contending that:

> Jews should be preserved as eternal witnesses to the truth of Christianity.

Gregory VII repeatedly sought to restrict Jews holding any office. It was Paul III who protected Jews from proposed expulsion from Avignon in France, but he was followed by the severe harshness of Pope Paul IV who cancelled letters of protection granted by past popes and accelerated the race to the Inquisition half a century later. We then have the case of Sixtus IV, who authorized the Spanish Inquisition under pressure from Ferdinand and Isabella of Spain. Thereafter, however, Sixtus IV tried to moderate the harshness of this miserable period by allowing peaceful relations with Jews within his domains in Italy.

In the 16th century we can turn to Leo X, who re-established privileges accorded to Jews in French papal territory despite the vigorous protest of the cardinals there. It was Leo X who ended the requirement of Jews wearing a badge in his French domain and let this obligation lapse into disuse within his Italian domain. He went further and encouraged Jews to practise professions and participate in the arts.

Later in the 16th century, we discover the leadership of Clement VII, who allowed

Jews to profess openly, established courts to settle disputes between Christians and Jews, and allowed Inquisition refugees to settle in Anacona on the Adriatic as a sanctuary. Clement VII also allowed Jews to practise their trades and their professions. Through the thickets of European history, we can perceive the papacy oscillating from protection to prosecution.

Honourable senators, the road to progress and humanity is by a steep and winding stairway until we approach the common era in the gates of the Holocaust itself.

It was Pius IX, in the middle of the 19th century, who ascended St. Peter's throne and who refused the right of Jews to live beyond ghetto walls, acquire land, engage in trade or enter into professions in Rome. In a throwback to centuries past, he even forbade Jewish doctors to attend Christian patients. All these prohibitions served as eerie yet precise forerunners of the infamous 1930s Nazi laws of discrimination and deprivation less than a century later.

Next we come to the heroic Pius XI who in 1939 issued an anti-Nazi encyclical following Germany's racist legislation and publicly told Belgian pilgrims:

> In spirit, we are all Semites.

Pius XI went even further and condemned Mussolini's laws "as a disgraceful imitation of Hitler's Nordic mythology." Reportedly the same Pius XI was planning even stronger denunciations when he died suddenly on February 10, 1939. Then, honourable senators, he was succeeded to the papacy by Pius XII.

The Vatican document makes reference to Pius XII and stated that he personally and through his representatives saved hundreds of thousands of Jewish lives. In one study done about this period respecting Rome and environs, a historian came up with the precise figures that 477 Jews were sheltered within the Vatican walls and another 4,238 found refuge in Rome's monasteries and convents. Yes, it is clear that in 1944, when Hungarian Jews were threatened with extinction, Pius XII did speak out loudly and clearly against the expulsions that ultimately led those Jews to the death camps. Of course, by then, Rome was safely in Allied hands. Perhaps the Vatican document might have made historical reference to French Cardinal Eugene Tisserant, who, in 1940, when the Nazi intentions of genocide were becoming clearer, wrote to a fellow cardinal in Paris of his futile urgings that Pope Pius XII issue an encyclical on what he said was the:

> ...individual duty to obey the imperatives of conscience.

Cardinal Tisserant went on in despair:

> I am afraid that history may be obliged in time to blame the Holy See for a policy accommodated to its advantage and little more.

Other Catholics can bear even stronger witness respecting that papacy's silence.

Honourable senators, while Popes may be "infallible," they are not perfect. Yet no one can doubt the leadership the present Pope, Pope John Paul II, has taken in reconciling the role of the church and the responsibility for the roots and exercise of anti-Semitism. He was the first pope since the founder of the papacy, St. Peter himself, to visit a synagogue. He was the first pope to visit a death camp, Auschwitz, located just 35 miles from his Polish birthplace. He followed Pope John XXIII's footsteps, who in 1959 ordered the first changes to Catholic liturgy to start to cleanse it of anti-Semitism, and the Second Vatican Council in 1962 when anti-Semitism and culpability were first denounced in Nostra Aetate. In 1988, Pope John II stated:

> I repeat again with you, the strongest condemnation of anti-Semitism and racism, which are opposed to the principles of Christianity.

Pope John Paul II was the first pope to establish relations between the Vatican and Israel and the first pope to condemn anti-Semitism both repeatedly and forcefully. In his recent book, entitled *Crossing the Threshold of Hope*, the Pope wrote with sensitivity and insight of the necessity for the reformation of relationships between Jews and the church. It is clear from a reading of a voluminous biography, entitled *Man of the Century*, that this Polish Pope was almost himself a direct witness to the Holocaust, living as a hidden Polish student priest in southern Poland during the war. Later, as a Polish Cardinal, before he ascended to St. Peter's throne, he even encouraged a priest to write an article criticizing Pius XII, provided that criticism was placed fairly in three contexts; historical, psychological and moral.

Honourable senators, we must note, of course, the strong statements of accountability by the bishops of France and Germany, the latter who declared in 1995 that Christians had not carried out "the required resistance" to the Holocaust and now held "a special responsibility to oppose anti-Semitism." Can we await a statement by the Conference of Bishops in Canada as to what role the church in Canada had prior to, during and following World War II in the documented unhappy attitudes of some of their priests and some of their adherents? May the newly appointed prince of the church in Toronto, His Eminence Cardinal Aloysius Ambrozic, himself born in Eastern Europe and reportedly interested in Catholic education, lead the way.

Honourable senators, I see this Vatican document as a useful first step in the right direction to correct historic wrongs and accept accountability. I hope the Vatican will find room to go further in the future, as even its adherents recommend, correcting the egregious errors of the past, perhaps moving from a "mea culpa" to a "mea maxima culpa." Whether the Vatican document's carefully delineated distinction between centuries of "anti-Judaism" as a religious teaching and the Nazi brand of anti-Semitism leading to the extinction, which the Vatican document says has "its roots outside of Christianity," is a distinction without a difference remains for theologians and historians to explore. What is the nature of the gulf separating these two friendless schools of ideas? Which school of ideas occupies which of St. Augustine's two cities remains yet to be seen. The least we can do, as Elie Wiesel reminded us, is to ask good questions.

Would it not be preferable that the Vatican fully open its files so that scholars can examine for themselves the historical truth of the Holocaust which, for most of us, remains beyond our imagination? In the first words of Pope John Paul II's papacy, "be not afraid." Yet to study this carefully crafted document is a step, another step in achieving what His Holiness Pope John Paul II has said and written and preached: "Never again."

Honourable senators, may we each be granted a period of quiet and thoughtful contemplation, as once again we approach, each of us, the Passover and Easter seasons.

RICHARD J. STANBURY: ON RETIREMENT

April 30, 1998

Hon. Jerahmiel S. Grafstein: Honourable senators, is there something in the soil or the air of southwestern Ontario that breeds Grits, particularly true Grits? I can think of the most famous offshoot, Kenneth Galbraith, and I can think of a family equally famous in Liberal circles, the Stanburys, father and sons; Judge Stanbury, Dick and Bob.

I first met Dick Stanbury, not in the salubrious region of southern Ontario where we were both born and raised, but in a small, panelled, basement family room in a modest bungalow in a suburb of Toronto, in North York, the residence of one Jimmy Mizzoni, then the President of the York Centre Liberal Association. There, one evening in 1961, I attended my first Liberal meeting for the purpose of organizing a Young Liberal Association in that riding. Dick was previously the President of the York Centre Liberal Association and had been elected President of the Toronto and York Liberal Association. In that capacity, he was guest speaker that evening, waxing eloquent in inspirational terms about the new Liberal Party and how young Liberal activists would be welcomed at all levels of the party structure. He was as good as his word. That evening, at my first meeting, I was elected President of the Young Liberal Association of York Centre. From that time, Dick and I became fast friends. Months later, I was elected President of the Toronto District Young Liberal Association and I became a member of his executive. Then, only months later, Dick and I were to serve on the National Liberal Campaign Committee after I became an officer of the National Young Liberals. In a few months, I had risen in the party from a rank outsider to the upper echelons of the party and was welcomed and treated as an equal by Dick.

Dick himself had risen from President of the Toronto and District Young Liberal Association to Chair of the National Policy Committee of the Liberal Party, and then on to the Presidency of the National Liberal Party of Canada. He served with great distinction and great respect in that capacity in the late 1960s and early 1970s.

What sparks of character led Dick to become a trusted colleague and advisor to Mr. Pearson and then to Mr. Trudeau, to Mr. Turner and to Mr. Chrétien, and to countless Liberals in every region of Canada and, beyond the seas, to Liberal International Optimism. Nothing could be so dark or disastrous that would befall the Liberal Party, or its personalities, that could not, with coolness and clarity, be turned around.

Dick was the coolest in the party, particularly when personalities or policies were in disarray or encountered deep difficulties. Dick was not a sudden flash in the pan. Dick had started at the grassroots and, by hard work, dedication and optimism, became an invaluable force in Canada. Dick has one other invaluable characteristic: he has never been hurtful, privately or publicly, to friend or foe. It is not in his nature. It is in his nature to appeal to the best, rather than the worst, in people and politics.

Dick was always strong at the grassroots, strong in his community in serving on library boards and hospital boards, strong in his chosen profession, strong in his church in serving as an elder in positions of the Presbyterian Church, strong in business affairs, strong in international commercial relations in Europe and in Asia, and always strong in every aspect of the work here in the Senate.

Despite personal trauma in his family, Dick and his wonderful and ever-cheerful helpmate, Marg, overcame all with optimism and equanimity. Dick was one of the spark-plugs for a small group of volunteers in Toronto that became the centre of power in the Liberal Party in the 1960s. His work led to the revival of the Liberal Party. Dick led in reform, from election expenses to policy on Medicare. I believe it was during his term as Party Policy Chairman that Medicare was introduced in Parliament in 1966.

Dick's small group included our former senatorial colleagues Keith Davey, Royce Frith and others. They believed in Mr. Pearson, they believed in the Liberal Party and, with unflinching dedication, they built Toronto and district into one of the finest and fairest political machines in the country.

Dick provided leadership on questions of national unity. Dick always insisted on policies of inclusion, opening the party at the grassroots to new faces, new voices, newcomers from Europe, Asia, South America, and Africa, all reflecting the changing demographics and profile of Toronto. He led on multiculturalism.

Honourable senators, nowhere in our written Constitution do we see reference to the invisible sinews of democracy, party politics. Dick Stanbury spent more than half a century engaged modestly and honourably in party politics; in particular, with the Liberal Party. He remains a model for us all.

To those of us in Toronto, Dick and Marg will remain Mr. and Mrs. Liberal. To Dick and Marg, may you both be blessed with many years of activity and action. To you and your family, the best is yet to come.

JACQUES HERBERT: ON RETIREMENT

June 18, 1998

Hon. Jerahmiel S. Grafstein: Jacques Hebert, Jacques Hebert, Jacques Hebert: voyageur, publisher, author, wit, raconteur, editor, pamphleteer, novelist, thinker, broadcaster, broadcast commissioner , catalyst, innovative organizer, humanist, bon vivant. All in all, Jacques Hebert is a most uncommon "common man."

I first heard of Jacques Hebert by his reputation as a civil libertarian well before I met him over a quarter of a century ago. When we met, we quickly discovered that we shared a deep affinity in our precise political outlook. Moreover, we shared a guru, a mentor of mine, the late and sorely lamented Fernand Cadieux, a sociologist and media thinker on par with Marshall McLuhan, yet virtually unknown in English Canada and, unfortunately, even in French Canada. Fernand Cadieux deeply influenced Jacques and the political and scholarly activist cohorts in Quebec and beyond, including Trudeau, Levesque, Seguin, Breton, Guindon, Falardeau, Pelletier, David, Dion, Marchand, Lamontagne, Sauve, Ryan, Roux, Gagnon, Juneau, Chaisson, Pitfield, Faibish, Strong, Meisel, Cook, Joyal, myself and countless others. It remains for future historians to document Cadieux's influence on Jacques, and all these men, and the influential role model that Jacques himself became for his generation in all of his works.

As for Jacques, that rather quiet surface of tranquil self-effacement camouflages the soul of a turbulent poet, of strong ideas and passionate commitments, who has always dreamed of what can be. George Bernard Shaw said:

Some people see things and say why, but I dream things that never were and say why not.

So it is with our friend Jacques.

Shortly after the Second World War, Jacques not only became the leading travel writer in Quebec, opening up new vistas of the world, but he led when he founded the leading French publishing house in Quebec and then offered especially low-priced books to make his authors accessible and known to the broadest sectors of the community. Jacques led again, when he founded and edited the weekly newspaper, *Vrai,* that challenged the one-eyed press that had been such a hallmark of the old regime, now the new regime, in Quebec.

As with his long-time friend, compatriot and fellow voyageur, Pierre Trudeau, in his heart of hearts Jacques remains a contrarian, schooled from his very youth to go against the stream, against the grain, against the conventional wisdom of his own milieu. Jacques believes in the power of the written word, and with a vengeance, as an author of over 35 books. At a time when the government had forged a close circle of ideas in Quebec, there was Jacques, and very few others, who bravely cracked that circle and went about preparing the groundwork for the Quiet Revolution. Revolutions eat their own, but this was not the case with Jacques. He was never prepared to exchange one system of closed ideas for another. He moved and acted to keep that new circle open to ideas of equality and accessibility.

Equality meant equality to Jacques. Equality was not an empty slogan but a word full of content and commitment. Therefore, he led again when he founded the Quebec Civil Liberties Association at a time when civil liberties were not very popular amongst the ruling cliques of his province. He led, again, as a catalyst for Cite Fibre in French and, even this year, in English.

No task was too small, no objective too grand to capture his time and attention. In the Senate, he revived his dream palace Katimavik, where he believes a new and united and different Canada will be spawned by a constant stirring and intermingling of our youth from every region. This common effort would create common values. This was one man's plan, Jacques's plan for national unity. Bring young people together on challenging tasks, and unity will be sure to follow.

Honourable senators will recall that he put his undoubted talents and energy to work as a founding President of both Canada World Youth and Katimavik. Honourable senators will recall his heroic fast in the antechamber of this Senate when he brought to public attention the demise of Katimavik .

Without Jacques, the Senate, for me, will be a lonelier place. We have shared such intense frustrations while observing the ebb and flow and drift, even the erosion, of the federalist idea, especially from those who profess the federalist idea. Distinctiveness for him did not require, and does not require, the crutch of constitutional recognition. This, to him, would be demeaning. Jacques was and remains a distinct individual in all of his works.

Jacques, we will sorely miss you, not only for the stimulus of your companionship but the unequaled pleasure of your company.

Albert Camus, that great French writer and humanist, once wrote that "even the darkest winter will give way to invincible summer." Jacques, may you enjoy countless summers, as we have been privileged to share the invincibility of your ideas and your friendship.

Albert Camus also wrote:

I love my country too much to be a nationalist.

So it is with my friend Jacques Hebert.

You will be sorely missed, Jacques. Goodbye, old friend. So long.

PHILIPPE GIGANTES: ON RETIREMENT

June 18, 1998

Senator Grafstein: Long before I met my friend Philippe Gigantes, I had heard of him as "Philip Deane." I had come to know his agile mind through his acute dispatches as a The *Globe and Mail* foreign correspondent based in New York and Washington three decades ago.

What an odyssey this elegant, articulate and graceful Greek-born adventurer has experienced. Son of Greece's greatest general and war hero, naval officer and gentleman, soldier, commando, bemedaled war hero, war correspondent, prisoner of war, humanist, broadcaster, world traveller, lover, author of 12 books, reporter, editorialist, gourmet, classical scholar and teacher, Cabinet Minister, UN official, legislator, true and clear Grit, Zionist, and advisor to kings and prime ministers and Secretaries-General of the United Nation. Philippe's colourful career gives true meaning to the oft-quoted but rarely exercised phrase: A life unexplored is not worth living.

From our very first meeting decades ago, Philippe and I learned that we shared a love of ideas, words, books, life and literature. Philippe has a unique gift and capacity to inspire friendship and loyalty .

Yet, honourable senators, how best to adequately celebrate Philippe's almost unparalleled life and extraordinary life accomplishments? Perhaps in quoting a poem written by one of Greece's greatest poets, Constantine Cavafy, in 1911, entitled *Ithaca,* we can echo some appropriate words. Let me quote:

> *When you set out on your journey to Ithaca,*
> *pray that the road is long,*
> *full of adventure, full of knowledge.*
> *The Lestrygonians and the Cyclops,*
> *the angry Poseidon - do not fear them:*
> *You will never find such as these on your path,*

if your thoughts remain lofty, if a fine
emotion touches your spirit and your body.
The Lestrygonians and the Cyclops,
the fierce Poseidon you will never encounter
if you do not carry them within your soul,
if your soul does not set them up before you.

Pray that the road is long.
That the summer mornings are many, when,
with such pleasure, with such joy
you will enter ports seen for the first time;
stop at Phoenician markets,
and purchase fine merchandise,
mother-of-pearl and coral, amber and ebony,
and sensual perfumes of all kinds,
as many sensual perfumes as you can;
visit many Egyptian cities,
to learn and learn from scholars.

Always keep Ithaca in your mind.
To arrive there is your ultimate goal.
But do not hurry the voyage at all.
It is better to let it last for many years;
and to anchor at the island when you are old,
rich with all you have gained on the way,
not expecting that Ithaca will offer you riches.

Ithaca has given you a beautiful voyage.
Without her you would have never set out on the road.
She has nothing more to give you.

And if you find her poor, Ithaca has not deceived you.
Wise as you have become, with so much experience,
you must already have understood what Ithacas mean.

BRIAN DICKSON, P.C.: EULOGY

October 20, 1998

Hon. Jerahmiel S. Grafstein: Honourable senators, rarely can we opine, without fear of inflation or exaggeration, on the designation of a truly great Canadian on his passing. Such is the precedent we can safely adopt on the premature passing of Brian Dickson, former Chief Justice of Canada. To call his passing premature is appropriate, even though Brian Dickson's life exceeded the allotted biblical span of four score years.

After his retirement as Chief Justice almost a decade ago, he never ceased to deploy his unquenchable and irresistible talents on behalf of Canada. He died peacefully in his sleep last weekend at his farm, close to his adoring family, near the horses he loved and the acreage he so carefully tended. Yet he was in the midst of a review of the military police for the Department of National Defence, after having chaired last year a civilian committee created especially to review our military justice system, so badly in need of renovation following the Somalia debacle.

For us in the Senate, his work is especially alive these last weeks as the Senate considers legislation respecting both the military justice system and issues respecting the independence of the judiciary. "But what did Dickson say?", I recall we asked ourselves several times just a few weeks ago. Then he agreed to appear before the Senate committee deliberating on Bill C-25, a bill to reform our military justice system.

What greater tribute can one pay to a jurist whose vision, words, ideas and works are still closely and hotly considered by lawyers and lawmakers alike? For Brian Dickson, always cognizant of judicial restraint, carefully and prudently led, and led again, and led again, to evolve our common law. His words burn ever bright as we debate anew issues respecting the independence of the judiciary, the reach and the limits of the Charter, or the line between law and politics in our Constitution.

Mr. Justice Dickson led especially on questions of minorities, whether the rights of the disabled or aboriginals, or the right to use English in the province of Quebec, or the right of a woman to decide on her own whether or not to have an abortion. On all these questions, Mr. Justice Dickson's decisions took the side of the disenfranchised and the weak.

All was not euphoric, however. I vividly recall the simmering dispute between Mr. Justice Dickson and Mr. Trudeau, a monumental clash respecting the power of the provinces in the repatriation of the Constitution. I recall watching Mr. Trudeau utter what he considered would be his last word on the Supreme Court decision, the majority decision led by Mr. Justice Dickson, in his address to the convocation in his honour at the University of Toronto. Then I turned to observe Mr. Justice Dickson, who sat in front of him, seething, in the audience. He was not pleased with Mr. Trudeau's last word.

We can even hear echoes of Mr. Justice Dickson's demarcation and convergence between legal precedent and politics in the last decision of the Supreme Court reference. History is still too green to judge which oak tree will stand.

Brian Dickson, ever and always a gentleman, was not an easy man for an easy time. He confronted all his tasks with unusual care, thoroughness and clarity of thought. Some of us on this side have read the recent decisions of the courts, so confused in their complexity that one can only hope that the example of Mr. Justice Dickson will win, anew, judicial converts for decisions of clarity, cohesion and judicial restraint.

Mr. Justice Dickson served his country in war and in peace in a way that earns him a special place in the pantheon of great Canadian jurists, along with Mr. Justice Rand and Mr. Justice Hall, whom he succeeded to the Supreme Court, and Mr. Justice Spence and Chief Justice Laskin.

Brian Dickson was more than an adornment to Queen and country, and his wisdom will be missed. Yet, honourable senators, what is missing from a simple recall of his many honours and many achievements? What influenced Brian Dickson to travel so often against the grain until the unconventional became the conventional? Was it the war, which took from him one limb? Was it the unceasing pain of that disability? Was it his study of the masters of common law - Bracton on the power of precedent; Blackstone on rendering each man his due; Mansfield on toleration of religious worship, or Brougham on reform? Or, was it closer to home? Was it his Saskatchewan roots and his western perspective that painted his own derived truth of man's inhumanity to man that caused him to press ever forward with relentless urgency for redress on matters that required redress? The collage of colours maketh the man. So we say about the great and grand life of Brian Dickson - a life worth living and a life worth remembrance.

Perhaps we can end with the words of Tennyson, who said.

A man may speak the thing he will...
A land of settled government,
A land of just and old renown,
Where Freedom slowly broadens down
From precedent to precedent.

So say we. Ave, Brian Dickson! May you rest in peace!

EDITH STEIN AND THE HOLOCAUST
CANONIZATION OF A CARMELITE NUN WHO DIED AT AUSCHWITZ

October 21, 1998

Hon. Jerahmiel S. Grafstein: Honourable senators, the theory of sainthood rests on elevating noble examples of miraculous lives lived by devout, innocent persons, exemplary and extraordinary in both character and conduct. Last week, the canonization of Edith Stein, a German woman of Jewish birth from an orthodox family who, well before World War II, chose to become a Carmelite nun, came as no surpise.

Edith Stein was not only a friend of Simone Weil, a great twentieth century Jewish writer and thinker who herself contemplated Catholicism at one time, but also she was a student of that outstanding Jewish philosopher Edmund Husserl, who wrote of Edith Stein:

> ...she was the finest student I ever taught...there was no more I could teach her...

Edith Stein's special Carmelite Order allowed no talk. Hence there is sparse written record of her thoughts or concerns. A selection of her ideas called *Writings,* and a book, *The Science of the Cross,* was published posthumously several decades ago. The Pope, both as a youthful philosophy student and then as a Polish priest, was said to have been deeply influenced by her teachings.

What do we know? We know that after her conversion in the 1920s, she taught philosophy and that special branch called phenomenology until she lost her teaching positions in 1933 because of her Jewish ancestry. We know that, in 1938, she was transferred from a convent in Germany to Holland to protect her from the Nazis. Later, she sought refuge in Switzerland, but no room could be found for her sister in Swiss convents.

We are told that in 1941, she returned to her convent in Echt, Holland, after a failed attempt in Gottingen, Germany, to save her parents from being transported to Bergen-Belsen. Shortly after her return to the convent in Holland, the Gestapo arrived. When the Mother Superior forbade the Gestapo entry, denying the presence of Edith Stein, the convent's heavy oak door was broken down. In the ensuing search, Edith Stein was discovered by her bedside, praying. She was quickly transported to Auschwitz.

There, in that dismal, devilish place, we are told she witnessed a rabbi forced to light his beard. When it burned, he was ordered to cut it off. She volunteered to substitute herself for that rabbi in the gas chambers. Later, when a Polish priest was to be taken, again she volunteered to replace him in the gas chambers and was refused again. In her own weakened, distressed state, we are told that she tended to the needs of others - the ill, the old, the starving. Selflessly, she risked her own fragile health against the rampant diseases of cholera and diphtheria, all to help others.

As a learned friend, Roy Farbish, wrote me last week so sensitively about Edith Stein:

> Finally they came for her, and so her invisible name was written in the smoke of the sky.

When they led Edith Stein away, her last words to her sister were: Come Rosa, we are going on behalf of our people.

We are now told that copies of her letters pleading for an audience with Pope Pius XII to warn him of the onset of the Holocaust and beseeching an encyclical on the evils of Nazism have yet to be published, and may reside in a library in Breslau, Poland.

We are also informed that she was taken to Auschwitz after Hitler was shown a photograph of Edith Stein at the head of a group of Dutch churchmen, Protestant and Catholic alike, who marched to protest the mass deportation of Jews to the extermination camps. As a reprisal for that event, 694 Jews were sent to the gas chambers.

Last week, the Vatican announced that Edith Stein would be elevated to sainthood. August 9 would be commemorated as the Roman Catholic Church's annual memorial to the "Shoah," the Holocaust. That date, the Pope declared, was ever to be the saint day of Edith Stein - Saint Teresia Benedicta.

What is one to make of these events? On the one hand, no one can question, Jew or Catholic alike, sainthood granted to Edith Stein. No one can question the Catholic Church's desire to commemorate the "Shoah," the Holocaust. However, what will Catholics or Jews take from this awesome convergence of sainthood and commemoration? What is the message to the Catholic masses? Will it be seen as another step in the reconciliation between faiths after centuries of studied, Catholic-led enmity towards Jews that, from a historian's point of view, lies amongst the corrosive root causes of the Holocaust? Will it be read as another attempt to colour or dilute or deny those root causes?

It is too early to judge. It is not too soon to ask the question. For me, the question remains locked by blank memories of my many relatives who were consumed by the Holocaust, merely and only because they professed Judaism.

As for me, each so condemned to death only for the sake of Jewish blood or Jewish faith became worthy of sainthood.

MICHEL CHARLES EMILE TRUDEAU: COMMENT ON HIS DEATH

November 25, 1998

Hon. Jerahmiel S. Grafstein: Honourable senators, were the Greeks right? "Take heart," Aeschylus once wrote. "Suffering, when it climbs the highest, lasts but a little time." But, honourable senators, were the Greeks right?

A great teacher and Rebbe, when he felt that he was about to die, wanted to make even his death a lesson. That night, the Rebbe took a torch and set out through the forest with his prized student. When they reached the middle of the woods, the Rebbe extinguished the torch without explanation. "What is the matter?" the student asked. "The torch has gone out," the Rebbe answered and walked on. "But," shouted the student fearfully, "will you leave me here in the dark?" "No, I will not leave you in the dark," called the Rebbe from the surrounding blackness. "I will leave you searching for the light."

So say we about the premature passing of young Michel Trudeau that left us all searching for the light. This we know: Michel's own brief and brightly burning inner light will ever glow in the fond memories of those who watched him from birth and shared his company, if even for a moment.

Regretfully, senators, our words remain imperfect. Words are inexact. Words are ill-fitting. Words are of little consolation for the loss of a child. Yet, words are all we have to bridge the deep abyss of such a loss.

Spinoza wrote that the basis of wisdom lies not in a reflection on death but on a reflection of life. So we remember the curiosity and courage, the lure of the wild on land and sea that so possessed and occupied the young and active mind and body of Michel.

Albert Camus, suffering the tragic accidental loss of his children, ruminated on forgetting the pain. Later he wrote:

"But sometimes in the middle of the night their wound would open afresh. And suddenly awake, they would finger its painful edges, they would recover their suffering anew and with it the stricken face of their love."

Can words, mere words, assuage the immutable grief of his family; his father, his mother, his brothers and his sister? What of the loss of a son to whom the sceptre cannot be left? Is it enough to say, "He worked his work, I worked mine." No. "Tho' much is taken, much abides." No. "That which we are, we are." No.

With this passing, can we learn more about the meaning of life or death? Perhaps. But we can hear. We can hear, from the vale, angels weeping.

Still, the Greeks haunt us. Sophocles wrote:

> The long days store many things nearer to grief than joy ....Death at least the deliverer.
> Not to be born is, past all prizing, best. ..
> Next best by far, when one has seen the light,
> Is to go thither swiftly whence he came....

Mercifully, Aeschylus wrote:

> God whose law it is that he who learns must suffer.
> And even in our sleep, pain that cannot forget,
> Falls drop by drop upon the heart,
> And in our own despair, against our will,
> Comes wisdom to us by the awful grace of God.

Honourable senators, why do we share their loss and pain so deeply? Could it be that a tender moment in our own youthful remembrance of things past has been stolen from us so swiftly and so brutally?

Thus we are diminished and can only pray for comprehension, if solely to fortify our own feelings.

May we recall the life of St. Viator, who as a youth, we are told, on account of his many eminent virtues, was much beloved by his elders, especially his mentor, St. Just.

So, we pray for Pierre, Margaret, the brothers and sister, that sweet peace conduct Michel's soul swiftly to the "bosom of Abraham," and let us say amen. *Mars omnibus communis.*

REMARKS TO ECOLE MAIMONIDES SCHOOL
OTTAWA, ONTARIO
CELEBRATING THE OCCASION OF ITS 21ST ANNIVERSARY

December 8, 1998

I come bearing greetings from Parliament to this unique institution and its founders, Rabbi & Mrs. Berger. It is the only trilingual institution of its kind in Canada. The school also reflects another miserable reality. Twice in the last four years, the school was fire damaged by unknown arsonists. On both occasions, the Ottawa community, of all persuasions, rallied. Classes continued almost uninterrupted. So I am here to salute the students, parents, teachers and supporters whose commitment and courage is a lesson for all Canadians.

Still, we are here to celebrate Ecole Maimonides School's 21st Anniversary. What do we think when we hear the name "Maimonides" - the namesake of this school? Just who was he? And, why name a school for an obscure 12th century, writer, philosopher and doctor?

Tonight, I've attempted to follow Maimonides advice on public oratory. Never speak publicly unless you have carefully prepared!

So, why is it that the words of Maimonides are alive, even more alive today, than they were almost 800 years ago when they were rewritten by hand and circulated to a small circle of scholars scattered in communities encircling the Mediterranean coast.

Maimonides led a colourful and incredible life. Born in Cordova, Spain in the 11th century, son of a great Rabbi and Judge, Maimonides was, at first, a rather indifferent student, who with his father and family was forced to flee first to North Africa and then later to Fez, Morocco, then to Acre and Jerusalem in Palestine and finally to Fostat, near Cairo in Egypt. His family fled rather than convert, or even submit to oaths demanded by Muslim or Christian fundamentalists or worse, risk charges of heresy and then martyrdom. His last days spent in Egypt saw him raised to the highest political post, achieved by Jews in captivity, Nasi, advisor to the Vizier and as Court Physician to the aristocracy. Yet by voluminous correspondence, by response for advice on ethical conduct, by incessant travels, he remained immersed in the dire straits confronting his co-religionists wherever they had migrated.

We are told that even King Richard the Lion Hearted, hearing of Maimonides' preeminent reputation as the leading physician sought to lure him to England, to serve as Chief Physician to him and to the English Court, but Maimonides declined.

His own life was fraught with peril. He was constantly on the move from place to place. Tutored first by his father, he started, with unusual determination at a relatively young age, in his early '20s, to become one of the renowned scholars and philosophers of his age. Maimonides set for himself an almost super human task. To single-handedly compile and codify the entire Jewish oral tradition practiced in exile for almost two millennium, deftly discarding practices inconsistent with the law. His aim was to complete a rational codex combining the written testament with the oral tradition - all written in a concise user friendly guide to a good life.

Maimonides' work was not without controversy. Maimonides, or "Rambam" - as he was called - the man, and his ideas have resonated down through the centuries, reverberating from hero to villain, denunciation to acceptance, from stimulant to irritant. From his Codex, called the *Mishneh Torah* to his letters ranging from the *Guide to the Perplexed* to treatises on *Logic* to manuals on *Medicine*, to epistles on Ethics, Conversion and even martyrdom.

Philosophers and theologians alike have studied his fastidious works. His ideas have emerged almost alone as a major theme, a cottage industry, on Jewish History and Medieval thought.

From Aquinas to Bacon, from Descartes to Kant, from Spinoza to Rosenzweig, from Strauss to Steinsalz, his works permeate and resonate in the ideas of others. The scope of his works spanned physics, ethics, logic, dietetics, poetry, metaphysics, mathematics, astronomy, psychology, algebra, biology and medicine. Yet the summa of his work rests on both the hidden and apparent belief found in the canon of the Scriptures. He warned that the delicate distinction between the mystical and empirical should only explored after mature study and preparation. His careful ideas on mysticism foreshadowed the later Kabbalah which reflected much of his theories.

When one approaches his work, one quickly detects his supreme care, prudence and humility.

In his epilogue to his major work, the *Mishneh Torah*, he wrote:

"I pray to God... every right person and intelligent person will realize that the task undertaken was not simple or easy of fulfilment..." "Agitated by the distress of our times, the exile which God decreed upon in the fact that we have been driven from one end of the world to the other... Some laws I explained on the road, some matters I collected while on board ship... I also devoted myself to the study of other sciences...

The reason to describe my situation...was my desire to justify my critics. They should not be blamed for criticizing me..."

Try to imagine, if you can, Maimonides carrying his books, scrolls and voluminous manuscripts with him in his travels from country to country, by ship and by land, always studying, always researching and writing on the run. Much of the *"Mishneh To-rah"* was finished in a cave while he kept hidden from religious zealots who were pursuing him. He was a student of Plato, Aristotle and Averroes - as well as other Muslim philosophers whose ideas he both rejected or incorporated in his works. He was a leading interpreter and disseminator of the work of the father of medicine, Galen.

Why does Maimonides remain such a towering figure? Because he attempted to bridge faith and reason by the pursuit of truth. His quest has both taunted and haunted thinkers and theologians to the present day. He had a particular and uncommon view about teaching. He believed that the best he could do was teach one student at a time. We also recall his poignant relevance to modern themes. You will remember he wrote *"Ani Maamin"* - *"I Believe,"* - the evocative prayer passing the lips of those engulfed or consumed by the Holocaust. No wonder that his reputation was summed up in the phrase - "From Moses to Moses, there were none like Moses".

One personal footnote. As a final request, Maimonides remains were disinterred in Egypt and brought to the Holy Land; re-buried in a small cemetery in the outskirts of Tiberias, on the road to Safed, in sight of the Mount of the Beatitudes, together with those of his father. I visited this tiny site which is also the resting place of a handful of learned sages, including a 16th century Talmudic Scholar "The Holy Shelah" from whom my mother's mother was directly descended.

Even the Chabad, from the times of the First Lubavitch Rebbe, was inordinately influenced by Maimonides. Read the Tanya - the first codification of Chassidic thought since the Baal ShemTov - the founder of Chassidism. Discover how the architecture of the Rambam supported certain of the ideas gleaned and glossed by Lubavitch.

So we are here also to honour this school in Maimonides' name. "Do not look at the stars, look at ourselves," he wrote. He was a bitter opponent of astrology. The future is as important as the past. The individual is more important than the State. The values of community can only be derived from each individual who can only achieve worth by hard work, careful study and careful conduct. He refused to become a professional Rabbi.

Everyday work was as important as thought. Thought was too important to leave only to professionals. Only in this way could each search and discover for himself that the laws in the Old Testament were not incompatible with either the search for the truth, or a better life.

This past September, the Pope issued his Encyclical entitled *"Fides et Ratio"* - *Faith and Reason,* which sought to bridge reason and belief through the scientific search for truth. So Maimonides' work bears revisiting for those of all faiths who are interested in this endless quest.

I am here not only to recall Maimonides, but the outreach of Lubavitch that continues to believe in education as the heart of Jewish survival and revival.

Not bad thoughts to ponder as we celebrate the trilingual essence of this school while approaching Canada's next millennium.

PETER BOSA: EULOGY

February 2, 1999

Hon. Jerahmiel S. Grafstein: Honourable senators, 250 years ago, in 1744, an obscure, impoverished Italian professor, Giambattista Vico, who had written a massive work, *Scienza Nuova,* or *New Science*, died not far from his birthplace in Naples. Like Thoreau, he did not travel very far in his lifetime from his birthplace to study the great ideas of the ancients. Yet his imagination, his "fantasia," as he called it, opened a new world of thought.

Many modern observers consider Vico and his masterpiece, *"New Science,"* the foundation of modern historical analysis. Vico studied history through a particular prism. He believed that history could only be understood by peering at the world through a detailed, methodical analysis of each culture. Each culture had unique, unduplicateable contributions to make to the ideas of history and civilization.

In its essence, Vico's work was the first modern dialectic of cultural pluralism. Our friend Peter Bosa, in his life and his work, exemplified Vico's theses.

Peter was born in 1927, in Friuli, an isolated border region of Italy in the northeast corner adjacent to Austria and Yugoslavia. It became a part of Italy only in 1866. This turbulent region was dominated in succession by Venice, Rome, the Vatican, Vienna and then Rome again. First, it was part of Venice's region. It then became part of the Austro-Hungarian empire, followed by the Italian monarchy. Finally, it became part of the Italian Republic.

As could be expected, the Furlan society in this century was divided, set between "reds" and "blacks," the church and socialists, the right and the left, and further fragmented by periodic eruptions of separatist movements. Into this hotbed of conflicting loyalties, in 1922, in Udine, then the capital of Friuli, Mussolini dropped his republican pretensions and started his march to the right.

The Furlan, the people of Friuli, are a passionate, robust society of hardy men and women, mountaineers and small farmers. In the frequent cycles of depression and political unrest, the Furlan began to emigrate. They chose, to a large measure, Canada. In Toronto, the Furlan represent a minority of Canadians of Italian descent, only approximately 50,000 of the 750,000. However, they developed strong bonds of community. They never forgot their roots or their singular dialect.

From this ambitious minority, a majority of civic and business leaders of Italian descent emerged in Toronto. Peter Bosa was a highly visible, most respected and much-admired figure of this vibrant community within a community.

When the earthquake hit his home region of Friuli, as was mentioned earlier, Peter led humanitarian efforts to help this impoverished region. Peter loved his family, his community in Canada. He brought a wise and gentle but perceptive mind to all problems confronting his community, his country and his church. He had a European aesthetic sense.

He combined an easy facility in Italian, of course, with English, French, Spanish, and a smattering of German - and he quickly picked up other dialects. He was a keen student of social issues and foreign affairs, serving with distinction as Canada's representative at international bodies such as the IPU and NATO. His life experiences, as an immigrant and as a student of Italy and of European history, made him a staunch federalist and an unforgiving foe of separatism.

Peter was deeply imbued with intellectual pursuits - whether theology, philosophy, politics or literature. He read widely and deeply. Yet in all things he was self-taught, for he arrived in Canada as a young immigrant with only a fragmentary education.

I first met Peter in 1961 when he was working in the Davenport riding, in the heart of "Little Italy," for Walter Gordon. We became fast friends. We served together on the Toronto and District Liberal Association and worked on the multicultural, labour and immigration committees. Both of us came from minority backgrounds and had a strong, mutual sense of being an outsider in a majority society. We both came to Ottawa in the mid-sixties to serve as ministerial assistants during the Pearson era. These strong bonds were resuscitated when I joined Peter in the Senate.

I believe that Peter was the first Canadian of Italian descent to be appointed to the Senate, and I know for a fact that it was one of the proudest moments - if not the proudest moment - of his life. His contributions to the Senate have been noted by others. Suffice it to say that he carried this honour with ease and distinction.

Peter was a gentle man; in all respects wise. Though quiet-spoken, he disguised his deep convictions and his much deeper beliefs. He was an indefatigable and dependable mainstay of the small "l" liberal group of activists that animated the Liberal Party on every front. He never forgot his humble origins, where he came from, how far he had travelled, or those in society less fortunate than himself.

Peter loved all things Italian. He loved wine. He loved making wine. He loved gardening, food, friends, music, opera, especially the Furlanian folk songs, but above all his family, his adoring wife, Teresa, and his two lovely children, Angela, Mark, and his grandchild.

When illness struck him recently, so suddenly and so savagely, he remained calm, quiet, an example for all. He only wanted to be healthy enough to come back to resume his work in the Senate. He loved the Senate in all its works. He remained a man of gentle persuasion and gentility. His wisdom, his quiet humour, and the pleasure of his company will be sorely missed and not forgotten.

Arrivederci, Pietro. Pax vobiscum.

DALIA WOOD: TRIBUTE

February 4, 1999

Hon. Jerahmiel S. Grafstein: Honourable senators, sometimes we in Parliament believe ourselves to be the lynchpins of unity, that it is mostly due to our efforts that we keep this country together. Sometimes we forget, and this occasion gives me pause to think about the activities of other active citizens who are interested in the country as citizens, and who play a superbly active, exuberant role in keeping the country together.

When I think of citizens like that, one of the first persons who comes to mind is the late Norman Wood, the husband of Dalia Wood, who was noted by Senator Fairbairn in her comments. Norman was an exuberant activist whom I met in the 1960s, before I met Dalia. Once he found out that I was interested in matters of national unity, he would phone me regularly and urge me to take a more active role in issues. I remember receiving regular calls and notes from Norman about following the true and straight Liberal and federalist path.

It was subsequent to coming to the Senate that I got to know Dalia quite well. She and I served on the committee dealing with the amendment to the Quebec language bill. It was during that period that her fire and her exuberance was so evident. She believed strongly that the notwithstanding clause respecting section 23.1 was an unfair, unreasonable and inexplicable limitation on minority rights in Quebec. It was that proposition which animated much of our discussion in that committee.

I wish to pay tribute to Dalia. I know that the light was dimmed when Norman left her. I should like to wish her Godspeed and good health. She will be missed.

KING HUSSEIN: EULOGY

February 9, 1999

Hon. Jerahmiel S. Grafstein: Honourable senators, the late King Hussein's grand-father, King Abdullah, the namesake of the new king, the first king of Transjordan, who was later assassinated before his grandson's eyes, met with Dr. Chaim Weizmann, the then leader of the Zionist movement, in the early 1920s, before Winston Chur-chill, who was then Colonial Secretary, envisaged and presented his plan for two new states, one Arab, one Jewish, on the East and West Banks of the Jordan. That eastern portion of the Jordan became Transjordan in 1921, and King Abdullah became King Abdullah I. Both wholly agreed with Churchill's recommendations. Israel became a state in 1948. It took 70 years, and much bloodshed, for a peace agreement finally to be signed between Jordan and Israel.

The late King Hussein, like his grandfather, became a leading activist of peace for his people, his neighbours, and all the people in that turbulent region. For this he will always be remembered in history. I say to him, "*salam alaikam*" to the late King, and "*salam alaikam*" to his son, King Abdullah II. Peace be unto you.

BILL PETTEN: EULOGY

March 9, 1999

Hon. Jerahmiel S. Grafstein: Honourable senators, I thought I should bring a central Canadian perspective to this otherwise fascinating tribute to our friend, the late Bill Petten.

When I think of the words "distinctive Canadian," I can think of no better example than Bill Petten. He was a distinctive man in many ways, but mostly in his words and his wit. His language and his Newfoundland mode of expression was so different that whenever I heard him, it brought a smile to my lips. When I say "whenever I heard him" or overheard him, I must say that Bill sat behind me after he stepped down as whip. I always heard two speeches in the chamber. One would be the Speaker on this side, or on the opposite side, and the other would be a low-level commentary in Newfoundland wit by Bill. During a very serious speech, I would sometimes break out in laughter involuntarily because of the crack or the comment or the anecdote that Bill would whisper in my ear as the Speaker was going through his routine.

I thought Bill was a very distinctive character in the language until I met Bernice. Her wit is probably faster and sharper than Bill's wit. I always imagined what their pillow talk would be like. I imagined Bill and Bernice together saying, "Well, have you heard this one?" That is what Bernice and Bill would always say to me.

I say this to Bernice: Bill left his mark through his wit, language and generosity of spirit. He left his mark as a great Liberal and a great Canadian, and he will always be remembered by myself and by my family.

EUGENE WHELAN: EULOGY

June 10, 1999

Hon. Jerahmiel S. Grafstein: Honourable senators, what praise can one even hope to lavish on Gene Whelan that he has not endlessly lavished upon himself? To ignore Gene's advertisements for himself would be to ignore his unique contributions to public life. You have only to engage Gene once to discover that almost all the blood-lines of Canada run through his veins from his beloved Ireland, to aboriginals, to France, to Eastern Europe. The fabled six degrees of separation simply dissolve in Gene's veins. What a combustible character is the distillation!

To say that Gene's gifts are unique is to diminish the definition of Gene's accomplishments - farmer, agronomist, small businessman, biologist, raconteur, public psychologist, orator, wit, politician, psychic, minister, consultant, diplomat and, finally, the greatest of all epiphanies in Canadian life, the Senate.

One might ask, honourable senators, why I would add my small, quavering voice to the thunderous, thundering paeans of praise that have erupted from time to time from leaders such as Pearson, Trudeau or Chrétien. I wish to note, for the record only, that only a distinct society like Canada could have formulated a personality like Gene's. In fact, he is stranger than fiction, and almost as incredible.

Gene can lay credit as one of our greatest Ministers of Agriculture since Confederation, and certainly the most memorable. Gene can lay credit to influencing Gorbachev and the new world order. Gorbachev was then Soviet Minister of Agriculture on his first extended trip outside Russia across Canada. Honourable senators, I ask you to cast your minds back to this memorable sight, Gene and Gorbachev, across Canada together. It was Gene who accompanied Gorbachev every step of the way. Gorbachev had the distinct privilege of having Gene fill his ears and eyes about western markets and democracy, and the productivity of the lush farms across Canada, all as a result of Gene's own policies.

Gene may well have been an unnamed author of Gorbachev's Perestroika policies.

Above all, Gene can lay credit as a staunch and vigilant guardian of "the liberal idea" within the Liberal Party. He could always be called upon to rail against the bastions of pomp and privilege, of always taking the side of the working Canadian, whether that Canadian was a farmer, a factory worker, a small businessperson, a clerk or a waiter. Gene was always on their side.

Honourable senators, I first met Gene in rather strange circumstances. It was well over 30 years ago when I was a young lawyer representing small interest groups opposing the Bell Telephone rate increase in Ottawa. One morning, I noticed a rather burly, homespun character lumbering up to the counsel table, laden with a jumble of papers, books and notes. At first I did not know what to make of him. As it turned out, Gene was then a shy, unknown and diffident back-bencher. He had personally intervened on behalf of his constituents to fight the increase in local telephone rates, because he felt they were unfair, particularly to the shut-ins, the disabled, and most particularly, to his rural constituents.

Gene and I sat together for many weeks at the counsel table, across from a large battery of high-priced lawyers. While Gene picked my brain about the theories of rate regulation, I picked his brain about the latest ins and outs of the Liberal Party. We took turns cross-examining Bell's experts and senior executives. They have never forgotten it.

From those days on, I became a lifelong admirer of Gene's shrewdness and political savvy. I found out that the gruff exterior and unmistakable twang camouflaged a soft, sensitive and, dare I say it, a romantic soul.

Several years later, I became deeply involved in the 1974 national campaign and the polls began to jump around. I thought I would pick Gene's brain once again. I began to call him regularly on the telephone and in person for advice. I found his assessments to be acute, accurate and precise, more deeply attuned to the public pulse than the polls.

Gene always demonstrated a quick first sense when it came to policies and people. It is not an accident that his perspicacity is still appreciated in every part of Canada, as demonstrated by the recent hearings he conducted as Chair of the Standing Senate Committee on Agriculture and Forestry.

Honourable senators, we have evidence in the gallery that the apple does not fall far from the tree. Gene's daughter Susan, now an elected member of the other place, whom I have come to know in the last few years, shares his acute political genes and gifts in great abundance.

How then to sum up the many colourful sides of one Gene Whelan? To say he is unforgettable is fact. To say his accomplishments are undeniable is historic. To say that he has always devoutly believed in the interests of the average Canadian is more than a truism. To say that Gene is an original never to be duplicated is the closest one can come to putting in one word, the sparkling, gem-like qualities of Gene Whelan. Gene is a Canadian original.

Gene, on a more personal note, the Senate will be a lonelier place for the loss of your Liberal conscience, and most certainly a duller place without your lively presence.

To shift metaphors, let me say, Gene, as you leave the Senate to wander out once again on the unsuspecting public and into the hesitant yet hopeful arms of your faithful family:

May the road rise up to greet thee, and the wind always be at thy back. Gene, keep your Irish up, and we will never let you down.

HEWARD STIKEMAN, Q.C., O.C: EULOGY

June 15, 1999

Hon. Jerahmiel S. Grafstein: Honourable senators, when the 20th century social history of Canada is written, pioneers of the professions, such as the late Heward Stikeman, will occupy auspicious space. Last Saturday, Harry Heward Stikeman, Q.C., O.C., known as Heward Stikeman, passed away at the age of 85, at his home in Bromont, Quebec.

Heward was one of Canada's outstanding tax lawyers. He rose to that position after a long and remarkable career in the public service. In 1939, he joined the predecessor to the Revenue Department and served there with great distinction until 1946. During that time, he acted as Government Counsel before the British Exchequer Court, then Canada's final appellate body for tax matters, and before the Supreme Court of Canada. He became the outstanding specialist in income tax. While in the department, he helped to prepare and shape all the Second World War budgets.

His career holds special significance to the Senate. In 1946, he considered it a leap upward in his career when he left the Department of National Revenue to become counsel to the Senate Banking Committee, mandated to investigate and recommend changes to Canadian taxation law.

That benchmark study led to the 1948 Income Tax Act. Taking his leave from public service, he joined Fraser Elliott to form a law firm called Stikeman & Elliott, specializing in tax law. A year later he was joined by George Tamaki. Led by Heward, they built their firm into a global law firm with offices across Canada, Europe and the Far East. In the process, he helped to transform not only the legal and accounting professions, but also business practices. In the early 1960s, he was joined by the Right Honourable John Turner, Q.C., P. C. the former prime minister, who served as a partner to that firm before his appointment to cabinet in 1965.

Heward was the author of numerous texts and articles on the tax system. He took special delight in editing tax reports, like the late Bora Laskin, who for years edited the Dominion Law Reports. He provided a signal service to the legal and accounting professions, helping to codify the burgeoning tax structure.

I first had the pleasure of meeting Heward in the mid 1960s and enjoyed a number of exchanges with him over the years. I can attest to his curious, probing, exacting and quicksilver type mind. He understood not only the arcane structure but also the social and public policy behind the tax system. On occasion, we acted as co-counsel on several exacting files, and I came to admire his ability to focus on problems and find solutions that were fair and defensible not only to the client but to the public purpose.

Heward, modest as he was, by his life's work, could lay credit to causing the legal and accounting professions to look outward to the world. In the process, the staid Canadian business leadership turned its attention outward to the globe. His work helped to reforge and refashion Canada and its major companies as players in a leading-edge trading nation. The work of the tax system and its practitioners was too often condensed and rarely praised. This is a deficit in popular thinking. A fair tax system lies at the heart of democracy and the rule of law. For democracy to work, acceptance of the tax system by our citizens depends on fairness and comprehension. Heward always argued for simpler, fairer tax rules. Heward fought against the Department of Revenue when it ran roughshod over simple questions of justice and equity within the tax system, as the department was bound to do time and time again.

Honourable senators, Heward's work goes on.

PAUL LUCIER: EULOGY

September 8, 1999

Hon. Jerahmiel S. Grafstein: Honourable senators, the North, the mysterious, inviting, inhibiting true North, aligns Canada as no other tangible or intangible bond. Our dearly departed friend Paul Lucier was born in Ontario and chose to settle in the North, in the Yukon, while still in his teens.

As the North defined Paul, so Paul helped define the North. Roustabout, sailor, trucker, boxer, inveterate card player, coach, mechanic, fire-fighter, ambulance driver, gun collector, hunter, wilderness guide, fisherman, politician, small businessman, Paul was a skilled jack of all trades. Almost of his life, he worked with his hands and his brain and, in the process, developed a simply marvellous rapport with working people - a rapport in which he had great pride.

A while ago, I travelled to the Yukon with several parliamentarians of both Houses. We stopped at a high lookout. Far below was a small, shimmering, diamond-like lake, and beyond, vast snow-capped vistas that stretched for miles in all directions. The air was crisp, cool, clean and invigorating. I asked one colleague, a member of the Bloc Quebecois, as we stood there gaping at the beauty of the geography: "All this is yours and mine. Why would you want to give it up?" He turned to me in deep reflection and said quietly, "I am not sure we do."

The North defines all of us in ways that we cannot imagine. For me, Paul exemplified the best pioneering spirit of Canadians who choose to live and work in the North. Paul was cocky, confident, tough, humorous, quick and self-sufficient, with a marvellous smile and an outrageous sense of humour.

I first met Paul in 1966, when I visited Whitehorse during an infamous national election campaign. Even then, you sensed that he was on the way up politically. As we strolled through town, there was not anyone who did not stop and say "Hello" and ask for a joke or for his advice about some matter, large or small. Who can forget Paul's dazzling smile, his chuckles, his quiet partisanship, his loyalty to friends and liberal ideas, which were self-evident and exemplary.

Paul was born and brought up in a French home in Ontario, and educated in a totally French environment. Yet, he had no time for French nationalists. He vitriolically opposed in this chamber, and elsewhere, Meech Lake. He felt Meech would not unite the country but divide it. He was, honourable senators, the first senator appointed to the Yukon, and he fought hard to gain recognition for aboriginal land claims in the North and elsewhere. It was only right, according to Paul. It was only fair.

Paul remained a fighter to the very end. He fought his illness with courage and quiet valour until finally it conquered him. He sat there just a few seats away, when he came back from time to time. He would always throw me an irreverent one-liner which never failed to break me up, even in the most solemn moments of this chamber.

Paul had a zest for life and a zest for living. He never complained, even when his eyes betrayed the pain that he was suffering. I was privileged, as many of us were, to call him a friend.

I extend to his wife, Grace, and his family and friends too numerous to mention, our deepest condolences.

I conclude with a paragraph from a poem written long ago by English writer Stephen Spender entitled *The Truly Great*:

"Near the snow, near the sun, in the highest fields, See how these names are feted by the waving grass And by the streamers of white cloud And whispers of wind in the listening sky. The names of those who in their lives fought for life, Who wore at their hearts the fire's centre. Born of the sun, they travelled a short while toward the sun And left the vivid air signed with their honour."

When Paul left this world, he left the air vivid with his honour.

Honourable senators, the surname Lucier is French, originating from the Latin word lucere which means "to shine brightly." Paul's plucky memory will ever shine brightly for all those who had the privilege to know him.

JEANIE W. MORRISON, C.S.R., MANAGER/EDITOR OF DEBATES AND PUBLICATIONS BRANCH: ON RETIREMENT

September 9, 1999

Hon. Jerahmiel S. Grafstein: Honourable senators, have you ever wondered where the Senate would be without the printed word? Are we not, after all, merely dealers in words? Where would we be, honourable senators, without the Debates of the Senate?

Without the printed word, senators would leave too few footprints in the sands of history. To mix a metaphor, our words would dissolve in ether, relegated to the dustbins of history. Some days, some might say, that would not be such a bad idea.

Still, from time to time we should remind ourselves that the craftsmen and women who sit before us in the well of the Senate every day, our Hansard reporters, serve as our indispensable link to public policy and history.

Jeanie Morrison, Editor of the Debates Branch, is retiring on September 24 next, after a most distinguished career. I thank Richard Greene for bringing her retirement to my attention.

Jeanie joined the Senate in February of 1983. She quickly became senior reporter, in 1989, assistant editor in 1992, and, finally, Manager/Editor of Debates in 1996.

One could not fail to note that she was one of the first two female court reporters to work at the Supreme Court of Ontario before she came to the Senate. When she came to the Senate, she was the first female senior reporter, the first female assistant editor and the first female Editor of Debates at the Senate Hansard

These many gender 'firsts' pale in comparison to Jeanie's unredoubted skills as a mistress of the English language. When we finish our work here, honourable senators, at the end of each day, the work of the reporters of Hansard has barely begun, and stretches late into the evenings. Jeanie has helped unravel the garbled syntax of my speeches, pointing out that participles should not dangle, that all words should not be capitalized, that a semicolon is sometimes better deployed than a colon, and that a period would simply do where I would tend to place an exclamation mark.

I am sure I speak on behalf of all honourable senators in wishing Jeanie an enjoyable and creative retirement when she leaves us here in the Senate on September 24.

We should remember that Jeanie has shown an interest in the Senate Hansard that goes well beyond professional bounds. Jeanie has been actively involved in the Canadian Hansard Association and the Commonwealth Hansard Editors Association, and has even paid her own way to conferences when the Senate was in the midst of yet another austerity program. In 1997, she was voted editor of the Canadian Hansard Newsletter. In every respect, Jeanie has been a superb professional, an exemplar to the staff of Hansard. Without their diligent presence, honourable senators, we would not even leave a footnote to the pages of history.

Rudyard Kipling once wrote:

> I am by calling a dealer in words, and words are, of course, the most powerful drugs used by mankind.

Jeanie's work with our words has enhanced the power of the Senate.

May I wish Jeanie Morrison the best of good health, enjoyment in her future travels and assure her of our gratitude by these few words for her superb and unstinting service on behalf of the Senate and all senators.

God speed, Jeanie!

DEREK LEWIS: ON RETIREMENT

November 25, 1999

Hon. Jerahmiel S. Grafstein: Honourable senators, we are here today to celebrate the long and illustrious Senate career of our friend, Derek Lewis, on his retirement - the quiet, modest man from Newfoundland.

Is it not appropriate that we pause and remind ourselves of the delicate balance the Senate plays in our public life, and the quiet, almost invisible principles that render our work here significant and credible?

When I first came to Ottawa in 1966 to work as the Chief of Staff to a Minister, I was advised that it was essential to learn about the work of the Senate. I knew very little about how the Senate actually worked.

On a sunny day in July, I sought an appointment through Torrance Wiley, an old friend and then Executive Assistant to the Honourable John Connolly, the powerful leader of the government in the Senate. I was immediately invited to see him. I attended in his beautifully panelled and sunlit corner office across the hall from the Senate chamber, now occupied by the current Leader of the Government in the Senate. Senator John Connolly left me with one simple message: If the Minister and I, as his senior staff person, would respect the Senate and its responsibilities, the Senate would respect our work, and my job would be easier.

Almost two decades later, when I was fortunate enough to be called to the Senate, I was immediately approached by an old friend, Senator Godfrey, the father of John Godfrey of the other place. Senator Godfrey handed me the red Senate rule book and said, "Respect the rules, and you will get respect from the Senate."

Shortly thereafter, the outspoken Senator McElman of New Brunswick advised me that the heart of the Senate was the work of its committees. While most of us are partisan, he reminded me that we can shape bad government policy through the quiet, unheralded and deliberative work of Senate committees. "Work hard at committees," he admonished me.

Then I encountered Senator Ian Sinclair, who at that time had just recently been appointed to the Senate. Formerly, he was the very successful chief executive of Canadian Pacific, one of the largest corporations in Canada, and a living legend in business circles. Senator Sinclair advised that his experience in business taught him that his best work - and hence the best work done in the Senate - is the work done by senators themselves. He suggested that hard work in the chamber and in the committees would bring its own personal satisfaction and personal rewards.

Finally, Senator MacEachen of Nova Scotia - formerly a leader of the government in the Senate - repeatedly reminded me, and all of us on this side, that in order to maintain our own persona's credibility and the credibility of the Senate, we must maintain at all times a respectful arm's length distance from the other place down the hall and from the other place across the street. Echoes of his advice reverberated in the Senate just yesterday, when Senator Murray raised the question of pre-study. Senator MacEachen was staunchly opposed to pre-study of government bills, as it had the undesirable effect of diminishing the credibility of the Senate as a chamber of sober second thought, as a chamber independent of the other place and of the other side of the street, independent in the eyes of ourselves and the public we serve.

Hence, honourable senators, for me there has been a delicate balance of principles at work in the Senate. The torch of power in the other place is always alluring, but if we get too close, the Senate and our work here can be burnt and turned quickly to embers and ashes. These were the first principles I garnered about the Senate. Principles and practice march best when they march together.

All of this, honourable senators, is by way of preamble to my tribute to our good friend Derek Lewis, who leaves us for a well-earned retirement. For me, Derek brought all of these principles alive. Derek respected this institution. Derek gained an encyclopedic knowledge of the rules and respected the practices of this place. He was the ultimate draftsman when it came to committee work. Derek was quiet, careful, competent, witty and deliberative. He always did his own work. He always retained a respectful arm's length from the powers that be.

In a phrase, Derek was a senator's senator, a public solicitor's solicitor. In that sense, he is a diminishing resource here in the Senate. For these reasons and for the loss of the pleasure of his company, his departure will leave the Senate sorely depleted.

Derek, your race is run. Your duty is done. You and Grace are heartily entitled to a good and healthy retirement. As they say in the Jewish tradition, "May you live in good health to 120 years." God bless.

MY PRIVATE MEMBERS BILL TO ESTABLISH A
PARLIAMENTARY POET LAUREATE

November 25, 1999

Bill to Amend - Second Reading - Debate Adjourned

Hon. Jerahmiel S. Grafstein moved the second reading of Bill S-5, to amend the Parliament of Canada Act (Parliamentary Poet Laureate).

He said: Honourable senators, in the beginning was "the word," then came a poem, and since that earliest time a fierce debate has ensued between myth and truth that has not yet, through the many millennia, been stilled or settled.

Metaphor, the intimate connection between language and thought, emerged as a touchstone of history.

Logic, from Locke to Bosanquet, essayed language. Yet they could not grasp the poetic mind. So poetry emerged unscathed through the ages, shrouded between history and science, between myth and truth, as the purest harbinger of literature and culture.

The great critic Owen Barfield once wrote: "The most conspicuous point of contact between meaning and poetry is metaphor." Metaphor, as Shelley argued, marked out the clouded realm between words and thought. Language was poetry before prose. The age-old question became simply: Does poetry make war on reason or is poetry the precursor to reason? And so the debate about the meaning of poetry and history rages on. Is history truth, or is truth better displayed in the sparseness or austerity of poetry?

Let us move smartly to the common era, to our cyberworld, from books to digital clicks. The rapid rise of the electronic media, now soon to be overtaken by the Internet, has instigated some pseudo-critics to argue, to stoke a false clamour, that the age of literature, and thus the age of poetry and prose, is coming to an end. To paraphrase Mark Twain, the announcement of literature's death is somewhat premature.

One can more forcefully argue that, in the digital age, the importance of literature, the essence of poetry, now becomes even more significant to a civil society than in earlier times. Poetry encapsulates popular history and popular memory in a way that history alone cannot.

How do we remember history? In the Davidic biblical period, it was the Psalms. In the Peloponnesian Wars, it was the Iliad. In the days of the first Common Era, it was the Sermon on the Mount. In the First English Commonwealth, it was the daunting poetry of Milton. Is not World War I, displayed in these pictures around us, best remembered by the poem In Flanders Field? Is not the shining moment in Camelot, the Kennedy era, best reflected by the poem of Robert Frost, recited on the cold winter day of President Kennedy's inauguration, "...and miles to go before I sleep..."?

Before European settlement of Canada, the poetic myths of aboriginal peoples permeated this land. Even Jacques Cartier was a poet. From the time he touched the land to be called Canada, our land became rich in poets and poetry.

There are over 1,500 published poets in Canada. We had the pleasure of the company of the late Jean LeMoyne in the Senate, who came here as a poet of renown. I am told that Canada has the largest number per capita of published poets in the world. All countries, large and small, come more alive through the words of their poets. We have a rich, if unheralded, inventory of poetry - from Atwood, to Callahan, to Klein, and Cohen, and from Johnson to Pratt to Birney to Scott. Louis Riel was a published poet. In French, from LaPointe, Miron, Legault, Henault or Roy, there continues to this day a rich and deep vein of poetry and creative imagination.

As we approach the next millennium, honourable senators, is it not appropriate that we recognize the role of the poet in Canada? From the 16th century, the Poet Laureate was recognized as a vital and cherished part of English life. This was heralded in Samuel Johnson's *The Lives of English Poets*. In the late 1930s, the Library of Congress in Washington appropriated this idea called a Poet Consultant to the Library of Congress.

What better way for Canada to celebrate our diversity for the next millennium than by establishing a Parliamentary Poet Laureate? By a simple means, we can bring Parliament and the Library of Parliament to a more visible, central place in our literary landscape that these institutions so richly deserve. By this simple act of Parliament, we can celebrate the artistry of poetry and unite poets, Parliament, and the people together in a greater union of creative harmony.

The process in this bill is simple and cost effective:

> The Speaker of the Senate and the Speaker of the House of Commons, acting together, shall select the Parliamentary Poet Laureate from a list of three names submitted in confidence by a committee chaired by the Parliamentary Librarian and also composed of the National Librarian, the National Archivist of Canada, the Commissioner of Official Languages for Canada, and the Chair of the Canada Council.

The duties of the Poet Laureate are, and are meant to be, minimalist. The Parliamentary Poet Laureate, during the two-year term, shall:

(a) write poetry, especially for use in Parliament on occasions of state;
(b) sponsor poetry readings;
(c) give advice to the Parliamentary Librarian regarding the collection of the Library and acquisitions to enrich its cultural holdings; and
(d) perform such other related duties as are requested by either Speaker or the Parliamentary Librarian.

Honourable senators, the duties encapsulated in this bill are meant not to be complex or onerous. Nothing should interfere with the work of the poet to write poetry.

Honourable senators, I commend this modest bill to you for your thoughtful consideration.

On motion of Senator Kinsella, debate adjourned.

ON NISGA'A ABORIGINAL SOVEREIGNTY
SECOND READING
February 10, 2000

On the Order:

Resuming debate on the motion of the Honourable Senator Austin, P.C., seconded by the Honourable Senator Fairbairn, P.C., for the second reading of Bill C-9, to give effect to the Nisga'a Final Agreement.

Hon. Jerahmiel S. Grafstein: Honourable senators, rarely can we in the Senate say that the legislation we are considering will have a profound impact on Canada and is of historic consequence or that the legislation marks a historic evolution, a turning point in the transformation of the very nature of our sovereign state. Such is the case of Bill C-9, legislation to implement the Nisga'a Final Agreement.

The treatment of aboriginals - or better stated, the mistreatment of aboriginals - predates Confederation and started from the first so-called discovery and, later on, occupation by European states of lands that came to be known as Canada, which in itself originates from an aboriginal word, "Kanata", meaning "meeting place".

Who in this chamber and who in Canada can deny that one of the most miserable and distressing chapters in the history of North America and South America has been our treatment of aboriginals. The federal government, proudly aided and abetted by the established churches of the day, legislated the Indian Act over 100 years ago, which incorporated European-style notions of racial discrimination by establishing bloodlines as a point of definition in the Indian Act. This proved to be both racist and exclusionary. The Father of Confederation, Sir John A. Macdonald, hoped that the so-called "Indians", the so-called "red man", would assimilate by these policies using isolation and then assimilation.

The churches, their missionary zeal and their schools were part of the problem. They have yet to fully atone for their collective efforts to take aboriginal children away from their parents to residential schools for the noble purpose of education, only to abuse them and seek to cleanse them of their aboriginal heritage.

The thinking of the Department of Indian Affairs was no different, backed by the power and prestige of the federal government and its provincial counterparts, all instigated by avaricious settlers and entrepreneurs.

For decades, the treatment of aboriginals went from bad to worse. Even the rights of citizenship were denied aboriginals. In the 1960s, the federal government, through the Hawthorn-Tremblay commission, defined the problem essentially in economic terms and recommended economic empowerment for the aboriginals, as quickly as possible, in order to provide equality of treatment to all aboriginals as citizens.

In 1969, the government white paper presented during the tenure of the current Prime Minister, who was then Minister of Indian and Northern Affairs, opened a new chapter calling for both equal treatment and affirmative action. The active search for a modern solution was on. It became an active part of the public discourse.

In 1982, the Charter of Rights propelled the public debate even further. Sections 25 and 35 recognized undefined aboriginal rights and aboriginal treaties. This was only just; it was only right.

Too few Canadians recall that Canada was saved from absorption by the United States in the War of 1812. It was the great Shawnee leader Tecumseh and his confederacy, siding with British and Canadian soldiers, who turned back the American invasion of Upper Canada. It was along the Thames River, not far from my birthplace in London, Ontario, where Tecumseh died in battle against the American invaders. Tecumseh rode north, from American lands to Canadian lands, to join the fight against the Americans here because he was promised fair treatment for aboriginal treaty claims and aspirations better than those offered or practised by the Americans.

Canada owes a deep social and historic debt to aboriginals; hence, the desire for economic and political justice. The establishment of the new Territory of Nunavut last year was a step in that direction.

Honourable senators, this proposed legislation presents us with a more complex challenge: how to restore fairness, equity and justice to those of aboriginal descent, with small pockets of population stretched across the country, on principles acceptable to the Canadian idea.

After years of negotiation, as Senator Austin so eloquently illustrated in his thorough and comprehensive speech in support on second reading, a settlement was reached between the Government of British Columbia and the Nisga'a of the Nass Valley, settling land claims and recognizing a form of self-government very different and distinctive from that ever seen in Canada before. This small band of less than 6,000 for years have long followed their own form of communal self-government.

No one can deny the need to renovate the aboriginal situation. There are now 80 negotiating tables across the country involving claims of over 10 per cent of Canada's land mass. The Minister in the other place stated that this settlement was not a precedent. However, yesterday, in a most moving address by Senator Gill, he eloquently, passionately and persuasively argued that other aboriginals will make good use of this settlement.

Let us turn to the Nisga'a model of governance. On a careful reading, we discovered some elements which are unique and different. They are so unique and different that I believe they have not been fully understood or digested by most Canadians. I traced the turn in the dialectic on aboriginal solutions since the Hawthorn-Tremblay report.

The egalitarian ideas of the 1969 white paper and the Charter of 1982 began to change dramatically during the debates on the failed Meech Lake Accord and Charlottetown Agreement. The Supreme Court of Canada entered the public debate with its decisions in the hope that these would elucidate and accelerate solutions such as the Calder decision.

With the publication of the Royal Commission on Aboriginal Peoples in 1995, the public debate abruptly and dramatically took another turn, shifting ground from support of the 1969 white paper's theory of individual rights and economic affirmative action, to promoting collective rights, special status and delicate theories of self-determination and a constitutionally approved third level of governance.

In the Nisga'a Treaty, we find that the Nisga'a, in the course of negotiations, substantially reduced the extent of their land claims and other claims in exchange for recognition of a new and different form of legally empowering governance.

In the Nisga'a Treaty, we find a distinction between the Nisga'a, called a Nisga'a citizen, and a non-Nisga'a resident on Nisga'a lands. Under the Nisga'a constitution, only Nisga'a citizens can enjoy full voting rights and full economic entitlement to the fruits of any settlement. Only the Nisga'a can define Nisga'a citizenship. There has been a delegation of powers here beyond the reach of future federal governments. Indeed, the 1982 Charter, in sections 25 and 35, provides for the recognition of aboriginal rights and treaties, and asserts that nothing shall derogate from those rights and treaties that were not defined at the time. The question is not only whether the federal government has the power to establish a third form of government, beyond the reach of future federal governments and Parliament, and without constitutional amendment. Under sections 25 and 35, these questions were and are being hotly debated. They are divisive constitutional questions. Even if these questions pass judicial scrutiny, is that the vision we want for a united Canada with the globe shrinking in the 21st century? We have yet to learn the bitter lessons of the 20th century respecting the clash between "ethnicity" on the one hand and open citizenship on the other.

Senator Gill stated persuasively and passionately the other day that all future aboriginal governments will not be "ethnic". He said that "...they will be a reflection of what we are entitled to be."

He went on with a very moving passage. He said:

This involves sharing the partnership. The more we are what we are, the more openness there will be between us. A distinct identity does not require the cultures to be separated; in fact, the opposite should be the case. A culture that is comfortable with itself can be open with others. It attracts interest. Its ethnicity is a part of the positive reality.

Who can quarrel with Senator Gill's statement? Yet, when one looks carefully at the words of the Nisga'a settlement, at the legislation, and beyond, as I have, and reads the Nisga'a constitution, one sees that the question of Nisga'a citizenship is left solely to the Nisga'a, beyond the reach of Charter principles. My concern would be that the definition of "citizenship" will be "ethnic" not as my colleague, Senator Gill, suggests. My concern is that, through the noble purpose of bringing delayed justice to the aboriginal situation in Canada, which screams for renovation, we may have unwittingly created "ethnic" feudal-like special status enclaves with two classes of citizenship that conflict with the higher notion of equal and inclusive Canadian citizenship.

Our work here, honourable senators, on this most important legislation, is challenging, delicate and difficult. It is not clear to me, after comprehensively reviewing the treaty, the Nisga'a constitution, this legislation, and the five volumes of the Royal Commission report on aboriginal peoples whether my concerns on this legislation are questions of principle or questions of clarification. I intend to abstain on second reading and carefully review the evidence presented before the Committee on Aboriginal Peoples which I know will be both exhaustive and thorough on these and my other concerns.

Hon. Ron Ghitter: Honourable senators, would the honourable senator permit a question?

Senator Grafstein: Yes, I would.

Senator Ghitter: If the concerns of the honourable senator become a reality, what does he believe the ramifications of that will be?

Senator Grafstein: Who can project into the future? There is one prophylactic to my own concerns. As this matter reaches beyond the boundaries of British Columbia, provincial assent will be required to 40 or so other negotiating tables. That is a prophylactic, but is it a salutary one? It is very difficult, as the Minister in the other place has suggested, to deny that this is a substantive precedent. If it is a substantive precedent, we could find ourselves in a position of having enclaves - and I use that word delicately - ethnic, racially-based enclaves across the country with different treatment of people who live within that particular enclave.

Having read the documents as thoroughly as I could, I wish to commend the negotiators who laboured arduously to try to bring together two different notions of Canadianism; the notion of equal treatment and that of ethnic identification. In many places in the legislation, you will see the reach of the Charter and the desire for Charter notions to pertain.

Let us look at the question very carefully. On Nisga'a land there will be a Nisga'a citizen - and remember that it is defined as a Nisga'a citizen. I always thought, honourable senators, that citizenship was a unique aspect of life in Canada, that it was open to every Canadian regardless of birth, race, or tradition. That idea was imported here.

I was not part of the negotiations. There were 20 years of negotiations; so it is facile for me to enter into this debate after a month of study. However, having read this, I must say that I have always thought that the highest architectonic of Canada is citizenship, that everything else flows from that, and that everyone here should be entitled to become a citizen. In the Nisga'a treaty, people are excluded. You cannot become a Nisga'a citizen, I do not believe - and that is why I want to await the evidence - unless you are born into the tribe. This sets up a different notion of citizenship; a conflicting notion of citizenship.

If Senator Gill's statement is correct that this will open up a larger vision of Canadian citizenship, I am open to that. However, I doubt that. I hope that my doubts can be allayed during the evidence given at the committee. I hope I am wrong. I hope my fears are misplaced. I will listen to the evidence and I shall read it in an open-minded fashion, but I have deep doubts about this. That is why I am abstaining here, despite my desire to renovate the horrible situation that aboriginals across the country face. I cannot bring myself to do that.

That is not a complete answer, but I hope that the evidence before the committee will help us all.

Senator Ghitter: From Senator Grafstein's reading of the agreement and the legislation, is it possible that a non-Nisga'a defined individual has no protection as normally afforded to Canadians under our Charter?

Senator Grafstein: No, that is not my position. Again, I wish to commend the negotiators and all the parties on this.

Senator Austin stated it quite well. As I understand it, when the rights of a non-Nisga'a resident on Nisga'a lands will be affected, he will be able to address those concerns. He will be able to be heard in the Nisga'a modality. He will have a right to be heard, but he will not have a right to vote. Perhaps when it comes to education there will be rights to vote. On questions, there will unquestionably be a distinct right to be heard, but they will not have a right to decide, to vote, or to access the decision making process other than to be heard.

That is my reading. As I have said, I hope that in the evidence before the committee these concerns can be allayed. There is a substantive and distinctive difference between the right to be heard and the right to vote as a citizen.

The Hon. the Speaker: Honourable senators, I must inform you that the time period for Senator Grafstein's speech and questions thereon has expired.

Is leave requested to extend?

Senator Grafstein: Yes.

The Hon. the Speaker: Is leave granted?

Hon. Senators: Agreed.

Senator Ghitter: I have one further question on this matter. Suppose that an individual is denied employment because he or she is not a member of the Nisga'a nation. In that circumstance, another Canadian could go to a human rights tribunal, at whatever level. Is it your belief that such an opportunity does not exist for a non-Nisga'a individual living on that land mass?

Senator Grafstein: Again, I am not clear about that. My preliminary reading is that there might be some rights under the Charter and under like legislation, because the Charter is not completely exempted here. There is, however, a Catch-22 here. Under the Charter, aboriginal rights are included but are not defined. However, they are defined subsequently and, therefore, are afforded equality of treatment under the Charter. The Charter has a Catch-22 to it. The question is: Is citizenship in the Nisga'a tribe open to all the Charter principles?

That is one question, and I do not know the answer to it.

Hon. Gerry St. Germain: Honourable senators, in speaking of Nisga'a citizenship, Senator Grafstein stated that he believed, from his reading and understanding, that citizenship flowed from ancestry and from being part of that ethnic group. My understanding, from the explanations that I have received, is that Nisga'a have the option of granting citizenship to anyone they so choose. Would that change your position at all?

Senator Grafstein: I should like to know what the qualifications are. Under our principles, there are objective qualifications. They are not discretionary. You come to Canada, you are a landed immigrant, and you can become, on objective principles, a citizen. In the United Kingdom, a Minister of the Crown can deny a person citizenship based on arbitrary conditions. That is not the case in Canada. After you reach a certain standard, citizenship is based on open principles. I do not know if that is the case under the Nisga'a constitution. On my reading, it is discretionary. That is one of the issues of evidence that I will be interested in listening to at committee.

Hon. Mira Spivak: Honourable senators, I have two questions for Senator Grafstein.

First, is it the honourable senator's view, with his concerns about the citizenship question, that the Nisga'a will have dual citizenship? Second, given those concerns, if the honourable senator wished to amend this treaty, could he give us some indication of how that process would then evolve? I presume the treaty would have to go back to all of the negotiating parties. Could the honourable senator elaborate on that?

Senator Grafstein: Honourable senators, I will deal with the last question first, because it is the fundamental question. I have given serious thought to it. Senator St. Germain raised the problem that we in the Senate have. The problem is that it is up or down. It is almost impossible to amend. I say that because, to be fair to the Nisga'a, they have given up substantive land and other claims in the negotiations. It puts Parliament, as Senator St. Germain pointed out, in an invidious position of deciding to vote up or down.

I do not know if there is an answer to this. I have given mighty thought to it. If this is a problem, and if my concerns are shared by senators on all sides, how do we change this in a way that will be fair to the negotiators who gave up positions at tables to reach a result and not hinder the other salutary aspects of this negotiation? It is a conundrum, and I do not have a fast answer to it.

I am sorry, I have forgotten your earlier question.

Senator Spivak: The question was whether it is your opinion that the Nisga'a will have dual citizenship.

Senator Grafstein: We just had this discussion the other day about Mr. Citizen Black and dual citizenship and what the rights of dual citizenship are. I do not disagree with dual citizenship -

Hon. John Lynch-Staunton (Leader of the Opposition): Within the same country?

Senator Grafstein: Let me finish. I do not disagree with dual citizenship as it applies to Canadians who hold citizenship in other countries, but it gives me great difficulty, Senator Lynch-Staunton, to bifurcate citizenship in Canada.

Were there other answers to this? I think there were, but I was not involved in the negotiations. We were not involved, nor should we have been involved. However, there might have been other models. That is for the committee to deliberate, as Senator Corbin points out.

Senator Spivak: Is this a template, then, for other things that might happen in Canada, or do you think this is a case of its own kind, sui generis?

Senator Grafstein: How can it not be a template? The Minister said it is not a precedent. How can it not be a precedent?

Senator Gill was very fair the other day when he said that other aboriginal groups will make good use of this - and why should they not?

Senator Lynch-Staunton: They do not want less, you are right.

Senator Grafstein: Our problem is: Is it a good precedent? It will be a precedent, despite what the Minister in the other place says. That is the danger. I hope it is a false danger, but, nevertheless, it is a substantive danger.

Hon. Noel A. Kinsella (Deputy Leader of the Opposition): Honourable senators, there are two areas that I should like to explore with Senator Grafstein based upon his comments.

First, continuing with our reflection on the notion of citizenship, I think it is necessary to underscore the importance of that question. It is important to the principle that underlies the bill that is before us, but, also, we have to mine that a little bit to see what it really means.

We must be mindful that the first Citizenship Act in Canada was passed only in 1945. There was a second one in the 1960s. We have been promised a new one by successive governments over the past few decades. We must also be mindful, in terms of the relationship of citizenship to rights, of the fact that, under our Charter of Rights and Freedoms, there are only three rights that are predicated on Canadian citizenship: the right to leave and return to Canada; the right to vote; and the minority education right.

Given the youthfulness of the whole idea under our parliamentary democracy of Canadian citizenship, and given the fact that most of our rights are applied to everyone in Canada, does the honourable senator think that perhaps this term "citizen" is an equivocal term, so that, when it is being used in this bill, it is not the same concept that is used even in the Citizenship Act, and is quite different from the notion of citizen that is in the Charter of Rights and Freedoms?

Senator Grafstein: I think that was the premise of Senator Gill's comments, namely, that there are different notions of lower-case citizenship. The word "citizenship" was used, however, in a legally and essentially constitutionally oriented framework. I think it was carefully chosen. I do not think it was lightly chosen. Because it was carefully chosen and because it appears at first sight, prima facie, to conflict with my notion of citizenship, and perhaps yours, it opens this question up, and maybe there should be a wider definition of citizenship. I have always thought that the essence of citizenship, in its legal and in its natural law state, was to be open to everyone - open citizenship based on open criteria.

Let me conclude, if I might. My maiden speech in this place dealt with the question of payment to Japanese internees. I chose that as my topic because I came across an invidious case of citizenship. There was a Canadian of Japanese descent in the Fraser Valley who had fought in the First World War and came back bemedalled; he then returned to the Fraser Valley to find that his land had been taken from him. He did not have the vote; he only got the vote because he became a soldier. The whole question of citizenship and voting became a real live topic for me.

I cannot think of anything more important that we can deal with as legislators than defining carefully and proudly what citizenship entails. This legislation opens this question - perhaps prematurely, but it opens the question. Therefore, we must deal with the question.

Senator Kinsella: That leads to my second area of concern. I listened carefully and took note that in the address of the honourable senator, he delicately used terminology like "ethnic group" or "ethnicity". He seemed, to my listening at least, to express some discomfort with a racial kind of definition. The Japanese redress speaks directly to the issue. That was racial discrimination. Therefore, a linkage exists in our history, perhaps in that part of our history of which we are not overly proud.

As the honourable senator gave his address this afternoon, was he struggling to avoid terms such as "race" that we ought not use? There has been, in part of the debate as I have read it, an attempt by some to define collective undertakings in racial terms. Given that race has no scientific base to it and given the history of the evil that has been perpetrated, would the honourable senator clarify what he meant and how we must expunge the notion of race from this consideration?

Senator Grafstein: The Honourable Senator Kinsella raises an interesting historic point, and I did spend some time looking at this.

The Indian Act imported a racial blood definition. This did not come from the aboriginal people. This came from the white man defining what the so-called "red man" was. This was a European form of definition and exclusion. Even the term "red man" is reprehensible to my mind. The definition in the Indian Act is reprehensible. Now we have this unbelievable paradox that the reprehensible notion of blood in the definition of the Indian Act, which was European and foreign to the aboriginals, may somehow continue on in this treaty.

I say that delicately because I do not know. I have no idea what it takes to be a member of the Nisga'a band. I do not know the answer to those questions. The honourable senator is right. I have been as sensitive as I could in my effort to move away from terms that I hope will be false hot buttons. This is a delicate situation and we are dealing with delicate issues. I hope honourable senators will address this issue as delicately, as fairly and as openly as possible.

MAURICE "THE ROCKET" RICHARD: EULOGY

May 30, 2000

Hon. Jerahmiel S. Grafstein: Honourable senators, hockey first introduced me to the French fact in Canada. Let me explain.

Born in southwestern Ontario in the midst of the Depression, sports was the only way to bring together kids in our ethnically rich neighbourhood. The dialects I first heard in my neighbourhood were Polish, Yiddish, Hungarian, Italian, Ukrainian, Russian, Czech, Dutch and others, but not French. Hockey made the difference. It was hockey that made me curious about one shelf of old French red Moroc-co-Leather-bound books crammed in a corner of my father's library next to a thick Polish-French dictionary with names like Zola, Maupassant and Hugo. My father explained that the Montreal Canadians were named after the first Canadians, who were French.

One of the biggest stories I remember from my early years was seeing a picture of Turk Broda in uniform when the great Toronto "Leaf" goalie joined the army and was replaced by Frank McCool, whose pictures I laboriously pasted in my most precious possession, my hockey scrapbook. The greatest news of all was about the "Punch Line," which pummelled our beloved Maple Leafs, and the biggest hero of all was the Rocket - Rocket Richard. On Saturday night, everyone in my hometown huddled around the radio to listen breathlessly to Hockey Night in Canada.

In 1944, an uncle living in Toronto invited me to visit and took me to my first game at the Maple Leaf Gardens as a birthday present. What a gift! It was a game between the Leafs and the Habs. I saw the Rocket for the very first time. Shorter, wider, even faster up close in person, the Rocket was simply poetry in motion. And he was tough. Nobody could push him around. I could not take my eyes off him. I remember his flashing eyes so wide open as he crouched low and raced over the blue line to score.

All that we as kids could do was pretend that we were him on our home rinks. He was the magic of hockey. Later, when I met him, he was still all about hockey. He was a simple man interested only in hockey.

This week, Maurice "the Rocket" Richard died after yet another valiant battle. His family insisted that no flag adorn his coffin. He did not need a flag. He was his own star. He was our hockey star. In my time, he was the greatest. He was Canadian. He was Canadian.

WILLIAM KELLY: ON RETIREMENT

June 20, 2000

Hon. Jerahmiel S. Grafstein: Honourable senators, the lamented looming retirement of the Honourable William Kelly will leave the Senate leaner, lighter, looser, and less learned. Bill, as we have heard, was a life-long Conservative. Before Bill was called to the Senate by the Right Honourable Pierre Elliott Trudeau, he was already a legend in my home province of Ontario. He was a legend in Ontario politics.

Bill was a key engineer who helped to construct, motivate and run the Big Blue Machine that was so successful for many decades in Ontario. If the truth is now to be known - since we are now making mea culpas - the truth is that the Little Red Machine in Ontario was modelled on the Big Blue Machine, with not inconsiderable success.

Bill was always a graceful and honourable opponent. He was tough, but fair. He was a strong, silent and influential advisor to successive provincial governments and premiers - governments and premiers who always clung or hung on to the middle road in Ontario. The fight in Ontario has always been for the middle ground and, dare I say, the progressive liberal middle ground. Bill was always a leader in moderation in all things, including in politics and in the Senate.

In his duties here, Senator Kelly approached his work with precision, passion and principle. Above all, he was a man of clear common sense. His work on committees, especially the committees dealing with intelligence, security and terrorism - that malignant disease of the last part of this century - is well known to all. He believed that Parliament had to play a more important and crucial role in its oversight on matters of national interest such as intelligence and security. He felt - and I believe he is right - that Parliament had not properly provided that oversight to which the public is entitled.

What is less known about Bill is his work on behalf of Canada overseas, particularly at the OSCE, where 55 countries, including Canada and the U.S., are voting members. As a rapporteur at that very distinguished body, he was responsible for drafting multifaceted, complex policy papers and then dealing with amendments that flowed in from 55 countries. Again, in Europe, Bill led the way with concision, skill and diplomacy. He navigated the ever difficult and complex shoals of international clashes. In the process, honourable senators, he raised respect for Canada across the face of Europe.

Bill, the Senate will miss you and your astute talents and capabilities. You helped to reconstruct and burnish the quiet reputation of the Senate, true to its mandate, as a chamber of sober second thought. Bill, you leave the Senate with a repository of distinguished work. Canada remains indebted to you for your outstanding qualities of passion and reason, all in the service of the Canada you served so well in war and peace. You will remain in my mind always as an officer and a gentleman. Bill, may the wind always be at your back. God speed!

CLAUDE BISSELL: EULOGY
MURRAY ROSS: EULOGY

September 20, 2000

Hon. Jerahmiel S. Grafstein: Honourable senators, I rise today to make a brief tribute to the late Claude Bissell and the late Murray Ross. As we embark on this joyous season of pre-election festivities in Parliament, we are agitated by all our political leaders who admonish that the contest for the hearts and minds of Canadians will be about values. It seems the common currency of values resonates here and reverberates more poignantly in the electoral wars now being waged to the south. What are we told about the nature or, indeed, the centrality of these values? What exactly do these leaders have in mind? Who are they trying to convince and about what? Before we seek to differentiate ourselves politically, must we not first attempt to better understand what we are seeking to differentiate ourselves about? Or is an electoral debate on values in reality a detour, a deception, a delusion, an allusion, or worse, a snare and a trap?

From our fragile perch here in the Senate, do we perceive an opening or a closing of the Canadian mind? Will the partisan political debate ruminate around higher expectations of pseudo family values, or will the political debate tend to "dumbing down," blurring values to the lowest consensual denomination? Will fact or fiction, reality or virtual reality be deployed in the ever elusive hunt for values to start this new millennium?

This pugnacious thought occurred to me, honourable senators, as I listened earlier this summer to the first political volleys over values and learned at the same time of the passing, first, of Claude Bissell, followed a month later by the death of Murray Ross.

Honourable senators might recall that Claude Bissell was first the youthful President of Carleton University in Ottawa and then the youngest university President, at 40, of the University of Toronto. Murray Ross, then Vice-President at the University of Toronto, became the first and founding President of York University.

These men led three of Canada's greatest academic treasures through an era of radical change. How they both would have lamented any "dumbing down" of political discourse about values! For them, the nature of a liberal education would have been the starting point, the crucial launching pad for any discourse on values. These academics were consumed by the defence of a liberal education - an elusive goal still under attack. Both emphasized the importance of a literary, aesthetic sensibility that lies at the core of the liberal idea. Both were excellent scholars and prolific authors, who in their own right set high standards of literary excellence in all their works. Both would have agreed with the late Harold Bloom, of Yale University, who wrote that most imaginative work, *The Western Canon*, on the importance of the study of literature at the core of education. Let me quote one small passage from Bloom's mesmerizing critique:

> The West's greatest writers are subversive of all values, both ours and their own. Scholars who urge us to find the source of our morality and our politics in Plato, or in Isaiah, are out of touch with the social reality in which we live. If we read *The Western Canon* in order to form our social, political, or -

The Hon. the Speaker: I am sorry, Honourable Senator Grafstein, but I must interrupt Your three-minute time period has expired .

Senator Grafstein: May I have leave to continue, honourable senators?

The Hon. the Speaker: No. I regret to say that the Rules Committee and the Senate have passed a rule that no leave can be accepted.

Senator Grafstein: I will continue tomorrow, then.

CLAUDE BISSELL: EULOGY
MURRAY ROSS: EULOGY

September 21, 2000

Hon. Jerahmiel S. Grafstein: Honourable senators, allow me to conclude a tribute to the late Claude Bissell, former President of the University of Toronto, and the late Murray Ross, former President of York University and a dialectician on values. Both would have agreed with the late Harold Bloom of Yale University , who wrote that most imaginative work *The Western Canon* on the importance of the study of literature at the core of education and the recovery of meaning. Let me quote one small passage from Bloom's mesmerizing critique:

The West's greatest writers are subversive of all values, both ours and their own. Scholars who urge us to find the source of our morality and our politics in Plato, or in Isaiah, are out of touch with the social reality in which we live. If we read *The Western Canon* in order to form our social, political or personal moral values, I firmly believe we will become monsters of selfishness and exploitation. To read in the service of any ideology is not, in my judgment, to read at all. The reception of aesthetic power enables us to learn how to talk to ourselves and how to endure ourselves. The true use of Shakespeare or Cervantes, of Homer or of Dante, of Chaucer or of Rabelais is to augment one's own growing inner self. Reading deeply in the canon will not make one a better or a worse person, a more useful or more harmful person. The mind's dialogue with itself is not primarily a social reality. All that *The Western Canon* can bring one is the proper use of one's own solitude, that solitude whose final form is one's confrontation with one's own mortality.

Let these words serve, honourable senators, as a modest elegy and eulogy for the late Claude Bissell and for the late Murray Ross, as tranquil reminders of the gossamer essence that lies at the heart of the age-old debate on values and the importance of first educating oneself to face at least the understanding of meaning and, at a bare minimum, the humility of one's own mortality.

PIERRE ELLIOT TRUDEAU: EULOGY

October 4, 2000

Hon. Jerahmiel S. Grafstein: Honourable senators, the hour is late, the evening draws nigh, the dreaded night is here, and so we come to honour Pierre Elliott Trudeau. How should we honour him? How he loved words, whether as a pamphleteer, essayist, teacher, satirist, memoirist, advocate, poet, or politician, he adored words. All his life he was most careful with his own words. Now, all we have to offer are our words to assuage the elusive feeling of loss to our own persona.

His crackling words first attracted our minds and our thoughts in the 1950s. Finally, even though we resisted, his persona captured our hearts. So we come to honour him for his words and his person.

In a strange way, looking back, it seems to me now, much of what I have said in the Senate was for a critical audience of one. I took care with my words in the Senate and relished his reactions in notes, encounters and conversations.

Why did he scorch such a significant space on the Canadian psyche? By the dint of his own energy and thoughts, he alone created a *novus ordo seclorum*, a new school of thought, a new lexicon of rights by the so-called breach birth of the Charter, a new uncommon Commonwealth. Surely, the final honour cannot be less than the accolade of acceptance by his most vitriolic opponents who, despite themselves, have adopted the Charter as their touchstone, just as his advocates have.

My first memories of Mr. Trudeau go back to the 1950s after I had first read his dashing essays on federalism. Our earliest exchange came in 1961, through a mutual friend, the late Jean David. We renewed more frequent exchanges during my first stint in Ottawa from 1966 to 1968.

He had a quick wit. On the day he finally announced his intention to run as leader of the Liberal Party early in 1968, he sent me an unsolicited photograph inscribed, "To Jerry. Next Year in Jerusalem Pierre." Earlier, I had turned down his offer of a job. To this day, I am not sure what he meant by that note. Whether he wanted me to go or to stay, or would we meet in the "Promised Land." In any event, I left Ottawa in 1968, right after his election as leader. In October 1972, he called for help during that ill-fated "Land is Strong" campaign, which I answered. In the midst of that campaign, I organized and co-chaired a surprise birthday party for Mr. Pearson, who was then dying of cancer. The surprise party was held in the intimate surroundings of the Maple Leaf Gardens for 25,000 Canadians, and we convinced Mr. Trudeau to act as host. It was to be Mr. Pearson's last public event. I recall the final exchanges between Mr. Pearson and Mr. Trudeau on that evening. The rest is history.

From 1974 until 1984, he asked me as a volunteer to supervise all of his television and print campaigns and so we carried on regular written and personal exchanges on ideas and policies.

Too many personal anecdotes flood across my memory plane, many intersected on public events. Allow me to focus my thoughts on the Senate and make a very partial public confession.

When I received a call from Mr. Trudeau early in 1984 to inform me of his decision to appoint me to the Senate, he described, in a quiet and complimentary way, the various private memos, some controversial, I had sent him over two decades. None had ever leaked; none had ever appeared in the press. He concluded with this line, "We need you in the Senate." He asked whether I needed some time to think about it. I said, "No, no, no." I was prepared to accept right then and there. I considered the appointment to be the greatest compliment ever bestowed upon me. However, I did allow that I was curious about one thing. I asked him why he had said, "We need you in the Senate." Then I heard the phone drop and a sudden burst of laughter. He picked up the phone and he politely apologized. He told me he thought I was the first person that he had ever appointed who had asked why. I told him, "I am serious, Prime Minister. I accept, but I still want to know why." Why did he need me in the Senate? He then told me something that I have never forgotten.

Pierre Trudeau wanted me to use the Senate as a platform for my own ideas, the same ideas, he said, that I had relentlessly pressed upon him and others in the party. He wanted the Senate to be a "house of ideas."

Shortly after my appointment to the Senate, the first issue that struck my attention was the debate of apology and compensation to Canadians of Japanese descent who had been incarcerated and had their property expropriated during the Second World War. On April 10, 1984, I tabled a motion in the Senate and, on May 8, 1984, I made my maiden speech on this subject. Mr. Trudeau opposed this measure. We could not forever resurrect the past, he argued. We could only change the future.

I and others felt that the case for Canadians of Japanese descent was different and could be differentiated on its facts from other similar claims. Mr. Trudeau argued vehemently that such differences would be overlooked. To do so would be an invitation for a flood of attempts to rewrite history. All we could do is not to repeat the failures of the past. We agreed to disagree.

When an apology and compensation were ultimately made by Mr. Mulroney's government, Mr. Trudeau gently chided me about the floodgate of demands and the expectation that this had indeed triggered, just as he had predicted. He rarely forgot, yet he never resented a principled or reasoned stand.

The next event we recall was the Meech Lake debate in 1988, right here in the Senate chamber. After Mr. Trudeau's retirement, he was most reluctant to return to public discourse. I and others convinced him that the principles captured in the Meech Lake agreement were more important than his person and that if he came to the Senate, he could make a difference.

The two-nations thesis was embedded in Meech Lake. Pierre Trudeau had fought against such a revisionist view of history his entire life. "Special status" or "distinct society" were code words for the two-nations thesis, he explained. I agreed. This he and many of us here could not accept.

Honourable senators, the Senate chamber echoes this evening with the eloquence of his speech and his responses. He sat in this chamber that day and argued here, alone, in the Committee of the Whole, for well over three hours. I have the transcript here. To my mind, that day he kept Canada on the fragile "One Canada" and "Canada, one and indivisible" course.

When the last referendum came, we enquired whether Mr. Trudeau had been invited to participate. We were surprised that we had not seen him on the hustings. We were told by the organizers that he was reluctant to do so. As the polls drew closer, many of us still believed that Mr. Trudeau could make the crucial difference. Calls were made to the No organizers in Ottawa and in Montreal to see how this might be done. In the last days, the No side support slid further and softened. Polls showed that the two sides were within several points of each other, within the margin of error. Still no invitation.

I concocted what I thought was a marvellous and simple plan. Mr. Trudeau, on that last Sunday before the referendum, after all the official television advertising had been completed, would take a casual morning stroll and then sit on a bench in the park near his house in Montreal. A CBC television camera crew would accidentally wander by. He would then give a final interview on that crucial Sunday and own the media on that day and on Monday, referendum day.

While Mr. Trudeau was reluctant, since he had not been asked earlier, I had reason to believe that he could have been persuaded to do so, even at that late hour. The organizers in Quebec would have none of it. I believe Mr. Trudeau would have been worth at least five additional points on the No side and again history would have changed. Honourable senators, it is for learned historians to speculate on that.

After the referendum came a resolution presented in Parliament respecting the "distinct society." I had heard from others here on this side and in the another place that Mr. Trudeau was in agreement. I could not believe that, so I called him several times. He urged me to make a long and forceful speech against the resolution in the Senate. That was the only time from the date of my appointment that he ever asked me to do something. Others convinced me that the resolution was not important and that I should remain silent. The resolution would fade.

Honourable senators, on December 14, 1995, I made the shortest speech I ever gave in this place against the motion to recognize Quebec as a distinct society. Let me repeat it:

> Come, let us now praise Canada, for Canada is a distinct society. The rest is commentary. Canadians, themselves, can count the ways.

This did not please Mr. Trudeau or anyone on this side or in the other place. I regret to this day that I did not follow his strong advice, for Mr. Trudeau believed that principles and practice march best when they march together.

Finally, honourable senators will recall the extradition bill and the discretion it gave to the Minister of Justice respecting the death penalty. Mr. Trudeau was delighted with the position some of us had taken against the measure.

When it came to the Nisga'a treaty, he again spoke quietly of his concern with respect to the compromise of some significant principles espoused in that measure.

I recount these events to demonstrate that from the time of his resignation 16 years ago as prime minister, he continued to actively follow events in Parliament, including the Senate, closely and with great and precise interest.

Honourable senators, how then are we to honour Mr. Trudeau? To hold fast to his ideas, ideas that many of us on both sides of this chamber share?

In 1979, after 11 turbulent years as prime minister, Pierre Trudeau's political fortunes had fallen to their lowest ebb. When the election started, the Liberals were lagging in the polls. The economy had been ravaged first by international then domestic inflation. The public had lost confidence in him. The regions were upset. The only area of public opinion where Pierre Trudeau still held an overwhelming lead was the leadership indices. Thus, I helped coin the phrase for the 1979 campaign: "A leader must be a leader."

Since that time, leaders of every political stripe in Canada, consciously or unconsciously, essay to measure themselves against the high standards set by Mr. Trudeau's innate and practised leadership skills and qualities. All others pale in comparison. Why so?

Pierre Trudeau came to politics and sought power, not for its own sake, but for a specific idea of Canada. His message was inseparable from his medium. The man became the medium. He envisaged Canada as a distinct society, a bilingual and multicultural society, and a just society fused by equality and inclusion. No one should be left out and no one should be left behind. Activist organs of government were to be re-engineered to be servants of the people. The Canadian Charter of Rights and Freedom would transform the political landscape. The individual would be placed above politicians or Parliament. In the process, alone, as I noted earlier, he created a new school of thought for us - a new and different commonwealth. Pierre Trudeau energetically, creatively and repetitively hammered home his singular message with persuasion, passion and precision designed to forge an unbreakable link with each Canadian, whether or not one agreed with him.

It is not strange, then, that each Canadian should personally measure his or her life experience against the larger-than-life figure cut by Pierre Trudeau. It certainly comes as no surprise that, on his death, each and every Canadian feels an indescribable personal loss, as if somehow one's own persona were diminished. The power and depth of that response across Canada is still unfathomable and unmeasurable.

Honourable senators, we honour Pierre Trudeau because today's political discourse vibrates and resonates anew with his obsession for equality rights - the demand for rights by one group or another, by one individual or another. Each claims rights based on the individual rights and freedoms he embedded in the Charter. Pierre Trudeau had that vision. These ideas would forge Canadians together into an exciting new crucible of identity, and that has been done.

For those who were privileged to know Pierre Trudeau up close and personal or from afar, his ideas are alive. His belief in forging one Canada, one and indivisible, now and forever, has been reignited, whether it be in the Citizenship Act or other legislation to come. His ideas refuse to be diluted or diminished. He cannot be forgotten. Pierre Trudeau's heartbeat lives on.

Rereading Pierre Trudeau's early essays, as I have this weekend, is a fresh pleasure. From that electric first encounter almost 40 years ago in a Montreal bar, his penetrating intellect forced one to think harder and more clearly and to be better than we deserve. I urge all new senators to read and reread his Meech Lake evidence in the Senate as a powerful reminder of what the Senate can do if we have the collective political will.

Let me conclude on a personal puzzle. From whence sprang Mr. Trudeau's fountain of ideas? I often asked him and myself that question. What motivated him? I began to read and reread carefully the ideas of Mounier, Acton, Newman, Maritain, Gilson, Berlin, and even the poet Saint-Exupery.

Trudeau prided himself as a contrarian who went against the grain, an anti-nationalist, especially when people wrapped the mantle of nationalism around them, which they needed for their own insecure comfort and needs. I reread the *Spiritual Exercises of St. Ignatius* and *the Interior Castle*, written by St. Teresa of Avila, and delved into the works of St. Thomas and St. Bonaventure. "Know thyself," "know thyself," these works proclaimed. Was it these thinkers or more simply the premature loss of a father we shared that forced one to think independently and differently, against the grain?

We shared a fascination with the mysteries of China and the Lubavitch movement. Above all, he relished the expression of ideas and phrases, both written and spoken.

When he came to office, he surrounded himself with creative thinkers, like his closest friends Gerald Pelletier; Jacques Hebert; the late and most lamented Fernand Cadieux; the unsung McLuhan of French Canada; Jean LeMoyne, the poet he appointed to the Senate; Eugene Forsey; Jean Louis Gagnon, that great Quebec Liberal who, in the 1930s, stood up alone against the Duplessis tide; Rod Chiasson; or my old friend and confidant, now in England, Roy Faibish.

One hour with Trudeau, honourable senators, became a gruelling intellectual workout, like an inept middleweight sparring partner against a heavyweight champion. Amplified by Mr. Trudeau's capacious memory, for he could remember precisely what one had said long after one had forgotten, he could always sneak in a jab or a telling counterpunch.

He frustrated us with his excellence just as he inspired us. Just as he relentlessly drove himself to inner standards of excellence, he inspired each of us to drive ourselves intellectually and professionally well beyond our meagre talents. In the same way, he concentrated his own bundle of energy and singular talent to drive Canada to be better than even we could dream. The dream lives on, inspiring us anew. Trudeau's heartbeat is alive. The mystery of Trudeau's persona still eludes us. We hardly knew him. No one did.

Deo gratias..Deo gratias. Pierre, thank God for the pleasure of your company. *Deo gratius. Dea gratius. Visio est tota merces... Visio beatifica.*

Vision is the full reward. Your vision is blessed. And so, honourable senators, the beat goes on!

HELEN ROSE GRAFSTEIN:
TRIBUTE ON HER 100TH BIRTHDAY

October 5, 2000

Hon. Jerahmiel S. Grafstein: Honourable senators, allow me to mark a milestone in the annals of my family. This week we celebrated my mother's one hundredth birthday. Helen Rose Grafstein was born in Yilza, Poland on October 3, 1900. She stemmed from an ancient line of rabbis on her mother's side. She landed in Canada in 1907 with her mother and her younger sister, following her father who had travelled and worked in Belgium until he arrived in Toronto a year earlier. Ultimately, she and her family settled at 35 Kensington Avenue in Toronto.

My mother met my father, also born in Poland, when he came to visit his older brothers in Toronto in 1927, after serving in the Pilsudski Legion in Poland. They fell in love, married in 1930, and moved to London, Ontario where my older sister and I were born and raised.

Tragedy stalked my mother's entire life. Her father was blinded in an accident just before World War I but, fortunately, lived to the ripe old age of 87. Her dearest, oldest cousin died in the Dieppe raid. Her mother died early due to the struggle and strain to provide for her family. My own father died prematurely in a car accident 50 years ago, and my mother was left to raise me and my sister. My sister died suddenly some years ago. Then my mother's beloved younger sister, Betty, passed away.

My mother worked practically all of her life to provide for her family, and yet her unquenchable spirit and private beliefs survived and surmounted all these family burdens and tragedies.

She loves clothes. "You are not dressed unless you wear a hat," she reminds us. She loves music. To this day, every Monday she attends choir practice and sings in a choir. Wednesdays she still plays bingo. Until recently, she was an avid reader of Hansard.

Let me recount one small, political story. During the last referendum, knowing of my concern, she asked me how it was going. She admonished me not to worry. She had read the question. The question was very confusing, she said. Quebec will never separate. Canada is too good to separate from. No one in their right mind in Quebec would ever separate from Canada. The only document to this day she still keeps in her purse with her is her faded citizenship certificate.

So, honourable senators, I seek your indulgence to salute her, to celebrate the centenary of her life. She believes nothing is really official unless it is in Hansard. May I wish her the traditional Jewish blessing to live as long as the lifespan of Moses. Mother, may you live to 120 years and may God's strong spirit remain with you.

LOUIS ROBICHAUD: EULOGY

October 19, 2000

Hon. Jerahmiel S. Grafstein: Honourable senators, I just want to add a brief word of tribute to Louis Robichaud and focus on only one point. Many other references to his illustrious career have been made, and made better than I could have. The one point that I want to draw to the attention of senators is one that others have talked about: Louis Robichaud's great and magical skill. To be able to speak without notes, without a text, for hours on end in a mesmerizing manner made Louis Robichaud one of Canada's greatest stump speakers.

There are few men or women in Canada who have this God-given talent. Louis could lift a listless audience of voters into a magical moment of unity. He could do it in either French or English. He could do it in such a way that when you left the room you had huge and repeated visions of his excellence and his scintillation. This magical quality is so rare that when we lose it in this chamber and we lose it in Canada, I think it appropriate that we should mark its loss.

I will remember the great moments and the great inspiration that Louis gave us all as young Liberals, this uncanny and magical ability to convince people that the country in which we live is a great one, and that one Canada, one Canada indivisible, is the highlight and the vision for all of us. Louis, I thank you for your vision, your contribution and your comradeship.

RAYMOND J. PERRAULT: EULOGY

January 31, 2001

Hon. Jerahmiel S. Grafstein: Honourable senators, I would be remiss as a Liberal from the most populous province of Canada, Ontario, and the most populous city, Toronto, if I did not add some words of tribute to Ray Perrault, because Ray has such a reverence for both Ontario and Toronto.

Ray's career has always reminded me of the movie, *The Loneliness of the Long Distance Runner*. I shall not repeat the accolades so eloquently made by our colleagues on both sides. I first met Ray in the early 1960s when I travelled as a young Liberal representative to British Columbia and Ray was one of the first people in the group that I met.

Three singular attributes struck me then and they remain with him to the present day. The first is Ray's voice. You will hear it in a few moments. It is a voice that you will never and can never forget.

His signature has always been his voice. When Ray leaves this chamber, we will lose I believe the best voice in the Senate.

The second attribute is Ray's joy of politics. I remember in the early 1960s and 1970s the man in the United States who best exemplified the joy of politics, who had a great voice and was a great speaker, Senator Hubert Humphrey. He could speak endlessly on any topic at any time in a wonderful way. He had a marvelous sonorous voice that one could never forget. He was a small-L liberal. For me, Ray had all of those talents in abundance.

Finally, honourable senators, we will all miss Ray's modest demeanour. The word "honourable" is a rich, wonderful-sounding word. I cannot think of another senator who so exemplifies the words "honourable senator."

Ray, we will miss you. As the Bible says, "Go from strength to strength," with your lovely wife, Barbara.

AL WAXMAN, O.C.: EULOGY

February 6, 2001

Hon. Jerahmiel S. Grafstein: Honourable senators, I rise in tribute to the late Al Waxman. Acting can be the most perilous of professions. An actor's persona becomes someone else's commodity, always at risk to the vagaries of public taste. Choices give way to the imperative of work and work in turn becomes fodder for criticism. To be an actor demands hidden reserves of confidence to overcome obstacles to recognition.

Behind the sparkling smile, Al Waxman husbanded this hidden confidence in abundance. Recently I wrote Al a long, discursive letter about his zestful autobiography. I quickly received a moving and cheery call. Al and I had been friends for over 40 years, since our student days at Western and then at the University of Toronto Law School in the 1950s. When we next met, Al laughingly said to me, "Think of it, Jerry. You are a failed actor and I am a failed lawyer. Now, who has had the more successful career?"

"You, Al," I said, "you, of course."

Back in the 1950s, Al chose insecurity over security, succeeding beyond anyone's imagination except his own. He never stopped working. His career resonated from acting to directing and even to songwriting, from *King of Kensington* to directing *Anne Frank*. From starring in *Death of a Salesman* to the avuncular police captain in *Cagney & Lacey*, Al never stopped improving.

My favourite was his portrayal of the venal Jack Adams in the hockey classic, *Net Worth*. For you see, he was inoculated early with the Talmudic gene for the endless search for personal perfection.

So let us all mark his cenotaph. Rarely does any actor transcend his time and place in Canada as Al did. He was quintessentially Canadian, choosing to live and work here though the lure of New York, Hollywood and even London beckoned. Nothing so exemplified Al's quest for personal perfection than the role he was slated to star in this summer at Stratford. He was to play the controversial Shylock in *The Merchant of*

Venice. He reckoned this posed a great critical risk. He was obsessed with striking the appropriate artistic balance, and so he did what he always did: He studied. He was never an accidental artist.

Honourable senators, Al Waxman was more. He owned other gifts. He had the gift of friendship and the gift of giving. There was no charitable event across Canada too large or none too small that he would not help.

Al, like all actors, vacillated between the hunger for celebrity and the hunger for self-improvement. Yet he never wavered in his gift of giving. He lived the Judaic ideal that dictates that charity is the highest human act of all.

May I tell one small political story, honourable senators. In the first Lastman campaign for mayor of Toronto, I asked Al to participate in a cultural task force to craft a cultural policy for the new Toronto. This, I thought, was necessary to counter the overwhelming support that Lastman's opponent was receiving from the cultural establishment in Toronto. Al joined our group with gusto and imagination. When Lastman's campaign badly sagged a week before the election date, Al called and said, "Let me take him out for a walk around Kensington to pick us his spirit and see if we can boost his numbers."

Al felt his celebrity would rub off. True to his word, Al did exactly that. He "mainstreeted" with Lastman and was instrumental in helping turn around the faltering Lastman campaign. Everyone knew Mel, but everyone loved Al.

The day after the election, Al called me and said, "Now, let's put that cultural policy in practice." He never stopped working.

Al loved his profession, but above all he loved his family. When his wife, Sarah, told me that he had died of heart failure, I told her, "That simply could not be. Al's heart could never fail."

Al, we are still dismayed that you left us so abruptly. We are still angry we were robbed, so prematurely, of your gift of company. So now, all I can say to you is, "Al, go to heaven."

May I conclude with a quote from Scriptures: "See the man who is diligent in his work. He shall stand before kings."

Al did and was.

GILDAS MOLGAT: EULOGY

March 1, 2001

Hon. Jerahmiel S. Grafstein: Honourable senators, politics, like the human condition, like character, has a dark and a sunny side. For me, the late most Honourable Gildas Molgat represented the very best in politics - the sunny side of politics, the politics of joy.

I first met Gil four decades ago in the early 1960s when I travelled to Winnipeg for a Liberal Party meeting. Gil was then Leader of the Liberal Party and Leader of the Opposition in Manitoba. Three things immediately struck me when I first met him: first and foremost, his sunny, smiling disposition; second, his sensitive interpersonal skills; and, third, his fluent, articulate and easy bilingualism.

Leading the opposition in Manitoba can be a lonely, difficult task. Gil was able to enter the cut and thrust of politics in that province, never losing his gentle and graceful manner.

The next event I recall was the dark and difficult period of the debates in this chamber on the GST, as alluded to today by the Leader of the Opposition in the Senate. Gil was the deputy leader at the time. He was most unhappy with the unruliness of the debate and the unseemly conduct on both sides. It was so out of keeping with his personal predilection to resolve issues by careful, quiet and fair diplomacy. Throughout that raucous period, he remained a man of deliberation and honour, convinced in his convictions, certain in his principles about the role of the Senate as a chamber of sober second thought.

Gil's career as a senator was exemplary. His innate skills shone through when it came his time to act as Joint Chair of the Special Committee on the Constitution. The other Co-Chair, you will recall, was another late great friend of ours, Mark MacGuigan. Their report was called the MacGuigan-Molgat report. Many ideas from that report were later incorporated in the Constitution of 1982. Then in the Special Joint Committee on the Reform of the Senate, Gil joined with Paul Cosgrove, Member of

Parliament for Scarborough, as co-chairs. That report, as others have mentioned, still bears reading today.

Who can forget the great dignity Gil lent to the chamber as Chair of the Committee of the Whole on the Meech Lake Constitutional Accord when Mr. Trudeau made his last memorable appearance in Parliament here on the floor of the Senate?

Incredibly, after being President of the Liberal Party, whip of the Senate, Deputy Leader of the Senate, Deputy Speaker of the Senate and, finally in 1994, as Speaker of the Senate, Gil continued to grow in stature on every task he undertook, large or small. As Speaker of the Senate, he was unparalleled in dignity, integrity and objectivity. The careful scholarship he brought to the opinions of the Speaker was not a facile pose.

Honourable senators, the role of the Speaker is never an easy one. Appointed under the Parliament Act by the Prime Minister, it is always difficult to separate one's loyalty and allegiance and still maintain the independence, integrity and objectivity required by the duties of that office. Yet, this is precisely what Gil did. Recently, when importuned to vote on a thoroughly contentious matter, he refused. Principle and integrity overruled the natural pull of loyalty and allegiance.

The full story of Gil Molgat as Speaker is yet to be told, but those of us who know only parts of his story will forever admire his invincible integrity. Gil Molgat, soldier, businessman, scholar, politician, diplomat, was a leader in all facets of his career, rising from the bottom to the top by the dint of his own energy and his own honour.

Honourable senators, "honour" is a word much used and much abused. Gil lived and died a man of honour. What better tribute can his colleagues here in the Senate pay to him?

In 1770, the great English parliamentarian Thomas Burke noted:

> It is the business of the speculative philosopher to mark the proper ends of government. It is the business of the politician who is the philosopher in action to find out proper means towards those ends, and employ them with effect.

Gil was relentless in his search for the proper means to make politics a profession of honour.

Honor virtutis praemium: Honour is the reward of virtue. So said Cicero. So say we about Gil Molgat.

EULOGY FOR THE LATE ROY ABRAHAM FAIBISH
MORTLAKE MORTUARY, WEST LONDON, ENGLAND

March 12, 2001

Barbara, Kristin, David, Holly and friends:

There is something awfully wrong here. I always believed that Roy would go on forever, cajoling, nagging, goading, even inspiring us, to the very end, as he did for over 40 years; that he would sprinkle dirt over me. The good die young, I taunted him.

What vocabulary can we adopt to describe our dearest friend Roy, who loved words so much. What would Roy say? What would Roy think? Where is he? And now we discover, to our chagrin, that we must fend for ourselves, alone.

Roy had a memory that refused to forget or forgive. As Elie Wiesel wrote, "For a Jew to forget is for a Jew to deny." Roy simply could not forget or forgive. Was it his capacious memory that caused him so much anguish because he could see clearer and farther than all of us. Perhaps Roy was frightened because he could see things too clearly. Was the endless flood of emails his way of relieving his inner torment and rage at a world that could do better? For Roy was a teacher and he taught us many things.

Early, he grasped the enonnity of China and its future leadership on the world stage. He hectored us to read books with great and delicate care. How he loved books. How many times I excitedly rushed to read a new book only to discover that Roy had already read the book, dissected it and discarded it. For he was, after all a child of the *"People of the Book"* and he loved and lived for books.

For some there are no questions. For others, there are no answers but Roy always divined both the right question and the right answer.

So our world grew darker and duller as the shadow of Roy's death passed over us. That bright, remorseless, pulsating light bursting with ideas is with us no more to rage against the gloom.

Just as Roy haunted us in life, he haunts us in death. What was the mystery of that relentless intellectual energy? Was the mystery hidden in the luminous caverns of his memory; or his obsession with truth; or his penchant for historical fact; or his unabiding hatred of racism; or his abhorrence of anti-Semitism; or is it buried deep in his inexhaustible need to explore his Jewish roots.

What was the basis of his limitless generosity to friends and to forgotten projects forsaken by others. And what of his unbridled hatred of Germans or Croats that he would never forgive or even his distaste for what he called "Black Hats." Yes, Roy was harsh on his friends, even rude to those who did not share his bias or fell below his expectations. Yet he was always harsher on himself. He would brook nothing less than clarity of thought.

Once, not too long ago I laboured long and hard over notes for a very short speech. Before delivery, I sent them to Roy for his comments. I heard nothing. This was most unusual so I called him as I frequently did and asked him what he thought. There was a long pause. "You Senator, you know better. You could do better." As usual, Roy was right. Roy expected much from his friends.

So the mystery of Roy continues to haunt us still. Exactly, what are we to do with this incalculable loss.

Kaddish, the ancient Hebrew mourner's prayer, in fact a celebration of life, starts with the words "Yiskadel Vyiskaddash, Shema Rabo", Magnify and Sanctify the Holy Name. Why Magnify? Why Magnify the Holy Name, which is limitless and beyond measurement asked Talmudic scholars through the ages?

The second Przysucha Rebbe, Simcha Bunim, A.H.L. the early 19th century Hassidic Master (who preferred rationalism to mysticism), and my great grandfather's Mentor, explained:

> When one of the Chosen die, one of the Chosen few, each death is so precious and the loss so immeasurable that the survivors must Magnify the Holy Name all the more to make up for the loss of even one such precious soul.

For Roy then, we must all especially Magnify the Holy Name.

So Roy, in this world:

> Your race is run,
> Your duties done,
> Your battles won;
> Now come to peace.

Barbara confided that now Roy may have finally found peace.

Barbara dear, I respectfully disagree. When Roy encounters the *Robono Shel Olam*, the Master of the Universe as he enters the grand celestial court, he will give him no peace. He will demand that he explain himself, to account for the misery of the last century. So the great debate will begin. Roy will give no quarter and ask none for eternity. Watch for the lightning and listen for the thunder.

Maybe Roy was like the great Rebbe, Simcha Bunim a.h.l after all. Or better the Kotzer Rebbe who wrote a book entitled *"The Book of Man."* The book was meant to include everything, everything concerning life and mankind, history and faith, the past and the future, and as Elie Wiesel describes, the grandiose project whose stunning aspect was that the author wanted his book to consist of one page alone. So every day he wrote a page and every evening he burnt it. And then started again.

This was so like Roy who wanted incessantly to correct the evils of this world and died always trying.

The day before his death I received my second last discursive email - one page, crammed with the history of the Ohel Rachel, the oldest Synagogue extant in Shanghai. I had asked him to use his good offices with the Chinese officials to restore its use to the Jewish Lubavitch community there.

Before drawing to a close, there was one thing about Roy that was clear and true. There was no mystery. Roy's love of Barbara. And more, Roy respected Barbara. He took such special pride in her accomplishments.

And Barbara's love and empathy and fortitude made way for Roy's needs.

Barbara let Roy be Roy!

Their relationship was a marvel to behold. And so we are all endlessly in her debt.

Roy did not have much time for the Greeks, for he knew too well their tortious and tortuous history. Nevertheless, Roy will forgive me if I end with a final thought from Aesychylus.

> "God whose law it is that he who learns must suffer. And even in our sleep, pain that cannot forget , falls drop by drop upon the heart, and in our own despair, comes wisdom to us by the awful grace of God."

Roy, we hardly knew you. We will never be able to forget you.

Stay with us forever, dearest Roy. Do not abandon us.

And let us say, Amen.

ROY ABRAHAM FAIBISH: EULOGY

March 15, 2001

Hon. Jerahmiel S. Grafstein: Honourable senators, the world of ideas is darker and duller with the sudden passage of Roy Faibish last week in London.

Roy was a friend and mentor for over 40 years. Rarely a week went by that we were not in contact by phone, fax or email. Roy was a genius. He was one of those remarkable yet unheralded Canadians who inoculated and stimulated public dialogue with some of the great policy ideas of the last five decades.

Born in a small town in Saskatchewan, educated at Queen's University, he served in the RCAF with distinction then found himself, first, co-opted to Alvin Hamilton as policy adviser and then as a speech writer and idea man for John Diefenbaker, an old family friend.

The Road to Resources, a National Power Grid, the opening to China in the 1950s, to name only a few, were all ideas that he generated. As a confidant and adviser to John Diefenbaker, Pierre Trudeau, Brian Mulroney and even Margaret Thatcher, he was unparalleled in the reach of his ideas.

Roy was a man of legendary generosity and loyalty.

While Roy was ecumenical when it came to people, he had little patience for Liberals, whom he felt lacked vision, with the exception perhaps of the late Paul Martin, Sr., and Pierre Trudeau. He was a Sir John A. Macdonald Conservative who dreamed great dreams of bringing Canada together from sea to sea to sea by massive development projects on the ground and for the mind. Roy owned great loves and harboured great hates. He hated anti-Semitism, and he abhorred racism and those who were soft on bringing war criminals to justice. He was a restless and rude seeker of the truth with whomever he encountered.

Roy refused senior positions in government, including a Senate seat. After a long career as a broadcaster and catalyst, he joined the CRTC as Vice-Chairman. Together with luminaries such as Jean-Louis Gagnon, that great Quebec crusader, Northrop

Frye and Fernand Cadieux, he helped transform the Canadian broadcasting and tele-communications landscape. His written dissents are still worth reading.

Twenty years ago, Roy decided to settle in England. He lived in a flat close to the London Library, which became his home away from home. He then bought a home on the coast in Northern Ireland where he retreated to recharge his batteries.

With the advent of email, my regular contact with Roy turned into a flood of daily email that pulsated through his unparalleled international intellectual network. Many so-called media moguls and newspaper pundits across Asia, North America and Europe owed their ideas to Roy, rarely with attribution. To Roy, ideas were like oxygen that filled every room he entered. To be his friend meant you were held more strictly accountable to rigorous standards of intellectual scrutiny. Whether it was Isaiah Berlin, Henry Kissinger, Zhou Enlai, Serge Klarsfeld, Pierre Trudeau or Brian Mulroney, all were swayed by his magnetic ideas. He loved books and he loved the spoken word. He was an "old China hand" and because of his deep interest drew many, including myself, into the mysteries of China. He knew poetry, political philosophy, literature, aesthetics, wine, theology, theosophy, quantum physics and technology. There is no area of intellectual interest that his probing curiosity did not explore in depth.

His passage leaves a vacuum in all those who came to know and admire him. Last week, at his funeral in London, I told his wife, Barbara, that I disagreed when she confided that Roy had finally found peace. When Roy encounters the Master of the Universe as he enters the grand celestial court, he will immediately demand an explanation - an accounting for all the misery of the last century. Then the great debate in the sky will begin. Watch for the thunder and lightening. Roy will give no quarter and ask no quarter. Roy had so many facets to his personality that he remains a mystery to even his closest friends.

Roy, we hardly knew you. The world is better, brighter and clearer for your sojourn here. Missed, you will always be.

TRIBUTE TO THE LATE ROY FAIBISH

May 5, 2001

Barbara, Kristin, David, Holly and friends. Almost 2 months have past since we heard of Roy's abrupt departure.

Roy was a man of so many talents - iconoclast, broadcaster, philosopher, speech writer, essayist, film consultant, producer, thinker, regulator, reader - the ultimate polymath.

Let me repeat, in part, the words of eulogy I gave in England. Perhaps, because of the vitality and endless flow of email and faxes I received from Roy, sometimes made more dramatic by exclamatory telephone calls, we always believed that Roy would go on forever, cajoling, nagging, goading, ever inspiring us to the very end, as he did for me for over 40 years; that he would sprinkle dirt over me. The good die young, I taunted him.

What vocabulary can we adopt to describe Roy, who loved words so much. What would Roy say? What would Roy think? Where is he? And now we discover, to our chagrin, that the taunting and daunting emails are no more. Now we must fend for ourselves to fill the void of Roy's capacious erudition.

Roy had a memory that refused to forget or sometimes made more dramatic by exclamatory and is for a Jew to deny. Roy simply could not forget or forgive. Was it his capacious memory that caused him so much anguish because he could see clearer and farther than all of us? Perhaps Roy was frightened because he could see things too clearly. Was the endless flood of emails his way of relieving his inner torment and toil, and rage at a world that he knew could do better? Roy, at heart, was a teacher and he taught us all many things.

Roy travelled the political spectrum from left to right. He was an early admirer of John Diefenbaker whom he knew as a youngster growing up in Saskatchewan. He worked for Tommy Douglas, then headed to Ottawa. He went to Ottawa as political activist and wrote speeches and policy papers for Mr. Diefenbaker. The "Northern

Vision" and the "Roads to Resources", part of Diefenbaker's Northern development policies, were phrases Roy coined that entered the Canadian political lexicon.

As Executive Assistant to Alvin Hamilton, Agriculture Minister in the Diefenbaker Cabinet, Roy orchestrated the first wheat deals to China in 1961 and attended with Mr. Hamilton on his first visit to Red China, deepening the wide net of contacts within the Communist hierarchy.

Early, he grasped the enormity of China and its future leadership on the world stage. "Why waste time studying and regurgitating Europe?" he admonished me in the early '60s. "Spend time studying China - the future is China". He hectored us to read books with great and delicate care. How he loved books. How many times I excitedly rushed to read a new book only to discover that Roy had already read the book, dissected it and discarded it. For he was, after all, a child of the "People of the Book" and he loved and lived for books. Every place he lived was crammed with books.

Roy's greatest delight came when he was made a Member of the Reading Room Committee of the London Library where he spent countless hours reading each week, devouring books old and new, when he lived in London.

We share a deep reverence for the late Fernand Cadieux. Only Cadieux could match Roy in the breadth and depth of his intellectualism and the knowledge of the great European and Asian philosophic masters which they both grasped and could relate to modern society concisely.

For some, there are no questions. For others, there are no answers, but Roy always divined both the right question and the right answer. Jewish sages remind us that, if we can find the right question, it answers itself!

So our world has grown darker and duller as the shadow of Roy's death passed over us. That bright, remorseless, pulsating light bursting with ideas is with us no more to rage against the gloom.

Just as Roy haunted us in life, he haunts us in death. What was the mystery of that relentless intellectual energy? Was the mystery hidden in the luminous caverns of his memory; or his obsession with truth; or his penchant for historical fact; or his unabiding hatred of racism; or his abhorrence of anti-Semitism; or is it buried deep in his inexhaustible need to explore his Jewish roots?

What was the basis of his limitless generosity to friends and to forgotten projects forsaken by others?

And what of his unbridled hatred of Germans or Croats that he would never forgive or even his distaste for what he called "Black Hats". Yes, Roy was harsh on his friends, even rude to those who did not share his bias or fell below his expectations. Yet he was always harsher on himself. He would brook nothing less than clarity of thought.

Once, not too long ago, I laboured long and hard over notes for a very short speech. Before delivery, I sent them to Roy for his comments. I heard nothing. This was most unusual so I called him as I frequently did and asked him what he thought. There was a long pause. "You Senator, you know better. You could do better." As usual, Roy was right. Roy expected much from his friends.

So the mystery of Roy continues to haunt us still.

Exactly, what are we to do with this incalculable loss?

When I learned of Roy's passing, Barbara confided that now Roy may have finally found peace. I respectfully disagreed. When Roy encounters the "Robono Shel Olam", the Master of the Universe as he enters the grand celestial court, he will give him no peace. He will demand that he explain himself, to account for the misery of the last century. So the great debate will begin. Roy will give no quarter and ask none for eternity. Watch for the lightning and listen for the thunder.

Maybe Roy was like the great Rebbe, the driven Kotzer, after all. The Kotzer believed if you could sum up Judaism in one word "truth" - EMAS. Rebbe Kotzer wrote a book entitled *The Book of Man*.

The book was meant to include everything, everything concerning life and mankind, history and faith, the past and the future, and as Elie Wiesel describes, the grandiose project whose stunning aspect was that the author wanted his book to consist of one page alone. So every day he wrote a page and every evening he burnt it. And then started again.

This was so like Roy who wanted incessantly to correct the evils of this world, to tell the truth and died always trying. The day before his death I received my second last discursive email - one page, crammed with the history of the Ohel Rachel, the oldest Synagogue extant in Shanghai. I had asked him to use his good offices with the Chinese officials to restore its use to the Jewish Lubavitch community there.

One word about Barbara. Barbara's love and empathy and fortitude made way for Roy's needs.

Barbara let Roy be Roy!

Their relationship was a marvel to behold. And so we are all endlessly in her debt.

With some distance from Roy's death, now that the shock has worn off, I came back from his funeral and rummaged through my 'Faibish' files and a chaotic picture emerges in my mind's eye about Roy, about the inner peace that could find no rest.

Roy was a good friend. He knew his friends better than they knew themselves. But Roy was not an easy friend. Roy demanded more from his friends than his demons, those inner foes fighting against his soul. Just what were these demands, which were always so urgent, immediate and consuming? Read a book right away! Send a cheque to an impoverished student who is doing esoteric research about Moldavia. Write a letter to an old Chinese revolutionary in fading health. He did a job for a recent academic refugee. Make a speech on Israel, make a speech on Canada's lack of development projects.

His letters, replete with barbs were erudite, rude, pitted with vitriol. As Roy harboured great love, he amplified his great hates. He hated silence, silence on the Krauts, or the Germans, or the French, or the Church. He criticized the silence on the Holocaust.

He made studies on war criminals, how they got away in law. When my son attended Oxford as a Rhodes Scholar, Roy he sent him a five-volume history on the Holocaust.

But Roy's great loves could blind him as well.

He found China could do no wrong. As the Tianamen Square massacre occurred, he traveled to China, visited the morgues and jails, learning the precise facts about who was hurt, who were killed and who were imprisoned. He came back dismayed, yet still enchanted with China.

He was enthralled by the poems of Anne Carson, the literate Canadian Poet. He loved Darwin and Yeats. And, while he loved the new poetry, he loved Yeats the most. He loved long, chatty lunches or dining on fine cuisine. He loved great wines. So, as I look back, I marvel at his great loves and his great hates.

Roy did not have much time for the Greeks, for he knew too well their tortuous history. Nevertheless, Roy will forgive me if I end with a final thought from Aesychylus.

"God whose law it is that he who learns must suffer. And even in our sleep, pain that cannot forget, falls drop by drop upon the heart, and in our own despair, comes wisdom to us by the awful grace of God."

Roy, with his capacious memory, refused to allow us to forget the evil past and he forced us to remember. To end with Roy's own words. I was preparing a book, an anthology on the Canadian writers' views of the Holocaust. I sought Roy's advice and begged him to write a chapter. He refused. Instead he sent me a letter which I published in the book. Let me read it:

"Dear Jerry:

The task you have set for me is too awesome, too awful, and too dreadful. It is beyond expression for me and I am unable to comply.

I am told that about one hundred thousand survived out of the six million Jews who were rounded up and sent to their deaths in Hitler's extermination and concentration camps.

This was in 1945. By 1945, my family had not yet recovered from relatives murdered by the Cossacks in the Great Peasant's Revolt in Modavia in 1907. Nor had they recovered from the murder of my great-grandfather by the Nazis in Jassy in 1943. By 1945, word was just coming through to my grandmother in New York that just two out of seven relatives who had been dragged off to Draney on July 16, 1942, by the Special Paris Police had survived the German camps in Poland.

By 1945, the family had not recovered from the telegram that told them that my uncle had been killed at Caen on July 18, 1944.

But in 1945, I was only seventeen, living safely in Saskatchewan. I am told that the last words of the distinguished octogenarian Jewish historian Simon Dubnov, as he stum-

bled through the streets of Riga in 1941 and was shot dead by the Gestapo, were 'Write! And record!'

I am sure his plea was to 'witnesses and survivors' of the 'Final Solution'; to 'poets and historians' of the future. I am none of these.

But of all the tens of thousands of pages that I have read by them about the Holocaust in my attempt to try to understand the Nazi evil and their racial hatred, the words of Primo Levi have left the deepest impression.

Levi ended his life when he could not bear the pain and the memory any longer. He refused to try to, understand the evil and the hatred that led to the 'Final Solution,' because, he said before his death, 'to understand is almost to justify.'

Roy Faibish"

We still cannot understand Roy. It is easy to justify his rightness, ideas and compelling personality that will never rest, or die, in the memory of his friends.

Roy, we hardly knew you. We will never be able to forget you. Stay with us forever, dearest Roy. Do not abandon us.

And let us say, Amen.

ERMINIE J. COHEN: ON RETIREMENT

June 12, 2001

Senator Grafstein: Because I barely knew Senator Cohen before she entered this chamber. I did not know her at all until she came here and I asked about her. I was told by my colleagues from New Brunswick that she had an outstanding reputation. I became more respectful as I watched her work here and watched her debate matters in this house on the side of minorities and others. In my view, her participation in the Senate is commendable.

Honourable senators, when one is stuck with not being able to match the eloquence of others, the best thing one can do is turn to the Bible for guidance. What type of salutation can one offer an auspicious person when they move on to another life or a different life? The best one that I could come across was the salutation that is traditionally given echoing Moses. Moses, as you know, lived to 120 years, so the normal salutation one would give is, "May you live to 120 years." However, on a deeper examination of the Bible, one understands that salutation is not an appropriate one for a woman.

Therefore, what is the appropriate salutation for an auspicious woman, a "woman of valour," as Senator Finestone has called her? If you turn to the Bible, there is a deeper and better salutation for Sarah. Sarah was the first of the four mothers, and she lived to 137 years. Therefore, the salutation one should direct to an auspicious woman is, "May you live to 137 years. May your life be long and fruitful." The word "joy" in Hebrew translates to the word "simcha." My father's name was Simcha. It means joy. The best salutation one can give you in addition to all that is, "May you have much joy, only simcha in the years ahead."

CHARLES BRADLEY TEMPLETON: EULOGY

June 13, 2001

Hon. Jerahmiel S. Grafstein: Honourable senators, I wish to make a brief tribute to the late Charles Templeton. He passed away last week.

As honourable senators are aware, Charles Templeton was an outstanding journalist, writer, editor, play write, actor, broadcaster, artist and politician. It is about his political career that I wish to comment briefly.

Mr. Templeton decided in the early 1960s to seek the leadership of the Liberal Party. I was actively engaged in the Liberal Party in those days and supported a former colleague of ours, Mr. Andrew Thompson, who was also seeking the leadership of the Liberal Party.

The only reason I wish to comment is that at the Liberal convention, Charles Templeton, who was a magnificent speaker and broadcaster, made one of the most outstanding political addresses I have ever heard, before or since. It was my task to help Mr. Thompson prepare his speech for that particular event. While Mr. Thompson did not reach the eloquence of Mr. Templeton, he certainly matched it in the same arena. I say that because had Mr. Thompson not stood up to the test and matched at least the level of the topic of Mr. Templeton, Mr. Templeton would have become the leader of the Liberal Party and history would have changed and history in this chamber would have changed.

I wish Mr. Templeton's family my heartiest and sincerest condolences. He was a great Canadian, a great speaker, and in time he could have been a great politician.

ON GENOCIDE OF ARMENIANS

June 13, 2001

Hon. Jerahmiel S. Grafstein: Honourable senators, this awesome resolution placed before the Senate by Senators Maheu and Setlakwe compels each and every senator to independently examine whether the frightful designation of genocide, ethical and legal, applies to the Armenian question of 1915 and the events following.

First history, first facts, and then policy. History tells us that Armenians have lived in the land of the Middle East from the shores of the Black Sea to those of the Caspian along the Mediterranean for millennia.

The Hon. the Speaker: I regret to interrupt Honourable Senator Grafstein, but I must bring attention to the fact that it is now six o'clock and I am obliged to leave the Chair unless honourable senators agree not to see the clock.

Hon. Fernand Robichaud (Deputy Leader of the Government): Honourable senators, I move that we not see the clock.

The Hon. the Speaker: Do honourable senators agree that we not see the clock?

Hon. Senators: Agreed.

Senator Grafstein: Millions have resided under various regimes since the independent Kingdom of Cicilia, the first Armenian Kingdom, which fell in 1375. Over the years the lands of Armenia were divided, re-divided, partitioned and re-partitioned into what is known as the Turkish Provinces, largely inhabited by Armenians, and Russian Armenia, now the Republic of Armenia, the largest portion of lands lying within the boundaries of modern-day Turkey. In the Caucasus, in addition to Armenia, Azerbaijan and Nagomo-Karabakh still obviously have a substantial population of Armenian descent. As you know, Nagomo-Karabakh remains a simmering problem to this very day.

Certain of the Balkan peoples emerged in the last half of the 19th century as nation states. The Armenian Question, however, within the Ottoman Empire, now the modern Turkish state, took a different and very revolting course.

Following the Russian-Turkish War of 1877-78, Article 16 was introduced under the Treaty of Berlin. Under that article, the Ottoman authorities were required to undertake local reforms in the provinces inhabited primarily by the Armenians and guarantee their security. Thus, as many historians have suggested, the Armenian Question was launched in the sea of international law in the modern era.

The evidence appears overwhelming that the Ottoman Empire would not implement its treaty obligations respecting Armenian human rights. In 1895-96, the Ottoman Empire provoked or allowed a series of massacres, with a cost of lives estimated to range from a low of 40,000 to a better number of around 300,000 Armenians. These massacres triggered a public outcry in the West, especially in England and France.

As a result of these massacres, Armenians contend that they resorted to self-defence for the preservation of their human rights. In their desire for independent status, Armenian discontent within the Ottoman Empire animated discontent amongst the Turks themselves for greater rights. The Ottoman authorities vacillated over the history of time toward its minorities, including the Armenians, sometimes protecting them and other times provoking violence and bloodshed.

A coup d'etat was staged in the Ottoman Empire on July 10, 1908. In the result, the Ottoman Empire adopted a constitution for the first time. Armenians anticipated that under a constitution, reforms would be introduced in the Armenian provinces to respect their linguistic and religious rights. The so called Eastern Question, in effect, primarily the eastern portion of modern Turkey, was again placed on the international agenda after the combined forces of Bulgaria, Romania, Greece and Serbia, all seeking greater "lebensraum," attacked the Ottoman state and defeated her, having reached within 25 kilometres of Constantinople, now Istanbul, in 1913. This violent interlude was called the Balkan Wars. Religion and nationalism combined with Christian nationalism to forment the historic claims of greater ethnic nation states. The operative political cry was the word "greater"; Greater Bulgaria, Greater Romania, Greater Greece and Greater Serbia, mostly at the cost of the Ottoman territories. Echoes of that nationalist agenda persist to this very day.

The European Powers met in Bucharest and London after the Balkan Wars to discuss peace terms between Turkey and the Balkan States which resulted in a peace settlement that ratified the loss of Turkish territory to Greece, Serbia and Bulgaria. The so-called Eastern Question was not resolved. The Eastern Question substantiated the Armenian claims, but the Eastern Question, respecting Christian Armenia, was never resolved.

Under constitutional Turkey led by the Young Turks, the divisions of powers from the central organs of state to those of provinces or regions substantiated by the Armenians within Turkey was never fully or fairly introduced. They never received what they were entitled to by those treaties. The question of internal autonomy of the eastern provinces, primarily occupied by Armenians within Turkey within the proposed reforms for protection of linguistic and religious rights, continue to be outstanding.

On July 3, 1913, at the initiative of the Russians, ambassadors met in Constantinople where they agreed to divide the seven provinces, those substantially inhabited by Armenians, into two parts within Turkey. On September 3, 1913, at a London conference, the decision included two administrative units, two inspector generals appointed by the great powers and agreed to by the Sultan. The two administrative units would each have a general assembly with Christians and Muslims represented equally. They would have the power to appoint and discharge officials. The administrative and judicial personnel, and police officers would be recruited from Christians and Muslims equally, reserving for the great powers the right to control and implement reforms through their ambassadors.

On February 8, 1914, Russia and Turkey signed an agreement giving effect to the above, and two inspector generals, one Dutchman and one Norwegian, were appointed. In July 1914, the inspectors were on their way to their posts when the First World War broke out. Turkey entered the war on October 12, 1914, on the side of the Germans against the Allies of the West - Britain, France and Czarist Russia. The inspector generals never reached their destinations. The question of Armenian reforms was then suspended.

In this interlude, the Turkish government then, apparently, based on the evidence presented on the history record, commenced a policy of mass execution, torture and forced displacement of Armenians, which in turn resulted in Armenian refugees seeking to leave Turkish lands.

Many Canadians and Americans of Armenian descent trace their origins to this and earlier Armenian refugee streams. On April 24, 1915, mass arrests of prominent Armenians, the intellectual and political elites, were made in Constantinople and in the eastern provinces. Many were tortured and murdered. Many were essentially displaced to Anatolia and beyond to Syria, Lebanon, Iraq, Persia and the Caucasus, where many perished either along the way or upon arrival.

Young Armenians drafted into the army were disarmed and transferred to labour battalions. Later, they were massacred in groups, leaving the Armenian population largely defenceless and subjected to forced displacement, deportation and massacres. Many were burnt alive in their villages and towns.

Many of those deported were comprised of old men, women and children. Upon reaching their desert displacement destinations, they were once more subjected to wholesale massacres in certain places, in particular a village called Musa Dagh, which attained special significance. I will return to that in a moment.

The Turks were joined by the Kurds and others in the slaughter, rape and pillage of these Armenian refugee streams. Having heard of the fate of their fellow Armenians and co-religionists, many could only offer feeble self-defence. A portion of the Armenian population died a tragic death in defence of their fellow Armenians.

I will take a brief aside, honourable senators, to say that in 1929, as Senator Joyal pointed out, Franz Werfel, a famous Czech writer, wrote a shocking book that he called *The Forty Days of Musa Dagh*. It was published in German in 1933. Shortly thereafter, the Nazis burned that book, along with others - a tragic but ironic fate.

Within the Ottoman frontiers, the policy of extermination and deportation continued, with the exceptions of Constantinople and Izmir. Massacres subsequently took place in Izmir, when the Turks defeated the Greeks and re-occupied that city in 1922. As a result of these massacres and deportations in Turkey, from 1915 and subsequent years, it is estimated that about half of the Armenian population - from a very low estimate of 800,000 to at least 1.5 million - perished, while the other half escaped to the mountains and were rescued by advancing Red Russians.

Many Armenians joined the Russians and many retreated to Russian Armenia while the struggle continued against the Turks. During World War II, Armenians primarily fought on the side of the Allies, with the high expectation that the promises made during the war would emerge, as Turkey was an enemy of the Allies. According to some figures, over 200,000 Armenians volunteered in the Russian Army, 20,000 Armenians fought on the Caucasian front, and another 5,000 Armenian volunteers fought with the French and the British as a separate unit in areas now known as Lebanon, Syria, Iraq, Israel and Transjordan. The British, French and Russian military leaders all applauded the soldiering of Armenians.

With the 1917 Russian Revolution, the territories in the Caucasus, known as Russian Armenia, established a provisional government to be known as the Soviet Republic of Armenia. After October 1917, when the great Czarist army dissolved as a result of the Russian Revolution, the Armenians continued fighting in the eastern regions of Turkey and gradually retreated until they reached the old Russian-Turkish border.

Under the Treaty of Brest-Litovsk on March 3, 1918, Turkey was given back its eastern provinces. On June 4, 1918, the Turks signed a peace treaty with Armenia in Batum and recognized the independent Republic of Armenia, located in the Caucasus. Under the Treaty of Sevres, in 1920, which designated the peace treaty with Turkey, this treaty recognized the rights of Armenians because of their military contribution especially against the Turks in the Caucasus.

After the withdrawal of Russian forces, thus delaying the Turkish-German occupation of Baku, the oil centre in the Caucasus, one month after the Treaty of Sevres, on September 20, Turkey attacked the Republic of Armenia. Unaided by the Allied powers, Armenia succumbed on December 2, 1920. A third of that territory was annexed by the Turks while the eastern portion later became a Soviet Republic. You will recall that when Stalin took over, he joined Georgia, Armenia and Azerbaijan in the Caucasus under the Soviet hegemony. In 1923, under the Treaty of Lausanne, the Armenian question within Turkey was left as an unresolved matter.

Senators will forgive me if I sketched this complicated, tangled history too quickly. I hope that I have not taken history too much out of context due to the brevity of this exposition, but I have concluded, based on the overwhelming evidence, that genocide, as defined under conventional and customary international law, took place. Indeed, the Ottoman war trials did take place after these events, but I have not been able to get access to those records or those conclusions.

In 1915, within the territories now known as Turkey, the evidence appears to be overwhelming that such was the case that genocide did take place. Let me quote from a fascinating book of history entitled *Europe* by Norman Davies, an outstanding British historian, published in 1996, at page 909. The section I am quoting is entitled "Genocide."

> On 27 May 1915, the Ottoman Government decreed that the Armenian population of eastern Anatolia would be forcibly deported. The Armenians, who were Christians, were suspected of sympathizing with the Russian enemy on the Caucasian Front, and of planning a united Armenia under Russian protection. Some two to three million people were affected. Though accounts differ, one-third of them are thought to have been massacred; one-third to have perished during deportation; and one-third to have survived. The episode is often taken to be the first modern instance of mass genocide. At the treaty of Sevres...the Allied Powers recognized united Armenia as a sovereign republic. In practice, they allowed the country to be partitioned between Soviet Russia and Turkey.

Adolf Hitler was well aware of the Armenian precedent. When he briefed his generals...on the eve of the invasion of Poland, he revealed his plans for the Polish nation: These were his words:

> Genghis Khan had millions of women and men killed by his own will and with a gay heart. History sees him only as a great state-builder... I have sent my Death's Head units to the East with the order to kill without mercy men, women, and children of the Polish race or language. Only in such a way will we win the lebensraum that we need. Who, after all, speaks today of the annihilation of the Armenians?

The term "genocide", however, was not used before 1944, when it was coined by a Polish lawyer of Jewish origin, Rafael Lemkin, who was working in the USA. Lemkin's campaign to draw practical conclusions from the fate of Poland and of Poland's Jews was crowned in 1948 by the United Nations "Convention for the Prevention and Punishment of Genocide." Unfortunately, as the wars in ex-Yugoslavia have shown, the Convention in itself can neither prevent nor punish genocide.

Honourable senators, I thought, to be fair to myself, that I would not only give this version of history but that I would seek to find out what the Turks were saying about these events. I turn to an excellent book published recently, entitled *Turkey Unveiled: A History of Modern Turkey*, by Nicole and Hugh Pope.

The Hon. the Speaker pro tempore: Senator Grafstein, I am sorry to interrupt you but your speaking time is up. Are you asking for more time?

Senator Grafstein: I would ask for leave to continue.

The Hon. the Speaker pro tempore: Is leave granted, honourable senators?

Hon. Senators: Agreed.

Senator Grafstein: Honourable senators, this book was published in 1996. I think it is cogent to see what Turkey says about these events. I will read to you a paragraph and a half on page 42:

> ...Turkish schoolbooks do not dwell on the subject. Subsequent events on the Ottoman eastern front, so important in the formation of European and American attitudes to Turkey, earn at most a few dozen lines. The grim tone of the half-told story in a leading textbook leaves it open to many interpretations.

This is a quote from a recent Turkish textbook:

> The Russians used the Armenians as a cat's paw. Thinking they would achieve independence, they attacked their innocent Turkish neighbours. The Armenian "committees" massacred tens of thousands of Turkish men, women and children. This made it hard to wage war on the Russians. So the Ottoman state decided in 1915 forcibly to deport the Armenians from the battlefields to Syria. This was the right decision.

During the migration some of the Armenians lost their lives due to weather conditions and insecurity ...the Turkish Nation [original emphasis] is certainly not responsible for what happened during the Armenian migration. Thousands of Armenians arrived in Syria and there lived on under the protection of the Turkish state.

The authors conclude:

> To Turkish schoolchildren, and other visitors to Turkish "museums of barbarity" in the east, the impression is given that the massacres were committed solely by Armenians on Turks. Those Turks who know that massacres of

Armenians occurred are left to conclude that since the "Turkish Nation" was not at fault, the Kurdish tribes must have been to blame. The truth is not so reassuring.

I thought I would place that on the record because it is important to put this in some kind of historic context.

Beyond other claims under international law, beyond a finding of genocide, other claims, both conventional and customary, respecting the provinces of Eastern Turkey are a much more complex and difficult matter. The resolution, thankfully, does not compel me to address those questions.

Suffice it to say that contesting claims, in the absence of a thorough review, are unreasonable. Such claims, considered independently, makes it almost impossible without a thorough review to render a fair opinion. The issue of self-determination within the boundaries of a recognized state invoke, as we know, great complexities and matters beyond the scope of this resolution. Once "genocide" is concluded, I have not, in the time available, considered the legal consequences.

The question of responsibility, while primarily on the 1915 Turkish authorities, opens up other questions.

While complicity in these crimes adheres to the authorities and the participants at the time, it is difficult to extend sanctions to legal entities or individuals. The question of genocide, however, is not a retroactive question. Under international law, as declared by the Nuremberg Tribunal following the Second World War, genocide is considered contrary to natural law and therefore is not retroactive.

What can one do under the present circumstances?

Honourable senators, before addressing the consequences, may we revisit the Armenian question from yet another perspective. Let me add some historical points of reference that might capture more closely our Canadian attention.

In 1896, shortly after Winston Churchill was commissioned as an army officer in England, he attended the Alhambra Theatre in London with a fellow officer for an evening of theatre and enjoyment. An entertainer, inspired by Salisbury, then Prime Minister of England, and the new Russian Czar's clamour of concerns about the Armenian massacres of 1896, sang these words in his vaudevillian style:

Cease your preaching,
Load your guns.
Their roar our music tells,
The day has come for Britain's sons,
To seize the Dardanelles.

Winston Churchill leaned toward his friend and asked, "Where are the Dardanelles, exactly?" That word, "Dardanelles," had historic consequences for Churchill and the British Empire, including Canada and Australia, and is closely related to the Armenian question that we are debating today.

Let me return to 1914. The British Empire troops from Canada and Australia, together with France and England, had suffered over one million casualties on the bloody trench fields of France. We see the pictures above us. Political leadership in Canada, the Empire and Britain were frozen, trapped by geography and mass mobilization. What was required was a strategic imagination, a strategic vision, to break the endless slaughter in France. Hence, the idea of attacking Gallipoli on the Turkish Straits of the Dardanelles, attacking the soft back of the tottering Ottoman Empire, then a neutral power but leaning toward the German adversaries. This was a very important strategic vision for a union of a Christian and Balkan league of states, together with the British Empire, all seeking greater living room to match the religious ideas of greater Serbia, greater Bulgaria, greater Romania and greater Greece. On the east, Czarist Russia planned to occupy the eastern lands of the Ottoman Empire. The narrow tactic was to free the waterways from the Black Sea to the Aegean Sea through the Dardanelles by the occupation of Gallipoli.

The Greek Prime Minister of the day had first offered 60,000 troops to recapture the European side of the Ottoman Empire. The connection of the Black Sea to the Sea of Marmora and then the Dardanelles to the Aegean Sea would open the sea lanes for both Imperial Britain and Imperial Czarist Russia, and they could attack and occupy what was considered to be the strategic lynch pin, Constantinople. Turkey was weak and unpredictable.

I recount this history briefly because this will establish the atmosphere surrounding the massacre and deportation of Armenians, which they commemorate, on April 24, 1915, a day before the imperial English attack on Gallipoli on April 25, 1915.

In September 1914, Britain had stopped Turkish torpedo boats and discovered Germans aboard. The Germans had moved to mine the Dardanelles, darken the lighthouses and cripple water transit. This was a flagrant violation of international convention, guaranteeing free passage of those straits.

German cruisers, flying under Turkish colours, attacked the Czar's Black Sea ports. Turkey finally became a belligerent on the side of Germany. The word "Chanak," located on this perilous passageway, became a rallying cry in Canada and the West and a strategic point of British attack.

In the circumstances, the Imperial War Cabinet, including the Prime Minister of Canada, Henry Borden, the Prime Minister of South Africa, General Smuts, and the Prime Minister of Australia supported the British war cabinet in its strategic attack on Gallipoli.

The Greek King, Constantine, married to a German princess, worried about Bulgarian intentions and German reactions, vetoed the Greek Prime Minister's offer of troops, so Britain was left without troops.

On February 19, the British naval attack force attacked the outward Turkish force guarding the lips of the Dardanelles. The Turkish defenders fled. The British marines landed and the start of the strategic onslaught against Gallipoli was underway. The

Greeks had second thoughts. Seeing that the first attacks were successful, they now agreed to send troops. Turkey, encircled, looked doomed. The Greek government fell. The Russians were encountering difficulties at home, which ultimately led to the Russian Revolution two years later.

On March 18, 1915, the British naval attack resumed on the Dardanelles. On April 25, the day after April 24, commemorating the Armenian catastrophe, the Allies landed at Gallipoli. Before the year was out, the Allies suffered well over 250,000 casualties.

Churchill, now politically burned because of his support for the Gallipoli venture, ruminated to his friend Sir George Riddell on April 29, 1915. These words were found in Riddell's memoirs. Churchill said, as he looked at a map of the region, the following:

> This is one of the great Campaigns of History. Think what Constantinople is to the East. It is more than London, Paris and Berlin rolled into one. Think what its fall will mean. Think how it will affect Bulgaria, Greece, Romania and Italy, who have already been affected by what has taken place.

The dreams of a greater coalition of Christian nations still occupied Churchill's strategic imagination.

To the surprise of all, the Turks defended and held. While they did so, the massacre intensified. The Western attacks were repulsed. One historian put it this way:

> The Armenians were available. They were Christian. They were clever. They were wealthy. They were suspected of sympathizing with the Russians and smuggling arms and plotting revolts and so the planned massacres began. Leaders were captured and tortured. The young were sent to labour, the old, the weak and the children forced to march toward Syria, Persia and Mesopotamia, where they were robbed, left naked, raped and left to die of hunger and exposure. And so a million or more died.

Churchill was demoted in the Cabinet on May 22, 1915. Ironically, in the British press, Churchill was called "England's Armenian."

I add this template of history to indicate how directly and indirectly other nations, including Canada, were involved in the events surrounding the Armenian massacres, which are the subject matter of our resolution.

Let me return to the word "genocide," first coined by Raphael Lemkin, in 1944, who was then working in the United States. Lemkin defined "genocide" in two ways: as the planned annihilation of a people and as a progressive process - a coordinated plan of different actions aimed at the destruction of the essential foundations of life of national groups with the aim of annihilating the groups themselves. Under this generic definition, clearly the actions of the Turkish authorities, up to and following

April 24, 1915, respecting its Armenian populations, would lead to an inescapable conclusion of genocide as defined by Lemkin.

Honourable senators, once we make this finding, in which I concur, what are we to do? Beyond the acceptance of the claim to genocide, other claims under international law, both conventional and customary, as it applies to the province of Eastern Turkey, are more complex and difficult.

Thankfully, the resolution does not compel the Senate to address these questions.

Let me repeat. Suffice it to say that any other claims, hotly contested, absent a thorough review, makes it almost impossible to render a balanced opinion on these other questions. The issue of self determination, often a tortured notion ripped from its international context, can cause great harm. Within a recognized state, it evokes great complexities, great factual issues and great philosophic and legal issues that are simply beyond the scope of this resolution.

The question of responsibility opens up other questions. Honourable senators should note the following statement made by a senior Turkish official on May 13, 1915:

> For the last month the Kurds and the Turkish populations merely have been engaged in massacring the Armenians with the connivance and often help with the Ottoman authorities.

This is grudging Turkish acknowledge of genocide. What therefore should be the sanctions? What was the role of the Ottoman war crimes tribunal? What should be done now? What are the consequence of a finding of genocide eight decades after the events? I can offer no ready solution to those questions.

I will draw the attention of honourable senators to two magnificent books that might help us address these questions, since Turkish governments past and present have barely acknowledged or appropriately dealt with these historic questions. In effect, what are the consequences of denial of historic truths on future conduct? What is the consequence of the Turkish denial of these historic truths?

First, I commend to honourable senators a book that was granted an award in this hall some months ago. That book, by a Canadian, Erna Paris, a long-time friend of mine, is entitled *Long Shadow: Truth, Lies And History*. The second book I commend to honourable senators is by Ervin Staub; it is entitled *The Roots Of Evil: The Origins of Genocide and Other Group Violence*.

My conclusion, honourable senators, is that nationalism married to religion always seems to activate the rawest nerves and instigate hate, defining, dividing and distorting the human condition. Memory and history require that first the truth be told so that the human condition can be exposed to this flaw of hatred, the roots of genocide, the human condition so often and so easily injected by greater calls of nationalism and religion.

The roots of evil lie not in the heart of darkness but more often in lip service and prayers invoked and taught to our children, when one person or one group is ascribed a higher place in the natural order of the human condition, where equality is displaced by theories of superiority. When one does not treat the stranger as oneself, we open the arteries to the heart of genocide. Thus, genocide lurks in the shadows and haunts us still. Will we ever learn from history?

This resolution is in itself a modest lesson in history . For that, we must commend our colleagues Senators Maheu and Setlakwe for bringing it once again to our attention.

THE MYSTERY OF THE NATIONAL LIBERAL CAUCUS
4TH ANNUAL ALLAN J. MACEACHEN LECTURE
ST. FRANCIS XAVIER UNIVERSITY

September 24, 2001

One should never correct someone who's made such a wonderful overly generous introduction, but I do want to correct two things. First and foremost, at that 1979 Campaign Rally with Mr. Trudeau, the central idea shared by his team, which we advised him to do was to reach out and touch people as he could do so successfully. You saw it that night. He could mesmerize a crowd. We told him, "You've got to talk about what people are really concerned about. You've got to do it in terms that people understand. You have to touch people." And so his own final preparation had nothing to do with any advice we had given. His speech was all about the Constitution. He concluded the speech on the Canadian constitution saying "and, and, we will bring it home." And I sat there, after helping to organize this rally and I said to myself, "That's it, we've lost this campaign!" The following morning I went to visit my mother, who, God bless her, is now 100, going to be 101 in October, and she's always been my one person focus group. I said, "Mother, what do you think?" And she said, "You know I like that man, Mr. Trudeau. He's a very interesting personality but I didn't quite understand what he meant by the constitution. Is that a breakfast cereal?" I knew then that the campaign was truly lost.

I am delighted to be here tonight because we know about Allan J. My topic tonight is the mystery of the national caucus, but the true mystery is really the mystery of Allan J. And the mystery within the mystery of Allan J. is his capacious mind, his very innovative and creative mind. And one never gets an insight into that mind and I see Sister Peggy Butts, a former colleague, and Dr. John Stewart. We've all sat in the caucus together. And the only time that you really understand the true genius of Allan is when you listen to Allan sum up a circumstance that everybody else thought they knew as well or better than he. And he adds a dimension or a multi-layered dimension that's exciting and interesting.

So we are gathered here once again for the 4th Annual Celebration here at St. F.

X. to celebrate a life in politics and most especially the political career of Allan J. MacEachen, the well-known icon. I say, more appropriately, the legend of party politics. Now, one lesson derived from the extraordinary works of Saint Francis Xavier is that while humility should characterize all conduct, timidity, he said, should not stifle the quest for truth, for hard truth. And so this exploration tonight - and you'll forgive me if I'm a little bit more serious than our previous speaker - this exploration tonight of politics and the root of our democracy, I don't think it could be more apt in light of recent shattering world events.

I have always believed, and I think I gain this from Allan, is that the first task of politics, and the first task of a politician is to ask questions and hopefully good questions. What is therefore the essence of politics? Politics is the pursuit and the possession of power. We see that Hugh's column is called "The Power Game." It's about power. Not surprisingly, we've always heard the repetitive cry from separatists, and it is always for more power. Even though the more power you give them, the less they are satisfied. You can never appease separatists with more power. For power, after all, is the magnetic attraction of politics. Power in the hands of the politician resonates between virtue and vice.

While virtue is the rational, the conventional reason for politics, all western philosophers agree on one common denominator, that power corrupts. All western masters of thought, architects of the western canon through the ages from Plato to Saint Augustine, from Montaigne to Blackstone, from Burke to Fox, from Locke to Hume. And John Stewart is one of the great experts on Hume, from Mills to Acton, from Vico to Berlin, they all shared one singular belief. All of them. The human condition is flawed and politicians no less and perhaps more than others.

Why? Because politics seems more measured by personal advancement, as Hugh Winsor pointed out, than by the march of progress. Politicians trade in ideas.

They deal with power and are naturally, because they are so close to power, more given to excesses of ambition, preferment and even avarice. Mother Teresa, we were told, was ever critical of politicians and she admonished "they did what they did for the love of power rather than for the love of people." So too the nature of the human condition, which Isaiah Berlin called the crooked timber of mankind.

Power remains the great temptation; perhaps the greatest temptation. All masters of the western canon differ only on the means to curb political power. Self restraint, they agree, is illusory. Power without checks and balances, without principles of restraint, cannot curb the natural impulses of a politician. So the search, the endless quest by western thinkers was to find the exquisite equilibrium between political progress and personal advancement, between unrestrained discretionary power and rules, between arbitrary action and the rule of law.

Politicians, these thinkers remind us, if left alone to their own natural devices, cannot but help themselves. They rigorously pursue ideas for personal advancement, to satiate their own personal needs and desires and pleasure. And power always needs company. One cannot be powerful alone. And please, if you'll forgive the gender reference, these human characteristics, these human flaws, are no different whether it's a man or a woman, especially in politics. A politician simply cannot function alone.

Politics is a group activity, almost a team sport. A politician needs groups like he needs oxygen. Politicians simply crave groups and crave crowds. And crowds, according to the Nobel laureate Elias Canetti, author of a magnificent work I recommend it to political science students, called *Crowds and Power* said, "Crowds are inseparable from people. Politicians like people behave differently in crowds than when alone." Canetti illustrated the pack theory of crowds. Crowds always follow certain rituals. Watch crowds applaud, both spontaneous and prompted in Parliament, or at the Air Canada Centre at a hockey game or at a funeral or at weddings. Crowds become packs with ritual behaviour. Such is the power and pull of packs. So the practice of politics is inseparable from the exercise of conducting and shaping crowd behaviour. Directing the pack. And those that dominate, rise to dominate groups, see that the public is really a consumer. They use the same tools that shape and drive politics. And of course the handmaiden, the power tool of all, the handmaiden of state power, is the political party.

Now what seem to escape even the true believers of democratic parliamentary governance are the endless daily conflicts over power rather than policy. Who decides? Who gets what? Rights have now become the lexicon but power really is the purpose. Parliamentary democracy marks the struggle for co-existence between the ancient power of the royal prerogative that now rests in our cabinet which is the executive prerogative within the parliamentary government, on the one hand, and members of parliament, on the other. With the conviction that power corrupts came the idea of alternation: the need for alternate party-led governments. Power was not to be the monopoly of the Crown's party. The clash between liberty and power, between rights and rulers, could only be achieved when the monopoly of power could be alternated under transparent, acceptable rules or conventions of conduct.

Now the philosophic rationale of governance, the state monopoly over power of others was always the ever-elusive and conflicting twin goals of liberty and equality. That search for liberty and equality obsessed all the masters of the western canon. Only through true transparent power-sharing instruments could liberty or freedom be tasted and shared. A civic society was premised on equality. Only by dividing and sharing power could a creative tension be struck in a civic society. Regretfully, we bear witness that this ideal, this western ideal, this democratic civic idea has not even permeated the majority of member states of the United Nations. The Wilson thesis of self determination was not coequal with democracy; never was. And so we have the United Nations still not really peopled with a majority of democratic states.

Now in the modern era in Canada, the heart of all political power rests in the darkest, most mysterious, least transparent, most obvious organizing organism: the national caucus. The caucus, in my view, is a rather opaque phenomenon that rests at the centre of our politics. Yet the caucus, given its apparent potency and power, is the least understood, most often by its own members. Caucus requires the most artful manipulation, especially in this media age as Hugh Winsor suggested, for the pursuit of personal and political power. To grasp the levers of state power requires art. And if the caucus is the child of the party, the thesis of political party, a balance rests as well on an independent party, independent from the caucus. The independent party, in turn, is premised on riding and party democracy. All to act as a counterweight to caucus power. Caucus power can be trumped by party power. Yet both are victims to the same orchestration to sustain the leader's discretionary power, at the expense of even notional party or constitutional checks and balances.

From the start, parties or factions or caucuses had as their operating objective the restraint of the power of others. Or better, the diversion of power and the restraint on absolute power: the sharing of power between the few and the many; the ferment for equality. That was the first origins of political parties: taking power away from the Crown into the hands of the many. The earliest English structures sought to limit the royal prerogative, the monopoly of the King's power, the heart of the King's power that was exercised by the King and the King's party: the royal party, the court party, the Crown party. That was the heart and that's how the absolute monarch sustained his power. So the birth of the earliest party formations was based on the restraint, on checks and balances against arbitrary absolute discretionary powers that facilitated power sharing. Pulling power from the pack, from the royal pack, was an early exercise in democratic reform.

The British historian - and John Stewart referred me to him a long time ago and he's a wonderful source of party history - Lewis Namier, in his extraordinary work on the backgrounds of English members of parliament and their party system, took a look at this question. He made a careful study of members of parliament, the first essential study of members of parliament. And he concluded that members of parliament relished the checks and controls. And they relished their mutual watchfulness and jealousy against the executive which demanded, and I quote, "...respect for public liberty against despotism." And he extolled the beauty, the excellence and the perfection of the British constitution founded on the rule of law, laws over men, laws to limit arbitrary power. That is what Namier said and it still holds true today.

Now enter the next seminal thinker, Montesquieu, the Frenchman, who so carefully studied and admired the British parliamentary system. He published in 1748, and I commend it to all of you, a book entitled *The Spirit of the Laws*, which recognized, again, that power corrupts. So he wrote these words, "...A monarch is ruined when referring everything to himself exclusively, reduces the state to its capital, and the capital to the court and the court to himself." Then as now, parliamentarians clothed their lust for personal power in virtue, in policies, in principles, in values, in conviction, in civilization, in progress, all mooted to be for the benefit of others. Yet, parliamentarians conspire to mandates so vague or so general in nature as to allow maximum arbitrary discretion. Only they and their party are the virtuous vehicle. Only they could decide. Virtue, or the appearance of virtue, could hold parties together; humility and restraint were, however, the victims of party politics. Besides, who could predict tomorrow's priorities we politicians would argue. So parliamentarians applauded themselves and we call ourselves honorable, all in the guise of selflessly pursuing power for others, not for ourselves. We call ourselves honourable because we're not doing it for ourselves; we're doing it for others. Virtue, therefore, became a monopoly, a commodity for a party. A tantalizing theme. A mantra repeated endlessly over and over again to not just members and their leadership but to the members themselves. We are the virtuous party. Trust us with power. The less restraints on popular mandate the better. Such is the political nirvana, a mandate with few promises. The vaguer the contours of the election's social contract with the electorate, the better. Trust our virtue. Trust our discretion. "Trust us" became the underlying current theme for election clashes for power. And in a candid moment, in a very candid moment, the witty, great, Liberal Prime Minister of England, Lloyd George was overheard to say "I am a man of principle and my first principle is expediency."

But I jump ahead of my theme. Blood feuds, vendettas, racked and divided the earliest party formations discovered in the evolution of every western society. Always done in the name of virtue and honour. While political philosophers trace the travail of the human condition through the annals of war and economics or biography, the same political observers or historians or constitutionalists, rarely take the time, with few exceptions, to trace the rise of the invisible influence of political parties, except almost accidentally. Read any history. Party politics is almost a footnote. This inattention to real power structures, resident with causes and parties, persists to the present day. The complexities of the caucus bred inertia, as Hugh Winsor pointed out in the media. It breeds inertia. It's too complicated. We can't quite cover that. Obviously, this shouldn't come as any surprise. There is no surprise. So, why is that so? Why is the caucus not covered? So little is written or noted about the rise and the nature of caucuses of political parties. By convention and tradition, votes or records are not kept in caucus. Votes are not taken. This comes as no surprise because it is by design that the very heart of all politics, the caucuses of political parties, operate as semi or secret societies. I only say semi because there are a lot of leaks from time to time, but really they operate as secret societies. Keeping their debates and discussions shrouded, purposely, in secrecy. And this secrecy is justified. It is justified by the notion that only by secrecy, only by privacy, only by caucus privacy can candid divisions be discussed and a caucus consensus emerge. Only by open debate within the privacy of caucus can members hope to share power, to diffuse power.

Such was the deal. The deal is: be secretive, be quiet, and you will share power. Decisions will be shared. The consensus of the caucus is relegated to the leader. And now the leader's cadre, armed with secret polls, can reject or scoff at any caucus consensus that differs from the executive. Yet progress and the advance of civic society have rarely depended on transitory public polls. The proper study of mankind, as Berlin suggested, is not linear. To gauge underlying sentiment, to pull the pack in arduous different directions requires energy, wisdom and conviction. The public outside the party and the caucus looks to the political structures for inspiration and direction. For decisiveness of action.

We want our politicians to be decisive. We want them to take leadership. We want to have clarity of thought. That's the public desire, the public sentiment; it is inimitable. We are repeatedly told that any political repository or repertoire of divisions and debates can only lead to loss of public support and of course, political power. Liberty and equality is purposely overlooked or quashed in the bud, in the need to retain power. So the choice between public debate, real public debate and division of ideas, on the one hand, and internal cohesion and symmetry and the image of unanimity, on the other hand, becomes a fundamental pillar of party politics and of caucus solidarity.

It is a closed circuit of logic. Leadership, now, relentlessly seeks external and consummate consensus by any and all means. Policy, personal preferment, patronage, the most potent of all political aphrodisiacs, sharing even notionally the experience of the exercise of power, to be part of an all powerful executive, to sustain the executive at all of its manifestations, to feel the warmth of the flame of power, to hope to be part of that inner circle, to be saluted, to share the insider's power stories with others, to brush against the emperor's clothes or his valets, as some observe, has become a noble purpose or pursuit almost for its own sake. The pull of the pack as Canetti said, is almost overwhelming. Of course, the ultimate desire of politics, like life, is to become immortal. To be remembered beyond death. To have a legacy, always laterally, becomes the paramount, if penultimate goal in the exercise of politics of any political leader. Do not forget me, for all that I have done for you, croons the last post of all politicians. Satiated with wasted discretionary power. Happily, poets remind us through the millennium that this, too, shall pass.

Now legacies have achieved in some western countries a rather garish level, reminiscent of ancient Rome. In the US, the presidential libraries avowed purpose is to brand into history the good works of each recent president for the benefit of revisionist history books. In France, each president leaves a colossal public work: the Centre Pompidu , Mitterrand's massive national library in Paris. Mercifully, in England and Canada, portraits, statues, plaques and books, seems to suffice to match our more modest public sentiment, more in keeping with "responsible" government!

Well friends, with that rather brief prologue (maybe not too brief), let me return to the topic of this lecture dedicated to Allan J. MacEachen, the master politician, the political organizer supreme, who served as such an effective advisor to prime ministers, as a Cabinet Minister (I think 11 portfolios in all), House Leader, Senate Leader, master of the rules of parliament - both the Senate and the Commons and, no less, a great master of that secret formation of Parliament, the national liberal caucus. The weekly meeting in caucus where all elected Liberals from the House of Commons, and all appointed senators, congregate to perform their weekly ritual, in private, while the media watches glowering in the corridors awaiting precise snippets of information to feed the indifferent instant news networks who are out there concocting the daily news. The national caucus has been so constructed and promoted to give the appearance and belief to its own members and observers and camp followers alike, the widest, most open debate affecting all people and all regions. That's the premise. Yet like a tango, it is most artfully orchestrated as an exercise resembling more a military structure and a military command formation. Like the military, treason or disloyalty is the greatest sin. To artfully pull from the pack takes extraordinary talent and resilience and self confidence.

Every Wednesday when parliament is in session, commencing at 10 a.m., time is tightly rationed and carefully choreographed in the national weekly caucus. Reports of the house leader, the whip, the senate, followed by regional and numerous special and policy caucuses, often leaves less than an hour relegated to 20 or so members who request an opportunity to address the caucus at large.

Those members that are not given to the regular genuflections and congratulatory comments articulate a rather narrow specific concern. Each member's plea resembles more, if you look at it in historical terms, the form of an ancient petition to the crown. A problem that seeks redress. The leader, like the royals of old, decides which of any members' petition he will even react too publicly. The raised dais, the seating structure, the format lends itself less to open debate than a formula for concise entreaties to the leader. And before each weekly meeting, the leader's cadre meets with the caucus chair to shape, anticipate and influence even more the caucus agenda. This ritual micromanagement of caucus consensus by the leader and his cadre operates in a strange way and from time to time, when warranted, the electronic media is allowed a few moments to tape spontaneous caucus solidarity, despite the caucus cant of privacy or secrecy. Rarely is the veil of perceived wisdom or the agenda or the priorities of the executive pierced by the caucus. And only then by a concerted chorus of member's concerns. Then such members are briefly applauded as if any change in the national priorities established by the executive, or any change in the national agenda established by the executive, is such a singular victory rather than the caucus doing its normal work, to act as a check on the executive.

Now in our political system of government, any leader quickly understands after election that he can only retain the support and confidence of the house if he retains the leadership and support of his own caucus. This as been distorted to mean absolute support for any and all actions. All legislative initiatives of the cabinet introduced into parliament rather than just money bills or significant matters related to election mandates. It's everything; practically everything. The caucus contains numbers necessary to support the leader and his chosen cadre.

And the confidence of the House, failing support of the caucus, the leader as Prime Minister is naked before the Governor General who holds the prerogative power to determine who will be granted the opportunity to gain the confidence of the House. Hence therefore, the caucus and power are inseparable, at its luscious prospect of power. Under this self imposed paradigm, any disloyalty is thus automatically deemed to be self defeating. Any disloyalty so called has become the metaphor to mean loss of power. Now if the past is prologue, and Allan J. has been both a participant and a ring-side observer, he would argue most artfully, that the illusive loss of caucus confidence intentionally or unconsciously, was always the first slippery step on the slide to loss of political power; to political oblivion certainly.

An accidental loss of a vote on a money bill by Mr. Pearson in his absence in 1967, led to his decision to resign ultimately as leader and Prime Minister. Mr. Diefenbaker's slide in caucus ultimately led to his political demise.

Thus it came as no surprise that that master of political power Mr. Mulroney, an alumnus of this university, purposely set about to micromanage his caucus solidarity. Mr. Mulroney is appropriately considered, and should be considered, a master of caucus control. We are told he used every personal and political wile, including daily use of his telephone rolodex, to note any caucus dissident and to immediately counteract it by contact, prefennent, persuasion, patronage (both personal and familial), message or the ultimate threat, to the thrust from the crowd. To be pushed from the pack. And we are told that a previous lecturer, Bob Rae, when he became premier of Ontario, allowed, at first - in a democratic fashion, an NDP fashion - a free and open debate in his caucus and his cabinet. But that soon changed - too late some say - to the tactics of caucus control, only to find that his caucus divisions had become so divisive and irretrievable, that it leads to his loss of power. Now some say, some observers say, Mr. Mulroney's absolute control of caucus, even when public support dissipated, was the cause of the Tory downfall.

Parties go through cycles. Mr. King, the great micro-manager always paid meticulous attention to caucus and party structures. Mr. St. Laurent, on the other hand, allowed party structures to atrophy. Hence the Pearson-led rejuvenation of the Liberal party of which AJ was a key architect, involved a grassroots revolution against the old cadres of power after the disastrous defeat in 1958. Those that lead that revival, and AJ was one of them, believed that only a democratically-elected grassroots party could become a check on the parliamentary wing, on the caucus, in order to regain and keep touch with the public as an open pathway to political power. Democracy in the party, in turn, would revive and restrain the caucus, satiated with power, while discarding the old, out-of-touch leadership cadre. Work out or get out was the clarion call to the grassroots riding executives and caucus members. The reformed party, by its constitution, would guarantee the party a strong and independent voice and a check on the parliamentary wing, from policy to leadership. That was the reform of the Liberal Party. That was the notion of the reformed Liberal Party lead in part by Allan MacEachen.

Now the modern party structure based on democratic ridings and provincial layers, has under the present caucus system, been transformed from an independent and democratic check on policy and personalities in the caucus, illustrated by Namier, and the independence of members that advance by John Stuart Mills, to one based on a caucus-centred mindset. In this ever contracting circle, this centralization of power, policy and pluralism has given way to personality and personal progress. And political progress to preferment. The classic role defined by John Stuart Mills, of the individual liberty of members as a check on the executive becomes, perforce, sharply curtailed and reined-in, even distorted. Hold your nose, I've been told, hold your nose and vote even though you don't like it. For good reason, control of the public agenda has emerged as the highest form, archetypical of modern political life. Control of caucus forms an essential part of control of the political agenda we are told.

Of course, the media brooks no dissent or division. The media can't stand division. With rare exception the electronic media can only hold one idea at a time. And I'm not referring to the print media because I think the print media is much different. But the electronic media, unfortunately, is what people watch. They don't read newspapers; they watch television. And the electronic media is too indifferent and mostly too inexperienced to evaluate differing points of view. So they can only report on caucus clashes without concluding that there are splits and dissents and division all rife but all, of course, all damaging. This is an implicit acceptance of Canetti's pack theory. Disloyalty becomes the metaphor for silence. So the contest for the daily control of the political agenda involves diffusion and absorption or distraction of problems rather than systematically solving any political problems that erupt. Get them off the table, clean them off, divide them, dissect them, but don't deal with them. The media will always move on. Collateral damage is done to political institutions but don't worry, the media as I said, are the media that have an attention span of yesterday's headlines. The pack affect is seen in the media itself, where so many slavishly follow the other in this new, immediate universe of so many different voices. And when you turn to the various television channels, what do you find? It's the same story told different ways, in different modes but it is the same story. It's not new. So they follow each other. So the popular and the sensational displaces the complex or the difficult.

Now the tightest, most invisible ring around the caucus is around the leader circle. A revolving faction, not new, but largely unnoticed and mostly misdescribed. In this leader-led, leader-driven caucus, the greatest sin, the greatest treason, was well articulated by Allan J. at his retirement dinner held in his honour that established this lectureship. Allan said, and I hope Allan I do not rip you out of context, that the iron rule of caucus progress and preferment for any caucus member, and I'm quoting here, "...is to never find himself in the way of having to say no to the leader." Criticism, carefully coached, kind criticism perhaps, but wide negative attacks never. And AJ developed strong critics within the caucus to almost an art form. So now both the caucus and the party appear orchestrated by the leader's faction. Party constitutions are, or seem to be, discarded or eviscerated. The orchestration is more evident in the parliament ring than the party ring, and now the house leaders of both houses, the whips, the chairs, the chairs of the regional caucuses, the chairs of the committees (except public accounts) are either appointed or if elected, indirectly assented to or orchestrated by the leader's circle. Advancement of a private members bill, appointment as a Chair, Parliamentary Secretary, Chairs of Committees and even as one whip recently proclaimed, invitations and trips abroad or invitations to dignitary's dinners, depend on adherence to the whip's line. Too often the Chairs are appointed as a reward more for their compliance than their competence, more for their dependability than their independence. And now, with the most recent amendments to the Parliament Act, last June, even new additional compensation to members' chairs and the like are essentially all but at the discretion of the leader. The number of discretionary compensation to members of caucus now exceeds $900,000 because of the new Parliament Act that was just changed a few months ago. Meanwhile, what's the situation in England? Hugh Winsor referred to this in his column not too long ago. In England, the Mother parliament, the four line whip is only applied to questions of confidence on money matters, which is of constitutional significance, and questions significant to the electoral mandate. It's limited. And then there are various other forms of whips but their four line whip, the big whip, is limited to the big, big issues. In Canada, virtually all votes are deemed questions of confidence. Free votes are sparse and misnamed then numbered as a measurement of a member's scope of independence rather than the reverse.

But let's take a look back now, stand back and take a look at history. Has much changed? Parties are as old as the bible. Tribes were the first natural political factions. Extended families became sources for both royalty and parties. The Western nation was forged when loyalty to the tribes was transferred to the king and country and then parliamentary democracy and more recently to constitutions and to the charter above parliament. So let's dance through the modern era. I'll try and do this quickly. But let's stop for a moment and pause in Medieval Italy, where no less a poet and writer than Dante wrote the *Divine Comedy* and *Inferno* essentially as political discourses. And Dante lived in Florence and there were two great party formations - the Ghibellines and the Guelfs - who dominated Florence and the other cities of Italy. And the Ghibellines and the Guelfs held diametrically opposed views. The Ghibellines supported the absolute power of the Holy Roman Empire, and the Guelfs supported the absolute secular power of the Pope. Nothing much has changed. This debate between the Guelfs and the Ghibellines were the seeds of the Hundred Years War and the Thirty Year Wars that so convulsed Europe. And we see echoes of it today in our recent unrest.

But let's turn back to England and the Act of Settlement in 1689. In 1689 in England, power was wrested, the prerogative was wrested from the Monarchy and the king's party, which led to restraint of the royal prerogative by parliament.

Power was transferred from the crown to parliament and shared within parliament. The division of powers was applauded by Montesquieu and studied as the English model. Blackstone said that the checks and balances were a device in retaining political virtue. Parliament would act for the people; loyalty to crown meant loyalty to parliament. Parliamentary institutions would act as checks and balances against each other when within parliament the crown now sharing its prerogative with the cabinet, the cormnons and the lords, each would check one another. There were checks and balances.

And so, they separated the law making powers in two. There was to be the lawmakers, the legislators, parliament and the courts. And the courts were to be separate and distinct, all with a view to checking power. Fifty years after the Act of Settlement, Montesquieu wrote these words, "so the purpose of the checks and powers [...] so that one cannot abuse power, power must be checked by the arrangement of things. A constitution can only be struck so that no one will be constrained to do the things that law does not oblige them to do or be kept from doing the things the law permits them to do. One must combine powers, regulate them, temper them, make them act. One must give power to balance so that to speak, to put people in a position to resist one another. This is the masterpiece of legislation that chance rarely produces prudence and is rarely allowed to produce." And so, the whole fight in powers which were to wrest power from the crown, from the executive into the hands of parliament through the party mechanisms.

If you take a look at things in recent times, I want to make one special note. At one time parliament was seen as a central organization in the country. And it's interesting that in recent times the Charter has displaced parliament and the crown in public esteem, in every region of the country including Quebec. I believe there is a shift in public support of the Charter as a unifying symbol due to the perception of parliament as a place of centralizing power while the Charter is seen as a source of individual rights, of decentralizing power, of power sharing. Now this should not be taken to mean that the courts are to replace parliament or for the courts to carry on what they now define as the democratic dialogue with the people.

Parliament is still meant to be supreme.

Our Fathers of Confederation organized powers based on the English system, the Liberal party in England, the Conservative party in England. But when they were first established, they were established for only one purpose. They were established, essentially, to get members of parliament elected. Both parties were there only to support the caucus and the leader. The heart of the party at that time revolved around the caucus. And Canada wasn't alone. Let me just quote from Robert Menzies, author of *The Prime Minister's of England*: "parliament might just as well not exist at present because legislation is first submitted to the caucus and once approval is given, then the subsequent debate in parliament becomes a mere formality." Now MacKenzie King was obsessed by the caucus and he was obsessed - and if you read the MacKenzie King record you'll see this - because he observed the disintegration of the Liberal party in England. And he did not want the Liberal Party of Canada to fall into the same trap of division. And so he, for one, was careful and meticulous about the caucus. Paul Martin Sr., who wrote an excellent biography, wrote this, "...that King saved his best oratory for the caucus and it was there to help mend intra-party differences regarding a particular policy." King would share. His technique of caucus was to share his internal thinking, to share his thinking, to share power or power decisions within caucus so that they could understand - members of caucus - and quarrel with his process of thinking.

Again, let me just read something here. And I've read the King's diaries this summer, not something I would do again, but it was interesting because his whole text was studded with references to the caucus, and he said this: "the desirability of having our differences fought out in caucus. Next day I spoke to the caucus pretty straight from the shoulder." Later on he said this: "I am saddened in my heart to see a great political party that has set the record like us over a century gradually disintegrating and getting to the point where it could totally disappear as the Liberal party in Britain because they were not their party men. Party men who were prepared to see that we had an effective organization." So King was the master of micromanagement of his caucus. He even appointed the caucus chairman. Yet he relished open and robust debate within the confines of caucus and caucus secrecy in those days meant caucus secrecy. And we are told he regularly wrote to party members in each riding to obtain a disparate grassroots opinion. He wanted to get a feel from the people in the riding as well as the members.

Now does this topic, and you've been so indulgent tonight, does this topic carry any relevance in these unpredictable times? Perhaps some lessons can be gleaned. Hopefully to draw attention to the deplorable state of critical debate and scrutiny in the Commons itself. Never has the Common's opposition been so divided, so weak and so totally ineffective. Never has the legislation or oversight been so sloppy and maladroit and John Stewart knows what I'm talking about, and so does Sister Butts. We sat in the Senate and we saw legislation coming across that hadn't been scrutinized by the Commons, by either members on our side or the opposition, and never have you seen such sloppy legislation. Never, in effect have the checks and balances in parliament taken a holiday. Meanwhile parliament is so divided and so fractious that it cannot even unite in the face of perilous common problems. Reform of parliament, I believe, should start with a very simple message and a very simple mission. Members of Parliament should act as members of parliament. Perhaps these recent earth-shaking events will service to shake up a call to lovers of parliamentary tradition, as all eyes will be turned once again to parliament. Divided when needed, say the masters of the western canon when it comes to parliament, but united when necessary. The caucus remains one source of the solution to parliamentary reform and I have three simple suggestions. One, there should be no whips except on budgetary matters, money bills and significant matters of public policy or questions related to electoral mandates.

Two, committee chairs should be selected by a more independent mode based on experience and competence, perhaps even seniority. Finally, allow one day a week for private member's bill without any executive control or hindrance, and allow one day a month for private members to interface with a clerk of the Privy Council in committee of the whole to hold the bureaucracy more accountable, which presently they are not. A profound danger, in my view, to peace, order and good government, lies in this over centralization of federal decision-making in the hands of a very narrow executive that hasn't changed in many years and in the bureaucracy. The power now resides in few hands in the executive around the leader and in the bureaucracy. It's become almost impossible with the modern complexity of government to oversee all these things. The system simply backs up. Parliament can do more. Over centralization is inconsistent with and suffocates the principles of liberalism. All wisdom does not flow from one coordinated source within caucus. Caucus and party malaise and disillusion can set in. Received wisdom from one source is simply not wise. Wisdom is rarely found in polls which represent only one narrow snap-shot of public sentiment at a time. Rarely do the polls look outside the box. Parliamentarians can do so and they can do so with some inspiration.

Now any paradigm of acute centralization, in my view is the Mulroney lesson, can ravage your party and at caucus. Obsession with linear, bureaucratic arrangements harnessed with a preoccupation with agenda control cannot avoid neglecting issues until they fester and crystallize beyond easy reform. And worse, when the only need felt is to micromanage equally large and small issues at the same time, the important is more often than not submerged with the trivial. And even a trivial division then becomes a major setback because of the paradigm of absolute control. Members of parliament should never forget that conventional wisdom always starts with the majority of one. Berlin defined liberalism as coexistent with pluralism. Regretfully, in recent time in my view, and this is a brief commercial, it is only in the Senate where open, extensive debates on matters such as Meech Lake, the Clarity Bill, the Nisga'a Treaty, and the Extradition bill and the Citizenship Act took place. By default, almost, the Senate has displaced the Commons as a check on the executive due as much to the vacuum in the Commons as to the desiccated opposition. Which brings me back to Allan J. MacEachen.

In 1979, it was Allan J. as Mr. Webster pointed out, who rallied the caucus and the party behind Mr. Trudeau's return. It was Allan J. when he became leader of the government in the Senate and leader of the opposition after his retirement from the Commons, who quietly instituted significant reforms that allowed the Senate to take its rightful place as an appropriate check and balance on the caucus, on the Commons, and on the cabinet. Almost immediately he objected to the long standing practice called pre-study where bills in the Senate would be pre-studied at the time of their introduction in the Commons, an amendment suggested by the Minister quietly during the Common's legislative process. This practice, he believed and we agreed with him, undermined the constitutional duty of the Senate as a chamber of second, sober thought. As a chamber independent of the Commons, they would act as both a check on the Commons and the Executive. The Senate's work should be visible and transparent for the sake of its own legitimacy and credibility, he argued over and over again in the caucus. Under his leadership, the Mulroney government was compelled to seek an election mandate on the Free Trade Agreement. Under his leadership, the GST was variously opposed not so much because of its philosophic disagreements because Allan felt, and we agreed, that the government lacked an election mandate for a massive reform of our tax system. In the Senate caucus, he never sought to control debate. There wasn't one time I can remember, and John Stewart was there and will affirm this, not once did he seek to control debate. On the contrary, he welcomed and relished the fullest and freest exchange of ideas. Then he would succinctly sum up in quite a brilliant and creative way, the consensus. Taking and weighing carefully all contesting viewpoints as expressed, and frequently amending his own views because of what he heard in caucus. Almost alone, he forced the national caucus and the Senate and the cabinet elect, to take notice that the Senate could not be relied upon as an invisible parliamentary rubber stamp. And since his time as the leader, the Senate has slowly regained a more appropriate place as a vital check and balance to both Commons and the cabinet.

You should recall that six out of the sixteen days of the Confederation Debates, concerned the Senate. Why? Because all fathers of Confederation were searching to strike an appropriate constitutional check and balance for the Senate against the Commons and against the Executive. And it's ironic, that the two national parties so obsessed with the current status of the Senate, the Alliance and the NDP have both failed miserably in their own constitutional duties as a check and balance in the Commons. No wonder that their current distortions within their own caucuses have been based on the politics of personality rather than the politics of conviction which brought them both to parliament in the first place.

One final aside about the Senate Academics have given undue and increased legitimacy to extra-parliamentary checks and balances. They have dismissed the Senate. They have encouraged the Courts to displace Parliament. Parliament, they preach, is no longer supreme. That topic, my friends, is the subject of another theme. The title might be "How the Principle of Parliamentary Supremacy Under the Constitution was Undermined by Constitutional Lawyers." But that dear friends, most indulgent friends, is for another day. Let me on the same note conclude where I began, the quest for truth. Truth, as Tolstoy the great Russian writer reminded us, has been, is, and will be, beautiful. Isaiah Berlin wrote he did not know if this was so but, as he continued, it seems near enough not to be too lightly set aside. Thank you.

LÉONCE MERCIER: ON RETIREMENT

October 24, 2001

Hon. Jerahmiel S. Grafstein: Honourable senators, my dear friend Senator Mercier, I have a public *mea culpa* to make. At times, I did not make Senator Mercier's life as a whip easy. I parted with him on votes and abstentions on some contentious issues where he had a direct interest in his responsibility as whip. Yet not once did he hold this against me. At all times, I explained to him my position in advance, and he quickly understood. He even called me a gentleman, which I took as the greatest of all compliments, especially coming from my dear friend Léonce.

Honourable senators, when we are appointed to the Senate, we automatically have the word "honourable" prefixed to our name. In my mind, Léonce will always be remembered as an honourable man, a politician, and above all a gentlemen.

Léonce, I will not say goodbye; I will say "au revoir." God grant you good health, and "bonne chance" in everything you undertake.

"THE MIRACLE ON 52nd STREET": CANADA LOVES NEW YORK WEEKEND

December 1, 2001

Hon. Jerahmiel S. Grafstein rose pursuant to notice of December 6, 2001:

That he will call the attention of the Senate to "The Miracle on 52nd Street", the Canada Loves New York Rally in New York City on December 1, 2001.

He said: Honourable senators, "Miracle on 52nd Street," the headline in the *Toronto Sun*, aptly described the Canada Loves New York Rally that erupted at the Roseland Ballroom on 52nd Street in New York on Saturday December 1, 2001. The headline was accurate. It was a "grassroots" miracle.

After September 11, Canadians shared the pain and tragedy with Americans. Canadians wondered what to do. As Co-Chair of the Canada-U.S. Inter-Parliamentary Group, I called colleagues and friends in the American Congress, both in Washington and New York, to commiserate. All were depressed and distracted by the situation amplified by the elaborate security checks necessary when they entered their own offices on Capitol Hill and days later by the anthrax scare that immobilized their offices and staff even further. Congressmen who lived in New York were confronted with all the problems in Washington, adding to the daily sorrow of living in New York. Canadians shared these sorrows and events deeply and poignantly, as it had happened to some of them.

What to do to show solidarity and support? The first idea was to organize a mass rally and benefit concert at the Skydome in Toronto to raise contributions for families of the victims. A few days after September 11, the Prime Minister held an open-air service where over 100,000 people gathered on Parliament Hill. The idea for a benefit concert received no traction as it was quickly overtaken by other concerts.

Friend and producer Gabor Apor said, "Jerry, your efforts are misplaced. You should organize something in New York." We approached municipal officials in Toronto who balked because they felt that such an effort would be perceived as counterproductive since tourism in Canada was in a dive. One leading businessman argued that such an effort would be misdirected and would be misunderstood in Toronto. Canadian retail sales were spiralling downward. We felt otherwise. A strong message had to be made in New York City, the media capital in the world, that we had to get things speedily back to normal or both our economies would cocoon and slide into recession. The terrorism threat was debilitating consumer confidence on both sides of the border.

Then, honourable senators, Mayor Giuliani made his magnificent speech at the United Nations, inviting those who wished to help America to come to enjoy New York and help get things back to normal. My wife Carole said to me, "Stop moping about this. Let's organize some volunteers."

A few days later, a handful of outstanding community volunteer leaders from health to the arts in Toronto were called together. They all enthusiastically endorsed the idea, knitted their various talents together to make it happen, organized a non-stop committee and set up an office. Others were quickly and easily added. Several undertook to raise out-of-pocket costs. One suggested we needed media support, and an advertising firm was contacted by a key volunteer to contribute the creative work under the direction of the committee. They generously agreed to donate their services to the committee. Another thought that a fire van to replace one of those demolished should be contributed to the New York Fire Department, and she quickly obtained a van as a donation. A victim's father volunteered to help in Toronto and New York.

Publishers of the leading newspapers in Toronto were called and full-page ads were requested. They all quickly and generously agreed. Leading executives in television and radio quickly agreed as well to contribute free media time. A wonderful logo was designed. Print ads were created and revamped to suit the committee's objectives. An ad was devised with Canadian stars in entertainment and sports produced by a Canadian producer, all of whom volunteered their time and services. They quickly congregated across Canada and in New York and L.A. to tape 30- and 60-second commercials. Street media, elevator and bus signs were generously donated after quick calls. I asked the Prime Minister if he would join in the commercial and he spontaneously agreed.

Another key volunteer suggested that the ad might be shown in movie theatres. A movie theatre executive was invited as a volunteer and agreed not only to have the cost of translating the commercial into film donated, but also to ensure it was launched with the Harry Potter movie about to debut in cinemas across Canada.

The committee agreed that November 30 to December 2, between the American Thanksgiving and Christmas, would be dubbed the "Canada Loves New York Weekend."

We approached Air Canada. They generously came up with a special package and then agreed that the package would apply not only to Toronto but also to Ottawa and Montreal. People in Vancouver, Halifax and other cities heard about the idea, and so Air Canada added special rates to those cities and other parts of Canada as well. A hotel chain in New York and Canada volunteered to obtain discount hotel rates in

New York. Another suggested that bus companies selling cut-rate packages should be contacted in order to ensure that students and others would be able to come to New York on an affordable basis.

Everyone said "yes." No one said "no."

Old friends in Montreal were contacted and conscripted. Then Senator Hervieux-Payette called and said that others in Montreal wished to join this effort as well, and a vigorous, high-powered, eminent organization of volunteers was quickly formed there. They speedily produced ads in French for both print and broadcast. This followed with a lively committee organized right here in Ottawa. Other groups across Canada and the United States, as they heard about the rally, joined as well.

A prominent Canadian living in New York was approached and a robust, dynamic volunteer committee of young Canadian professionals and executives working in New York was quickly established there. They worked non-stop from the very start.

Since we discovered that hundreds of thousands of Canadians live within Greater New York, the Committee felt it was important that Canadians coming from across Canada should converge with Canadians living in Greater New York.

With barely one month to organize the event, the committee concluded that the presentation of the van should be made to Mayor Giuliani and the Chief of the NYFD. Ambassadors in Washington and Ottawa were enlisted, as were two ranking American congressmen, both great friends of Canada. Contact was made with the Mayor's office with an invitation for him to attend a rally that would take place on December 1.

A frantic search discovered that the historic Roseland Ballroom was available. The New York owner was contacted and generously made the ballroom available at very nominal cost. Venue insurance was donated by a key volunteer's Canadian firm in New York. A website was created and an 800 number was donated in order to focus all the outreach activities. The website received thousands of hits from across Canada and the United States.

Reaching the tens of thousands of Canadians who lived in New York was a daunting challenge.

One international magazine donated an ad in its Manhattan edition. Use of email was deployed. It just was not enough.

We called one of the owners of the large screens in Times Square and told our story. He agreed not only to provide time on his screen, but volunteered to obtain the assent of all other screen owners in Times Square to broadcast our message in New York as well.

Another key New York volunteer obtained access to the Jumbotron at Madison Square Garden to broadcast our call for the rally there. Yet another persuaded the Empire State Building to be lit up in Canadian colours, and it was done on November 29.

Mayor Giuliani graciously issued a proclamation which officially declared December 1 "Canada Loves New York Day" in New York. Then the White House was contacted and President Bush promptly issued a presidential message that was put on the wire services commending the "Canada Loves New York" Committee for its efforts. Let me quote briefly from President Bush's message. He said:

> The United States and Canada are strongly linked by ties of family, friend-ship, trade, and shared values. Our countries have stood shoulder to shoul-der in war, peace, trial, and triumph, and we again stand together today to defeat terrorism. I applaud the "Canada Loves New York" Committee and the Canadian people for making this event possible in celebration of our sol-idarity. By responding to Mayor Giuliani's invitation to come to New York, you demonstrate your love for this remarkable city and build on the special heritage our countries share as lands of freedom and opportunity.

The committee felt that, if we could induce 3,000 to 4,000 Canadians to attend, it would send a wonderful message across America and Canada. All agreed it was es-sential to snap things back to normal, to overcome the fear of flying and resume air travel, and to help thaw consumer paralysis, so evident in both the United States and Canada.

Canadian artists, including opera singers working in New York, were enlisted to donate their talent.

Senator Hervieux-Payette who helped organize the Montreal committee insisted that a longer show especially for Quebecers with more Canadian talent was necessary. Thus, a wider panorama of Canadian talent was sought and quickly assembled with the help of volunteers in Canada and especially in New York.

Pamela Wallin was hastily called upon for her contribution as MC. With her excel-lent, ebullient talents, she helped make the rally memorable.

At the last moment, the committee was approached by rank and file policemen in Toronto who had raised over $100,000 by selling over 15,000 T-shirts door to door. They wished to hand the cheque directly to the NYPD Benevolent Fund for Victims. They wanted to ensure that the money reached the right source. We agreed to have them join us in the presentation ceremony. We invited the Police Chief and the Fire Chief of Toronto and their counterparts in New York to join the presentation.

I then approached Charles Pachter, one of Canada's leading artists, to create a commemorative painting for this event. His generous gift would be transformed into a commemorative poster and given to Canadians attending the rally as a lasting sou-venir. Some 5,000 were printed. The first of the three artist's proofs of this emotive painting was to be presented to Mayor Giuliani, and later one to President Bush and one to Prime Minister Chrétien.

A Canadian clothing company owner designed and produced a special "Canada Loves New York" cap to be given to those attending the rally, and volunteered on the committee himself. He also deployed, through his email system, extensive lists, and all volunteers helped enlist other through email lists as well.

The Prime Minister agreed to a photo opportunity boarding a bus in front of Parliament Hill to help promote the event. It was covered by all the media across Canada and picked up by American television to help boost public awareness in both Canada and the United States. Special postcards of the Pachter painting were generously printed by yet another key volunteer and were handed out on airplanes, buses and hotels as an invitation to the rally.

University newspapers in Ontario and Quebec were called upon for their help and support, and they gave it.

The media in both Canada and the United States, especially the networks, allowed us to boost our activities in the days leading up to the rally.

Public relations experts volunteered their invaluable services, consuming virtually all of their time.

As December 1 approached, members of the committee did not know what to expect, or even how to calculate how many would come. We had no accurate way of predicting. The volunteers were to be overwhelmed and gratified. The doors were to open at 1:30 p.m. at the Roseland Ballroom.

To our surprise, the lineup of Canadians started at 9 a.m., on 52nd Street, and then streamed along 53rd Street, 54th Street, 56th Street, 57th Street, 58th Street, 59th Street, 60th Street, and beyond. Canadians then lined up along 8th Avenue and Broadway. The various estimates concluded that up to 26,000 Canadians converged around the Roseland for the rally. Indeed, 53rd Street was blocked off. Those who were unable to enter the ballroom, or the festoon-closed-off 53rd Street, where a jumbotron was hastily added, lingered and then moved happily on to enjoy the sights and sounds of New York. Not one complaint was heard.

Canadians had come from as far as Whitehorse and Newfoundland for the weekend. Many did not get even close to the ballroom - and not one Canadian complained. The tough New York police officers, charmed and disarmed, marvelled at the patience, politeness and the genial spirit of the thousands and thousands of Canadians who lined up for hours and still could not witness the rally.

Two red-coated Mounties became instant celebrities at the Roseland and as they strolled along Broadway.

For me, the most poignant story centred on a group of young disabled Canadians from Toronto's Variety Village who wanted to come to the rally. A key volunteer quickly arranged to have bus and train facilities donated. These young disabled people travelled for 15 hours on Friday, November 30, to attend the rally. Given a prominent place, they joyously wrapped themselves in Canadian flags, and were painted in the Canadian colours.

The Prime Minister, on a trade mission in the southwest United States, completing in Los Angeles on November 30, the day before the rally, made a special detour in order to join the thousands and thousands of Canadians who had come to participate in the Canada Loves New York Day. He was cheered and welcomed on the crowded streets of New York by his fellow Canadians.

The finale of the presentation was marked by three Canadian opera singers who sang a haunting rendition of God Bless America. There was not a dry eye inside or outside of the room. The Fire Chief of New York, with tears in his eyes, thanked us for such an inspiring and emotional event. The Chief of the NYPD was equally overwhelmed. Mayor Giuliani whispered to me after the event that it was one of the most inspirational moments he had experienced since September 11. He said he was simply overwhelmed.

At the end of the presentation, I asked the mayor publicly to make one promise. When things got back to normal, when things were running smoothly in New York, we invited him, all New Yorkers and all Americans to come and visit Canada. He enthusiastically accepted.

As Canadians left the Roseland Ballroom and drifted away from the surrounding area, Mayor Giuliani thanked me again for our committee's organizational efforts. I told him that his appreciation for our efforts was misplaced. Yes, it was all the volunteers who worked so selflessly and quickly to facilitate a response to his most compelling invitation at the United Nations. Most of all, I told him, the volunteers discovered that all you have to do is ask Canadians to do the right thing and then move out of the way. They will do it and do it in overwhelming numbers!

Just trust the Canadian people and they will surprise you every time.

On Saturday, December 1, tens of millions of Americans and Canadians on both sides of the border and overseas witnessed, via television and by listening to the radio, the "Miracle On 52nd Street." An all-Canadian grassroots miracle did take place in New York City.

God bless Canada. God bless America.

Hon. Senators: Hear, hear!

SHEILA FINESTONE: ON RETIREMENT

February 2, 2002

Hon. Jerahmiel S. Grafstein: Honourable senators, on occasions such as this, it is incumbent upon us to be brutally frank and candid about our departing colleague, the Honourable Sheila Finestone.

Sheila was not always the easiest person with whom to deal. When I first encountered Sheila, she was explosive, opinionated, feisty and the newly-minted Member of Parliament for that great riding of Mount Royal. We had a barbed and rather frosty exchange. It is fair to say we even clashed.

I did not know anything about Sheila Finestone at the time, or her background. Unlike me, she was always very definitive in her views and was not easy to persuade. Then I discovered that her father was the great Monroe Abbey. Monroe Abbey was a civic leader in Montreal. He was influential not only in the Jewish community there, but also as a national leader across Canada. Monroe Abbey was an activist in the Canadian Jewish Congress. As a 12-year-old youngster, I had the privilege to hear Monroe Abbey speak at a community function in the late 1940s in my hometown of London, Ontario. He was impressive, persuasive and a tireless advocate for lost causes, for immigrants and for religious freedom. Monroe Abbey stood against racial discrimination. He was in favour of sports and law reform, and he was a staunch, lifelong Zionist. Monroe Abbey was a member of the Order of Canada as well as a Q.C. Monroe Abbey was named after James Monroe, the fifth President of the United States, the father of the Monroe Doctrine and a drafter of the American Constitution.

Honourable senators, the apple does not fall far from the tree. Sheila has left a lasting trace of activities, ranging from women's, children's, privacy and human rights to international peace and harmony, not only in Canada, but abroad. When you attend international meetings, more often than not, someone will come up and say, "Do you know my friend Sheila Finestone?" Sheila has always had a grand and great range of interests and intensity. Above all, Sheila has had and still has a fire in her belly for the underdog.

Honourable senators, not only was Sheila Finestone a great member of the House of Commons, but she was also a great senator. It is not very often that members of the House of Commons make the transition and become equally important and potent as a member of this chamber.

I extend these words to Sheila Finestone's family. To Sheila, I offer the traditional blessing that she, like our matriarch, Sarah, live to 127 years and have a long and fruitful life.

Happily, honourable senators, I learned just a month ago, when Senator Finestone and I travelled abroad together, that she plans to continue to be a resident of Ottawa.

Sheila, I have a number of tasks that I intend to talk to you about because we need your help, creativity and energy. I promise not to clash with you too often. I will be calling you soon.

You have made us proud and privileged to be your friends. God speed.

PETER GZOWSKI, C.C.: EULOGY

February 7, 2002

Hon. Jerahmiel S. Grafstein: Honourable senators, I rise in tribute to the late, unforgettable, Peter Gzowski. My first fiery encounter with him was in 1956 on the campus of the University of Toronto. I was a law student active on many fronts, and Peter was the radical editor of *Varsity*, the University of Toronto's excellent and well-respected daily newspaper.

Peter was irascible, opinionated and brilliant. Rarely was he easy to convince. We clashed frequently and held heated debates in his office and on campus about almost everything. Yet we kept in touch. We shared a wide circle of friends and business partners. Later, in the 1960s when I was practising law in Toronto, he came to me with a mutual friend, Ken Lefolii, an equally inspired Canadian writer, editor and publisher with a magnificent idea to start up a new weekly magazine to be called *"This City."* The magazine was to focus with an elegant inner eye on the cultural and intellectual life of the city, the prism that the national media had neglected. The thesis was valid then and it is valid now.

We agreed to combine to float the idea, but failed to gain economic support or enthusiasm. This preoccupation with the inner city manifests itself today in the electronic and print media but, at the time, it was revolutionary.

Peter and I shared a love of the printed word, but for me, Peter's great talent was his insatiable curiosity about the undiscovered Canada - his unquenchable curiosity about the unheralded Canada. His curiosity forced Canadians to become curious about themselves. For that, Canadians remain eternally in his debt, and he will not be readily forgotten. He will be missed as the ultimate Canadian catalyst. In a word, he was excellent. He relished and practised excellence. What better legacy can a man bequeath to his country than an unrequited curiosity and love of country.

DAVID PAUL SMITH: WELCOME TO SENATE

October 2, 2002

Hon. Jerahmiel S. Grafstein: Honourable senators, I rise to welcome our newest senator, David Paul Smith - such a simple name for a political master. Brother Smith comes to the Senate at the height of his political, business and legal powers. He bears the well-warranted, deserved reputation as the best political organizer of his generation. A political activist from his youth, he was enlisted by his mentor and mine, Keith Davey, then chief Liberal organizer in Ottawa, after he left the presidency of the Young Liberals in the sixties.

Once ensconced in Ottawa, Senator Smith became an instant protege of Mr. Pearson, who designated both himself and David as double "PKs"- kids whose fathers and grandfathers were pastors, men of the manse. Pastors' kids have always deeply influenced Canadian public policy. It was Mackenzie King who created the first external affairs organism in the East Block in the 1920s, composed of pastors' kids - sons of missionaries who inculcated the social gospel as the first organizing idea of our foreign policy, which reverberates to this day.

David comes from a renowned family of evangelical preachers; hence, his first two names. You will hear the echoes of that eloquent tradition in his speeches and his knowledge of the Scriptures, Old and New. You will also hear the rhythms of great gospel music, of which he is a fervent follower.

David worked for Walter Gordon, then joined me as an assistant to John Turner in the mid-sixties when we assembled the book of John's speeches, entitled *The Politics of Purpose*, which still stands the test of time today.

Together with Lloyd Axworthy, we worked assiduously to make John Turner Prime Minister. Loyalties die hard amongst Liberals and so do misconceptions. It was John Turner who inspired the youth vote in 1968. It was David's idea to establish the 195 Club, composed of mostly Young Liberals who stayed with Turner through the last ballot and continued to support him thereafter. It was Turner who captured the

Young Liberal vote in 1968.

Honourable senators, David and I shared common digs in Ottawa in the sixties. Together with Lloyd Axworthy, we managed successfully the floor fight at the Liberal convention to introduce Medicare. Memories fade, but we still recall the proponents and opponents of what was to become a cornerstone of Liberal policy.

David then went to Osgoode Hall Law School and then on to Queen's University, where he uncovered Tom Axworthy and where he met and later married Heather Smith - now a pre-eminent justice of the Court of Appeal of Ontario - raised a talented family, and commenced the practice of law. He then ran for municipal office in Toronto, rising to Deputy Mayor.

Honourable senators, perhaps I will conclude on another day.

DAVID P. SMITH, P.C.: WELCOME TO THE SENATE

October 8, 2002

Hon. Jerahmiel S. Grafstein: Honourable senators, I beg your indulgence once more to conclude my welcome to our newest colleague, Senator David Paul Smith. Let me pick up where I left off the other day.

While continuing as Deputy Mayor of Toronto, Senator Smith continued his practice of law. While the practice and business were his preoccupations, federal politics was and remains his passionate obsession.

David decided to run for Parliament, and run he did, successfully. As a member of the House of Commons, he chaired a special committee reporting on disabilities, and then in turn led the successful lobbying to include disability rights in the Charter.

He joined the Cabinet as Secretary of State for Small Businesses and Tourism, where he served with imagination and energy, two of David's natural gifts.

I recall - and Honourable Senator Lowell Murray may recall - that during the Charter and amending formula debates, there was great difficulty as a result of the opposition's very acute and intelligent lobbying in the mother of all Parliaments, the British Parliament. Provincial lobbyists as well as opposition members did a good job of seeking to convince some members of the House of Lords and the House on the other side that there should be major concerns with respect to the amending formula and the Charter. Mr. Trudeau sent David as a government troubleshooter to persuade reluctant British parliamentarians to accept the amending formula in the 1982 Constitution to overcome these well-organized and very acute objections. His persuasive powers were and are legendary. For these and other contributions, he proudly received a rare Queen's Counsel appointment from the federal government.

When he retired from Parliament in Ottawa, he was never far from politics in Ontario, involved in every national campaign at the most senior levels since the 1960s. He became Campaign Chairman in Ontario and the National Campaign Chairman under Mr. Chrétien in the last election. Meanwhile, he rose to the pinnacle of the legal profession as managing partner of Fraser Milner Casgrain, and helped build his firm into a national presence.

He makes his home in the heart of Toronto - he is a neighbour of mine - and summers in Cobourg. He led the Liberal Party to almost a full house in Ontario in the last three federal elections, a feat never before matched in Canadian political history.

He is a world traveller - there is no corner of the globe unfamiliar to his curious mind and capacious memory. His keen sense of humour will be a pleasant distraction from his more sober duties here in the Senate.

Now our friend David starts a third career in politics as a Senator for Ontario, from Cobourg, his country home. While I can say without fear of exaggeration that David is prepared for the Senate, I wonder if the Senate is prepared for this burly life force called David.

An Hon. Senator: Three minutes!

Senator Grafstein: Rarely has an individual been so fully armed and loaded and ready to take on the exacting and self-effacing tasks confronting a senator.

While we survey the current political landscape, the old road maps in Canadian politics are of little value and offer no hints to the future. Rest assured, David will be among the skillful guides around the difficult political shoals, waterfalls and cascades awaiting all of us on this side of the aisle and the other in the current Parliament.

With your indulgence, honourable senators, may I have another moment?

An Hon. Senator: No.

The Hon. the Speaker: Honourable Senator Grafstein, I regret to advise you that your three minutes have expired

NICHOLAS W. TAYLOR: ON RETIREMENT

November 7, 2002

Hon. Jerahmiel S. Grafstein: Honourable senators, I have had the distinct pleasure of Nick's company for over three decades. His infectious smile, wit and spirit never flagged from the first moment I met him. I am sure, when he leaves the Senate, it will never leave him.

I asked myself, as I listened to these magnificent tributes to Nick, how I could describe him in one word. That word, I believe, is "maverick." For most of his private and public life, Nick was a loner, a contrarian, a man unafraid to stand against conventional wisdom. As you all know, Nick was a Liberal in Alberta. For me, liberalism and Taylorism became synonymous with Alberta. In the Senate, as Senator Joyal pointed out, he never succumbed to the instincts of the herd, nor to the convention of loyalty above loyalty to his principles or to the independence of the Senate itself. In a way, the Senate was established as a maverick institution, and Nick has always been loyal to that tradition. Nick's principles and practices have rode well because they always rode together. He always followed his maverick instincts and always stood tall in the saddle on his stirrups of principle. Nick, you have left your brand in the Senate and you will not be easily forgotten.

On a personal note, when I introduced my clean water bill, it was Nick who encouraged me when he agreed to take the bill to his committee to thoroughly study it and unanimously endorse it. I thank you for that encouragement and I wish you and your family all the best in the future.

JOE CLARK, P.C.: TRIBUTE

June 3, 2003

Hon. Jerahmiel S. Grafstein: Honourable senators, I rise to pay tribute to the Right Honourable Joe Clark. He and I entered party life at the same time, in the early 1960s. I have watched him rise from a Ministerial Assistant to a Member of Parliament, to the leader of his party, to the Prime Minister, and then on to a very distinguished career as Minister of External Affairs.

He has always been a formidable adversary, an energetic party activist, and an outstanding and potent debater in the House of Commons - in summary, a true man of the Commons, following in the footsteps of John Diefenbaker, who was also a great lover of the Commons.

I have only one quibble, and it relates to one small aspect of the grand tribute paid to him by the Right Honourable Brian Mulroney, when he said that Mr. Clark was the second best Foreign Minister of this century. I would beg to respectfully quibble with him. I believe that the first and most outstanding Foreign Minister of this century was the Right Honourable Louis St. Laurent, closely followed by the Right Honourable Lester B. Pearson. Where Mr. Clark's rating is after that, I leave to history.

ROMANCING THE STONES: A MODEST LESSON IN THE "NEW POLITICS" OF THIS 21ST CENTURY OR, AS SIR MICK JAGGER PROCLAIMED "TORONTO IS BACK AND IT'S BOOMING!"

August 12, 2003

Pierre Trudeau once pondered that media was akin to "electronic cannon."

That electronic cannon, the global media launched a sudden, brutal frontal assault against Toronto and Canada magnifying the SARS scare across the world.

So what lesson can be gleaned from the historic Rolling Stones Concert? Can a complex intersection of public and private interests and actors be quickly mobilized to transform public policy and launch a counter attack by reversing the same powerful cannons of the global media?

Are governments ready for this new global media warfare?

Too often, bureaucratic structures, disarm themselves into ineffective cudgels of public policy. Organized in separate, communist-like pillars, segregated by bureaucratic self-interest, all made less effective by three confusing, competing levels of governance. Such overlapping government asymmetry, appear confused and unable to serve public needs when national emergencies erupt so suddenly gutting public opinion.

Hence the American story of unpreparedness before September 11th. Hence the delayed feeble response time when issues such as bad blood, bad water, SARS or the Mad Cow Disease suddenly pre-empt other stories. Thinking outside the box, outside traditional lineal government overlapping structures, calls for a different paradigm of public policy to suit this new virtual reality.

Public health and public safety have catapulted on to the global stage and inflamed public opinion as preoccupations of this new 21st century accelerated by global media inter connectivity. The speed of economic dislocation is always deeper than imagined. These lightning, almost accidental events, have left governments careening across departments, unprepared and under organized, and thus bereft of swift remedial effective public policy.

Rarely is cost a factor. Rather this complacent disarray of governance lack appropriate responses due to the misuse, or worse disuse of public power. So, the public remains stunned, confused and confounded.

Rarely, in the heat of confusion, is the power of public purse strategically applied to careful, cost efficient targets of opportunity.

How come? Why so? Obviously, clarity of ideas is on leave. Energy to execute ideas is on vacation. Of course, the appetite for risk is limited. So copious levers of public policy are rarely deployed effectively. Inertia combats energy, as governments refuse to cut a swath across bureaucratic lines of activity or engage the private sector. So governments languish, like Gulliver, tied down by the strands of the departmental Lilliputians, each department more obsessed by its own narrow bureaucratic needs than the public good.

A "new politics" inspired by quick silver supple leadership can easily bring order out of disorder, comfort out of chaos, all at a minimalist cost to the public purse. All that is necessary at the federal level is for a tiny SWAT-like committee of politicians to stand ready, on guard, energized and active, matched by the already superbly organized PCO, that can mow a fresh path across departments and levels of governance to quickly reconfigure the government levers as weapons of choice and weapons of effectiveness.

One modest yet stark lesson is the "Romance of Rolling Stones". How then to use rock music as an engine of public policy, domestic and international.

Overcome the "coalition of the anti's", as Pierre Trudeau would say ready - to spring up against any new idea.

Then harken to Sir Mick Jagger who early targeted the "whingers" who, are for the most part, led by largely uninformed media who often fail to research all the facts.

So what to do? First, float a compelling idea like a free Stones Concert supported by government and allow public opinion to shape and tailor the idea.

The idea behind the Rolling Stones Concert was to project simply and quickly a positive message around the globe in such a way to capture the curiosity and awareness and interest of global media.

In the midst of the SARS crisis in May, governments languished. Conventional wisdom at all levels of government held that marketing into the eye of the storm of the SARS crisis would be costly and ineffective. The Dixie Chicks and Billy Joel and other stars were canceling concerts. Indeed, when governments did advertise, millions of dollars were wasted because there was no singular projectile or magnet of global attraction that could draw away the negative perception of SARS danger to public health in Toronto. So the political objective was simple. To quickly override the negative perception ingrained by both global television and print, endlessly repeated across all world news networks, underscored by continuous alpha numeric digital messaging that Canada and Toronto were unsafe destinations for tourists.

Few grasped the deep, darkening economic implosion across Canada ignited by the SARS crisis which was so catastrophic. Within weeks, 19,000 low paid hospitality workers (waiters, chambermaids, dishwashers, etc.) found themselves out of work in Toronto alone. Another 20,000 others were on work share in Toronto, making barely enough to cover even their monthly rent. Tourism across Canada in every region from PEI (with loss of the Japanese tourists) to Niagara to Banff were devastated. New car purchases for rental at airports were cut back by 20%. An estimated some 10,000 to 15,000 less new car purchases this fall would reverberate into the auto industry. Further, hotels and airlines and tourist destinations and restaurants and theatres were on the cusp of bankruptcy. Taxi drivers were ravaged by minimal cash receipts and higher insurance.

Consumers confidence across Canada ebbed as did retail sales across Canada.

Then "Mad Cow" struck the global media with a vengeance, putting cattlemen, meat workers out of work across the West and Ontario, reducing food store and fast food sales. Meanwhile, conventions, concerts and film productions continued to cancel, even further greasing the skids towards economic disaster. The GNP faltered. The economic dislocation seemed spinning on an endless cycle of losses to the Canadian and Toronto economy, fitfully waiting to be borne by the ultimate victim - the taxpayer.

A quick fix was needed. A powerful global quick fix. Both Dennis Mills and I had come to the same conclusion: so we joined forces to do something about this bad situation.

One key was to project a vast picture of hundreds of thousands happy, healthy fans seen crowded together at a sunny outdoor concert, cheek to jowl, and arrange to have that picture flooded across the globe for hours, reversing the same global media that had so ravaged tourism and the beef industry. One need not delve too deeply into Canetti's "*Crowds and Power*" to uncover keys to success!

Make sure the hospitality workers and SARS front line fighters were not forgotten. Establish a benevolent fund for each group so that $1.00 from each ticket and net proceeds of the Concert after cost recovery would be available for them.

There could a quick and cost effective turn about! The beef problem could be muted. American and Japanese politicians' objections to Canadian beef, supported by their bureaucracies and interest groups could also be overridden by going over their heads to the masses via the global media.

Not only could the Rolling Stones, those global icons, be transformed into a global projectile of public policy on par with the Pope, but the positive message could be enhanced by adding a sterling cast of Canadian and International rock stars targeted to every demographic age group - from 70 to 7.

Remember the Stones provoke news and entertainment coverage!

Design a populous, accessible venue, replete with affordable tickets, food, open, safe and sound for fans and families alike.

Ensure the disabled and SARS workers received the best views of the concert stage. Magnify the message still further. Invite political elites; the Organization for Security and Co-operation in Europe Parliamentary Assembly ("OSCE-PA") in Rotterdam (Parliamentarians from 55 countries from Vladistock to Vancouver), 190 Permanent United Nation Delegations in New York, and then the entire United States Congress in Washington. Enlist Consul Generals across America and Ambassadors across the world to invite local dignitaries in their regional spheres of influence.

A picture is worth a million words. The challenge was to exhibit that picture around the globe cost effectively. Take the existing broadcast networks led by CBC, our public broadcaster, to produce a two hour special simulcast, joined by MuchMoreMusic, a leading national private cable broadcaster, and fill them with 12 hours and more of a star studded concert flooded with sunny side up pictures of Canada and Toronto.

Provide affordable packages by air bus and train, especially from America so that fans, young and old alike, would affordably flock to Toronto to celebrate the historic experience for classic rock fans everywhere. Allow millions of fans around the Globe to join electronically for at least a part of the psychic experience.

Gain vital endorsement and total support from your own GTA caucas and then seek further support from concerned civic groups.

Make sure that a creative consortium is forged together all three levels of government, together with the private sector inspired by Molson, one of Canada's premier event managers, led by entrepreneurial Dan O'Neill and Jo-Anne McArthur of Mostar and supported by Doug Brummer of A&P/Dominion, the artists led by Michael Cohl, the world's premier concert promoter, together with astute Steve Howard of Toronto, who collectively assembled the best experts, a global international all star team of concert managers from the U.K., U.S. and Canada to join Molson to micromanage the concert. Watch the legendary Michael J. Elder of Toronto, Benny Collins of California, Riley O'Connor of the House of Blues and then Jake Berry of the U.K., join the singular Bob Singleton of Mostar to put the puzzle together with precise planning.

Ensure that the municipal services from policing to transportation, to waste removal, cleanup, to emergency services, to parking anticipate all problems and superbly organize for every eventuality. Obtain the crucial early support of Chief f, who leads the police, to specially prepare themselves to be Ambassadors of Goodwill rather than enforcers so that all actors at the event would be prepared to project the same idea of a happy safe city to the world.

Help the audience to prepare itself to play its part as typical, nice, well-mannered Canadians joined by tens of thousands of American and international visitors so that the global media would record, repeat and project the positive message - simply, that Toronto and Canada are healthy, safe venues, free of SARS.

Use the presence of the global media to project that Canadian beef must be healthy if tens of thousands of fans are seen munching happily on Canadian beef prepared at the longest barbeque line in history, all manned by BBQ champions invited from around the world organized by Shane Carmichael.

Entice CNN and the other curious TV networks to record this event. Carefully seek print coverage in the opinion-making major dailies such as the New York Times, the Wall Street Journal, the Chicago Tribune and the other regional newspapers, especially all the major news services.

Don't forget the International Herald Tribune, the global English newspaper or the Financial Times. Inspire print magazines to do photos and retrospectives of the record breaking event, like Time, McLeans and People.

What skeptics could not grasp was that time was of the essence! Only weeks to prepare in what would normally take a year or more.

Yet the two year experience planning of the Pope's visit last year allowed Dennis Mills and other experts to eradicate any missteps. Canadian tourism could recover quickly if there was a quick turn about this summer, so that booking cycles, normally 12 to 24 months or more, would reopen for tourists and conventions.

Yet, skeptics still failed to grasp was that the Stones' concert itself was only the sparkling, captivating tip of the iceberg in the micromanagement of electronic cannons. Below the surface prepare a carefully designed media plan to broadcast across the networks, not only in Canada, but across North America and then target the far corners of the Globe. Add the expertise of Fran Curtis of New York, David Jones of Molson, Rene Blackman of House of Blues.

Prepare carefully for three waves media coverage. First wave before the concert, the second wave during the concert and third wave after the concert.

Have the second wave of media led by a CBC Television Special combined with cable's MuchMoreMusic, a day long stream of "info" entertainment studded with one song by each artist. Ensure that these were broadcast across Canada targeted to capture over 50% of the Canadian viewing.

Get Standard Broadcasting to work with CBC on a two hour radio concert of music to distribute simultaneously across Canada, and carried by both private and public radio broadcasters alike.

Realize that all waves, both radio and television signals would spill over into Canada's primary tourist basin located within 300 miles south of the Canadian border across America from coast to coast at no additional cost.

Arrange the same two hour CBC T.V., simulcast a show to be beamed to 800,000 American service men and women serving in 178 countries and including Iraq, Korea and Japan as well as all U.S. territories overseas from the Pacific to Puerto Rico via American Forces T.V. and Radio. Asked that all 178 U.S. ships on all the high seas also be allowed to receive the show. As well, make 12 hours of MuchMoreMusic and the 2 hour "simulcast" available to the Department of Defence for satellite to all Canadian service men and women overseas, including our fighting forces in Afghanistan, and our peace keepers in Bosnia, the Golan Heights and Egypt. Agree that these broadcast to these far flung service men and women could be repeated for a third wave.

Allow close circuit feeds to all cities across Canada requesting the feed including Calgary and Edmonton and St. John's and so on, so other willing Canadian cities can join the full 12 hour concert feed without cost. Make sure all broadcasts include and repeat a short spectacular special infomercial of Toronto and Canada produced specially and quickly by a Canada's renowned film maker, Norman Jewison.

Negotiate for a tape delay of the 2 hour show to the Space Station in outer space via NASA Johnson Space Station to heighten global interest and one hour T.V. special featuring the best of the 12 hour show to be broadcast across Canada and later repeated across Canada and our spillover Canadian basin in the United States. Prepare yet another one to two hour global special to be shown later and repeated in the United States and to be sold to all foreign markets across the globe as yet another musical infomercial for Canada for the third wave.

What was the impact of this fusillades of global media? Was it powerful enough to scorch the SARS scare from the global media?

Preliminary studies show that CNN and its world affiliates broadcast 18 live segments (including the Four Premiers - Ernie Eves, Ralph Klein, Gary Doer and Lorne Calvert, serving Canadian beef and BBQ to thousands of happy and healthy munching fans from across America and overseas).

Positive segments appeared on all three major entertainment channels - E, Access Entertainment and Entertainment Tonight, the top graded American TV show, NBC's Good Morning America as well as TV coverage on the regional outlets of NBC, ABC, CBC, CBS and Fox in most, if not all, regional markets across America, especially Canada's major tourist targets in the northern states, all major cities including New York, Boston, Chicago, Detroit, Los Angeles, Miami, Washington and so on.

Add a surprisingly effective Internet show to the second wave of global media - an innovative twelve hour WorldWide Webcast distributed first by CBC across Canada, and through the good offices of Microsoft Canada, throughout the United States, via MSNBC, then around the Globe by Microsoft through Windows reaching 300,000,000 people, from South America, to Asia, to Australia and throughout Europe.

Preliminary studies indicate the Webcast, called "Toronto Rocks WorldWide Webcast", received 1,000 hits per seconds rising to 1,800 hits or so a second for an estimated 75 million hits in just a 12 hour period. Compare this shattering global reach to the recent *New York Times* analysis of the U.S. top rated Web Sites in the United States this June. E-Bay received 43,000,000 hits and Amazon received 23,000,000 hits in that 30 day period.

As for print and photos, preliminary analysis indicates that over 564 stories appeared in all major and regional newspapers across America the next day alone and in other foreign dailies. As for radio, the National Public Radio carried behind scenes interviews, "info", entertainment and broadcast to 300 America radio stations across America and overseas without accounting for other rock stations around the world.

Billboard & Variety, the entertainment bibles, presented glowing reviews of the concert for their global readership. Ensure in the third wave, a one to two hour special to be distributed across the globe retains 10% of the global proceeds for the two benevolent funds.

Hopefully inspire a DVD to be produced and sold across the Globe - all projecting a positive image of Toronto and Canada.

The third wave will also include stories in magazines and newspaper and possibly books to recapture retrospectives, this historic record breaking musical event.

Not to be forgotten was third language coverage. The commercial of the Stones coming to Toronto was translated into 10 languages by OMNI, Canada's premier multi-lingual service shown first on OMNI, then in Rotterdam at the OSCE Parliamentary Assembly before Parliamentarians from 55 countries and then distributed to all OMNI foreign language network contacts across Europe, South America and Asia as public service announcements.

So the story of the "new politics" is still being written. While it may be premature to project if the "new politics" will overtake and leave behind the "old politics", failure to grasp both realities and opportunities to promote public policy to the masses in the 21st century comes at our economic peril. Music can be a powerful instrument to transform domestic and international policy if carefully deployed.

All would have not been possible without the enthusiastic spirit of dozens of Canadian companies, unions, workers and volunteers who answered the clarion call and rarely said no.

"Old politics" suffers only from lack of imagination rather than lack of assets, lack of energy than ingenuity. It is so simple to deploy the existing levers already built into the existing government costs that can so easily be fielded at little or no additional cost to the taxpayers.

For all involved, the federal, provincial and city governments, the private sector, the artists, the workers and the Canadian public, this was a Win-Win-Win-Win-Win-Win situation.

Preliminary, partial, economic impact studies showed hotels filled, taxis had their best days since September 11th, credit card usage spiked to 22%, consumer confidence returned, retail sales and services exploded, restaurants and fast food boomed, while Toronto and Canadians feel proud and happy. Car rentals and photo supply sales rose sharply. All this happened in Toronto followed by waves across Ontario and Canada.

The "New Politics" is all about recapturing the global media. In the last resort, all these tailored elements combined to make the Rolling Stones and their Friends Concert more than a historic event for fans and viewers alike. An indelible brand of 'can do' spirit was ignited anew in the Canadian psyche.

Even politicians can be right!

Early on, John Manley predicted more Americans would invade Canada than the War of 1812.

He was accurate. Americans came in the tens of thousands.

This record breaking musical concert raucously announced that Toronto and Canada was open for fun and business. Sir Mick Jagger caught the message. "Toronto is back and it's booming." So is Canada!

One day after, one Toronto newspaper declared "WE ROCKED!". . . . "It was exactly what we needed."

Exactly.

•These not so exclusive excerpts are from a book yet to be written perhaps to be published and probably to be entitled *ROMANCING THE STONES - A Modest Lesson in the 'New Politics' of the 21ˢᵗ Century.* Or, as Sir Mick Jagger proclaimed, "Toronto is back and it's booming!" Hopefully to be written by Senator Jerry S. Grafstein, Q.C. and co authored by Dennis Mills, M.P.

LEO KOLBER: ON RETIREMENT

October 22, 2003

Hon. Jerahmiel S. Grafstein: Honourable senators, I also rise to pay tribute to Leo Kolber. Leo Kolber, Leo Kolber, Leo Kolber - a concise and clear name for a concise and clear-minded man. Leo and I arrived in the Senate within weeks of each other, close to two decades ago, and so have been colleagues and really great if not argumentative friends since that time.

Leo is an impatient man, and I will not try his patience much further today, for Leo is not patient with fools, pomp, cant or ceremony. He is a man of concise and clear common sense. He prides himself, rightly, on his ability to cut quickly through matters, whether business or politics, to reach the heart of any complex problem. This is a rare and great gift, which he has amply demonstrated in both his business and senatorial careers.

Leo is a builder - a builder of great buildings, great networks of friends, and political coalitions. He helped to build one political coalition that I believe helped save Canada.

He has applied his same rare gifts to philanthropy and causes ranging from the arts to education to health, as we have heard here today. If you probe him, you will find that he is a proud, pugnacious Canadian and a fierce, fearsome, proud Jew. This pride comes at a time when his co-religionist rights as an equal citizen are being challenged around the globe.

Honourable senators, Leo has now become an author. I can hardly wait to read the index to see if my many kindnesses to him have been reciprocated in that volume. I remain confident that when he leaves the Senate in a few months, he will not vacate the public arena and will continue to provide his insight, clarity of thought and energy all in the aid of the public good.

His life, his late wife, Sandra, and his family have filled a unique niche in the Canadian mosaic. Leo, old friend, may I conclude, by giving you a traditional salute - L'chaim! To life!

CLAUDE RYAN: EULOGY

February 11, 2004

Hon. Jerahmiel S. Grafstein: Honourable senators, I rise to pay tribute to the late Claude Ryan. Suddenly, Quebec and Canada have suffered an irretrievable loss: the resonating, meticulous, fair minded voice of Claude Ryan, an unforgettable Canadian, a thoughtful advocate of Quebec's interests within Confederation and a staunch advocate of Canada.

When history of this era is written, it will paint a prominent portrait and clear a place for Claude Ryan. Many of us bore witness to that era and followed Claude Ryan's opinions with great care. Quebec produced a most remarkable generation, especially five powerful individuals who began as activists, critics and journalists and emerged as powerful political leaders. In the process, these five individuals changed the course of history: Pierre Trudeau, Rene Levesque, Jean Marchand, Gerald Pelletier and Claude Ryan. All could trace their affiliation to L'Action Catholique Canadienne and all were acquaintances, if not friends, and all became antagonists.

Each approached the idea of Canada in different ways. Their internal debate became our national debate, and each was a devout democrat. All five were deeply influenced by two great thinkers: Cardinal Newman, a well-known Catholic philosopher, and one unknown Canadian thinker, Fernand Cadieux.

Mr. Cadieux was born in New Brunswick, settled and worked in Montreal as a teacher, then came to Ottawa in 1968 as a resident thinker in the Trudeau government. Each Wednesday evening, at the bar in the Chateau Laurier, Cadieux would hold forth, with a drink and cigarette in hand and, like Socrates, talk and teach and dazzle his circle of acolytes. Cadieux deeply influenced each of these five famous men with his ideas, which, like Marshall McLuhan's, addressed the clash between the power of the media and the power of politics. The impact of television and radio lay at the heart of his ideas.

Cadieux died suddenly and tragically. Claude and I, as friends, attended his funeral in Ottawa. At the funeral, I asked Claude why French Canadians had not written about Fern and why Fern, who had not left a written record, was not noticed in the French press for his wide and pervasive influence. Ryan suggested that I write such a piece for Le Devoir. I told him that my French was not adequate and, therefore, I was not up to the task. "Not to worry," said Claude, "you write it in English, and I will translate it myself and publish it in Le Devoir," which he did several days later.

Claude Ryan was interested in and open to ideas, but he was unbending in his analyses, unremitting in his opinions, always honest about the facts and always, always a democrat. Canada has lost a great mind and a great Canadian. I regret that we will never see the likes of him and his colleagues of that era again.

His passing marks the end of an era of great Canadian history. Canada will miss him and so will I.

HARRISON McCAIN, C.C.: EULOGY

March 23, 2004

Hon. Jerahmiel S. Grafstein: Honourable senators, I rise to pay tribute to the late Harrison McCain, a strong, bold name for a strong, bold personality.

I was surprised and saddened to learn of his passing. I recall a chat that we had just a few months ago when I called for his political advice. Harrison, in that high, shrill, down-east voice, said: "Now Jerry, give me those arguments again." And I did. He said: "I will get back to you."

A day or so later, he called back and said: "You are wrong. You should not do that. Here are the reasons why. See you later." Boom, and he hung up. That was Harrison McCain: quick, to the point, very effective and no wasted words. He had a sharp political instinct and he had sharp political judgment. He was a great entrepreneur, a great Maritimer, a great Liberal, a great small "l" liberal and one of the greatest Canadians of his generation.

His late sister, Eleanor Johnson, was also a great friend. I recall that when I first went to a rather conservative educational institution with my young son, she saw me cringing at the back of the hall. I was not used to that environment where everyone in the room, except for me, was a Conservative. She called out in that same high-pitched McCain voice: "Jerry, you come right up here with me. Us Liberals have to stick together!" I will never forget that.

Honourable senators, it is with great and deep regret that we witness the passing of Harrison McCain. I will never forget his voice; I will never forget his flashing eyes; I will never forget his puckish humour nor his great social conscience. He will be greatly missed by all who shared the pleasure of his company. My condolences to all members of his family, which is also a great Canadian family. Their extraordinary contributions to our country are yet to be fully measured or fairly applauded.

"SHOAH" AND THE POWER OF MEMORY
NOTES TO COMMEMORATE THE FIRST ANNUAL HOLOCAUST MEMORIAL DAY PURSUANT TO C 459, AN ACT OF PARLIAMENT

April 18, 2004

Today is an historic day.

And, Jews have never treated history lightly. Why?

Because history has always provided so many mixed reviews for Jews. In the last 1,000 years, one out of every three Jews was murdered. In this last century, the murder of Jews accelerated. In the modern 20th century, two out of five Jews were murdered. So, for Jews, history must always be weighed carefully. Jews must always keep in mind the dismal mathematics of history.

Yet today is an historic day. Today we commemorate the "Shoah." Today a brand new page has been added to Canadian history. For today we breathe life into Canada's law for the first time. May I thank members of the Parliament, from the Commons and the Senate, who were the sponsors of this Bill. May I specifically thank my colleague in the Senate, Marie Poulin who at my request introduced the Bill to the Senate.

C-459 is an Act of Parliament to commemorate the Holocaust - "The Shoah" - on each and every year and, according to our ancient Hebrew Calendar.

What is the "Shoah?" Does the "Shoah" lie beyond words? Beyond poetry? Beyond music? Does the "Shoah" reside beyond human communication, as some observers have argued. If so, how then are we to even communicate the word "Shoah"? The word "Shoah" itself cannot be easily translated for the word "Shoah" only approaches words like catastrophe or cataclysm or annihilation by burning. So the word "Shoah" still lies hidden beyond our feeble imagination!

Our Rabbis tell us that whenever we are confused, whenever we cannot comprehend the incomprehensible, whenever we cannot find answers, we are duty bound to search out good questions!

Some times good questions are better than bad answers!

The first question we might ask ourselves today is what then is the "Shoah?" The "Shoah" was not an event. It did not occur on one day. Or one month. Or even a year. The "Shoah" was a process to reach a certain conclusion. The "Shoah" was to be the Final Solution. The "Shoah" then was a culmination, an awesome conclusion to lifetimes of small, almost, disconnected acts. Slowly these disjointed, disconnected acts, like drops of water turned into rain. Then a storm. Then a torrent. Then a tidal wave. Then this tidal wave turned into a flood that uprooted out and swept out Jews wherever they lived, even in their small, peaceful, isolated communities. This flood was of such monumental misery and scope, that it left no individual Jew or family untouched by its awesome tide, or undercurrents, or cross currents.

Each and every sign, each and every signal, large and small alike, like rain drops at first evaporated, or were suppressed, or generally ignored, or explained away, or rationalized, or muted, or neglected, by Jew and Gentile alike. Who could understand or expect the scale of the unexpected? Who could predict that such a process would be so precisely planned or minutely engineered? Who could comprehend this incomprehensible? What reason could rationalize the irrational? What civilized countries could have designed such plans or collaborated to organize themselves in such a way, each abusing their own Rule of Law, towards the people of the book whose origins and faith and historic message was so based and bound up with the Rule of Law! That civilized nations would collaborate on the perversion of the law, on the Final Solution, was beyond our reason.

So, the "Shoah" seeped out, not from barbaric states but civilized ones. What were the drops and dots that did not connect! Only a taunt here! A rant there! A dogma here! A teacher there! A preacher here! A government leader there! A mugging here! A march there! A bureaucratic policy here! A government programme there! A window breaking here! A book burning there! A synagogue scorched here! Graffiti there! Media here! A chorus of voices at an international forum there! A native leader's outburst here! A joke there! Just here and there! Just here and there! Just small, unconnected drops!

So, what then is the question? What are we to remember? The Hebrew word for memory is "Zachor!" What is the power, the engine of our memory?

The Rabbis tells us that "Zachor" is not a passive word. "Zachor" looks backward and forward. Yes, we must never forget the past. But we live in the present. "Zachor" is an imperative verb! "Zachor" - cannot ignore the present. So the answer to our question is simple, simple action! The power of memory is the engine to energize the present. To energize us to act! What actions can each one of us take to refuse history another lesson? Can one person change history? Can one person make a difference? The Bible gives a resounding affirmative. The answer lies in individual action - in deeds, in "Mitzvot" - acts large and small - alone, alone, alone and hopefully together. The first Mitzvah is never to remain silent but to speak out!

Martin Luther King once mused that the words of his enemies never disturbed him. It was the silence of his friends.

And the Kotzer Rebbe reminded us that the first duty of a Jew, as Jew and as a citizen, is to awake to take individual responsibility. Awake from our slumber. Awake from our complacency. Become alive and alert to any word or any act, large or small, that heaps disrespect or hate on "the Other." Fight lies with truth, he taught!

Treat the stranger as yourself, so the Bible admonished us!

Do not do unto others that which is distasteful to yourself. So, the great Rabbi Hillel, himself scourged only for his beliefs, taught well before the Common Era.

Above all, don't fall asleep. Don't become lazy. Don't pass the buck to others! Don't become so tolerant that you tolerate intolerance.

This generation, our generation, has a special responsibility! We are chosen! Why? We were witnesses! Each generation of Jews is admonished to think as if each one of us were slaves in Egypt. We are taught to remember at Passover that we, each one of us, sought freedom from oppression! So we should force ourselves, each of us, to relive the Shoah. We do so as that experience will oblige us to use all of our powers to work and strive that the Shoah does not reoccur in this time, in this present, in our time. Recent history argues that we have already forgotten "Zachor." We cannot remain silent. For silence is acquiescence and, acquiescence brought us the Final Solution!

The souls of the "Shoah," the sparks of their souls can still find no rest! Indeed, as the Kabbala says, their vessels were broken! The sparks of their souls escaped their broken vessels. Their souls will not rest and cannot rest! Their vessels will not be repaired! There will be no "Tikkun." There will be no restoration. There will be no repair until there is "Chai Olam!" Peace in the world. So let us repeat two words - Mitzvot, Deeds, and Shalom, Peace! Without action against hate, whenever or whichever or from whomever it erupts, can be no rest. There can be no Shalom without Mitzvot!

From today, the new law, commemorating Yom Hashoah, this new Rule of Law will spread across our land. Hopefully this law will inspire every city, town, village, every house of faith and every school to use this new laws as a simple lesson of how a civic society teaches itself to guard against historic and present barbarism.

So let us say, Shalom, Salaam. Peace! Amen!

JACK MARSHALL: EULOGY

October 6, 2004

Hon. Jerahmiel S. Grafstein: Honourable senators, my late father was a decorated veteran of the Polish army and fought in the war for Polish independence following World War I. From early childhood, I was always fascinated with military matters and war stories I heard from veterans. Before I came to the Senate, I articled for Senator Croll and learned of his outstanding military career: rising from Private to Lieutenant-Colonel in his regiment, and his service overseas with such distinction during World War II before returning to Canada in 1945, then being elected in Spadina as the lone Liberal member in Toronto.

When I came to the Senate, now over two decades ago, I came to know Jack Marshall and discovered his equally fascinating military record of a proud and courageous service at Normandy and beyond during World War II.

Jack was an outstanding advocate for veterans' issues, a strong voice for his region and island home in Newfoundland, and a staunch supporter for a united Canada. As a proud Jew and a proud Canadian, he made me proud to feel privileged to be his colleague here.

Jack will be missed by friends and political foes alike for his humanity and his wit, for all who came to know him could not fail to respect him for all his works.

We extend to his family our deepest condolences. As we say according to Jewish tradition, may his soul be bound up in the bonds of eternal life.

RICHARD H. KROFT: ON RETIREMENT

November 17, 2004

Hon. Jerahmiel S. Grafstein: Honourable senators, I first encountered Richard Kroft in Ottawa almost four decades ago in 1965 when I came to serve as John Turner's Executive Assistant. John Turner then was the most junior minister to the Pearson government. Richard, on the other hand, was the lofty Executive Assistant to the powerful and most senior Minister of Finance, the Honourable Mitchell Sharp. In those days, Richard - always called Richard and never by a diminutive of the name - was ever elegant and suave. He sported a graceful pipe, which was allowed in the halls of Parliament in those days, and was clothed in immaculate English-cut jackets. He spoke in quiet, measured tones, befitting all the magisterial sounds that emanated from a mandarin minister's lair.

Always debonair, Richard came from a most distinguished Winnipeg family whose father and mother held august positions in the Winnipeg Liberal establishment. His family was multi-talented. I, on the other hand, was a rather green, inexperienced, impatient, political activist from the streets of Toronto, ever-anxious to change the world. Despite our differences in approach, we always shared one common political objective, to further the policies and principles of the Liberal Party, and so we became fast friends and confidants.

Now, while Richard was a loyal member of the Sharp-Chrétien circle, I became successively a member of the Keith Davey crew, the Turner clan and then the Trudeau tribe. When Richard was finally summoned by Mr. Chretien to serve in this chamber some six years ago, I asked him what had taken him so long. It did not take Richard long to catch up. He rose swiftly through the Senate ranks to hold the position of Chair of the Standing Senate Committee on Banking, Trade and Commerce, which I now hold. Although we disagreed on measures from time to time, especially the role of the Senate in the Clarity bill, Richard was always sound and considerate in all of his views.

We will miss his wise counsel, but are consoled by the fact that now that he has been liberated from the travails of the Senate, he will speak up freely and wisely in Canada's interests in the future as he has done so ably in the past.

I extend to him safe passage as he returns to the arms of his wife, Hillaine, to his wonderful and talented family and to the tranquility of private life. No doubt we will hear words of wisdom from Richard in the future.

Finally, honourable senators, I confess that Richard and I share a deep, dark secret - a love of Winnipeg. My daughter-in-law and the mother of my three grandsons was born and bred in Winnipeg. I have observed that the wind and the cold at Portage and Main has enlarged the warmth in the hearts of all Winnipeggers. We are so grateful to share the warmth of Richard's friendship.

DAN IANNUZZI, O.C.: EULOGY

November 25, 2004

Hon. Jerahmiel S. Grafstein: Honourable senators, this week we learned that Mr. Trudeau is climbing up the charts to become Canada's Greatest Canadian. Why? For the simple idea of Canada as a 'distinct society': a bilingual and multicultural society. This week, we learned as well of the sudden passing of Daniel Iannuzzi, the visionary dreamer and co-founder of Canada's, and the world's, first multilingual television station in Toronto, who tried to breathe life into Mr. Trudeau's idea.

Dan was also a founder of the Canadian Italian daily, *Corriere Canadese*, which he started in 1954 at the tender age of 20. Over the years, he acquired and published a number of other third-language newspapers.

Dan shared the intellectual direction of his enterprises with his wife, Elena Caprile, and the business direction with his long-time partner and brother, Paul.

Dan, a Montreal-born Canadian of Italian descent, dedicated his life and work to eradicating systemic discrimination in our society against third languages and third language groups, especially those of Italian descent.

If Dan had problems, it should be said that his heart was larger than his body. He could not bring himself to say no to a writer, producer or artist with a problem and, in his business dealings, he was the eternal optimist. He was probably too optimistic.

For years he fought for a national multilingual, multicultural television service across Canada. He could not persuade the regulators to make it a part of the basic service. As I said, Dan wanted to breathe life into the idea of a bilingual , multicultural Canada.

I first met Dan over 30 years ago. I was a co-founder of CityTV that changed television to reflect the face and voices of the streets of Toronto. We enlisted Dan as the producer of our weekend segment on multilingual programming.

This segment quickly outgrew its allocated weekend time slot, so Dan and I set off to co-found the first full-fledged multilingual television service, the first fully independent multilingual television service broadcast in over 20 languages weekly in Toronto, the very first of its kind in the world.

Beneath the radar of these new programming services were fierce battles with regulators, media buyers, advertisers and competitive broadcasters who first opposed, then sought to augment, these services by carrying their own third-language service.

Dan has suddenly left us. Who will take up the leadership to fight for the equality of multiculturalism and third-language treatment on the public airwaves?

Our deep condolences to his wife, Elena, his family and brother Paul, who stood and fought these battles beside him with grace and ferocity.

Dan was a pioneer. Perhaps he dreamed too greatly, but those dreams came to be shared by millions of Canadians from coast to coast to coast.

HERBERT O. SPARROW: ON RETIREMENT

December 13, 2004

Hon. Jerahmiel S. Grafstein: Honourable senators, I too would like to add my words in tribute to our great friend Herb Sparrow. I came here at a time when I thought the place was populated by giants. I certainly found out in short order that, while Herb was small in stature, he was a giant of a senator.

He advised me to do one thing. When I spoke to any matter, he would say, "Have you read the bill? If you did not read the bill, you cannot speak in Senate or the caucus." That piece of advice rings in my head to this day, and I remember fondly the idea that one should not speak in the Senate on a matter unless one has read the bill and the material. It has been great advice to me.

I cherish the fact that Herb gave me that advice, and I lend it as support to all senators. It is excellent advice. As legislators, we should read the bill.

Herb's contribution here was outstanding. When he spoke, whether in caucus or the Senate, I found that I had to nod with affirmative enthusiasm on practically every issue. He was certainly on time, on line and always right.

PHILIPPE GIGANTES: ON HIS DEATH

December 14, 2004

Hon. Jerahmiel S. Grafstein: Honourable senators, our dear friend Philippe Gigantes has left us. What can we say about this true Renaissance man, who represented the best of the old and the new world? Perhaps the best tribute would be to repeat what Philippe proclaimed about himself.

He said that he was a great lover. He loved literature and art, he loved poetry, he loved journalism, and he loved politics. He was once asked what was his religion. He answered that it was journalism and politics. He loved writing, and he was an excellent writer. He loved youth, he loved the Senate, he loved to speak, and you will recall the great GST debate when he made one of the longest, if not the longest, speech in this chamber. He loved to listen to the speakers, and he loved good food and clothes. He loved to travel, he loved languages and he was adept at many languages. He loved good friends and stimulating conversation. He loved Mr. Trudeau. He loved the Liberal Party. He loved Israel because he loved all democracies. He loved courage and he was a courageous soldier. He loved his roots in Greece but, above all, he loved Canada more. Yes, Philippe Gigantes was a lover of Canada.

We will never forget his loves and his hates. We will remember his hates as well as his loves, for he was a very, very passionate man. Our hearts go out to his wife and family who loved and cared for him. To them our deepest condolences.

Above all, we will miss the pleasure of his usual spirited company. I say to him in Greek, Philippe, we love you.

ORIGINAL AND LONGER VERSION OF AN EXCERPT IN: *PIERRE,* McCLELLAND & STEWART 2005 EDITED BY NANCY SOUTHAM

2005

JERRY GRAFSTEIN
Friend since 1957; policy and media adviser, 1972-84

In 1972, Pierre Trudeau was not very happy with me. While for years we had been members of a circle who regularly exchanged intellectual fusillades, I had played a leading role in John Turner's leadership campaign in 1968. When Turner stayed on until the last ballot, Trudeau was not pleased.

As for me, I shared Pearson Liberals' unease about Mr. Trudeau, because of his earlier broadsides at Mr. Pearson before he ran as a Liberal in 1965, and especially since his decision to drop the Election Writ in 1968 before Parliament could pay tribute to Mr. Pearson. Mrs. Pearson was miffed, to say the least - less about Mr. Trudeau's earlier criticisms and more about his treatment of Mr. Pearson after becoming Prime Minister, especially since Mr. Pearson and his aides had quietly give Trudeau special scope and opportunities for his leadership aspirations.

Then, after the outburst of "Trudeaumania" in 1968, Trudeau's 1972 national campaign, heralded as an "Encounter with Canadians", and bearing the campaign slogan "The Land is Strong", had begun to flounder and fall flat. Public adoration of Mr. Trudeau's charisma and charm had changed to public chagrin. Liberals were sinking in the polls. The Toronto Liberals, whom Trudeau had failed to cultivate after his sweeping 1968 Victory, sat back. A Conservative government was looming.

Several weeks after the launch of that disastrous 1972 campaign, I received a call from the PMO, inviting me to meet with the Prime Minister on his next campaign swing through Toronto. The Conservatives, under the brilliant direction of the "Big Blue Machine" in Toronto, were steadily gaining momentum. I had barely spoken to Trudeau for several years; his campaign team remained leery of Toronto Liberals. We met at the Prince Hotel, the Japanese-style hostelry that Trudeau favoured.

Pierre Trudeau had one uncanny knack. Dispassionately, he could separate himself from his persona and performance, and analyze his own strengths and weaknesses as if reading an X-ray.

After the usual family pleasantries, he asked, "How are we doing?" "You, Prime Minister, are losing Toronto," I rejoined.

"Why so?" he asked softly.

"Because, you, Sir, have failed to engage Liberals. Besides, Liberals in Toronto are unhappy with your treatment of Mr. Pearson, and now he is dying." (By then, Mr. Pearson was suffering from cancer). Trudeau fell silent and pondered, chin in hand, looking down.

Then he slowly raised his head, captured me with his penetrating look, and asked quietly and firmly, "Is there anything that can be done to change the situation?"

I knew that was why he had invited me. I Immediately responded.

"Yes, there is something that can be done". "What would that be?"

"We would have to transfer the love and affection the Toronto Liberals have for Mr. Pearson to you."

His eyes narrowed and then lit up. "Is that possible now?" he asked, given that we were in the midst of the election campaign.

"Yes, I believe it is possible", I said. "How?"

"You, Sir, could throw an intimate surprise birthday party for Mr. Pearson. Toronto Liberals know that Mr. Pearson was dying. Toronto Liberals are sitting on their hands. All that we would need would be Mr. Pearson to attract them back."

"Would it work?" he asked.

"It can only help and it cannot hurt."

"Where would you propose to hold such an intimate surprise birthday party?"

"At the Maple Leaf Gardens of course".

Trudeau almost broke up. "Where?" he laughed. "At the Maple Leaf Gardens".

"Why do you think you could fill the Maple Leaf Gardens when our campaign crowds have been sparse?"

"Because, Sir, every Liberal in Toronto would want to come and have a last chance to pay their respect to Mr. Pearson."

"Would you help organize it?" "Yes, on three conditions." "What are they?"

"First, your campaign team agrees not to interfere. Second, we must convince Mr. & Mrs. Pearson to attend, which I believe is possible with the help of Keith Davey, Jim Coutts, and others. Finally, you have to agree yourself to work that whole day in Toronto until midnight."

Pierre Trudeau was most curious about the third condition. "Why is that important?"

"Because, Sir, Liberals work hard in Toronto. Meanwhile, your campaign has been working half time and has been meandering."

Trudeau agreed and immediately instructed his national campaign chairman, Bob Andras, to support the event. We quickly set out to put the restless Toronto Liberal machine not only in motion but in high gear.

Keith Davey, Jim Coutts, Royce Frith, Dick O'Hagan, and I attended on Mr. & Mrs. Pearson's corner suite at the Park Plaza Hotel, which Mr. Pearson always preferred. Despite Mrs. Pearson's initial reluctance, Mr. Pearson overcame her irate vocal objections and agree to be the "surprise" guest at "a surprise birthday party in his honour." He was bemused by the idea and anxious to help the party.

Dorothy Petrie (later Davey), a superb Liberal organizer, agreed to be Co-Chair. One call to Harold Ballard, who revered Mr. Pearson, gave us the Gardens. Dorothy and I set out to call every Liberal candidate and riding president in the greater Toronto area to get their commitment to bring five hundred or more from their riding to the rally.

Elvio DelZotto (then in the baking business) agreed to provide a six-foot-tall birthday cake, billed as "the biggest birthday cake in Canadian history". Popular Canadian musicians were enlisted to volunteer their talents. A snappy downtown Toronto media blitz was quickly deployed. Liberals came alive in Toronto. We decided to calibrate the seating capacity of the Gardens to eighteen thousand, confident of an overflow crowd. We prepared a wagon top outside on College Street, from which Pierre Trudeau could address the disappointed throngs unable to enter the Gardens.

The City buzzed with excitement. Mr. Pearson's appearance was not announced to the media. The event was billed as a Liberal Rally to rejuvenate the Liberal team. The local media woke up. Liberal organizers were quietly informed about the "surprise guest" and outdid themselves to bring as many Liberals supporters from their ridings as possible by bus, car, and transit. A curious public appeared in droves.

At the rally, over twenty-eight thousand people showed up, effortlessly filling the Gardens and overflowing onto all the streets around. Trudeau spoke to those jostling outside just before the event. Loudspeakers were made available so outsiders could listen to the program inside.

Royce Frith, then a broadcaster, was MC for the event. All the Toronto Liberal candidates were on the stage to bask in the glow of their two inspired leaders. Mr. Pearson was introduced as "the surprise guest." The giant birthday cake was wheeled in, candles ablaze, and Prime Minister Trudeau, Mr. Pearson, and all the candidates clustered around the cake and joined to blow out the candles, followed by a rousing chorus of "Happy Birthday." That was the image that would be pictured in the papers and TV.

Mr. Pearson spoke briefly and beautifully. There was not a dry eye in the jammed arena. Then Mr. Trudeau spoke. A stirring national anthem followed as the audience roared with one voice and the evening came to a tearful and emotional end. Volunteers streamed out of the building, energized with the new sense of purpose.

It was only 9 p.m. Mr. Trudeau came backstage to thank the organizers and take his leave. I asked him where he was going. He seemed surprised. He thought his job was done. I reminded him of his promise to work until midnight. He laughed and asked, "What is left to do?" I motioned him into a small room backstage, where there were a thousand or more small white cardboard cake boxes lining the walls. I then invited him to autograph every single white box.

Eyeing the huge stacks of cardboard warily, he asked "Why?" I told him when he finished his final task, I would tell him. I smiled and said, "Toronto Liberals, our work is never done" or - as Keith Davey would put it with apologies to Yogi Berra - "it's never over until it is over".

He began to autograph each box with his scrawled signature "Best regards, Pierre", "Best wishes Pierre", "Thank You Pierre", "All the Best Pierre". Shortly before midnight, Mr. Trudeau completed his task. I then told him that each small cake box would now be hand-delivered to each newsman, radio reporter and commentator, TV anchor, TV reporter, and (for that matter) disk jockey in Toronto, and to each member of the national media covering the Campaign. The national TV news coverage was upbeat that night, with sympathetic shots of the audience.

The next morning on CFRB radio, an ever-caustic Trudeau critic, Gordon Sinclair, with the largest listenership in Ontario reported on the rally at length. The lines went something like this: "Even that arrogant Trudeau cannot be that bad. Look how he treated Mr. Pearson." That refrain was repeated endlessly in television, radio, and print. The media warmed to Mr. Trudeau, as did the Toronto public. The Tory momentum slowed. The Polls in *Toronto star*ted moving up. Don McDonald held his seat in Rosedale. The Liberal government held on as a minority government.

Throughout the many political challenges ahead, Toronto formed the bedrock of Trudeau's support that enabled him and Liberals to achieve such historic milestones as the Charter of Rights.

Two years later, in 1974, Trudeau, now fully supported and engaged with Pearson Liberals, won a surprising victory and recaptured a strong majority government.

Trudeau never forgot the lesson. The Land Was Strong. So was Pierre Trudeau. So were Liberals!

LOUIS J. ROBICHAUD: EULOGY

February 1, 2005

Hon. Jerahmiel S. Grafstein: Honourable senators, Louis Robichaud was a legendary figure who I came to know as I sat behind him here in the Senate chamber. He and his Liberal colleague Charlie McElman ran New Brunswick on a "small l" liberal agenda for over a decade. One of my greatest pleasures in the Senate was to watch and listen to Louis when he spoke in debate. He was, by legend and by fact, one of Canada's greatest "stump" speakers, in both English and French, in all of Canadian history.

When you sat and watched him, you could see the sparks of that brilliance. His spirit, his words, his energy, his mesmerizing talent to persuade his fellow Canadians is one of his lasting legacies. He set such a high standard for public rhetoric that we poor speakers today can only hope to approach the high standards he set. He will be missed, but he will never be forgotten.

ROYCE FRITH: EULOGY

March 22, 2005

Hon. Jerahmiel S. Grafstein: Honourable senators, beyond a doubt Royce Frith was the most elegant and dashing male senator in figure and dress during my time in this chamber. He was as fussy about grammar as he was about the cut of his suits and the colour of his suits and ties. He was a vibrant member of Cell 13, organized by Toronto Young Liberals during the dark days of the 1950s and dedicated to renovating and renewing the then moribund Liberal Party. Other founding members of Cell 13 include former outstanding Senate colleagues Keith Davey, Dan Lang, Richard Stanbury and John Black Aird.

When I joined the Liberal Party in the early 1960s, Royce, ever the outspoken activist and strategist, was already a legendary figure - a distinguished lawyer, actor, singer, speaker, broadcaster, raconteur, gourmand, and lover of literature, plays and poetry - and a very special favourite of Mr. and Ms. Pearson.

It was Royce who was called upon to be the Master of Ceremonies at countless Liberal revival meetings, dinners and fundraisers. It was Royce who chaired the last public mass meeting that took place in the form of a surprise birthday party for Mr. Pearson at Maple Leaf Gardens during the 1972 election, just before Mr. Pearson passed away due to a tragic illness.

Later, when I joined Royce here in the Senate, it was a delicate matter to meet with him privately in his office just behind this chamber, where he was usually involved in an electronic chess game with himself. You interrupted his next move at your peril.

When Royce was appointed High Commissioner to London, I told him he was the first Canadian since Vincent Massey who would not have to acquire bespoke suits tailored in Saville Row because his wardrobe already satisfied the high station of a British public figure.

Royce, ever the graceful man, full of energy, verve and wit, a connoisseur and bibliophile, could become fussy, stubborn and impatient when it came to compromising

Liberal principles or policies, incorrect grammar in speech, or imprecision in legislation, either in English or French.

Honourable senators, Royce will be remembered by friends and political foes alike for the joyful pleasure of his company. He was and he will be always the essence of the definition of an honourable gentleman.

POPE JOHN PAUL II: COMMENT

April 12, 2005

Hon. Jerahmiel S. Grafstein: Honourable senators, with profound humility I hesitate to rise to pay my meagre respects to Pope John Paul II; born Karol Wojtyla in Wadowice in 1920 - the same year that the Battle of Warsaw was fought and the Bolsheviks were defeated.

His father and mine, also born in southern Poland, less than 100 kilometres away, served in the Pilsudski brigades in that momentous battle for Polish independence. This slender but splendid thread was noted again over a year ago during my last audience in Rome with this charismatic personality.

More than common Polish roots, the Pope's transformation of the Church, its teachings and practices towards Jews and Judaism and its policy towards Israel shattered the Church's previous history and drew me and those of my faith to him.

Honourable senators, all progress is by a winding staircase. The Pope spoke out repeatedly and forcefully against the rising scourge of anti-Semitism. He was the first Pope to visit a synagogue in Rome, to visit Auschwitz, to visit Jerusalem, to pray at the Wailing Wall, to pay his respects at Yad Vashem and to recognize the State of Israel.

In his 1994 book entitled *Crossing the Threshold of Hope*, given to me by my great friend and mentor, the late Emmett Cardinal Carter, which I cherish, John Paul II wrote these words in his own hand.

Listen to his own words:

> *Through the plurality of religion ...we come to that religion closest to our own...that of the people of God of the Old Testament ...*

> *...The declaration Nostra Aetate represents a turning point...since the spiritual patronage (of Jews) is so great, the...Council reminds and promotes a mutual understanding and respect. ..*

Remembering in his hometown where his school backed upon a synagogue, the Pope wrote these words:

> ... *both religious groups were united ...by the awareness that they prayed to the same God.*

The Pope continued:

> ...*a personal experience. Auschwitz ...the Holocaust of the Jewish people shows to what length a system constructed on...racial hatred and greed for power can go...*

He wrote:

> *To this day, Auschwitz does not cease to admonish ... reminding us that anti-Semitism is a great sin against humanity ...*

Allow me to repeat the Pope's words, "anti-Semitism is a great sin against humanity." The Pope went on to write:

> ...*a truly exceptional experience was my visit to the Synagogue in Rome ... the history of the Jews of Rome...is linked...to the Acts of the Apostles.*

POPE BENEDICT XVI: COMMENT

April 21, 2005

Hon. Jerahmiel S. Grafstein: Honourable senators, I rise to pay respects to His Holiness Pope Benedict XVI. As a student of the church, always rich in symbolism, to take the mantle of St. Benedict, the patron saint of Europe, offers interesting insight into the Pope's stewardship in the future direction of the church.

I had the opportunity to meet the Pope when, as Cardinal Ratzinger, he visited Toronto in 1985. He was there to speak at a mass public meeting at Varsity Arena entitled, *An Evening with Cardinal Ratzinger.* I was delighted to attend and join 8,000 enthusiastic members of the audience in this moving event organized by our great and good friend Dennis Mills and made possible by the generous support of Frank Stronach.

Earlier, the late Cardinal Carter invited me to a small, private dinner to meet this eminent cardinal. I knew of his participation as an advisor to the Cardinal Archbishop of Cologne in the sessions of Vatican II. I was surprised to find myself as the only non-Catholic in this small, select company that included my friend and one of Canada's and the world's greatest outstanding scholars, Father Jim McConica, then President of St. Michael's College. I learned more of Cardinal Ratzinger's participation as a key adviser in the formulation of Vatican II. I was told by Cardinal Carter and my friend Dennis Mills and Father Jim McConica that we would share a common interest in the changing attitude of the church as manifested by Vatican II.

During the dinner, I was allowed ample time to enter into a direct discourse with the new Pope. I came away deeply impressed by being in the presence of a superior, brilliant mind, deeply engaged in the momentous issues of Vatican II and, above all, his humble and very gentle demeanour.

As Pope John Paul II did, I believe Pope Benedict XVI will surprise all as he forges a different path for the church, assaying, as his predecessors have, to fill the capacious footprints of the first fishermen.

The name "Benedict" comes from the Latin word for "blessing." May we hope that the new Pope's work brings blessings to his followers and the entire world.

CHRISTINA McCALL: EULOGY

May 3, 1988

Hon. Jerahmiel S. Grafstein: Honourable senators, I rise to pay tribute to the late Christina McCall.

If I had a favourite saint, it would be the Apostle St. Thomas, the eternal skeptic, who questioned and doubted the conventional wisdom of his peers and raised questions about the very nature of the human condition.

For me, it could not have been more appropriate that Christina McCall's funeral service be held at Saint Thomas's Anglican Church in the heart of old Toronto, for she was, as all great journalists are, a creative skeptic.

Great writers, like candles, illuminate the darkness enveloping the human condition. The writer's art is to pull together disparate threads and weave them into an authentic, vibrant story, making sense of what apparently is senseless. So it was with Christina McCall.

To those who treasure the written word, Christina was herself a treasure. Breathtakingly beautiful, she carried herself with effortless grace and looked the part of the elegant Rosedale matron that she was. Yet beneath this elegant veneer was a vulnerable, restless, energetic, insightfully brilliant writer. She had a deep, velvety, smokey voice and dark, melancholy eyes. Christina spoke purposefully, quietly and slowly. It was always difficult to concentrate on the subject at hand because of the charm she exuded. She was admired by women and men alike, and entranced and enchanted all who came to know her. My mother taught me that a lady wore a hat and gloves. Christina did, and she was. She wrote as beautifully as she looked. Because of her own complex personal experiences, she could parse the complex passions and contradictions at play and that were displayed within the body politic. For her, there was never a glass ceiling.

Christina became a leading political chronicler of her time, on par with Bruce Hutchison, Bill Wilson, Pierre Berton, Blair Fraser, Charles Lynch, Doug Fisher, Peter

Worthington, Geoff Stevens, Tony Westell, Richard Gwyn, Jeffrey Simpson, Lawrence Martin, and her one-time husband, Peter Newman, and at times she outshone all of them with her luminous prose and exquisite insights.

As a writer and journalist, she was meticulous in her preparations. She always came prepared with research and notes that she took copiously. She would pause to reread her notes and relaunch her enquiries. Christina could penetrate to the essence with soft, rapier-like questions, always touching the inner core of any subject she was exploring under the prism of her own personal microscope.

She was the very model of journalist and writer, and we will not likely meet her equal again. While she wrote of the foibles and the failures of politics, she never ever tarnished its noble purpose.

To capture the metaphor she wrote of Pierre Trudeau, her beauty and brilliance "haunts us still." With her passing, the still unlimned political anatomy of our country is darker and dimmer because her bright light was so prematurely extinguished.

To her three beautiful, loving daughters and her husband Stephen, we can only share a portion of their pain upon her passage and the marvellous remembrance of glowing moments passed. Her own words, lustrous words, will forever carve a lasting memorial to her memory.

Christina.
Your work well done!
Your battles won!
Now come to rest.

THE ROLE OF PARLIAMENTARIANS IN COMBATING ANTI-SEMITISM
OSCE CONFERENCE IN CORDOVA, SPAIN

June 9, 2005

Here in the heart of Cordoba, we sense the wheels of history turning yet again. Cordoba has been drenched in the historic cycles of tolerance and discrimination. From early Roman times before the Common Era, Jews settled in this region called Sepharad mentioned in the Bible by Obadiah.

From Roman times is the Visigoths, Iberia especially, from 711 C.E., when the Moors of Morocco, the Al Andalus came to govern regions of the Iberian Peninsula until The Reconquest was complete in 1492 when the last Arab Kingdom of Granada was defeated, Cordoba has resonated between two ideas - multiculturalism and multi-religion and tolerance on the one hand and exclusivity and discrimination and intolerance on the other. For over 300 years, the Al Andalus governed Cordoba and transformed it into a leading city of both Europe and the Middle East.

And it was here in 787 that the Caliph of Cordoba, Abdur Rahman, the great Muslim Moor instructed his successor son, Hisham, and his government officials on the importance of tolerance towards all of his subjects, Jews, Christians and Muslims alike.

> "Remember, my son, that these are God's kingdoms, God who gives and takes away at his leisure . . . Be just to all men, equally to the poor and the rich, for injustice is the road to ruin; at the same time be gentle and merciful with those who are dependent on you, for they are all creatures of God. Trust the government of the provinces to wise, experienced men and punish without pity those ministers who oppress the people."

Abdur Rahman, Caliph of Cordoba
787 C.E.

During the reign of the Al Andalus, Mosques, Churches and Synagogues were built side by side. In Cordoba, the greatest Jewish philosopher Maimonides was born in the 12th century and commenced one of his greatest works, "*The Guide to the Perplexed.*" The core of his belief was that reason and religion complimented each other. For this idea, his books were burned in Cordoba by his Jewish co-religionists. Also born in Cordoba, was Ibn Rashid known as Averroes, one of Islam's greatest philosophers and a close friend and contemporary of Maimonides, who sought to prove that there was no contradiction between religion and reason since both emanated from the Spirit of God.

His Muslim co-religionists burnt Averroes' books. Both were physicians and scholars who taught that revelation and rationality could be synthesized and harmonized.

These men of reason and others who believed in tolerance and reconciling faith with philosophy were perceived to be a threat to all three religions.

During the period of Al Andalus, Cordoba blossomed in the sciences - medicine, mathematics, botany, navigation, astronomy - and the arts, poetry, literature, architecture, painting and music. All this, as a centre of moderation, erudition and culture, came to an end with the Reconquest that led to the Spanish Inquisition accelerating in 1492.

Moderation had been overtaken by extremism near the end of the 12th century when the fanatical Almohads invaded from North Africa forcing conversion or emigration to the north, Jews and Muslims alike. And in the old Visigoth north, this fueled the notion of Reconquest infused with religious fervor. Massacres erupted anew. Public humiliation was practiced. Badges of shame were demanded of both Jew and Muslim, anticipating much later Nazi practices.

So a dark cloud hovered over the Iberian Peninsula and descended when both Jews and Muslims were expelled, forcibly converted or massacred, smothering its multicultural society and reducing its status as a centre of educational and aesthetic leadership. Books had been collected in voluminous libraries, literacy in multiple languages was the norm. Paper came to be manufactured. Cordoba's markets teemed with exotic goods and foods. Trade and government were open to all faiths and minorities were protected and encouraged to participate. By the tenth century, Cordoba rose to become the greatest centre to both Jewish and Islamic scholarship in the known world. 1492 ended this golden period of history. It took almost 500 years for Spain to recapture that virtuous cycle of tolerance and openness to all religions and rationalism.

So it is fitting that this historic Conference combating anti-Semitism should be situated here in Cordoba - witness to so much hope and despair about the human condition.

Before I turn to the topic at hand, when one pulls back the veils of history and turns to leaders who advocated intolerance, from Julius Caesar who had granted Jews a Charter of Liberty, confirmed by Augustus to Saladin when he reconquered Jerusalem and dealt fairly to all religions, to Charlemagne who issued Europe's first declaration of tolerance, to Frederick the Great in 1740 when he affirmed the principles of tolerance, to Napoleon who demanded equality of treatment for all citizens in Europe, that one sees the virtuous cycles of tolerance matched by cycles of discrimination that led to the tragic excesses of the three miserable "-isms" - Nazism, Communism, and Fascism - and recalls such leaders as Hitler and Stalin, that we can appropriately place this conference more fully in its historic context.

THE ROLE OF PARLIAMENTS IN COMBATING ANTI-SEMITISM

So here we are in Cordoba at this historic conference on combating anti-Semitism sponsored by the OSCE. I am privileged to share this Panel with two outstanding OSCE-PA colleagues, the President of the OSCE, Alcee Hastings and Gert Weisskirchen, Member of the German Parliament who serves as the Personal Representative of the OSCE Chairman-in-Office on Combating Anti-Semitism.

It might be useful to remind ourselves how we got here. The origins of this conference cannot be separated from the origins of the OSCE. In 1974 the Helsinki Process was at its core, a remarkable compromise. The Soviet Union and its eastern allies agreed with the western democracies that if its borders would be respected, in turn they would agree to a regime respectful of human rights.

From that historic bargain called the Helsinki Accords emerged the OSCE, the largest international organization dedicated to human rights, political rights, economic and democratic development.

The Helsinki Process led directly to the formation of the OSCE - The Organisation for Security and Cooperation in Europe.

From the Copenhagen and Paris Declarations in 1990 to the 1992 Charter of European Security, from the Lisbon Declaration in 1996, culminating with the Berlin Resolution in 2002 and the Edinburgh Declaration in 2004, the Parliamentary Assembly of the OSCE, the Parliament of Parliamentarians from 55 Member States from Vladistock to Vancouver has insistently and consistently raised its voice against the ugly revival of anti-Semitism and intolerance.

Last year, at the OSCE Ministerial Conference in Sofia, Bulgaria, the OSCE took a further concrete step. The Chair-in-Office appointed three personal representatives to follow up on resolutions against intolerance. First, our colleague, Gert Weisskirchen was named Personal Representative of the OSCE Chairman-in-Office on Combating Anti-Semitism and Intolerance.

Anastasia Crickley was appointed as Personal Representative on Combating Racism, Xenophobia and Discrimination, focusing on Intolerance and Discrimination against Christians and Members of Other Religions, and Ambassador Omur Orhun was appointed as Personal Representative on Combating Intolerance and Discrimination against Muslims.

But a brief word about the leadership of parliamentarians involvement in this historic process. Just before the Berlin OSCE Parliamentary Assembly in the spring of 2002, I received a call from Congressman Christopher Smith, the Chair of the

OSCE Helsinki Commission in Congress about a resolution we had earlier discussed with Gert Weisskirchen and others about anti-Semitism. He advised me that other Congressmen, such as Congressmen Alcee Hastings, Steny Hoyer and Ben Cardin, had enthusiastically supported this Resolution. He asked me to join them to convince all our parliamentary colleagues at the forthcoming Berlin meeting. I immediately agreed and this Resolution went forward to Berlin. It was unanimously approved and adopted after debate in Committee and ultimately by the OSCE Parliamentary Assembly as a whole. This Resolution in turn triggered a series of conferences across the face of Europe and in Washington. Twice in Vienna, in Berlin and in Washington, Copenhagen, Oporto, Maastricht, Rotterdam, Warsaw, Paris and Rome. The list goes on! This process was from outset led by Parliamentarians. The same OSCE Resolution passed in Berlin in 2002, inspired the United Nations and Kofi Annan to hold the First UN Conference on anti-Semitism just over a year ago. Of course Spencer Oliver, the Secretary General of the OSCE-PA, a friend, was a valuable guide to the processes of these international forums.

So the role of parliament and the leadership of parliamentarians in combating anti-Semitism and intolerance have been intrinsic to changing public opinion about the magnitude of the problem of anti-Semitism itself.

Why are parliaments and parliamentarians essential to this struggle against hate and intolerance?

The history of anti-Semitism can be traced to governments and to parliament as well as organized religions.

Czarist Russia's government was the instigator of Pogroms and instrumental to fomenting the infamous Protocols of Zion.

Modern anti-Semitism was systemic in governments for all the wrong reasons.

It was the French government that covered up the Dreyfus Affair. And it was the French Parliament, pressed by the media that raised the issue in the French Parliament that ultimately led to Dreyfus' redress.

It was the German government and German Parliament that passed the infamous Nazi Nuremburg laws.

It was Vichy France and other parliaments across Europe that passed and implemented compliant laws.

Yet it was parliamentarians, in America and England, that first raised the spectre of the Holocaust, when both governments and media, chose to ignore the emerging signs.

In free and democratic societies, parliaments are shaped by public opinion.

Parliaments also shape public opinion. Misconduct erupting within civic societies or within government usually receives their first public debate airing within parliamentary forums.

Opinion polls are deeply shaped by consensus reached in parliament. Parliaments can educate!

Parliamentarians must educate themselves on steps to eradicate anti-Semitism before they educate their constituents.

So what can parliaments and parliamentarians do to eradicate the roots of ancient scourge of anti-Semitism that sustain intolerance, hate and discrimination and violence towards the "other."

1. Public debate. The OSCE Resolution can be an excellent catalyst to foment such debate in each parliament. Silence is acquiescence and always leads to license. License leads to incitement. Incitement leads to violence.
2. Governments and committees of parliament can study in detail how to attack the roots of anti-Semitism still embedded in each civil society.
3. Governments can compile timely, cogent statistics on hate incidents and publicize them regularly.
4. Governments can renovate and legislate stronger anti-hate laws.
5. Governments can encourage anti-hate law enforcement. May I commend the ODHIR for organizing meetings in Toronto where, just last month, curricula are being developed for police forces across the OSCE space, based on enlightened police practices of the Toronto Police Department, my home city?
6. Education. A number of countries have led the way in education. Germany, Bulgaria and others. We have heard now on education strategies in many Member States. Many have adopted no change in education. We need to accurately measure the nature, implementation and impact of these recent developments.

Elie Wiesel correctly advised us in the Berlin Conference that "a child can be taught to love or to hate." Early education and continuous reinforcement at the primary, secondary and university levels can ultimately dilute the springs of discrimination of the "Other" including politically incorrect private or public discourse. Work should continue to cleanse religious text and teachings of anti-Semitism. It was the fervor of Pope John XXIII and Vatican II that marked a sea of change in religious teachings. John Paul II was the first Pope to visit a Synagogue, Auschwitz and the Yad Vashem. John Paul II understood public opinion. He understood the power of his position. He spoke forcibly and regularly against the rising tide of anti-Semitism. Public education is an endless process. This work must be continued by the leadership of the Church and joined by all other denominations.

Why critics ask, the preoccupation on anti-Semitism? Why not generalize?

Why? Discrimination exists against the "Other," against Christians and Muslims and other faiths as well. Why then anti-Semitism? Why not a macro approach? A macro approach to all forms of intolerance blurs the solution to specific forms of discrimination as the Representative of Germany so clearly pointed out yesterday. Anti-Semitism is the oldest discrimination. Each form of discrimination is unique.

Each form of discrimination emanates from different roots and requires different solutions. It has been said, with some irony, that discrimination starts with Jews but never ends with Jews.

Ethnic cleansing of Jews was the unique contribution of Nazism in the 20th century.

Now anti-Semitism has re-emerged with renewed power and vigor in the 21st century. After 1989, when the wall came down, I believed the "anti-Semitism" dossier would become part of the dustbin of history. I was wrong.

It has re-emerged in a powerful form abetted by the convergence of communication via the Internet. So solutions are complex in our free and democratic societies.

What are common are the desire and the objective of all parliaments to ultimately erase all forms of discrimination.

What is being asked in Cordoba is simple. Just as parliaments and governments are bound by the UN Charter of Human Rights, so it is a truism that the UN Charter is episodically enforced against its own members. The Charter is embedded the rule of law in all democratic nations of the world. Even those that are not democratic have agreed to the UN principles of the Charter. At the heart of the UN Charter is a simple idea. Do not treat others differently from how you would treat yourself.

There's great debate about ending this public process in the fight against anti-Semitism and intolerance. This would be wrong. National strategies require years to implement. Just as the OSCE took years to transform the OSCE space, we parliamentarians recognize that the work of respecting the "other" will never end until anti-Semitism and all forms of intolerance no longer manifests itself in our region for which we have public trust.

Governments and parliaments must be held to account, as we heard, while some governments have started a national strategy, many had lagged behind. Regular meetings to share best practices culminating with an annual meeting that audits and measures each Member State against their commitment to the Berlin process is essential if we are to eradicate the rising problems of anti-Semitism and intolerance. The work is just beginning.

Let us put principles and practices to work. Principles and practices march better when they march together.

HUMAN RIGHTS AND ANTI-SEMITISM
DR. BERNIE VIGOD MEMORIAL LECTURE
ST. THOMAS UNIVERSITY, FREDERICTON, NEW BRUNSWICK

November 21, 2005

At the outset, may I pay tribute to my friend and colleague Noel Kinsella, Leader of the Opposition in the Senate, who persuaded me to accept your kind invitation?

Senator Kinsella has been an avid advocate against all forms of discrimination and a fighter for human rights.

It was with deep double trepidation that I accepted your gracious invitation to speak here at St. Thomas University on Human Rights. This lecture was named in memory of your colleague Dr. Bernie Vigod, a University Professor and a leader in Human Rights and the ongoing struggle combating anti-Semitism - the oldest on-going virus of discrimination. To join the roster of distinguished visitors for this lecture is a rare privilege and the cause of my first trepidation. I doubted whether I could rise to the eloquence of your former speakers on the question of "human rights" in Canada.

Allow me to address the second reason for my trepidation with a minor mea culpa. I have been a lifelong student of the Catholic Church since my University days! I confess I was a sometime member of the Newman Club at the University of Western Ontario because of my interest in another student. There, it was Cardinal Newman's *Essays on the Idea of the University* that first persuaded me that faith, reason and science could be reconciled. Cardinal Newman went further and advocated the essence of a liberal education through the study of great literature which it was and is! If 1 had a favourite Saint, it would be St. Thomas, the Apostle. This University, however, is named after another St. Thomas, St. Thomas Aquinas and herein lays the basis of my major hesitation. While St. Thomas, the skeptical apostle, sought to reconcile faith and reason, it was St. Thomas Aquinas some centuries later who agreed with St. John, that there is one and only one exclusive path to God. That was only through the gateway of Christ.

You all know that Aquinas, a Dominican Priest, was and is one of the most studied and revered of Catholic scholars. In the 13th century, as a student at the University of Paris, he set out to assemble what became two major works of Catholic thought that resonate within Catholic Scholarship to this day. Aquinas is quoted more than any other scholar except St. Augustine and probably more than any other scholar in Vatican II. His *Summa Contra Gentiles* (1259) was a scholarly theological synthesis written to arm defenders of the faith against disbelievers. *"Summa Theologiea"* was completed in 1273 using Aristotelian metaphysics and style logic to construct a complete and comprehensive paradigm of Christian belief.

It was Aquinas who changed the early Church's notion of Jewish ignorance of the true path of Christ's teachings to the idea that educated Jews were not only ignorant but deliberately defiant about the only one true path to salvation. He went on to argue that Jews were decides not only of "Christ as a man but as God" (ST 3, 947, 5 and 3).

Thus Aquinas fortified that stream of Catholic thought that became the predominant stream that changed the tolerant flow of the early Catholic attitudes towards Jews. That stream advocated singularity not pluralism, exclusiveness, not inclusiveness to the life beyond!

Much earlier in the 3rd century, St. Augustine in his masterpiece *The City of God* took another benevolent view that the Jews around the world were providential since only they bore witness to the authentic older scriptures upon which Christianity relied.

Some could draw direct line from St. Thomas Aquinas' magnum opus *Summa Theologiea* to the Inquisition in 1492 and beyond to the horrors of the 20th century. In the 12th century overlapping Aquinas' scholarly progression lived one of Judaism's greatest scholars and doctors, Maimonides. In his writings he sought to reconcile revelation with reason and science. His great work is entitled *Guide to the Perplexed*. For his efforts, Maimonides was scorned by Jewish Orthodox co-religionists and his books were burned. Today, Maimonides is revered by Jews and Gentiles alike as an iconic figure who led the way toward the Enlightenment from the gloom of the Middle Ages. Maimonides' contemporary in Cordova, Spain, was Ibn Rashid, a Muslim doctor and scholar later called by his Latin name, Averroes, who also sought to reconcile reason and faith. His writings were also burned by his Muslim co-religionists for his efforts.

Yet, they both remain as beacons of light from the dark middle Ages to the Enlightenment and beyond to the Age of Reason and our generation. While both their works were studied by Aquinas with care, it was Aquinas' ideas that led the Church for generations to advance in a different, narrower direction.

Then came Erasmus "the great humanist" some centuries later! Erasmus chose a somewhat ambivalent different way when, during his era, churchman sought to justify the burning of all Hebrew manuscripts. Erasmus rose up. He publicly supported Johannes Reuchlin, a Catholic scholar of Hebrew texts, who battled against this tragedy when Reuchlin was accused of heresy. Erasmus argued strenuously that if being a good Christian meant hating Jews then assuredly the population of his era consisted of very good Christians indeed. Still Erasmus shared the biases of his time.

And, Paul Johnston, the eminent British historian, noted in his *History of Jews* an interesting parallel in history with advent of printing in the Middle Ages alluding to the advent of mass media in our day.

"The notion that Jews knew the truth but neglecting it preferring to work with the forces of darkness - and therefore could not be human in the sense that Christians were already well established . . ." and dehumanizing crude images of Jews ... "could now proliferate."

I will not navigate through the various edicts, proclamations, statements or encyclicals through the ages as they oscillate between isolation and condemnation of Jews on the one hand to tolerance and grudging acceptance on the other.

The Church was always divided between Popes and Kings and Scholars who urged toleration and respect, if reluctant, acknowledgment, for Judaism and Jews, while others took the darker, narrower path.

Yet, here we are at the beginning of the 21st century, in many ways no closer to those who would still preach exclusionary religious practices as the core of religious belief. Progress has been made! Great, if fitful, strides have been taken. It was Pope John XXIII through Vatican II who sought to cleanse Catholic Church's ancient liturgy against extreme declamations against Jews. Vatican II was completed after John XXIII passed away. But still, Nostra Aetate marked a turning point for the Catholic Church to start anew to reconsider Catholic liturgy and catechism respecting Jews. It launched the beginning of the beginning to transform the Church's teachings from harsh criticism of Jews to acceptance of common historic religious roots while accepting historic religious differences. Step by step advances have been made through recognition and acceptance that there are more paths to God than one and only one exclusive way. Notions of exclusivity, especially notions of religious exclusivity, seem to lie at the heart of discrimination against the "Other." Some recent studies have drawn a direct relationship to orthodox religiosity and secular anti-Semitism.

Pope John Paul II who I was privileged to meet first, through the good offices of the Honourable Stanley Haidasz in the '60s and later in audience on a number of occasions, through a mentor and friend, the late and great Emmet Cardinal Carter and finally in Rome, just some months before he passed away last year. It was John Paul II who took up the thread of leadership started by John XXIII propelled by Pope Paul VI to reconcile the Church's teachings with the recognition of Judaism's unique contribution to faith and monotheism. As Pope John Paul II came to call Jews "The elder brothers in faith."

Many here are familiar with Pope John XXIII's pioneering work that launched Vatican II.

Other churches in Canada have slowly followed suit. Several years ago, the Lutheran Church of Canada announced it had revised the historic teachings of Luther who publicly preached and castigated Jews and whose anti-Semitic diatribes were incorporated in Lutheran texts. Both Luther and Calvin adopted the logic and declension of Aquinas on Jewish questions, and if even more extreme in their diatribes.

So few can deny religion sits at the centre of the most ancient of all discrimination anti-Semitism - discrimination of the "other." Anti-Semitism remains the oldest pandemic of prejudice in recorded history.

Now history also teaches that discrimination may start against Jews but never ends with Jews.

I, therefore, hold simple, perhaps self-serving theses, about the human condition, human rights, and anti-Semitism. If anti-Semitism, in spoken and written word, both in public discourse and in private conversation is eradicated, other equally violent and distasteful forms of discrimination will slowly dissolve as well. Then the full force of all God's creatures can be exploited for their uniqueness and authenticity to the fullest potential, provided their pathways are pathways of peace and tolerance.

But that is the desired future. What of today!

After 1989 when the wall came down I thought I could close finally my dossiers on anti-Semitism. A new era of human rights was dawning. A new world, a new society, a new international civil society, was being created before my eyes. A new world of human rights ignited by the Helsinki Process in the 1970s beckoned in the 1980s.

My optimism about washing away discrimination against Jews was never greater when in 1989 when the Berlin Wall came tumbling wall. I believed that moment finally marked the end of the most murderous century in history. Let us recap by some numbers:

1. In the 11th century, one out of the five Jews were murdered.
2. In the last Millennium, before the 20th century, two out of every five Jews were murdered.
3. Then when we reached the 20th century ("The Killing century") the mathematics accelerated. In the 20th century, over two hundred million human beings were slaughtered and, the Jews were always at the head of the list. One out of every three Jews was murdered.

Mathematics teaches Jews to be alert. Mathematics keeps us awake. Still Jews, despite these murderous mathematics through the ages, maintained their fidelity to monotheism - to one God!

To reiterate, when the Wall came down, I believed that the three miserable 20th century "isms" had finally been vanquished - Nazism, Fascism and Communism - all anathema to Jews. Why, because Jews were always at the top of the list targeted for liquidation. My optimism for change increased dramatically again by the leadership of John Paul II in bringing down the Berlin wall. He helped gain Poland's independence, the birth place of so many Jews, including both my parents. He was an inspirational supporter of Solidarnosz, a coalition open to all citizens. He had witnessed the Holocaust at first hand in Poland during World War II.

But that optimism was not to be! Anti-Semitism is alive and well today - even in faraway places where few Jews live, such as Japan. Yet, all progress is by a winding staircase.

What have we learned? What is the message of the Holocaust? What is the lesson of the most savage planned act of history - the so-called "Final Solution?" What is the heard of all human rights?

Hate always starts with words. Words can incite. Words turned into orders can kill! This is the tragic lesson of history. This is the bitter lesson of the European history still scorched in our memories. It starts with words.

Scholars tell us discrimination's job is to elicit fear! Fear and loathing of the "Other." Discrimination's oxygen is to demoralize, demonize and delegitimize the "Other!" Only by denigrating the "Other" or as Freud say only by "transference" of our problems to others can the weak rationalize their own faults and their own weaknesses and limitations.

Let's return to words! Universities are constructed on words. "In the beginning was The Word". Discrimination always starts with a word, then a phrase. Always a taunt. Perhaps a joke. Then gossip. Then conversation. Then a speech or a sermon. Then a lecture. Always a march replete with banners. Usually a book. Then a policy. Always abetted either a free or directed media! Then a state program followed by the expectation that the state program will be executed. And so it was!

Put yet another way, silence, is acquiescence. Acquiescence breeds licence. Licence breeds legitimacy. Legitimacy leads to incitement. Incitement inevitably is followed by violence.

So, what have we learned?

In Canada, our Parliament, our word factory of freedom, can act as the vital vocal bulwark and a vital centre against discrimination. So too our schools and universities also constructed on words which are turned into thoughts, can be easily transformed into verbal ramparts against hate, and for human rights.

Too often, even Jews censor themselves and fail to speak out at obvious outbursts of anti-Semitism. Four synagogues were scorched or defaced in four provinces across Canada in the last five years, yet it took the firebomb of a Jewish School Library in Montreal to arouse the Canadian public.

In March, Jews around the world celebrate the ancient story of Purim. You may recall how Esther, Hadassah, the namesake of Jewish women's organizations around the world, became the Queen of Persia. You'll recall, to be chosen Queen, Esther kept her Jewish identity hidden from her King.

Haman, the King's Advisor, angered and fearful and envious of Jews, issued an edict authorizing genocide of the Jews throughout the one hundred and twenty-seven provinces of the Persian Empire stamped and authorized by signature ring of the King - an Order of the State!

Mordecai, Esther's uncle sent an urgent message to Esther in the Royal Palace.

Petition the King! She refused, fearful of the consequences. She understood that anyone who entered the presence of the King without his consent could be executed.

When Mordecai heard Esther's response and her refusal, he sent her another message admonishing her. He said, "Do you think that you will be spared because you are in the Royal Palace? Why do you think that you were elevated to that place that you would refuse to fulfill your responsibilities to protect your people?"

Of course, the rest is history. Esther convinced the King, who angered at Haman's prevarications immediately executed Haman. The king allowed a message to go forth, through Mordecai, to the Jews in the 127 provinces to band together and protect themselves against slaughter and genocide. This they did!

One moral from that story, no individual can remain silent in the face of adversity.

No one can hide or transfer the responsibility to others. The first role of a citizen in a democratic society is to wake up his co-citizens to any dangers to our civic society. As Pierre Trudeau once argued "discrimination against one is discrimination against all."

So what to do? What progress has been made? The OSCE, the world's largest human rights organization which flowed out of the Helsinki Process in the '70s - composed of 55 states including Canada and the United States (where I am privileged to serve as a senior officer) - has developed an international consensus around four action items to root out anti-Semitism. It was repeated in the OSCE Resolutions against anti-Semitism that finally convinced even Kofi Annan, the UN Secretary General, to convene the UN's very first conference against anti-Semitism, just last year. Thus conventional wisdom respecting anti-Semitism was slowly changing even at such a remote outpost as the UN.

In the last five years, when the ancient scourge of anti-Semitism reared its head in the heart of Europe, many parliamentarians of the OSCE refused to be silent. With colleagues from Germany, France and America, we studied the problem, drafted resolutions and got unanimous OSCE approval. These resolutions goaded OSCE Ministers to act. To further educate ourselves, seminars were held to develop an activist agenda against anti-Semitism across the face and space of Europe. In the last five years, I've attended a number of such meetings in Copenhagen, Berlin, Vienna, Paris, Washington, Rotterdam, Rome, Maastricht, Edinburgh, Oporto, and most recently in Cordova this June. And there were others. An action plan to combat anti-Semitism was slowly forged and adopted. The action plan is simple and focused. These are the main planks in the action platform:

1. Bring the issue to public attention in the Parliaments of the 55 Member States of the OSCE especially whenever and wherever outbursts of discrimination and anti-Semitism erupt. Persuade Parliaments to go beyond resolutions and study this phenomenon in their country, armed with regular statistics.
2. Examine and amend domestic laws dealing with hate crimes, especially on the Internet.
3. Teach law officers and local police officers in all OSCE states, how to best implement and enforce "anti-hate" laws by creating core curriculum and specialized training. Combating hate crimes require great sensitivity in their enforcement.
4. Foremost and finally, inspired by parliamentarians and governments, encouraged civic society and educators to meet voluntarily and develop curricula for primary, secondary and post secondary schools to inculcate and educate our youth against hate and discrimination.

Elie Wiesel, at the major OSCE Berlin Conference on Anti-Semitism two years ago, said that you can teach a young child to love or hate. It all depends on education.

Meanwhile there have been dramatic, if fitful, advances along all the frontiers to combat anti-Semitism.

OSCE Foreign Ministers gave further high-level political recognition to the seriousness of anti-Semitism at their December 2003 annual meeting in Maastricht. There they took the formal decision to spotlight the need to combat anti-Semitism by deciding to task the OSCE's Office of Democratic Institutions and Human Rights (ODIHR) to serve as a collection point for hate crime information.

ODIHR is now working with OSCE member states to collect information on hate crimes legislation and to promote "best practices" in the areas of law enforcement, combating hate crimes, and education. ODIHR established a Program on Tolerance and Non-Discrimination and now has an advisor to deal exclusively with the issue, though funding continues to be a problem.

At their December 2004 annual meeting in Sofia, OSCE Foreign Ministers welcomed the Chair-in-Office's decision to appoint three special representatives for tolerance issues, including a special representative for anti-Semitism, to work with member states on implementing specific commitments to fight anti-Semitism. In addition, the Foreign Ministers accepted the Spanish Government's offer to host a third follow up anti-Semitism conference in June 2005 in Cordoba. All 55 Minister's attended. I was part of the Canadian delegation to that event which I aided in organizing.

Regretfully, Canada was a reluctant participant in this process.

As I said, the United Nations also took important steps in the fight against anti-Semitism reversing the ugly anti-Semitic dialectic that erupted at the so-called UN Conference on Human Rights in Doha, South Africa. The June 2004 seminar on anti-Semitism hosted by Secretary General Kofi Annan was a small step to reverse the excesses of the Doha UN Conference! Another concrete measure was a resolution of the United Nations Third Committee in November 2004, which finally called for the elimination of all forms of religious intolerance, explicitly including anti-Semitism.

Education remains the most potent antidote for anti-Semitism and all other forms of intolerance!

For example, a remarkable conference in Stockholm in 1998 was convoked out of concern for the decreasing level of knowledge of the Holocaust particularly among the younger generation, Sweden, the United Kingdom and the United States decided to take a lead and address the issue collaboratively. They formed an International Task Force. The Task Force for International Cooperation on Holocaust Education, Remembrance, and Research (ITF) emerged from this initial effort.

Today the ITF, an informal international organization operating on the basis of consensus, and without a bureaucracy, consists of 20 countries. ITF member states agree to commit themselves to the Declaration of the Stockholm International Forum on the Holocaust and to its implementation. Current members of the ITF include Argentina, Austria, Czech Republic, Denmark, France, Germany, Hungary, Israel, Italy, Latvia, Lithuania, Luxembourg, the Netherlands, Norway, Poland, Romania, Sweden, Switzerland, United Kingdom and the United States. In addition, four other countries (Croatia, Estonia, Greece, and Slovakia) maintain a liaison relationship with the ITF.

Regretfully Canada has not joined the other 20 nations in this crucial International Task Force focused on education and research. It is my modest hope that this lecture might stimulate Canadian participation in this global effort to eradicate the oldest pandemic of prejudice in the world - anti-Semitism.

What of anti-Semitism in the 21st century Canada. What are the facts?

There are no single overall Canadian statistics sources about hate crimes in general or anti-Semitic incidents in general. There are four pools of statistics.

B'Nai Brith Canada's League for Human Rights has tracked anti-Semitism outbreaks across Canada for 22 years. This March, the League reported 857 incidents across Canada, the highest number in 22 years, and up 47% from 2003 including the first ever incident in Canada's newest Territory - Nunavut!

The Pilot Survey of Hate Crime by the Canadian Centre for Justice Statistics released in 2004 which compiled records of 12 police forces from the years 2001 and 2002 are relevant. That survey across Canada found that 25% of the 928 reported hate crimes were anti-Semitic in nature once again making Jews the largest single target group. That study also found that Jews were the most likely group to be targeted by a hate crime in the 12 jurisdictions that participated in the study.

Less than 2% of the Canadian population is Jewish, yet over 25% of all hate crimes were targeted towards Jews.

Toronto Police Services is one police force that produces an annual Hate Crime Report. The Report is available online.

That Report indicates that there were 163 hate crimes in the Toronto area in 2004, representing a 9 percent increase over the previous year's figures of 149. Page 9 of that report indicates that the victim group most targeted were Jews (59%). In addition, there were 18 in multi-based categories, i.e. that fit into more than one group and could include Jews, so those figures might be higher.

Police tracked lesser incidents. A significant portion - name calling - at schools would not count as a "crime". Yet, most were directed against Jews.

York Regional Police in Ontario also produce a hate crime stat report through their diversity office ("Policing in a Multicultural Community"). That service reported 105 hate crimes in 2004, compared to 92 in the previous year. While the community is quite diverse, 72 or 68.6% of the 105 hate crimes reported to York Regional Police targeted Jews - making Jews the most targeted group in that region as well. The next most targeted group was Blacks (12 incidents) while three cases targeted the Muslim community.

Despite these alarming and miserable Canadian statistics, I have yet to convince my Senate colleagues of the need to study the OSCE Resolutions on anti-Semitism although I have attempted to do so for almost four years.

Let us return to the Catholic Church.

We have just celebrated and commemorated the 40th Anniversary of Vatican II Encyclical *Nostra Aetate* that marked a remarkable turning point in Jewish/Catholic relations. As I said earlier, that profound and remarkable reform was launched just before Pope John XXIII ascended to the Holy See in the late 1950s and was broadened in equally remarkable ways by his successor, Pope John Paul II. Vatican II returned to the ideas of the early Church's attitude from Augustinian times when Jews were to have a protected if restricted place within Christianity and the ancient scriptures were revered.

Aquinas' writing, as I have said, help reverse that more tolerant policy of the early Church.

The old policy of St. Paul, had declared that Jews were deaf and blind and thus ignorant to the recognition of Jesus' divinity. Then along came Aquinas who argued in *"Summa Theologiea"* that a clear distinction must be made between Jews who were ignorant and those who were educated, and still refused to recognize Jesus' divinity.

Ten years before Aquinas was born, the Lateran Council in 1215 promulgated the first comprehensive restrictive edicts separating and isolating Jews in society and in the work place.

Aquinas' scholarly works gave that separation a growing respectable intellectual basis. These restrictive laws were ultimately codified under the Nazis. And so came the Holocaust.

I believe human rights cannot be obtained by revelation or miracle though I may believe in both from time to time. Respect for human rights can only be embedded in the individual psyche, by respect, dialogue and education.

So, the late '50s marked the start of a historic sea of change - the beginning of a change in the world in the relationship between Judaism and Catholicism. The Church's agents for change included the Superior General of the Jesuits, Father Janssens (the Black Pope), Cardinal Tisserant of France, then Cardinal Roncalli of Italy and then Cardinal Montini of Italy, Cardinal Bea of Germany, amongst others. Each was uncomfortable with Pope Pius XII's ambivalence towards the so-called "Jewish Question" before and during World War II. They agreed with the rationale that charges against the Jews as "deicides" and the "perfidity" of the Jewish people must be expunged from the teachings and the liturgy of the Church. These teachings rested too near the heart of anti-Semitic teachings - first based on religion and then expropriated by the secular domain. They understood that the latter could not be changed without the first.

On October 18, 1958, Cardinal Roncalli became Pope. Later, as John XXIII celebrating his first Mass on Easter Sunday, in April 1959, he suddenly interrupted Easter Mass in St. Peter's Basilica and he instructed offensive words of culpability against Jews be expunged from the text of the Mass immediately. This was the dramatic start of Vatican II and the start of that profound change in the Church's relation to other religions, especially towards Judaism.

Catholic thinkers such as St. Augustine, St. Bernard of Clairvaux, St. Ignatius Loyola, the founder of the Jesuit Order, whose early successors were Jewish "conversos", and in our century, many scholars such as Jacques Maritain and others, all were concerned about these textual references that criticized the Jewish people. They all preached and taught tolerance and mutual respect.

After Cardinal Roncalli became Pope John XXIII, the spirit of reform accelerated.

Vatican II was inaugurated by pre-council meetings. A consensus developed that the Jewish/Catholic relations file be classified "as urgent Vatican business." The death of John XXIII in June 1963 in the midst of Vatican II preparations seemed to slow down the accelerating impulse for reform and the reform forces. The Jesuits and especially Cardinal Bea, an old Jesuit himself, took the lead in addressing the Council three times in three years which led to its final text adopted 1767 to 250 which was issued October 28, 1965. This Encyclical, after paying tribute to the people of the Old Testament, continued and I quote:

> *"Christ's passion" cannot be blamed on all Jews then living without distinction nor upon the Jews of today. Although the Church is the new people of God, the Jews should not be presented as repudiated or cursed by God, as if such views followed from the Holy Scripture. All should take pains, then, lest in catechetical instruction and in the preaching of God's Word they teach anything out of harmony with the truth of the gospel and the spirit of Christ.*
>
> *The Church repudiates all persecutions against any man. Moreover, mindful of her common patrimony with the Jews, and motivated by the gospel's spiritual love and by no political consideration, she deplores hatred, persecutions, and displays of anti-Semitism directed against the Jews at any time and from any source."*

So began the reform process where the substructure and subtext of Catholic teachings was slowly altered. The Old Testament did not replace the New. Both were valid. The New Covenant did not erase the old Covenant between God and the Jews. Both were authentic. And, the idea that Jewish revelation was older and authentic and thus Christianity did not invalidate Judaism saw a change in the evangelical approach of the Church as it related to Jews. In light of these changed policies, the Church's mission to convert Jews was no longer deemed appropriate or necessary.

Some were not satisfied with the pace of change that slowly evolved from Nostra Aetate within and without the Church. Cardinal Bea, a leading advocate acknowledged that the Encyclical was a start but only a start. He was quoted . . . "Two years are not enough to change ways of thinking forged over two thousand years. . . . It is after the Council that we must labour to disseminate both its spirit and principles and gradually discover concrete structures for improving Catholic - Jewish relations. It will be a long struggle demanding patience and perseverance but is the only way to produce lasting fruit." So Cardinal Bea decided that more formal structured institutional changes were necessary. He persuaded the reformers in the Vatican of the necessity to establish "the Office for Catholic-Jewish Relations" which would accelerate and sustain this important work through mutually respectful and active dialogue.

Cardinal Bea believed that dialogue, interaction and education only could reduce the ancient antipathy toward Jews.

John Paul II seeped in his own experiences and observations in Poland during World War II, gave the Jewish Catholic dialogue increased symbolism, energy, action and public demonstration. He was the first Pope to visit a synagogue, the first Pope to visit a death camp, the first Pope to recognize and visit Israel in 2000, especially the Western wall and to lay a wreath at Yad Vashem. In his speeches and actions, John Paul II, still constrained by reactionary forces within the Church, continued the reform thrust of John XXIII and gave the reform agenda added public momentum by these symbolic gestures.

The large footsteps left by Pope John XXIII and Pope John Paul II are being filled with renewed vigour by Pope Benedict, the 16th.

When Cardinal Ratzinger became Pope, his first message was to Rabbi Segni of Rome renewing Pope John II's dialogue with the Jews of Rome who had lived in Rome before the coming of Christ.

On his first visit outside of Rome to Cologne, Germany this year, Pope f visited the old Cologne Synagogue in the heart of Germany where Jews had settled for over 1500 years. This was yet another important symbolic Papal gesture.

Was Nazism a Christian phenomenon? This question has been laboriously debated. Cardinal Cassidy from Australia, a leader in Vatican II and beyond, in his recent text, *Rediscovering Vatican II, Ecumenism and Inter Religious Dialogue* and Professor David Novak, an author of *Daber Emet - To Speak the Truth* - in a scholarly reaction to Nostra Aetate, agreed. While without the long history of Christian anti-Judaism and Christian led violence against the Jews, Nazi ideology could not have taken out nor carried out, and while too many Christians participated in or were sympathetic to Nazi atrocities against Jews, and while other Christians did not protest sufficiently against those atrocities, Nazism itself was not the inevitable consequence of Christian teachings. If the Nazi's had been successful, the Nazis would have turned their murderous rage more directly against Christians. Many Christians risked and sacrificed their lives to save Jews during the Nazi regime. Thus Cardinal Cassidy concludes recent efforts in Christian theology to repudiate unequivocally contempt of Judaism and the Jewish people must be encouraged.

Cardinal Cassidy continues, and I quote:

"Irreconcilable differences between Jew and Christians will not be settled until God redeems the entire world as promised in the scriptures. A new relationship between Jews and Christians will not weaken Jewish practices; Jews and Christians must continue to work together for justice and peace; Both recognized each in their own way, the unredeemed state of the world."

In 2000, then Cardinal Ratzinger published an Article in the Vatican Paper *L'Obsservatore Romano* - to dispel a disturbing statement of the Vatican Congregation of the

Doctrine of Faith. "Dominus Jesus" - that argued that followers of other faiths were gravely deficient in respect of salvation. Cardinal Ratzinger's article was entitled "*Abraham's Heritage - a Christmas Gift.*" This article provided fresh impetus and encouragement for the Catholic Jewish dialogue. "The faith witnessed in the Jewish Bible is not merely another religion to us, but the foundation of our own faith." So wrote Cardinal Ratzinger.

Pope Benedict XVI, then Cardinal Ratzinger, had played a crucial role resuscitating in the Jewish Catholic dialogue.

In 2000, four independent Jewish scholars from all facets of Jewish religious life published a document entitled "*Daber Emet: A Jewish Statement on Christians and Christianity.*" Daber Emet means to "Proclaim the Truth." The following Remarkable Statements were articulated which caused heated criticism on both sides of the Jewish Catholic divide.

1. Jews and Christians worship the same God - the God of Abraham, Isaac and Jacob.
2. Jews and Christians reap authority from the same books, the Tanach or the Old Testament.
3. Christians respect the claim of Jewish people upon the land of Israel.
4. Jews and Christian respect the moral principles of the Torah - they all were created in the image of God and all can improve their lives and conduct by standing against immoralities and idolatries that harm and degrade all.

To allay the concerns of the Vatican Statement, "Dominus Jesus" Cardinal Cassidy placed Cardinal Ratzinger' s Response in this context, and I quote:

"Referring to the very negative Jewish reaction to the document Dominus Jesus, *'Abraham's Heritage - A Christmas Gift' affirms:* 'It is evident that, as Christians, our dialogue with the Jews is situated on a different level than that in which we engage with other religious. The faith witnessed to by the Jewish Bible is not merely another religion to us, but is the foundation of our own faith.' Cardinal Ratzinger then gave what has been called 'a new vision of the relationship with the Jews.' After tracing briefly the history of God's dealing with the Jewish people, the cardinal expresses 'our gratitude to our Jewish brothers and sisters who, despite the hardness of their own history, have held on to faith in this God right up to the present and who witness to it in the sight of those peoples who, lacking knowledge of the one God, dwell in darkness and the shadow of death (Luke 1:79).'

The article includes the following interesting comment on relations between Christians and Jews down through the centuries:

"Certainly from the beginning relations between the infant church and Israel were often marked by conflict. The church was considered to be a degenerate daughter, while Christians considered their mother to be blind and obstinate.

Down through the history of Christianity, already-strained relations deteriorated further, even giving birth to anti-Jewish attitudes that throughout history have led to deplorable acts of violence. Even in the most recent, loathsome experience of the Shoah was prepared in the name of an anti-Christian ideology that tried to strike the Christian faith at its Abrahamic roots in the people of Israel, it cannot be denied that a certain insufficient resistance to this atrocity on the part of Christians can be explained by the inherited and anti-Judaism in the hearts of not a few Christians.

For the Cardinal, it is perhaps this latest tragedy that has resulted in a new relationship between the church and the people of Israel, which he defines as 'a sincere willingness to overcome every kind of anti-Judaism and to initiate a constructive dialogue based on knowledge of each other and reconciliation.' If such a dialogue is to be fruitful, the Cardinal went on to suggest that it must begin with a prayer to our God first of all that he might grant to us Christians a greater esteem and love for that people, the people of Israel, to whom belong 'the adoptions as sons, the glory, the covenants, the giving of the law, the worship and the promises; theirs the patriarchs, and from them, according to the flesh, is the Messiah' (Rom. 9:4-5), and this not only in the past, but still today, 'for the gifts and the call of God are irrevocable' (Rom. 11:29).

Cardinal Ratzinger then went on to propose to Christians that they in their turn might pray to God 'that he grant also to the children of Israel a deeper knowledge of Jesus of Nazareth, who is their son and the gift they have made to us.' His final conclusion reminds us of the sixth statement in Dabru Emet: 'Since we are both waiting the final redemption, let us pray that the paths we follow may converge.'"

So friends, the laborious work of human rights between religions continues. For me you will understand that the heart of reform, the heart of human rights is dialogue and education. Perceiving the "Other" as different and celebrating the joys of those differences to replace the fears and loathing of differences that so perturbed the inner psyche of many must be our collective goal. Education of parents and youth, in schools and churches, on the streets and in homes, at the primary, the secondary and university level in my view, are the major keys and chords to dissolving this ancient animosity as best we can in our time.

Let me conclude, as I began, with a personal note. My father's family were students and followers of a certain long line of Hasidic Rabbis - one of them was called the "Kotzker Rebbe" who lived and taught over 150 years ago in Southern Poland. He taught that first rule of conduct for Jews is to tell the truth, especially to one's self.

The "Rebbe" despaired of the world. So each year he set out to write a history of the world on one page. And each year when he finished and read that one page, he was deeply disturbed and dissatisfied. So, each year he burned that one page and each year, started anew!

What do you say to those who look to the future and await the Kingdom of God?

When God arrives, both Jews and Christians will argue who was right or who was wrong? Both can be assured that God will surprise us all, as he has done so often in the past, when he addresses the question of "Human Rights."

Let me say, I admire the Catholic Church. I love and admire Canada. But there is great work to do in our endless quest for "human rights!"

Let us begin!

CHARLES V. KEATING: EULOGY

November 25, 2005

Hon. Jerahmiel S. Grafstein: Honourable senators, I wish to add my condolences. Charlie Keating was a lifelong friend. We met over 40 years ago. He was an active member of our party and an active supporter in all our political endeavours. I do not want the house to be confused with the fact that not only was Charlie a great Canadian, but he was a great and outstanding Liberal, a good friend and a stalwart also. His energy, his creativity, his commitment and his passion, not only for the party but also for the country, was undiminished.

I was saddened to hear this morning that he had passed away. I am unhappy that I will not be able to attend his funeral, but to his family and to his friends, and on behalf of his friends in Ontario, we will miss him.

IAN SINCLAIR: EULOGY

April 26, 2006

Hon. Jerabmiel S. Grafstein: Honourable senators, I, too, would like to rise in tribute to the late Ian Sinclair. He had been appointed just before I arrived in the Senate, and we were sworn in at the same time. We should not look back too far, but in those days, this chamber was populated with premiers from every region. Outstanding academics, outstanding legal and medical experts were here. None was greater in this chamber than Ian Sinclair, who was able to become a master of many disciplines. He was a master lawyer, a master when it came to regulations and administration, a master when it came to economics and a master of business. Above all, we saw him in the Senate as a master senator.

Shortly after I was appointed, Ian called me to his office. His office was spotless and his desk was clean. He had two piles on his desk. I was quite curious, first of all, curious to be invited to his office, although we were friends, and became closer friends while we were here. I was also curious about these two piles. One pile was bills from the House of Commons and the other pile was bills that were in progress in the Senate. I could see that the bill in front of him had been marked up.

Ian sat behind this massive desk, and he was a massive man himself. He looked up and said, "We have one problem in the Senate." I said, "Ian, what would that be?" He said, "Senators do not read. The House of Commons is bad, but we are equally bad. We do not read. We do not read our legislation. We are called upon to vote, but many times, when we have a debate, either in committee or in the chamber, it is obvious that many senators have not read their material." He said, "My one word of advice to you as a senator is to read. If you do read that legislation, you will be surprised about what is in that legislation, and you will be surprised about the mistakes that the other place has overlooked." I felt that was good and thoughtful advice. This advice was passed on to me, and I pass it on to new senators.

One final word about Ian. He was a man among men. He was a great titan of business. He was a superb lawyer. He was a great Canadian, and his talents, which were truly multi-faceted, will be sorely missed. To his children and to his grandchildren who proudly bear his name, our hearts go out to him. We hope to see his talents again, but I am doubtful. Nothing has been so combined in one man as these many talents and his great humility and love of this country. He will be missed.

JOHN KENNETH GALBRAITH, O.C.: EULOGY

May 2, 2006

Hon. Jerahmiel S. Grafstein: Honourable senators, I rise to pay tribute to the late and great John Kenneth Galbraith. John Kenneth Galbraith: an imposing name for an imposing figure and a most imposing and formidable mind.

In 1958, in my final year at law school, I read a book, *The Affluent Society,* written by John Kenneth Galbraith. That book had a major influence on my youthful and impressionable mind. Suddenly, economics, law, political science and sociology, which I all struggled with at Western, came together for me and demonstrated what was possible with a liberal political attitude and mind.

In 1961, I founded a journal called *"The Journal of Liberal Thought"* to generate liberal ideas. I wrote to John Kenneth Galbraith and he responded. He went further and articulated and assisted me in things that I should explore and people I should contact to assist, including Barbara Ward, who, at that time, wrote a stunning article for that journal.

Mr. Galbraith and I shared common roots, I discovered. We were both born in southwestern Ontario. Both his father and my father were Liberal Party workers. We considered ourselves true Grits and shared an early admiration for Mitch Hepburn when he was on the rise - not in his latter years.

Mr. Galbraith and I kept in touch. I read each and every one of his books. In 1974, when wage and price controls were issues in the land - and senators on the other side will recall that time - Mr. Trudeau could not make up his mind about what to do after the election, having fought the election against wage and price controls. The last person he saw who convinced him that wage and price controls were possible was John Kenneth Galbraith. Mr. Galbraith was influential in that regard because one of the most important pieces of work that he had done during the war was a study of wage and price controls.

John Kenneth Galbraith's career as a gadfly, writer, diplomat, political speech writer and an adviser was scintillating. He could write with great panache. He had wit and he could turn a phrase. He coined the phrase "conventional wisdom" and once told me that conventional wisdom is usually always wrong or always late. He was a contrarian.

In 1997, the Governor General saw fit to award Mr. Galbraith the highest honour we can bestow on a Canadian, the Order of Canada. I was privileged to be one of the few to be invited to that ceremony.

After his passing, Mr. Galbraith's son said that his father was not dead. His father was alive. He was alive in his words, in his thoughts, in his books. I believe, honourable senators, that the best way to judge John Kenneth Galbraith is to read once again each and every one of his books. He had much to say to my generation, and I think he has much to say to the present generation.

His ideas are alive. He will live on. He will be missed. We offer our condolences and our best wishes to his children and his grandchildren.

LORD KENNETH THOMSON: EULOGY

June 13, 2006

Hon. Jerahmiel S. Grafstein: Honourable senators, I rise to pay tribute to the late Lord Kenneth Thomson. I first ran into Ken Thomson over 45 years ago. I introduced myself, saying, "I am delighted to meet you, Lord Thomson"; and he said, "My name is Ken; what is yours?" Thereafter, we developed a very warm and friendly relationship.

I ran into him in my early years going downtown on the subway. An underground passage connected my office to his office around the corner, so I met with him from time to time at a coffee shop in the food area underneath our buildings. Of course, one would always run into him at any major charitable event in Toronto because he was an avid supporter of the arts.

Ken Thomson, in my view, was brilliant. He was modest and a visionary who transformed his father's print empire into a virtual internet-savvy conglomerate. In the process, he became one of the richest men in the world and certainly the wealthiest Canadian.

He was a lover of the arts and his living monument will be the Art Gallery of Ontario. He was a collector of Cornelius Krieghoff and the Group of Seven. His efforts propelled those artists into the world art community.

Last Wednesday night I raced to Toronto for a surprise birthday for Tom who is a clothier in Kensington Market. Tom, who owns Tom's Place, is a Hungarian refugee and his friends were throwing a party for him. Ken Thomson was there; he was one of Tom's best customers.

Whenever I called Ken Thomson, he was ready to help. For me, Ken Thomson was the quintessential Canadian. He was brilliant, modest, hard working, a gentle man and a gentleman. Our hearts go out to Marilyn, his family and his extended family.

Ken, your race is run, your victory is won, now come to rest, Godspeed, God bless.

EDWIN A. GOODMAN: EULOGY

September 27, 2006

Hon. Jerahmiel S. Grafstein: Honourable senators, I rise to add my words of condolence to the Goodman family. Eddie Goodman and I were lively, if rarely amicable, friends, and political contestants for the heart of Toronto and Ontario. Sometimes he won and many times I won, but we were always friends.

I would like to tell a story to elucidate our relationship. He was the Chairman of a Conservative convention when Mr. Diefenbaker ran again in 1966-67 for the leadership. Mr. Diefenbaker became a mentor of mine when I first spoke to him upon my arrival here in 1965. He called me to his office and told me about the "dos and don'ts" of Parliament, and we became fast friends, despite the fact that in the Liberal Party he was considered an ogre. At that convention, I called his office for an observer pass, and he sent me two seats, insisting that I bring my wife. We sat behind Mr. Diefenbaker at that convention. Eddie Goodman was the Chairman, but he and Mr. Diefenbaker were on the outs and, therefore, not on good speaking terms. Eddie walked down the aisle and, when he saw me sitting behind Mr. Diefenbaker, said, "What are you doing here?" I turned and pointed to "The Chief," who turned around and said, "He's with me." Goodman replied, "Grafstein, you're impossible." I was, and so was Eddie.

I want to wish Eddie's family all the best. He was a great Canadian and he will be sorely missed, not only by his friends, but also by those who were his honourable opponents.

JUNE CALLWOOD, O.C., O. ONT.: EULOGY

April 19, 2007

Hon. Jerahmiel S. Grafstein: Honourable senators, I rise in a belated tribute to the passing of an extraordinary Canadian and a good friend - June Callwood. June was a beautiful woman inside and out. June Callwood; what a lovely name, fresh as spring and as inviting as our trees and forests.

June was more than an acquaintance. She became a friend and advocate for any good cause that warranted public attention, especially for the underdog. June was quiet, graceful, elegant and witty; her gentle demeanour hid an inner will of steel and a heart of great passion and compassion for people and unpopular causes.

People rightly called her "the conscience of Canada," but June was more. She was a woman of many talents, a Renaissance person, a writer, a commentator, an author, a licensed pilot, an avid swimmer and sportswoman, and always an articulate spokesperson for the neglected underside of our society.

June was the first advocate - I believe the very first advocate - for those suffering from AIDS, at a time when it was not popular in our country. She was always the first to take on unpopular causes and transform public opinion.

June had no enemies. No one ever said an unkind word about her. She was blessed with legions of friends and admirers.

June, your race is run, your battles done, your victories won; now come to rest.

Our hearts go out to Trent Frayne and June's wonderful and talented family and friends. Regrettably, honourable senators, I doubt that we will see the likes of a June Callwood again in our time.

To you, June, pax vobiscum, Godspeed.

DAN HAYS: ON RETIREMENT

June 13, 2007

Hon. Jerahmiel S. Grafstein: Honourable senators, today we hail Dan Hays and bid him farewell as he takes his leave from the Senate. Dan was appointed to the Senate six months after me and has served almost a quarter of a century in this chamber. We share several common bonds. We were both appointed by Mr. Trudeau; we both graduated from the greatest law school in Canada, the University of Toronto Law School; we are both deeply interested in constitutional matters; and, finally, we have had and continue to have a lavish relationship with the Liberal Party of Canada.

I will not retrace Dan's contributions to the Liberal Party, to the Senate or to his province. These have already been delineated, and I will not make them more fulsome than they already are.

Let me briefly touch on some personal characteristics that, from my perspective, made Dan Hays a model senator. He represented his province with coherence, civility and commitment. He made wise and thoughtful contributions to the business of the Senate. Dan was never swept up in the short-range politics of the moment. Once, when Dan was asked to deliver a piece of unhappy news to me about my role in the Senate, a role I had sought for years, he did so candidly, concisely, carefully and co-gently.

We will miss Dan's careful deliberation and contribution to the Senate in the grand tradition of a great friend of ours, his late father Harry Hays, who made an outstanding contribution not only to this chamber, but also to the other chamber, to the Liberal Party and of course to his province.

To you, Dan, to your wife Kathy and to your entire family, we can only wish you energy, health, happiness and a long life. You are starting a new career. I am confident that you will bring the same competence and energy to bear as you have to the Senate.

Let me end with these two Latin words: carpe diem. Pluck the flower of today; smell the roses. The best is certainly yet to come.

MAURICE RIEL, P.C., Q.C.: EULOGY

November 21, 2007

Hon. Jerahmiel S. Grafstein: Honourable senators, I rise to pay belated tribute to the late Maurice Riel, who served as Speaker of the Senate for less than a year, from 1983-84, and who was the Speaker who inducted me into the Senate.

Maurice Riel was a distant relative of a controversial Canadian, Louis Riel, but Maurice was the least controversial of public men. He was an outstanding international lawyer who was respected in Canada and overseas, particularly in France where he was held in the highest regard. He was a great speaker, honourable senators, and a greater listener. He was elegant of dress, quiet of demeanour, a lover of good wines, a wonderful conversationalist and a delightful raconteur.

Maurice was an intellectual. We both shared a love of French authors - he in French and I, struggling, mostly in translation. We discussed Proust and, if you will forgive me, Baudelaire and de Maupassant, Sartre, Malraux, and especially Albert Camus, who was a particular favourite of his and mine. One day, in a rather long-winded speech, I quoted Albert Camus. After my speech, I received a note from Maurice delicately informing me that I had mispronounced "Camus." "Camus" is spelled C-a-m-u-s. I had pronounced his name with a silent "s." Maurice, ever the thoughtful linguist, believed that I should have pronounced the "s." After an animated discussion, we agreed that we would refer the question of appropriate pronunciation to a mutual friend of ours, Maurice Druon. Druon was - and is - an outstanding French novelist whom I had met when he spent some years studying at Glendon College in Toronto. He had hosted me in Paris at the Academie Francaise, the highest authority of French arts and letters. It turned out that Maurice knew him better than I, and it turned out that they were good friends.

We agreed to refer the matter to Druon for arbitration, as he was then, as now, the Secretaire Perpetual of Academie Francaise in Paris. A month or so later, he responded in writing and advised that "s" at the end of the surname Camus could be pronounced or not. For instance, Camus cognac is spelled the same way, but the "s" is pronounced. However, Druon felt that the better usage for Albert Camus' name was with a silent "s" as he had come from Algeria and that was more common usage there.

I raise this, honourable senators, to show that Maurice was a most meticulous and honest man, both as an intellectual and as a man of deep culture. His wit and wisdom and the contributions he made here will be sorely missed. He was a man of honour, grace, intellect, idolism and probity. He believed in a strong, united Canada and, as a member of the Senate and as Speaker, he embellished and elevated the stature of all members of this chamber.

A Greek philosopher once said that one's first duty is to be true to oneself. Maurice was true to himself, his party and country. Pro partee, pro patria. To our dear friend, you go to a better place. Dea optima maxima. For God, the best and the greatest. Nil non mortale tenemus, pectoris exceptis ingeniique bonis. We possess nothing in this world that is not mortal except the blessings of heart and mind. Thus let it be with our dear, departed friend Maurice. My condolences to his wife and family. Requiescat inpace, dear friend. Rest in peace.

ROSS FITZPATRICK: ON RETIREMENT

January 31, 2008

Hon. Jerahmiel S. Grafstein: Honourable senators, I simply cannot believe that Senator Ross Fitzpatrick is leaving the Senate. I have known Ross for almost 50 years. We met in Ottawa in the 1960s to serve as young, energetic and ambitious, bushy-tailed ministerial executive assistants in Mr. Pearson's government of all talents. To us, he was always Mr. Pearson.

Quickly, all of us came to respect Ross. He was mature beyond his years; he was quiet; he was humble, a man of few but incisive words, so unlike myself.

Ross was and is a great listener and a greater doer. Ross has, as a few of you know, a quick and rather wicked sense of humour, which I have been able to enjoy over the years sitting beside him here in the Senate. We became fast friends, and even though over the years may have disagreed from time to time on personalities or policies, we never exchanged a word in anger or disrespect because we are both loyalists, Pearson-ites, Trudeau-ites, Turner-ites, Chrétien-ites, Martin-ites and now loyal acolytes to Mr. Dion.

To recap Ross' success story, it is probably one of the most remarkable and untold Canadian success stories, almost unrivalled by anyone in this chamber or, indeed, Parliament in recent history.

Ross rose by the sheer dint of his own efforts from a modest background as a farm boy in the Okanagan where his grandfather and father were fruit farmers. He worked his way through school, first at the University of British Columbia and then on to the University of Maryland and Columbia University in the United States, gathering distinguished degrees along the way. Ross quickly caught the eye of John Nicholson, then a leading politician and baron, if you will, a minister from British Columbia, who was postmaster general, along with other portfolios, a very sensitive and political job requiring political skill, diplomacy and finesse. Ross had all these mature attributes in abundance. We all admired Ross for his smooth handling of contentious issues. He made everything look so easy, but when we tried ourselves, we saw how difficult it was.

We worked together on John Turner's leadership campaign in 1968, and Ross was a marvellous grassroots organizer. When he left Ottawa, he returned to British Columbia and built a remarkable business career in resources, transportation and real estate and especially in the creation, as others have pointed out, of one of Canada's, if not North America's, leading wineries in his beloved Okanagan.

He was a CEO in companies and resources in aerospace and did business not only in North America but throughout the Americas, in Asia and Africa, a remarkable story of Canadian entrepreneurship.

There is not a private cause - from health care, to the arts, to the environment - where Ross has not been a leader, a mover, a shaker and a donor. He was active not only in British Columbia but elsewhere in Canada and in the United States. In the United States, he has great friends in Congress who say to me: "How is my friend Ross Fitzpatrick?"

There has not been a federal or provincial political campaign in British Columbia where he did not take a leading role. He quickly became the confidante not only of politicians in Ottawa, but also mayors and premiers in his beloved province.

Ross was, as others have pointed out, one of the two key outside and long-time loyal advisers to Jean Chrétien. A great deal of Mr. Chretien's remarkable political success can be attributed to Ross who, over the years never failed to provide him with tough, clear-headed and always sound and grounded advice.

I have the privilege of his cogent insights when I served as Chair of the Banking Committee. He persuaded the committee to study interprovincial trade barriers that restrain Canada's markets, productivity and trade within Canada. It will be, I hope, a landmark study when completed.

Ross leaves the Senate, but he does not leave his energetic commitment to the public good or to politics. I wish him great and good health as he returns to his beloved Okanagan.

I will miss him because it will be almost impossible to get a seatmate like Ross who can put up with me. I wish him and his family, and particularly the graceful and lovely Linda, who has always been at his side, best wishes.

Ross, the best is yet to come. Godspeed.

OSCAR PETERSON: EULOGY

February 12, 2008

Hon. Jerahmiel S. Grafstein: Honourable senators, I want to join with Senator Banks and Senator Oliver in paying tribute to the great Oscar Peterson. When I, too, was a law student, I first came across him at the King Cole Room at the Park Plaza in 1956 when he celebrated all his talent with another great Canadian, Peter Appleyard. It was there that the magic of jazz, previously unknown to me, came alive.

Over the years I got to know Oscar reasonably well. I met him on a number of occasions, most recently after the tsunami in Southeast Asia several years ago when we put together a charitable event to which stars donated their time. Oscar was one of the first to respond to our call. He played for that CBC concert, and we raised over $15 million at the event.

I want to pay tribute to Oscar, to his family and to all jazz lovers throughout the world. Wherever you go in the jazz community around the world, be it Ronnie Scott's in London or the Village in New York, if you mention that you are Canadian, the automatic reply is, "Oscar Peterson." The two are inseparable - Canadianism and Oscar Peterson. May he rest in peace.

CHARLES CACCIA, P.C.: EULOGY

May 6, 2008

Hon. Jerahmiel S. Grafstein: Honourable senators, I rise to pay tribute to the late Charles Caccia, who suddenly passed away over the weekend. Charles Caccia was a friend and a Liberal stalwart for over 40 years.

Born in Italy and educated throughout Europe, he immigrated to Toronto and became involved with COSTI, the Toronto Italian community services outreach organization helping immigrants and others to adjust to Canada.

Charles was a man of the left, so much so that sometimes he was ignored by members of the Toronto Italian community, where he was respected for his honesty but where his views were not always fully appreciated.

He was an academic of note. He became a Professor of Forestry at the University of Toronto and became interested in environmental issues.

I first became acquainted with Charles in the early 1960s when he and I worked the streets of downtown Toronto for the Liberal cause. When his hero and mentor, Walter Gordon, left Parliament and left the Davenport riding seat open in 1968, after a very raucous, contested nomination of over 5,000 people at the coliseum at the CNE, Charles won the Liberal nomination. After that, he continued to hold the Davenport seat for 10 successive Parliaments until 2004, when he returned to academia.

After a very distinguished parliamentary career as a backbencher serving on many committees, Charles was appointed as Minister of Labour under Pierre Trudeau, and then became Minister of the Environment under John Turner.

With his environmental expertise, Charles became almost the godfather of environment issues within Parliament and beyond into the wider community. When he left Parliament, he continued and started teaching as a Fellow at the prestigious University of Ottawa Institute of the Environment.

Charles was a formidable personality. He was a thoughtful, well-read, independent, prickly, outspoken, at times aggressive left-wing Liberal who was consistent and passionate in his views. He was relentless and he was also an outspoken champion of the labour movement and working Canadians.

Charles loved Canada. He believed in and fought for one Canada. He was a true believer.

In his latter years, Charles served as Chairman of the Canada-Europe Parliamentary Association and encouraged me to become active at the OSCE Parliamentary Assembly in Europe, where he felt that Canada needed a consistent and constant voice for human rights and issues of interest to all Canadians.

Charles will be sorely missed in the Liberal Party, where he brought a perception, an attitude and a strong voice that is growing dimmer and dimmer, not only within the party but across Canada.

Our condolences to his devoted family. To know Charles was to never forget his honesty, his courage, his independence, his passion and his commitment for a progressive reform agenda for all Canadians.

RAYMOND JOSEPH PERRAULT: EULOGY

March 5, 2009

Hon. Jerahmiel S. Grafstein: Honourable senators, I also rise to pay tribute to Ray Perrault. I first encountered Ray in the early 1960s when I was an advance man in the Pearson regime and I went out to British Columbia for the first time. Ray was then the Liberal leader. He shared a remarkable resemblance to a great American politician, Hubert Humphrey.

Ray celebrated the politics of joy. He was a happy, joyous warrior. He was a partisan, as some senators opposite have said, but he was a great comrade at arms, and he never took things personally. As people know, Ray was a great talker. What people do not know is that when he was the Liberal leader, he was also a great listener. He listened carefully to people.

I come from a small town in Ontario. When I first went to British Columbia, Ray told me that if I really wanted to understand Canada and the West, I had to go into the interior of British Columbia, which I did. There I began to see not only the magnificence of Canada but the magnificence of British Columbia.

Ray was a true liberal. He was not a large-"L" Liberal but a small-"l" liberal. On Liberal causes, you would always find Ray on the right side of the rainbow. He was a sports enthusiast, bar none. He was a baseball and hockey fan. He drove us crazy talking about British Columbia versus Toronto, saying: "We have a great basketball team, a great baseball team and a great hockey team." Ray always felt that nothing could be better in the world than those sports teams from British Columbia.

I want to take issue with some of the comments made by Allan Fotheringham. I do not think Ray was Dr. Foghorn at all. I think Ray reached Churchillian heights. He spoke with great articulation, and every once in a while, he reminded me of one of his great heroes, Winston Churchill. Once in a while, Winston Churchill's cadences could be heard in Ray's speeches. Ray was great and he touched us all.

Ray, your race is run, your victories won. Now go to rest, and all my best. Godspeed to Barbara and the Perrault family.

MAURICE DRUON: EULOGY

April 23, 2009

Hon. Jerahmiel S. Grafstein: Honourable senators, I rise to mourn the death of France's greatest intellectual and cultural icon, Maurice Druon.

As France's pre-eminent literary figure, Maurice was a lover of all things French and a vitriolic protector of the French language. He railed against colloquialisms and, more recently, against political correctness.

He loved English. He taught in Canada briefly and relished Canada. I was proud to call him a good friend.

He had a mythical career, first as a cadet in the French cavalry school when the Germans invaded France in 1940. Ignoring the orders of Pétain, the Vichy leader, to lay down their arms, he and his school staved off two German divisions for two days in the Loire.

Receiving honours for their heroism, he and his cadets were allowed safe passage to the unoccupied zone of France, the Cote d'Azur. There he met his equally brilliant uncle, the author and musician Joseph Kessel, where they wrote and produced a play.

He became a leader of the French Resistance. In 1942, he escaped to Spain and finally landed in London, where he joined De Gaulle and the Free French.

Asked by the Resistance to write an inspirational song, he and his uncle wrote *Le chant des partisans - The Song of the Partisans -* that became the rallying cry of the Resistance. He wrote the French lyrics, which translated say:

Friend, do you hear the black flight of the crows on our plains?
Friend, do you hear the death cries of a country in chains?

This song was broadcast twice daily over BBC and rivalled *La Marseillaise*, the French anthem, in popularity.

After the war, he became a prolific writer, creating historical works and novels in quality and quantity not seen since the days of Alexandre Dumas.

In 1966, at the youthful age of 48, he was elected to the Academie Francaise. In 1973, he followed the footsteps of Andre Malraux and became the Minister of Culture of France, and then a deputy, representing an area in the heart of Paris.

As a staunch protector of the French language, he became Secretary Perpetual of the Academie Francaise, the pantheon of the French elite in the arts, science and literature.

Once, he called me to convince me to join his efforts to raise funds to fix a leaky roof over Napoleon's tomb at Les Invalides, which I did. I was rewarded with a sparkling dinner at the Academie Francaise, where he hosted me.

One Senate story: I had a disagreement with the former Speaker of the Senate, Maurice Riel, who was also a respected French linguist and expert, and a great lover of French literature. In a speech in the Senate, I quoted Albert Camus. Maurice immediately criticized me for mispronouncing Camus' name because I had not pronounced the final "s." Maurice insisted that I should have pronounced Camus with a spoken "s." We agreed to have the issue arbitrated by Maurice Druon in Paris and so we wrote him a letter. I was pleased that Druon supported my pronunciation.

Maurice Druon loved the English language, praising the speeches of Winston Churchill. He started a controversy when he said some years ago:

> French no longer respect the language because they no longer love themselves and no longer loving themselves, they no longer loved what was the instrument of their glory - their language.

So said Maurice Druon.

Maurice Druon was proud of the bilingual nature of Canada and proud that French Canadians had joined in his effort and the effort of his compatriots in the survival of his greatest glory - the French language.

Honourable senators, we will miss him, his wit, his profound knowledge and his pen. While Maurice has passed away, his bright memory, his novels, his words and his friendship will live on to the end of time. Au revoir, cher ami.

YOINE GOLDSTEIN: ON RETIREMENT

May 7, 2009

Hon. Jerahmiel S. Grafstein: Honourable senators, I rise to pay brief tribute to our colleague, Senator Yoine Goldstein, and to deal with a false belief.

There is a false belief in this chamber and other places that each Jew knows every other Jew. Frankly, I did not know Yoine Goldstein before he called me shortly before he was appointed to the Senate. I knew of him, as Senator Smith says, but I did not know him.

He sought my advice and my advice was very simple. I said: "If you get to the Senate, focus, work hard and you will be immensely satisfied and gratified by the things you do and the work you undertake."

He worked hard and he was rewarded; he was a quick study. He quickly became a member of the Standing Senate Committee on Banking, Trade and Commerce, which I chaired, and he played a very important role in that committee.

Yoine has left a large footprint in a very short period of time, so I will not reiterate what all honourable colleagues have said. I can only wish him and his wife a traditional Jewish salute, that he should live to 120 years.

Jews greet other Jews by this greeting, saying "You should live to 120 years," because Moses lived to 120 years. There is a symbolic, unconscious message within that message, which is that Moses became a leader and started his first career at the age of 80. A great Rabbi once told me to try to emulate Moses. Do not worry about old age because Moses, our greatest teacher, became a leader at age 80, which he did.

To Yoine, I wish you well. I wish you the other traditional Jewish greeting, which is "from strength to strength"; and I wish you Godspeed. I know you have only started. You have had several careers and you are about to start your greatest career. We do not know what it is; we wait with breathless anticipation.

WILLIE ADAMS: ON RETIREMENT

June 10, 2009

Hon. Jerahmiel S. Grafstein: Honourable senators, I am rather angry today about Willie's departure. Everyone is praising him, and I am upset that he is leaving, because he has left me with the responsibility for what he and I started with our good friend Charlie Watt some nine years ago.

Nine years ago, Willie, Charlie and I were having dinner in the parliamentary restaurant. I was upset with the water crisis in Walkerton. Willie and Charlie said, "Why are you so upset? We have lived all our lives with bad water. It is just coming to your attention for the first time."

It was that conversation that led me to my almost decade-long quest to have clean drinking water for everyone across the country, including in the Aboriginal communities.

I have always believed that drinking water is a question of equality and that it is unfair that we should have clean drinking water in the Senate when there is not clean drinking water in the far reaches of this country.

Those bills are still on the Order Paper, Willie, and you are leaving. I am upset because your support has been invaluable.

I will relay an incident for honourable senators. There has been a great debate in committee about bad drinking water. We have heard reports from one government agency after another telling us how good the drinking water is, and how they are improving the product.

Willie said to me one day, "I can help you with that." The following week when he came down from the North, he brought me his house water filter, which was black. He said, "This is the drinking water that they think is clean, and that is what my family has to deal with every day."

Willie, the mission continues. We will discuss water today, tomorrow and as long as I am here.

Hon. Jerry S. Grafstein. Q. C

There is no question that you have the best smile in the Senate. You have the brightest eyes in the Senate. May your smile and bright eyes continue to shine on all those who have had the privilege of your company.

DOUGLAS FISHER: EULOGY

September 29, 2009

Hon. Jerahmiel S. Grafstein: Honourable senators, I rise to pay tribute to the late Doug Fisher. Doug Fisher was a giant of a man. He was oversized in everything he did: war veteran, librarian, teacher, miner, forest ranger, political giant killer - he defeated C.D. Howe, Member of Parliament, hockey fanatic, political commentator and journalist par excellence.

For me, the passing of Doug Fisher marks the end of the Canadian giants of journalism Blair Fraser, Bruce Hutchison, Charlie Lynch and Bill Wilson, just to name a few. All of those journalists were members of the fourth estate. They understood war and understood peace. Each was a coherent, cogent writer who had a deep, facile knowledge and sense of Canadian history, Canadian politics, Canadian personalities and international affairs. That knowledge radiated in each of their columns.

We will not see their kind again.

Doug, whom I first met when he was running as an NDP candidate in Toronto, was different. I was an active organizer in York Centre when he ran a distant third as the NDP candidate; but we came to know each other, and I came to respect his erudition.

Doug, as many men on the left of the political spectrum, abhorred Liberals. He had that secret streak: he was a secret admirer of conservatism. This streak seems to run through many of our friends in the NDP. However, we shared some common interests. He was a book lover, and whenever we met on the street or for coffee in the West Bloc, we played a little game. He would ask, "Have you read this book?" I would say, "Yes, and by the way, Doug, have you read this book?" "Of course," he said. We were both voracious readers. He read everything. He was a collector of newspaper clippings, which became a treasure trove for him when he launched his career as one of Canada's most informed, intuitive and political journalists.

He made some exceptions in his hatred of Liberals. He admired John Munro, especially because John shared his love of hockey when Doug served as Chairman of Hockey Canada. Doug, as you recall, co-authored a definitive history of Canada's sporting heroes. Doug admired John Turner and John Diefenbaker because, like him, they were fervent believers in Parliament.

We also shared an admiration for my late father-in-law, known as "What-a-Man, Sniderman," who was an outstanding baseball pitcher and hitter in the 1920s and 1930s in Canada.

Honourable senators, the fourth estate has fallen and become fragmented. No longer will we see giants such as Doug Fisher, so influential in the public affairs of this nation. We are the worse for it and we will not see his like again.

My condolences to his family and his many sons, some of whom have followed in their father's footsteps and taken up distinguished careers in the media.

It is said that stars light our horizon long after the stars themselves have vanished in space. Doug's memory and his prodigious written record will live with us as a bright testament to his greatness and brilliance. He will be remembered as a man who wore proudly the mantle of every man.

DR. STANLEY HAIDASZ: EULOGY

October 29, 2009

Hon. Jerahmiel S. Grafstein: Honourable senators, I, too, rise to pay tribute to the late Dr. Stanley Haidasz. Stanley was the epitome of a truly multilingual, multicultural Canadian - a new image of Canadian citizenry that he helped to create and to promote, despite serious opposition, as others have said.

Born in Canada of Polish roots, he studied medicine at the University of Toronto and completed his post-graduate education in cardiology at the University of Chicago. After starting his medical practice, he became interested immediately in public affairs. He became the Member of Parliament for Trinity in 1957, a riding in the heart of Toronto. He was defeated in 1958 in the Diefenbaker landslide. He ran again in Parkdale in 1962 and represented that proud constituency in five successive elections until 1978 when he was appointed Senator. He retired from the Senate in 1998.

Stanley was much more than the sketchy outline of his political victories. He was a unique Canadian. I came to know Stanley in 1962. As President of the Toronto District Young Liberal Association, my job was to organize young Liberal groups in each riding in Toronto. Stanley knew virtually everyone in his riding. Everyone had an immense respect for him because he practised medicine, and most people were his patients. In addition, he had an immense following amongst young people. As a result, we had a strong and active young Liberal organization. Some of us in this room benefited from the relationships we developed there, as Senator Eggleton pointed out.

Stanley was multilingual; he spoke a number of languages. He was a scholar, deeply religious and proud of his Polish patrimony - a patrimony we share. One day, he called to invite me to a meeting of a young visiting Catholic prelate from Poland. He was the dynamic Archbishop of Krakow, Father Wojtyla. We discovered in our conversations because of Stanley that both our fathers had served in the Pilsudsh brigade after World War I that led to the independence of Poland.

After I told that story to the Archbishop, he and I became friends, and my friendship with Stanley was forged into that bond. Later, that gentleman became Pope John Paul II. He was a great advocate of Stanley Haidasz. As others have mentioned, Stanley was honoured by the Pope receiving the distinguished Order of Saint Gregory.

As a doctor in 1966, Stanley was one of the foremost advocates of Medicare at a Liberal policy convention in Ottawa. I participated in that policy fight. As a doctor, he fought for Medicare on the floor of that policy convention that led to the establishment of Medicare. That fight should not be forgotten.

In 1972, Stanley went on to become, as others have said, the first Minister of State for Multiculturalism. He helped transform Canada from a unilingual to a bilingual and finally multicultural Canada. It was not easy. He was a gentleman of the old school. He had a capacious knowledge of everything. When we served here in the Senate on many committees, everyone was amazed at his deep erudition.

Honourable senators, Stanley Haidasz left a deep impression on the body politic of Canada. Unfortunately, I do not believe we will see his like again. Our condolences go out to his family. His light is diminished, but he has left a starry trail of accomplishments that will be forever remembered.

ROMÉO LeBLANC: EULOGY

November 3, 2009

Hon. Jerahmiel S. Grafstein: Honourable senators, I rise to pay tribute to the late and great Roméo LeBlanc.

I first met Roméo when I came to Ottawa in the 1960s as Chief of Staff to a Minister in the Pearson government. Roméo was the go-to man for advice. He was available for all bushy-tailed, overeager, overambitious young assistants, as many of us were.

Roméo was an unusual man and a most unlikely politician. He was modest, almost shy, unassuming, humble and so unlike most public or, in particular, political men. He was a great listener. He was truly bilingual, or might I say, trilingual. He spoke careful, impeccable English; he was articulate in French; and he spoke grassroots Acadian. As a teacher, journalist, broadcaster, press officer, writer and speaker, he loved both the written and spoken word. He was a great speech writer and an excellent and compelling, if modest, speaker in the Churchillian style. He was a simple man, always refusing to take credit for his many accomplishments and always refraining from the limelight. Both Mr. Pearson and Mr. Trudeau cherished the written and spoken word, and his words and advice to them were highly regarded and respected.

I will also remember Roméo as an approachable politician who had a golden gut. He did not need to read polls. He could tell you what the public opinion was on any issue. He was a remarkable Canadian who made a difference in all that he did and to everyone he met. Our hearts go out to Dominic, my friend, and to his family. His light will continue to burn brightly in our memory. Godspeed.

JOHN BRYDEN: ON RETIREMENT

November 24, 2009

Hon. Jerahmiel S. Grafstein: Honourable senators, I also rise to pay tribute to my friend, John Bryden, who sat in the chair behind me in the Senate, and would volunteer to me, sotto voce, his homespun, salty, always-funny comments about the speakers and the Orders of the Day. I will miss those comments, John. They kept me awake during most of the debates.

Honourable senators, John is a quiet man; a man of few words; a man with a razor-sharp, steel-trap mind; and a very great wit. We have heard that he is a teacher, scholar, lawyer, public servant, businessman, farmer and a political organizer par excellence.

Politics, or the DNA of politics, runs very deep in his province. John hails from New Brunswick. I have always considered New Brunswick a truly distinct society. I recall Senator Charles McElman, who became an iconic figure here, and I recall the late and great Louis Robichaud, the former Premier of New Brunswick, one of Canada's greatest political speakers. Every once in a while, we heard him regale this Senate, and I remember his words to this day.

John was a creative force behind Frank McKenna and his landslide election victories in New Brunswick. It was unheard of and unheralded in political history to win all seats in a province. It had never happened before, and will never happen again.

New Brunswick has produced great, energetic and fertile minds like the late Roméo LeBlanc; our Deputy Speaker, Senator Losier-Cool; Senator Ringuette, our colleague over to the left; of course, the always-astute Senator Robichaud; and, never to neglect my seatmate, Senator Day, a capable and energetic senator if there ever was one.

However, John was more than that. He is a contrarian, with an independent streak of mind which gives him great credibility and unshakable honesty. His force of personality shaped this chamber in a quiet and persuasive way, and he was a great star - a quiet star - on the Standing Senate Committee on Legal and Constitutional Affairs, where I served with him from time to time, having been kicked off a number of times while John survived.

I will miss John's wit, his companionship and his political insight. I wish him good health and long life. John is a man for all seasons and for all good reasons.

MARCEL PRUD'HOMME: ON RETIREMENT

November 25, 2009

Hon. Jerahmiel S. Grafstein: Honourable senators, I rise to pay homage to my old friend, Marcel Prud'homme. When I look around this chamber, I see two senators who have known me the longest, David Smith and Marcel Prud'homme, although I have known Senator Smith longer.

I first met Marcel in 1961 in Montreal when I was President of the Toronto District Young Liberals Association and English-speaking Vice-President of the National Liberal Federation. I met Marcel when we came from Toronto to ask: What does Quebec want? That was the subject matter. Marcel then came to Toronto.

We were the first to ask what Quebec wanted and that question has reverberated through this chamber and Parliament ever since. I still do not know what Quebec wants, but I think I can sum it up in one word - more. I learned that from Marcel.

I made a careful investigation of Marcel after I met him. He was quite an interesting character. He was a cadet military officer as I was; he was a Liberal as I was; he was a strong federalist as I was. I think when it came to social policy, I was to the left of Marcel. However, Marcel became my greatest fan. Whenever I made a speech after I came to the Senate - Marcel was in the other place - he would come to listen.

I will miss you, Marcel. I will miss your surveillance, your monitoring, your debate, your interference, your delays all the great things that an independent senator has. I will miss that.

Having said all that, Marcel, this life is full of strange ups and downs. The other day, Marcel came to me, put his arm around me and he said, "You know, Jerry, you and I aren't so different after all." I appreciate that because I now believe that I am a member of 'the distinctive society' of Quebec if I am no different than Marcel. I believe that I am as distinctive as he is and I accept the fact that he and I have had visceral and deep differences of opinion.

However, the beauty of this chamber, as others have said, is that this is a place for people to be heard and to use their independence to speak aloud. I have tried to use that while I have been here and Marcel has done the same. He has been truly an independent and contributed to the independence of this chamber. Democracy depends on independence. In that sense, I commend him for his efforts over the years.

FAREWELL ADDRESS TO THE SENATE ON RETIREMENT, RESPONDING TO OTHER SENATORS

December 9, 2009

The Hon. the Speaker: Honourable senators, pursuant to rule 22(10) of the Rules of the Senate, the Leader of the Opposition has asked that the time provided for consideration of Senators' Statements be extended today for the purpose of paying tribute to the Honourable Senator Grafstein, who will be retiring from the Senate on January 2, 2010.

I remind honourable senators that, pursuant to the rules, each senator will be allowed only three minutes and may speak only once.

However, it is agreed that we continue our tributes to Senator Grafstein under Senators' Statements and that Senator Grafstein hold his comments until the end of Senators' Statements. We will therefore have 30 minutes, not including the time allotted to Senator Grafstein's response.

Is it agreed, honourable senators?

Hon. Senators: Agreed.

Hon. James S. Cowan (Leader of the Opposition): Honourable senators, I rise today to pay tribute to our colleague, Senator Grafstein. However, I will admit to you that the prospect is a little daunting. How do you pay tribute to a force of nature disguised as a person?

Some of you may remember the old film *Zelig*, about a character who just happened to be everywhere anything important was happening, anywhere in the world. Senator Grafstein has been rather like that. However, instead of a hapless Woody Allen character, Senator Grafstein has usually been a moving force behind whatever it is that everyone else was clamouring to be a part of.

Industry Canada, the department established to be a powerhouse for Canadian innovation policy, began as the Department of Consumer and Corporate Affairs in 1967, established under Prime Minister Trudeau. Yes, Jerry Grafstein was there, as a special adviser during its founding period.

In Washington, everyone knows Jerry Grafstein. The inauguration of President Obama? Absolutely; he was there.

Even the Pope famously referred to the fact that there were only two people he knew in Toronto - two people in our nation's largest city - and, yes, one of them was Jerry Grafstein. As we learned a few weeks ago, they happened to meet a number of years before, through the good graces of our former Senate colleague, Senator Stanley Haidasz.

As we in this chamber all know, Senator Grafstein is just like that. If something needs to be done, he is there and ready with a plan before most people even realize a problem exists.

Senator Grafstein was born in London, Ontario, where he attended the University of Western Ontario. He then went on to study law at the University of Toronto. He was called to the bar of Ontario in 1960.

From a very early age, Jerry was a dedicated Liberal. Over the years, he has held various positions in the Liberal Party of Canada, from the riding level to the national one. However, titles do not begin to convey the depth of his commitment to Liberal ideals, principles and a vision for Canada.

In 1966, Jerry founded and edited the *Journal of Liberal Thought*. He was Executive Assistant to the Right Honourable John Turner when he was Registrar General of Canada. He served as an adviser to the Ministry of Transport and the Canadian International Development Agency, and was a member of the Department of Justice Advisory Committee. Senator Grafstein co-founded and was President of Red Leaf Communications Company, the advertising consortium that served the Liberal Party so well for so many years. Senator Grafstein also found time to practise law with the well-known Toronto firm of Minden Gross, which he joined in the 1960s and helped to build to its current status as one of the leading firms in the country.

In 1984, he was summoned to the Senate by Prime Minister Trudeau. Some people like to present the Senate as a sleepy chamber, filled with people who do not do much of anything. I invite those people to meet Jerry Grafstein. Here are just a few of the highlights of projects he has been involved in while with us.

Senator Grafstein has been an active member of numerous inter-parliamentary groups and associations in Europe, Asia and Latin America, including the Inter-Parliamentary Union and the Canadian NATO Parliamentary Association.

He served for more than a decade as Co-Chair of the Canada-United States Inter-Parliamentary Group. In July 2007, he was elected Vice-President of the Parliamentary Assembly of the Organization for Security and Co-operation in Europe, the largest governmental human rights organization in the world.

His community involvement is legendary. He was Co-Chair of the 1988 Toronto Economic Summit Preparation Committee; he was a member of the executive of the 2008 Toronto Olympic Bid Committee; he spearheaded the 2001 "Canada Loves New York" Weekend to help New York in the aftermath of 9/11, the Rolling Stones concert in Toronto in 2003 to help that city recover from the SARS crisis, and the Canada for Asia telethon in December 2004 that raised $15 million to help victims of the 2004 tsunami. He was named an honorary commandant of the U.S. Marine Corps and an honorary fire chief of New York City.

Senator Grafstein has served on just about every standing Senate committee over the course of his 25 years. He chaired the Standing Senate Committee on Banking, Trade and Commerce, and is the longest serving member of the Standing Senate Committee on Foreign Affairs and International Trade.

Senator Grafstein has introduced a long list of private members' bills - including, of course, Bill S-201, to establish a national portrait gallery; but that is only one. He introduced a private member's bill that established the Parliamentary Poet Laureate, and co-sponsored one that established Holocaust Memorial Day. He introduced a bill to add suicide bombing to the Criminal Code, Bill S-205, which has now passed second reading in the other place. His bill on clean drinking water is now also in the other place, and there remains a long list of his private member's bills on the Order Paper here.

Our distinguished colleague may be leaving this chamber, but he has made sure that the rest of us have plenty of work to do after he is gone.

He is a member of the Canadian Institute of International Affairs. He has published articles, given lectures, appeared on panels and led conferences on technology, television, cable, film, broadcasting and finance.

Senator Grafstein is a patron of many arts and health organizations. He served as a Governor of the Canadian Opera Company and on the board of the Shaw Festival, the Stratford Festival, the Toronto Film Festival and the Festival of Festivals. I guess where else can one go after working with all these other prominent festivals but to something called the Festival of Festivals?

Honourable senators see what I mean; Senator Grafstein must be a force of nature. No mere human being could ever pack so much into one lifetime.

Senator Grafstein, I know that for you, retirement from the Senate just means one more milestone has passed and it is time to look to the next. It is impossible to believe that you will ever lead a quiet life.

We all look forward to watching in admiration as you alight on your next project - the Grafstein tornado begins to move again.

Senator Grafstein, I extend our warmest wishes to you, your wife, Carole, and your sons, Laurence and Michael.

Hon. Marjory LeBreton (Leader of the Government and Minister of State (Seniors)): Honourable senators, two and a half decades ago, Senator Grafstein entered this chamber. Today we say goodbye as he takes leave of the Senate early in the new year. It is difficult to imagine this place or the Liberal Party without him, and I am sure it is equally difficult for Senator Grafstein to imagine it.

All honourable senators are well aware of Senator Grafstein's past in the Senate, his legal background and his long involvement in the media through the co-founding of CityTV. Named to the Senate in January 1984, a month before Prime Minister Trudeau took his walk in the snow, Senator Grafstein has participated on any number of committees, as has been outlined by my colleague opposite, but he is perhaps most identified with his work on the Standing Senate Committee on Banking, Trade and Commerce, where he served as Chair.

In this chamber, he has been both prolific and tenacious in introducing, reintroducing and re reintroducing private bills on any number of subjects that are of particular interest to him.

As a parliamentarian and as a private citizen, Senator Grafstein has shown a deep, abiding affection for his home, his beloved city of Toronto. He is one of the biggest and best supporters imaginable for the city of Toronto and has proven this time and time again. Whether it was his involvement in mayoralty races, or rock concerts featuring the likes of the Rolling Stones and the promotion of tourism in the wake of SARS, Jerry Grafstein has been a true champion for Toronto.

As all honourable senators know, Mayor David Miller has decided not to seek another term. We will await with interest to see what role our honourable colleague plans to play in the upcoming mayoralty campaign .

I would be remiss if I did not point out that Senator Grafstein has consistently worked for years to strengthen Canada's ties with our biggest trading partner and closest neighbour and friend, the United States of America. Honourable senators agree, I am sure, that stronger relations between our two countries are always worth pursuing, for the benefit of Canadians and Americans alike. There are many citizens on both sides of the border who sincerely thank Senator Grafstein for all of his efforts in this regard, most particularly, as Co-Chair of the Canada-U.S. Inter-Parliamentary Group and for organizing the "Canada Loves New York" event in the wake of September 11, 2001.

Senator Grafstein, on behalf of all Conservative senators, I wish to extend our best wishes to you and your wife, Carole, and your entire family for a healthy and happy retirement, although, like Senator Cowan, I have my doubts that you will be retiring. Rather, you are taking forced leave of this place and will now zero in on some new endeavour on which to focus your extreme energy.

Hon. Serge Joyal: Honourable senators, it is a privilege to be able to pay tribute today to Senator Jerry Grafstein upon his retirement from the Senate. Although we are losing an esteemed colleague, we will be keeping a close friend.

I will not speak today of the bonds that cement our friendship; there are other more appropriate venues for that. Rather, I will remind honourable senators of the principled positions that Senator Grafstein defended during his 26 years in the Senate.

The most important was the recognition of the value of human life as the fundamental principle at the heart of our rights and freedoms. He fought for such rights 10 years ago in this chamber when an extradition bill introduced by the government of the day allowed the Minister of Justice to permit the death penalty to be applied against a Canadian citizen abroad. Senator Grafstein thought there could never be two sets of principles for Canadian citizens, one for protecting them at home and another discretionary one abroad. He believes in the fundamental principle of the sanctity of life, equal everywhere and at all times.

We lost that amendment here; but a year later, the Supreme Court vindicated that principle in the case of United States v. Burns, and last year, the Federal Court reaffirmed that point in the case of Ronald Smith.

The second principle that Senator Grafstein holds as part of his commitment to action is the protection of minorities and the defence of the vulnerable in our society. By the mere fact of their greater weight, majorities tend to disregard the condition and plight of persons or groups who are less influential or powerful. At the top of those who must fight for recognition are the Aboriginal peoples. Senator Grafstein has introduced or supported amendments, motions and inquiries to support their right to self-government, their right to live in dignity and in decent health, as well as their right to speak their language.

Senator Grafstein is also concerned with the plight of youth and the rights of the child. He has supported the opportunity for a second chance for those youth caught in the web of criminal justice, especially those from a poor and violent family background. At one point, he got removed from the Standing Senate Committee on Legal and Constitutional Affairs for his point of view.

The Senator believes in the role of government - not necessarily of more government, but of better and smarter government. As Chair of the Standing Senate Committee on Banking, Trade and Commerce, Senator Grafstein launched and had a study completed to enhance the protection of consumers in the financial service sector. He opposed the mergers of banks, as ultimately the risk generated by bad investment decisions would have been borne by taxpayers.

He does not believe that equal opportunity can be left solely to the interplay of market forces. He is what I would call a "liberal democrat." He is convinced of the value of a free market, but with an eye to the strategic redistribution of wealth to those living under the accepted standard in an affluent society.

He is also a committed Canadian. He has always seen his initiatives as those of a nation builder, of an effective central government working toward binding the various regions, groups and communities of our country. His support of a portrait gallery for Canada is just such an example.

He remains attentive to the cultural richness and contribution of French Canadians throughout the country. An active participant in the debate involving our constitutional future, he is preoccupied with the way institutions of Parliament are defined in our Westminster system of government. He did just that in defending the role of the Senate as an essential house of Parliament during the Clarity Act debate.

He also kept an eye on the challenges of protecting the environment, regarding access to clean water in particular - a global preoccupation.

At the international level, his initiatives were also directed toward peace in regions where neighbouring nations have not yet been able to define the terms of peaceful cohabitation. The Middle East, the fight against anti-Semitism, the development of international institutions to better mediate the settlement of conflicts, in particular at the OSCE, have all been objects of his everlasting commitment.

Honourable senators, do you have any idea how many bills, motions, inquiries, questions, amendments, interventions and speeches Senator Grafstein has given or made during his 26 years in the Senate Chamber? It is quite a few.

Today, I thought it would be appropriate to review some the principles and values that Senator Grafstein has stood for. They are at the heart of his commitment to action and offer a stronger description of the stature of the person we are saluting today as he leaves the Senate. Thank you, Senator Grafstein.

Hon. W. David Angus: Honourable senators, I have admired and respected my friend, the Honourable Jerahmiel "Jerry" Grafstein ever since I came to the Senate in the spring of 1993. Indeed, over the intervening years, I have come to regard Jerry as the quintessential senator. I say this, honourable senators, for the following reasons.

First, Jerry has a passionate love for his country, Canada, and a deep and abiding respect for our system of parliamentary democracy. He understands and honours Parliament, and believes truly in responsible government and the rule of law.

Second, he has an impressive knowledge and understanding of our social, economic and cultural history and heritage. This extends to how our rich, pluralistic society has evolved and shaped the tolerant values of our wonderful nation as we know it today and as our Fathers of Confederation hoped it would be. They toiled long and hard to find a balance to the vast regional and cultural disparities facing them as they worked to craft the British North America Act and the related laws and agreements.

Third, Senator Grafstein believes profoundly in the Senate as conceived by Sir John A. Macdonald and his colleagues of the day. Jerry ardently supports the process of sober second thought, the protection of minority rights, and the advancement of regional interests. He has demonstrated this ably and in a most articulate way over the many years he has represented the vast metropolitan city of Toronto and its multicultural populous.

Fourth, Jerry has a unique capacity, believe it or not, to be objective. He has proven time and again that he is able to rise above strict partisan interests and to do what he considers, and indeed is, the correct thing. I personally observed him in this mode in the Standing Senate Committee on Banking, Trade and Commerce as, together, we dealt with the thorny issues around the new bankruptcy and insolvency legislation three or four years ago. This was repeated more recently with the bill designed to remove excise taxes on watches, jewellery and other similar items.

Fifth, Jerry Grafstein likes the Senate basically the way it is, subject only to certain necessary minor reforms necessitated by the passage of time. Indeed, Jerry is against a triple-E Senate, but he is a triple-E senator. He is educated, energetic and entrepreneurial.

Some Hon. Senators: Hear, hear.

Senator Angus: Sixth, and finally, honourable senators, Jerry is a man of strong character and integrity, true to a fault to his values and principles. As his friends and colleagues, his roasters and toasters, proclaimed the other night, Jerry consistently is a good Liberal. He is faithful to and a practitioner of the principles of Sir Wilfrid Laurier and Pierre Elliot Trudeau. I mention these names in this chamber with trepidation, but I do so out of honour and respect for my friend Jerry and for all of my friends and colleagues on the other side.

At Jerry's dinner last week, there was also absolute unanimity that Senator Grafstein, given the slightest opportunity, will talk your ear off. He is the wrong man to meet on a street corner when you are rushing to a meeting for which you are a little late. Honourable senators, we all know this about Jerry, but we still love and admire him a lot, not only for what he says, but also for all the great and public spirited things he does - from organizing Rolling Stones concerts in Toronto, to finding housing for Hurricane Katrina victims in New Orleans, or for supporting 9/11 victims in the Big Apple.

We love him for his belief in the family unit, his wife Carole, brilliant sons Laurence and Michael and his wonderful grandchildren we were able to meet the other night. We also love him for the pungent aromas that he emits while savouring a fine Cohiba cigar or other very special Cuban stogie. Yes, Jerry is a sartorial gentleman, maybe even the Beau Brummel of the Senate, with his beautiful silk shirts and ties that are matching to a fault. What a guy!

I will truly miss my friend Jerry and value the time I spent with him on Canada-U.S. issues and on the Banking Committee, which has already been mentioned.

I learned one hell of a lot from you, Jerry. For that, I will be eternally grateful.

Senator Grafstein is a gentleman. He is a loyal friend, a great Canadian and an outstanding senator. We will miss him a lot here. We wish him much happiness and success as he moves on to his next interesting endeavour, whether it is in business, public service or both, as a broadcaster or a publisher, or even a mayor. Go for it, Jerry. Thank you for making this Senate a better place over the past 26 years.

Hon. David P. Smith: Honourable senators, I rise to pay tribute to my friend Jerry Grafstein, whom I have known for over 45 years. I even knew him in his twenties, if you can believe it. I was somewhat younger or you would be paying tribute to me today.

Those were the young Liberal days. When we look back on that period, we think of Lester Pearson, Walter Gordon, Keith Davey and the song with the lines, "Those were the days, my friend. We thought they'd never end." However, they did and we moved on.

We worked together on countless campaigns. In fact, I cannot resist mentioning one of them, the 1964 provincial leadership campaign. A man by the name of Andrew Thompson won; some honourable senators may have known him, though maybe not as well as you should have. In any event, those were the days.

Senator Cowan spoke about Senator Grafstein's legal career and Senate accomplishments. I want to touch on how he helped to make democracy work at the party level. If it does not work at the party level, then it does not work . There are people on both sides of the house, such as Senators Meighen, Finley, Nolin and Angus - who have I left out? - who have all helped to make the Conservative Party and the Liberal Party work. Those two national parties are a form of glue that helps to keep the country together, and I believe that.

Senator Grafstien has done that work at all levels. At the riding level and then, in the 1968 leadership campaign, we had both been John Turner's executive assistants. Jerry came before me and then I worked for Turner. Many people do not realize that in the 1968 convention, Turner had the largest portion of the youth vote. Many people assumed that Trudeau did. It was a friendly convention with a good ending and everyone got behind Mr. Trudeau, however we had rounded up most of those young people to support John Turner.

Jerry has also been involved in the Red Leaf group that creates imaging, advertising and things like that.

Jerry gives new meaning to the word "energy." I do not need to explain that. All honourable senators know that. It is just simply there.

Another role I want to reference is the way in which he has somewhat filled the shoes of someone like David Croll, who was a patriarch of the Jewish community. Jerry has represented that community in a fair, balanced and, I think, objective way on lively issues. I fully and totally respect that. Those will be very hard shoes to fill.

Jerry has also been a friend. It is hard to believe now, but when he was appointed to the Senate in January 1984, I was in the other place. I hosted a dinner for him upstairs at Cafe Henry Burger with a dozen of his friends. We had another dinner for him last week and there were 25 times that number.

The place was packed; it was a sell out; it was an extravaganza. You do not see too many shows like that - it was an incredibly tremendous tribute. None of us who were there will forget it.

Jerry, you will be missed. Yes, someone will succeed you and fill the seat, but they will not really fill it because you are irreplaceable. Some of your causes and issues have been addressed, but there are still motions and private members' bills that have not yet come to fruition. The seeds have been planted, watered and will be harvested. As time goes by, your legacy will be even stronger.

It will be on the record that Jerry's family was snowed out today. Carole will still kick him out of the house most days because he will have many other things to do.

All the best to the family and to you, Jerry. You will be missed. You are irreplaceable.

Hon. Joyce Fairbairn: Honourable senators, it is with both sadness and pride that I say farewell to a longtime friend and colleague, Senator Jerry Grafstein, who has energized the Senate. Certainly, he has energized our caucus ever since he entered this chamber in January 1984. He brought with him his skill as a lawyer and as a longtime political adviser for the Liberal Party in Toronto. He has been an icon in Parliament and in this chamber.

I first met Jerry in 1966 when he came to work with a vigorous new cabinet minister, the Right Honourable John Turner. He was a first-class assistant in helping to set up the Department of Consumer and Corporate Affairs. He was a young Liberal and full of advice. He is still a young Liberal. Not only was he full of advice and a great fundraiser, he was also profoundly admired by all of us. His passion for his city and his country is deeply rooted. His friendship with, and knowledge of our neighbour, the United States, has grown tremendously over the years. He is the longest-serving Co-Chair of the Canada-United States Inter-Parliamentary Group, with 15 years in that capacity. He is recognized not only as a senator but as a respected representative of this country, determined to maintain an open door when discussion and help are needed. When he is not deep in politics, he is an invaluable community organizer.

He spearheaded the slogan, "Canada Loves New York." Almost 30,000 Canadians heeded that slogan and went to New York to offer assistance after the 9/11 terrorist attacks. He is also well known for his work to bring the Rolling Stones to Toronto on July 30, 2003, as the disaster of SARS moved across our country. The concert had an attendance of about 500,000, including me. It was recognized as the largest outdoor ticketed event in world history. The concert was also noteworthy in my view because I saw, as I rolled in from Lethbridge, Alberta, that they were selling Alberta beef in support of the Canadian beef industry, which had been suffering because of mad cow disease.

All in all, Jerry has had a great life on the Hill. I remember how young we were - and still are - on the other side of this building, as were the Leader of the Government in the Senate and others. We were friends and we are still friends. In every sense, it has been a great opportunity for us to serve with him in Parliament, not to mention all the rest that he has done for the place he cares so much about, Toronto.

I thank you, Jerry, for everything you have contributed in the Senate for the last 26 years. We will miss you. I will miss you. I will miss watching the wonderful shirts that you wear, in particular the pink one. I remember that shirt and will think of you. All of us will miss you.

As you go, I hope that one day there will be a portrait gallery. I will be ready to support you in any way and anything that you wish to do, and to find your special events in the future, because you will have another great future. I tell you, Jerry, your presence here will never be forgotten.

Hon. Art Eggleton: Honourable senators, I hope you will not consider this a prop, but I have in my hand the Order Paper and Notice Paper that is before the house today. With the departure of Senator Grafstein, it is about to become a lot thinner because more than half the pages are taken up with motions introduced by Senator Grafstein. While some honourable senators might welcome that reduction, I think the chamber will be the poorer for not having all these contributions from Senator Grafstein. As is evident by reading this paper, he has done a great deal of research on the issues and commits to them with a great deal of conviction and passion. He has made an outstanding contribution to Canada in doing so.

As was pointed out, he made contributions outside the chamber in many of his organizations where he represented the Senate in Europe and in the United States with the Canada-U.S. Inter-Parliamentary Group. He has contributed outstanding work.

I cannot help but think that he quickly grasped the idea that someone with a title of "senator" would do well in relations with the United States where the title of senator carries much weight and opens many doors. He has been able to open many doors and meet and become acquainted with many people. He has used that strength to the benefit of this country in its relationship with the United States. We are so much better off because of the kind of contribution he has made.

I must mention Toronto, of course. Jerry was a strong supporter and adviser to me during my 11 years as Mayor of Toronto from 1980 to 1991. No mayor could have a better citizen of their city than Jerry Grafstein. No mayor could have a better builder, booster and promoter of a city than Jerry Grafstein. I was pleased to have been a mayor of a city that had him as its citizen.

Of course, his many contributions to Toronto have been cited by some of my colleagues this afternoon. I cannot help but mention, once again, the Rolling Stones concert in July 2003. By that time, of course, I was not Mayor; I was here and was Chair of the Toronto caucus. I was happy to lend my support. All kinds of people said to me: It cannot be done! They cannot organize a concert in 30 days with stars like that and expect 500,000 people to come. It is impossible.

Never tell Jerry Grafstein that anything is impossible, because he can do the impossible. That was another great contribution to Toronto in helping us to recover from SARS and to tell the world that Toronto was, indeed, a safe place to come.

Thanks to Jerry Grafstein's enormous effort, we are in the Guinness Book of World Records, as Senator Fairbairn said, for having the largest ticketed concert ever, and all organized in a short period of time.

Jerry, thank you for all those contributions to Canada, to international affairs and to human rights issues, which I know are close to you. I, above all, thank you for your contribution to Toronto. I look forward to a continuing friendship with you, Carole and your family.

Hon. Tommy Banks: Jerry, I will break ranks here and speak directly and personally to you, and briefly. You have heard from others and you will hear from others who are better equipped than I to articulate the ways in which you have made this place better. The Senate of Canada will be a different place without you. We will save a lot of trees, as Senator Eggleton pointed out.

I thank you personally because of the fact that, as we have heard, you have been moving at 200 miles an hour in every direction all the time, and despite that peripatetic nature, you have always been there to answer questions. You have been a valuable mentor to all of us, but to me in particular, throughout the past years that I have been here. I thank you for that.

In particular I thank you for your prescient understanding and grasp of the water problem. You alone, among all of us here in this place and in the other place, understand what is at stake here, and have tried to do something about this problem. I hope that we will be able to continue that valuable work for the good of our country. Thank you, Jerry.

Hon. Peter A. Stollery: Honourable senators, I will say a couple of words about Jerry, my old friend and sometimes seatmate, on a slightly different and brief note.

Jerry and I have been here for a long time. We have known each other for more years than I care to mention. Over those years, we have occasionally had disagreements, as people do. The characteristic of Jerry that I want to impart is that he has a great gift of never holding it against you when you have a disagreement. He is the most charming and easy-to-get-along-with guy after you have had a disagreement, of which we have had a few over these many years.

Jerry, I thank you for your company and your good humour.

Hon. Terry M. Mercer: Honourable senators, it is a pleasure to take part in a tribute to my friend Jerry Grafstein. I have known Jerry for much longer than I have been in the Senate. I knew him, obviously, when I was national director of the Liberal Party, and back in the days when I lived in Toronto and was a party activist there.

The description of Jerry being everywhere is absolutely true. We could spend the entire afternoon telling interesting and funny stories about Jerry. Some of them might be embarrassing, so we will leave those out.

I remember one specific day when I was in the Senate. Jerry and I met and talked about what I thought was an important problem. He agreed with me. He said, "You know, we have to do something about this." I said, "Yes, we will talk about this again."

The next day I came to the chamber ready to talk to Jerry. The Order Paper process was ongoing, and the next thing I knew, Jerry was standing up introducing a bill on the subject that we had discussed. I was still discussing what to do and Jerry was doing it. That, indeed, was Bill S-217, to establish a National Philanthropy Day, which is now in committee in the other place and hopefully, will eventually become law.

Jerry, you have set such high standards for us, both for your energy and for knowing what to do. Senator Angus and Senator Fairbairn have talked about the standards you have set in the dress code here. The one good thing about your not being here is that we will not be measured against your sartorial standard.

I have been to Washington once with Jerry. I was travelling with the Standing Senate Committee on Agriculture and Forestry, under the then Chair, Senator Fairbairn. Senator Len Gustafson - a Conservative senator from Saskatchewan, a great guy - and I were there, and Senator Tkachuk might have been there as well. There were two Canadian committees in town, so someone organized a reception for the Canadians with American senators and congressmen.

When we walked into the room, most of us did not know anyone, or we recognized a few faces that we had seen on television. However, when Jerry walked into the room, not only did he know everyone, but everyone knew Jerry. I am told a number of great stories about Jerry's ability not only to be known on Capitol Hill in Washington but also being known, or at least purporting to be known, in various good restaurants around the city of Washington.

You are a hard act to follow, Jerry. All of us in this chamber, on both sides, will miss your energy on the Canada-United States Inter-Parliamentary Group. The work that you have undertaken and the standards you have set, with which others are trying to keep up, will be long lasting. Also, much of the legislation that you have introduced has passed, or is in the process now.

As someone who has been in the Senate only six years, I hope that when my time is finished here, I can accomplish at least 10 per cent of what you have been able to do. Thank you, Jerry.

Hon. Jim Munson: Honourable senators, I asked this serious question this morning of the senator, and I will leave this question with you, Senator Grafstein. It is an extremely important historical question, and there is always a set-up guy in politics: What was Sir Wilfrid Laurier really like?

Hon. Jerahmiel S. Grafstein: Honourable senators, thank you for those most generous words. My late father would have been surprised. My late mother would have said, "Not nearly enough."

Honourable senators, I have always been curious about the words, "maiden speech." By custom, it designates the first speech a parliamentarian makes when a parliamentarian enters a house of Parliament. What do we call a farewell speech in Parliament when we are no longer a maiden? I leave that to honourable senators' imagination.

It has been over 25 years since I was first summoned to the Senate by Mr. Trudeau. When he called to appoint me, he said, "We need you in the Senate; take your time, Jerry, to think about it."

I told the Prime Minister I did not need any time, that I accepted. "This is the greatest honour anyone has ever bestowed on me," I told him. "However, Prime Minister, I do have one question."

Mr. Trudeau laughed. "What is your question, Jerry?" he asked. I asked, "What did you mean when you said, "We need you in the Senate'?"

Mr. Trudeau laughed again and I heard the phone drop. A second later he apologized and said he did not mean to laugh. He said, "Jerry, you are the very first person I have ever appointed who asked me why."

"Well, Prime Minister, why?" I repeated. "Why am I needed in the Senate?"

He responded so graciously, and he said these words - I made notes at the time: "You have provided me with great ideas. Now I want you to use the Senate as a platform to share those ideas with the Canadian public."

Honourable senators, I have tried. Sometimes I succeeded. Many times I failed. However, I have been motivated by three pieces of advice that Mr. Pearson gave me when I first entered politics and I sat beside him. He told me these three things: Aim high, work hard, and be fair.

Some time before my appointment, Mr. Trudeau told me at a meeting, "Jerry, you have great ideas, but you have not overcome one problem that you have."

"What is that?" I said. "I do not have any problems."

"Yes, you do," he said. "Each time you advocate a great idea, automatically and spontaneously, a coalition of 'antis' spring up to fight any good idea. Your job as a politician is to navigate around that coalition and get to the other side."

Then he said these words that I have never forgotten: "Never give up."

Honourable senators, each day when I awake at the Chateau Laurier, I say a short Hebrew prayer: *Modeh ani Lefanecha* - Thank God who has awakened my soul to live another day.

I walk a hundred steps from the Chateau Laurier across the historic bridge over the Rideau Canal and look up to the statue of my great political hero, as Senator Munson mentioned, Sir Wilfrid Laurier, and give him a morning salute. Then I take another hundred steps, past the East Block, and the most beautiful building in Canada looms into sight. What a sight it is. I see the Parliament buildings, the Peace Tower and, on top of it, the Canadian flag flying. I remember the courage of Mr. Pearson, who introduced the flag in the face of great division in this country. I swear every morning that I will do my very best that day for the privilege of serving in the Senate and here in Parliament.

Honourable senators, I have served under eight Prime Ministers and twelve leaders in the Senate. I want to thank all of my colleagues, but especially the current deputy leaders, Senator Tardif and Senator Comeau, who have the most complex jobs in the Senate. I want to say how much I admire both of them.

Hon. Senators: Hear, hear.

Senator Grafstein: Of course, I salute my own leader, the graceful Senator Cowan, and the Leader of the Government in the Senate, Senator LeBreton, both of whom lead us here so very ably. Thank you so much.

May I thank the reporters who have reproduced - do not be shocked - almost 5 million words of my speeches, resolutions, comments and reports.

I would be remiss if I did not mention the researchers of the Library of Parliament who have responded to my needs.

To Mark Audcent and to the legislative staff who drafted my bills, motions and resolutions with skill and professionalism, I thank you.

For the many courtesies offered to me by the Speaker, his predecessors, by the Deputy Speaker, and to all the table officers, my sincere appreciation for your patience and advice. I have learned much from all of you.

Of course my special appreciation goes to my executive assistant, who is sitting up in the gallery, Mary de Toro, who leads my mighty staff of one, the wisest woman on Parliament Hill who has kept me from making disastrous mistakes.

My first decision when I came to the Senate was what name and what designation I should use as senator. I chose my first given name, Jerahmiel, although people have called me Jerry. People have been curious about why that name and not my customary name, Jerry. Jerahmiel is mentioned only once in the Bible. He was the son of the last King of Israel. The name means "the mercy of God." It is meant to remind the holders of that name to remember that they are here to help the less fortunate. My other designation as senator is Metro Toronto, to remind me of the great city of Toronto and the regional base of the key of my responsibilities here.

What lessons have I learned in the Senate? Honourable senators, I will not predict the future. I have always worked hard in the past and in the present. In the process, I became a much better criminal lawyer, a substantial constitutional lawyer, as my friend Senator Nolin has become, and an expert international lawyer. The future, honourable senators, I leave to you.

The precious gift that the Fathers of Confederation bestowed on the Senate and senators was independence and the freedom to make choices. That is what Sir John A. Macdonald and the Fathers of Confederation gave each and every one of us. Most of my choices I shared with my party and my leader, and sometimes I disagreed and did as Mr. Trudeau advised, spoke my mind to the discomfort at times of my leaders and my colleagues on this side.

I have served on all the committees of the Senate, and I have been kicked off several committees several times when I did so, and I do not regret it. I always believed that the Senate acts best when it is true to its mandate as a chamber of second sober thought. The Senate has always made mistakes when there has been a rush to judgment. "Principles and pragmatism," so said Lloyd George, "march best when they march together."

This chamber, following the teachings of the great Blackstone, is a chamber dedicated to checks and balances . To check and balance the executive and the other house of Parliament is our constitutional mandate. Hence, we should not place our trust blindly in government. Governments do what they do and do what they want and do what they must. It can be best summed up in Psalm 146: "Put not your trust in princes." We are here to speak truth to power. That is our constitutional duty.

I recall my maiden speech when I advocated an apology to Canadians of Japanese descent. Mr. Trudeau, who had just appointed me, disagreed. He argued that we cannot correct the past but can only improve the future. I disagreed with him on the facts. Citizens of Japanese origin had been deprived of their rights and property during the war, and there was no evidence whatsoever provided to me or to the Prime Minister at the time to call in or question their loyalty to Canada. I advocated for an apology, and ultimately it was given by Brian Mulroney, and I respect him for that.

I recall the extradition bill, as Senator Joyal pointed out, passed by a Liberal government in haste, with barely a debate in the other place. Under that bill, the Liberal Attorney General of Canada of the day would have had the power to extradite Canadians to a state that practiced capital punishment even though Parliament had abolished capital punishment under Mr. Trudeau after a fantastic and unbelievable fight across the country. The government wanted that bill. They wanted it then. They urged it was important because of pending decisions.

I disagreed, and so did my colleague Senator Joyal. Together, with other colleagues in this chamber, we kept that debate going for several months, but finally we succumbed to our leadership and to government pressure. Senator Joyal and I decided to make our arguments in the Senate at third reading as if we were arguing before the Supreme Court of Canada because we felt that that bill would be ultimately challenged and would be shown to be unconstitutional. We sent the Senate Hansard, a public document, to all the judges of the Supreme Court, and we were so pleased over a year later when the Supreme Court of Canada upheld our major arguments.

I remember another important debate on a resolution introduced in the other place declaring Quebec "a distinct society." The government introduced that resolution here shortly after the referendum. I angered my colleagues on this side, I angered the Prime Minister, I angered the leader of the Senate, my great friend Allan MacEachen, and other colleagues on this side, when I refused to support that resolution. I gave the shortest speech I have ever given in the Senate, and I repeat it here now: Canada is a distinct society. All the rest is commentary.

While Quebecers are different, so are Newfoundlanders, so are Acadians, so are hundreds and hundreds of Aboriginal tribes and many other groups in Canada. Honourable senators, I believed then and I believe now in one Canada, bilingual and multicultural - one Canada.

One of my most stimulating periods was as Chairman of the Standing Senate Committee on Banking, Trade and Commerce with Senator Angus as my congenial Deputy Chairman. Together, with a total consensus of all members on both sides, we did a number of important, sharp and pointed studies dealing with consumer protection of the financial securities sector, the volunteer and charitable sector, the demographic time bomb, stemming the flow of illicit money to Canada and others. Hopefully the work we commenced on hedge funds and derivatives, started well before the last financial meltdown, and the work on reducing interprovincial trade barriers to make Canada one dynamic competitive marketplace will be completed by others in the Senate.

Being a Canadian senator offers unique opportunities to travel and to participate in international affairs. One of my most satisfying experiences have been as Co-Chairman of the Canada-U.S. Inter-Parliamentary Group. I was elected to that office by members of Parliament in both houses for eight successive terms and served for over 16 years in that position.

The Canada-U.S. Inter-Parliamentary Group was founded in 1959 and recently celebrated its fiftieth anniversary. During my term in office, with the support of colleagues on all sides, bipartisan, we transformed that organization from one annual meeting with the Americans to an active, vigorous advocacy group meeting with state legislators, governors in every corner of America, in addition to regular meetings on Capitol Hill in Washington with congressmen and senators to advocate one thing, Canada's interest.

We learned that all politics are local, and so we have to work at the local level in the United States, and hence our meeting with state officials and governors. All problems in the United States affecting Canada start at the local level and, if detected early enough, can be diluted if not resolved.

After each meeting, honourable senators, as I will do later today, we tabled a complete report of our activities to the Senate to ensure that the senators who were interested could benefit from our experience. We were not there to represent ourselves. We were there to represent Canada, and that is why we tabled these reports.

I want to thank my current Co-Chair in the house, Gord Brown, and my current American Co-Chairs, Senator Amy Klobuchar of Minnesota and Congressman James Oberstar of Minnesota, who is the only member of our group who has served the Canada-U.S. Inter-Parliamentary Group longer than I.

When I first came to the Senate, I was able to travel to a number of international organizations consistent with my work on the Standing Senate Committee on Foreign Affairs and International Trade, where I and my colleague Senator Stollery have been the longest serving members. I decided that I would focus my activities where Canada and the United States both had a vote, the Organization for Security and Co-operation in Europe Parliamentary Assembly, which flowed out of the Helsinki Accord in 1974, currently with 56 member states from Vladivostok to Vancouver. There I became an active member on the executive and served as an elected member for 15 years. This organization is the largest Parliamentary Assembly dedicated to human rights, economic rights and democratic rights in the world.

I became a witness to history serving as one of the heads of election monitoring in Russia, Ukraine during the Orange Revolution, Georgia during the Rose Revolution and on the Independence Referendum for Montenegro and many others. Senator Di Nino has also served on a number of those committees with great skill and expertise.

I learned how precious democracy is and how important democracy building is for the future of the world. I worked closely with elected presidents of the assembly, and I want to pay special tribute to two recent Presidents: Congressmen Alcee Hastings of Florida and Joao Soares, the head of the Portuguese Delegation and current Vice-President of the OSCE Parliamentary Assembly, who have done outstanding work travelling the length and breadth of the OSCE space. We have become great personal friends.

A spark plug in this organization, which is headquartered in Copenhagen, is Spencer Oliver, the long serving Secretary General, who is the most brilliant and knowledgeable American I have ever met, with a deep and penetrating insight into foreign affairs. He has become one of my closest friends in public life.

While at the OSCE-PA, I served as leader of the Liberal group there, and I finally resigned this year after 12 years. They elected me as Liberal Leader Emeritus Perpetual, a title I will cherish all my life. I do not kid myself: I achieved these offices overseas because I was Canadian, because the world respects Canada and Canadians who represent Canada.

I think the Senate should have a brief explanation, particularly those senators who have been mildly critical of the numerous OSCE resolutions combating anti-Semitism on the Order Paper that I tabled and that are still on the Order Paper. Why those many resolutions?

After the Berlin Wall came down in 1989 - and I was in Germany before and after the wall came down, I thought I would finally close my dossier on anti-Semitism. There was hope for a new world order. But it was not to be. The UN had passed an invidious resolution equating Zionism with racism. Anti-Semitism was on the rise not only across the face of the earth and around the globe, not only across Europe, but also in South America and in Canada. In 1994, a diligent congressman from New Jersey, Chris Smith, approached me to work on a resolution to combat anti-Semitism and to present it to the OSCE Parliamentary Assembly annual meeting. I agreed. We were joined by Congressman Steny Hoyer, now the majority leader of the Congress and one the most powerful men in the United States, a good friend; Congressman Alcee Hastings; Congressman Ben Cardin, now a Senator from Maryland; Gert Weisskirchen of the German Parliament and parliamentarians from Italy, France, Austria, Ukraine, Poland and others.

That first resolution was passed by a bare majority. Thereafter, across the face of Europe, in Copenhagen, twice in Berlin, Oporto, Cordoba, Rotterdam, Edinburgh, Vienna, London, Rome, St. Petersburg, Kazakhstan, Madrid, Washington and so forth, we continued the thrust of those resolutions, parliamentary, ministerial and side meetings.

There were two chilly experiences. I spoke on these resolutions in the Berlin Reichstag at the very podium where Hitler had declared the Nuremberg Laws in 1933. I spoke in the Hofberg Palace at the very same place in Vienna where Hitler announced the Anschluss between Germany and Austria in 1938 that most historians agree ignited World War II. This work continued, meeting after meeting, and finally, honourable senators, I brought one of these resolutions to the Senate in 2002. It was passed in

2004 and was referred to the Standing Senate Committee on Human Rights. That committee held meetings for a day or so, and then, without explanation, decided not to complete its work. It is the first time I can recall that a resolution passed by the Senate was not followed by a committee of the Senate. I urged members of the committee to complete their work, but without success. I decided to put down resolution after resolution on the Order Paper until there could be some closure and conclusion to this matter. I was pleased some years ago that the UN would use those very resolutions to hold a one-day conference on anti-Semitism, the first of its kind at the UN. I was delighted when the British Parliament did a landmark study on this topic several years ago and published it. I am pleased that, finally, parliamentarians on the other side, under the leadership of Mario Silva and Scott Reid, are holding hearings on combating anti-Semitism. I live in hope that the Senate will consider its findings and add its considerable expertise and credit to its recommendations.

I have learned two things about this topic, "anti-Semitism," the oldest of all prejudices. First, that discrimination starts with Jews, but never ends with Jews, as one great Danish Prime Minister once said. Second, what to do? Education is the answer. The Nobel Prize winner Elie Wiesel said these words at the Berlin conference: "You can teach a child to love or you can teach a child to hate." So education is an answer.

A word about Senator Di Nino: I admire very much his work with respect to human rights not only at the OSCE but also with respect to the Dalai Lama. He has been a great and compatible companion at the OSCE, and he will continue to do great and important work over there. My congratulations to him.

Senators, I am coming to the close, but before I end, I would like to say a word about the current atmosphere in the Senate that I dislike. While I am as partisan - as everyone knows - as any senator, and will vigorously attack on behalf of my party and on behalf of my principles, I also believe in political companionship and congeniality that rises above partisan politics.

I do not enjoy those who downgrade the Senate, the institution we are all privileged and summoned to serve. I have made good friends on both sides of the aisle here and in the other place.

I take my leave of this hallowed hall with no regrets. I tried my best, and if I failed, I have failed trying to do my best.

Honourable senators opposite will forgive me if I remind them that my great parliamentary hero was and is Sir Winston Churchill, whose printed works and speeches I have read avidly. When Britain was in the most desperate straits in the early part of the World War II, he gave this advice to his colleagues, and this is my advice to my colleagues on this side: KBO, keep buggering on.

As for my colleagues on the other side, I recall that Sir Winston Churchill in his dotage confessed that he had always been a Liberal. Good advice.

If I have succeeded, I owe it to my late father and the great mentors I have encountered in politics: Mr. Trudeau, Mr. Turner, Mr. Chrétien and Mr. Martin, and, of course, Keith Davey, our former colleague, who taught us all on this side to love the

Liberal Party.

I will not say goodbye, but au revoir. On January 2, I start my third act. Regretfully, you have not heard the last of me yet.

To my wife who might feel trepidation on my return to Toronto: Do not worry. I have lots of new projects that will keep me eternally occupied.

All the very best to all of you, Godspeed and thank you so much.

Hon. Senators: Hear, hear!

LORNA MILNE: ON RETIREMENT

December 14, 2009

Hon. Jerahmiel S. Grafstein: Honourable senators, Senator Eggleton inspired me to talk about Lorna Milne's father.

First, I helped run Phil Givens' campaign against William Dennison. Phil was a Liberal, ebullient, a world figure, a world-class speaker, and opposite him was a modest NDP gentleman by the name of William Dennison who had a lisp. He conquered his lisp through training with a speech therapist. By the dint of his own personal discipline, he became a solid speaker. We felt that with Phil Givens talking about the famous Moore statue in the centre of Nathan Phillips Square, and the city of Toronto being a world city with great ideas we could conquer and really crush William Dennison who was supported by the unions in Toronto.

I learned a serious and important lesson about politics in that campaign because Dennison had a banner that I have never forgotten. It was one of the hard lessons you learn in local politics. He would make a speech, and Phil would beat him at each debate and Dennison would complete his speech by pointing to the sign that said, "You have to respect the taxpayers' dollar." We were talking about the world and he was talking about respecting the taxpayers' dollar. Dennison beat Givens hands down.

The lesson to be learned is to always remember to respect the taxpayer's dollar.

When Lorna became active, she moved away from her NDP roots and joined the Liberal Party. Two great and powerful women were the keys to the success in Ontario politics for the Liberal Party for some time. The first was Dorothy Petrie, or Dorothy Davey, the wife of Keith Davey, who was a powerhouse. We ran a number of campaigns together. I cherish my thoughts of Keith Davey, but Dorothy was an equally powerful organizer, one of the best organizers we ever had in Ontario, and she brought along Lorna Milne. They became good friends, and Lorna stepped into her footsteps and became a superb organizer for the Liberal Party in Toronto.

I wish all the best to Lorna and her husband Ross. I have fond memories of them. They were great public servants, but they were greater Liberals.

DAVID ALAN JOHN NUGENT: EULOGY
GIVEN AT ST. PAUL'S ANGLICAN CHURCH, TORONTO
September 9, 2013

David Alan John Nugent, a stout, staunch, anglo Irish Norman name that reflects the simple yet complex persona of our dear departed friend, David. How do I encapsulate, in a few minutes, a friendship that lasted over 30 years.

Soldier, sailor, salesman, skier, skeptic, sportsman, gourmand, gentleman, world traveler, adventurer, elegant Beau Brummel - a wit and a wag - lover of all things beautiful, and a believer. A man of deep loyalties and great passion and pride, loyal to queen and country, Canada, and a passion for Catherine, the love of his life. And pride in his large family, sons, daughters, brothers, nieces and nephews is unquestionable.

Let me start with the opening lyrics of "Hallelujah," written by my friend, Leonard Cohen:

"I have heard there was a secret chord
That David played
And it pleased the lord but you don't really care for music, do you?
The fourth, the fifth,
The minor fall, the major lift
The baffled king composed halleluiah."

David's life was so like those lyrics, that lifting song.

David was not an easy man to know or understand. He was driven by his own music, his own secret chords, by his own drummer but, once you penetrated his fearsome demeanor, you discovered a warm, gracious, wonderful companion with great talents, skills and an astonishing array of interests.

We travelled to South America and across Europe with our wives in tow - met his fascinating friends and did interesting things together.

David loved life. He had such a zest for life.

Nachmanides, the medieval Jewish philosopher, wrote of such men - that his flesh and his soul are jealous of each other and cling to each other - and are loath to let go. But let go he did, as we all do. Each soul is a spark, encased in a case broken in creation. Each spark, each a particle of energy floats through the heavens until the spark collides and joins with his one true beloved. Then these two sparks cast a bright powerful light eternally. So it was with Catherine and David.

Three short vignettes about David and me:

We met and witnessed Catherine and David's early tempestuous relationship. When they decided to marry, David asked me to propose a toast to the married couple. I hesitated as I held serious doubts about this longevity of this marriage. He urged me to be honest, not to embellish my toast. I summed it up in words which David repeated me on each and every wedding anniversary thereafter.

At the time, I said that their marriage was a triumph of optimism over experience.

Once, together in Rio de Janeiro, David insisted we play golf. I hesitated, as David was a superb golfer and I was indifferent at best. Yet, David insisted and who could resist him?

David arranged for us to play at the most exclusive club. Nothing but the best for David. The golf course was a not-too-tailored jungle, hilly with deep dark roughs, dotted with waterfalls and pools of water everywhere. It was for me a first glance at a living nightmare. David hit each ball clean and straight down the narrow winding fairway. Most of my shots ended in the rough or in the water. David would patiently walk over, help me search for my lost ball for a moment, throw down another ball into the fairway and said "hit away".

I could hardly wait to finish, covered in sweat. Once at the clubhouse overlooking the picturesque scene of my disastrous round, David ordered two tall cold drinks, smiled and raised his glass in a toast and said sweetly "Challenging, wasn't it?" And not another word about my disastrous game. David, always a true gentleman.

Earlier, Catherine, Carole, Cathy Bratty, that sparkling trio, had joined forces to organize a ball for wonderful charities. Husbands were required for each event to make generous donations, at least a table or two for each event. However, the ladies did not want to waste a good table on themselves so they located us at the rear, usually near the kitchen door. David labeled us the table near the door gang. After several of these events, David groused about the location to Catherine.

At least, he complained, if we are to sit by the door, at the next gala we should be located near the front door, closer to the outside bar. From then on, we were elevated to sit near the exit door, but close to the bar. A minor triumph. He also labeled our exclusive club the rainbow coalition.

Before his death, Vince Paul and Nancy were part of our exclusive club. Imagine, David said, three Roman Catholics, two Anglicans, one a true believer, one protestant and two conservative Jews.

Truly a rainbow coalition. Once in Rome with David, Catherine, Rudy, Cathy, Vince and Nancy, I had secured a private audience with Pope John Paul II for Carole and myself. Carole refused to go. She insisted I make arrangements for all the others to attend. Vince attended the private audience as me with Cathy Bratty as my wife. I got invitation for the rest of us to join the general audience following. David sat beside me and whispered with a chuckle: "Think about this, the table by the door gang with Pope John Paul II, and it took a good Jew to make these arrangements."

We visited Catherine and David during their sojourn on the Riviera. Several times David arranged to meet us on a luxurious yacht in Monaco and later toured us around like royalty in his aqua blue Rolls Royce. Gracious and interesting as always.

For my 60th birthday in Paris, David arranged a sumptuous dinner at Lasserre, followed by a special birthday surprise at a party at the Ritz, hosted by his pal, Karl Lagerfeld. As a surprise, David had arranged for me to meet my dream girl, Catherine Deneauve. After fortifying me with a few drinks, he introduced me to her. I could not utter a word, not a word. Quietly, he apologized in exquisite French to Ms. Deneauve and said he would be right back. He took me back to the bar, gave me another stiff scotch and said "Now don't blow it this time. I think she likes you." We returned to the party room and, once again, David made the intro, I was speechless. David, graceful as always, again apologized to her for my bad manners. We left her puzzled. David told me under his breath "Two strikes and you're out my friend".

The memory of that night in Paris still stings and David never let me forget it on each birthday. David was a friend, the consummate gentleman who loved fine food, fine cars, great wines, aromatic Cuban cigars and all things beautiful. He had old world manners, always rising quickly to greet a woman and then kiss her on her hand or attend to her seating. He was always immaculately tailored and stood out in a crowd with his sartorial splendor.

He had such a zest for life. Indeed, he was larger than life in every way. He was a member of the airborne division of the British army, and a member of the U.K. special forces. Always true to his soldier's code of silence, he never gave us a glimpse of his dangerous missions, except to say that they were demanding. A truly remarkable and modest man for so many extraordinary accomplishments.

Let me conclude by final lyrics by Leonard Cohen:

"I did my best, it wasn't much,
I couldn't feel so I tried to touch
I told the truth
I didn't come to fool you

And even thos some went wrong
I'll stand before the lord
Of song
With nothing on my tongue but halleluiah"

David, dear friend you race is run your battles won your labour done now come to rest halleluyah, and let us say amen.

JIM (JAMES ALLAN) COUTTS: EULOGY

January 2, 2014

Suddenly, Canada is a smaller place.

Political life in Canada will never be the same without Jim Coutts, nor will the Liberal Party. Born and educated in Alberta, not exactly a habitable space for Liberals, Jim was a contrarian and he ran as a Liberal in the early '60s, which brought him to the attention of Mr. Pearson and Keith Davey. Mr. Pearson brought him to Ottawa as his appointed secretary. Jim never looked back.

Like all born and bred westerners, Jim was an unconventional thinker, a contrarian, and he was nearly always right. He was an idea man par excellence - he knew how to execute his ideas. He was a true and clear grit. He was a true believer in the liberal party, a political force he served with dedication and energy. He gave his all to the liberty party, and his all was a deeply considered, thought-out belief in its political principles. He never did things by half measures. He went all out, all the time.

Jim had the gift of friendship and, if you were blessed to have him as a friend, you knew he always had your back. He was a rare, honest and honorable politico who gave much more to politics than he took. He prized loyalty to leader, the liberty party and friendship, above all else.

Jim loved beautiful things: Canadian paintings, photography, antiques, beautiful women, Canadian landscapes, the western prairies, and the wilds of the Canadian North..

He was a passionate man who believed in the Liberal Party as a progressive force for the good. He privately scorned his political opponents but smiled at them in public. His face was his shield, always smiling happily but he could boil on the inside at the slightest display of disloyalty to leader and party or his vision of one Canada which he shared with Pierre Trudeau.

The sweetest words would flow from a telephone call from Jim, who would say: "Jim here. Jerry, I have an idea" I prided myself being an idea man, but Jim could always come up with an idea, a tactical strategy that was different, unconventional and better.

He was an avid reader with a capacious curiosity. He had a grand passion for books which he collected and shelved with precision. His homes overflow with books, his dearest possessions. He loved to travel and developed an international network of key operatives. Jim was a rational man but also very emotional. He would shed tears when he heard a great speech, especially one that he helped to write.

He and Keith Davey resurrected the Liberal party when Jim became Mr. Pearson's Executive Assistant, and Keith became the liberal party's director in the early '60s when Mr. Trudeau won his landslide. Mr. Trudeau wanted a fresh start and the old "reliables" like Jim and Keith were left out of the loop.

After the disastrous "Land is Strong" campaign in 1972 that ended in a minority, Mr. Trudeau reflected on the new reality We lobbied to have Jim return as Principal Secretary. Mr. Trudeau was reluctant but, after some false moves by Mr. Trudeau and his staff, Jim was brought back to the centre of power, and so was Keith.

Then came the 1974 campaign, "Zap, your wages are frozen", and then the 6-5 campaign. This was followed by the disastrous campaign of 1979. Mr. Trudeau could not turn it over. The spark was gone, gone for a number of reasons. So Mr. Trudeau resigned to Jim's consternation, and Keith's also, for that matter.

But it was Jim, Allan MacEachen and Keith who persuaded Mr. Trudeau to renege on his resignation and return. The problem was that the Liberals were popular but Mr. Trudeau was not. Yes, Mr. Trudeau was perceived as a leader but not one who was liked.

It was Keith and Jim who levered the 1980 election "Low Bridge" campaign, where Trudeau made the same speech once or twice a day, ducked the press and stayed below the radar. Trudeau stayed on message despite himself. Jim helped to write that speech.

After a couple of weeks of campaigning, Mr. Trudeau was absolutely bored, repeating the same things twice a day. He approached me, as Jim knew he would. I was prepared with Jim's advice. "Mr. Prime Minister, you are a creative man, say the same thing your own way, but stay on message."

Trudeau did and he won.

I recall Jim helping Tom Axworthy write a speech for the victory party at the Chateau Laurier. "Welcome to the '80s" Mr. Trudeau proclaimed, and we did. Jim was in tears as he listened to this speech he had helped draft. He took out his big white hankie and blew his nose and then steeled himself with the prodigious work ahead.

Shortly after the 1980 campaign, 8 of us were invited to dinner at 21 Sussex to celebrate the return of a Trudeau government. Mr. Trudeau went around the table and asked for ideas. "What should be our priorities?" He asked. "The constitution", I said, "Repatriating the constitution with a bill of rights and you will have a legacy." Mr. Trudeau turned to look at Jim and the two silently nodded. They had already discussed this idea so Mr. Trudeau, with Jim's advice, devised the tactics strategy, to repatriate the Constitution with a Charter of Rights. For that brilliant work alone, Jim is entitled to a secure place in the history books of Canada.

Earlier, when serving with Mr. Pearson, he helped devise the tactics to get the new flag passed by doubters, including some of the Liberal caucus. Jim was also a key strategist in persuading the Liberal party convention in 1966 to adopt Medicare. So, on the flag, Medicare, the repatriation of the constitution, three historic Canadian achievements, Jim helped make all three a reality. We should not mourn Jim's passing, but we do.

Jews believe that death means that the soul, the spark, that particle of energy, is liberated from its physicality, but the spark burns on, as bright as ever.

Now, those of you Liberal sinners who will not go to heaven, too bad.

For those few of you that might enter the pearly gates, I can tell you now where you will find Jim - in the grand celestial courtroom in the sky where the master of the universe sits in daily judgement as there is so much work to be done. Sitting beside him or her, will be Jim Coutts advising the grand creator what to do.

So beware you sinners, there is still time to redeem yourselves and serve the liberal party. Let me end on a lyric by a friend of mine, Leonard Cohen:

> I've heard there was a secret chord
> That David played, and it pleased the lord but you don't really care for music, do you?
> It goes like this the fourth, the fifth
> The minor fall, the major lift
> The baffled king composing hallelujah
>
> Hallelujah, hallelujah
>
> hallelujah, hallelujah
>
> I did my best, it wasn't much
> I couldn't feel, so I tried to touch
> I've told the truth, I didn't come to fool you and even though it all went wrong
> I'll stand before the lord of song
> With nothing on my tongue but hallelujah
>
>
> Jim, hallelujah.
> And let us say amen .
>
> Jim, the beat goes on, and so do you.

A REVIEW OF *ELUSIVE DESTINY*:
THE POLITICAL VOCATION OF JOHN NAPIER TURNER
BY PAUL LITT, UNIVERSITY OF BRITISH COLUMBIA PRESS

July 9, 2012

"He who does not make known his own history, runs the risk that .. the media and ... histori-ans will construct a history for him, using whatever information they have, regardless of whether their information is accurate or not."
- Osama Bin Laden in a letter to a lieutenant
Circa 2010

Reason ... is the slave of the passions ...
- John Hume
A Treatise on Human Nature 1740

The true statesman is not one who gives orders to his fellow citizens so much as he is one who devotes himself to their service.
- Pierre Elliot Trudeau
Vrai 1958

ELUSIVE DESTINY - The Political Vocation of John Napier Turner, is a gripping, sometimes soaring and too often painful account of the life and times of John Turner and the Liberal Party in the '60s, '70s and '80s.

Unlike other anodyne self-embellishing published accounts by key contemporary actors, or outside observers who had their own special hook to advocate, Paul Litt's book is a balanced, well-researched and elegantly crafted biography. Litt clinically and objectively dissects the public and not-so-private life of John Turner gleaned from public and private archives, coincident personalities, supporting players and sources of discontent that festered within the body politic of the Liberal Party. Even of those participants and close observers, Litt paints a fresh montage of new, surprising revelations.

"How Can You Hope to Unite the Country if You Cannot Unite the Party?"

Deftly stripping away the varnish from John Turner's star-crossed life, Litt uncovers a searing passion play, a potent concoction of strong competitive personalities, the magnet of power, venal party politics, raw ambition, self-interest and high public purpose. With crushing honesty, he illuminates the dark, even reprehensible, actions of so-called party players, and their willing wingmen, and the origins of the onslaught of the internecine, tribal wars that bedeviled the Liberal Party during those three turbulent decades.

Clandestine and not-so-clandestine conspiracies became a miserable realty of party life. Loyalty to the Leader, the attraction of translating liberal principles into activity, the paramount duty to promote national unity and to advance Canada's domestic and foreign interests, all the hallmarks that traditionally fused the disparate factions of the Liberal Party, were ripped asunder, motivated by personal pique, triggered by imagined slights and ruthless petty egoism that vaulted personal ambition above party and, at times, Country. The Freudian principle of the "narcissism of small differences" was in play. The old Liberal saw - "How can you hope to unite the country if you cannot unite the party?" - was shredded by even its most ardent advocates. Anonymous wounding gossip coloured the darker shades of the underside of politics. This divisive factionalism, once the characteristic of the Conservative Party, which had kept it from power for decades, now, like a virus, infected the uppermost echelons of the Liberal Party, once noted as the party of unity and loyalty to the Leader, as its dual operational code. The self-defined "natural governing party" was seen to be ripping itself apart, and from the inside. Lyndon Johnson once opined, "You know the difference between liberals and cannibals ... cannibals eat their enemies." This, too often, was the miserable new norm.

In retrospect, what still amazes is the absence of either shame or remorse by the instigating players. As if internal party politics, played by amoral, rancorous rules, is doomed to travel a different route in public life rather than personal character or intellectual probity. Narcissism seems to rule. Is power, at all costs, the goal? Was this to be the "new norm" of party politics or the "norm"? Is hypocrisy the name of feigned virtue? These are profound questions implied by Litt's expose.

Has the Liberal Party cleansed itself and moved on beyond this sordid period? Perhaps certainly not, unless the players, in the mode of reconciliation, admit their errors, or at least expiate themselves, refrain from future repetitions, and inoculate others against this mean conduct.

Unnoticed by public observers is the loss of "character" in public opinion and public opinion polls as an element or aspect of measurement of leadership qualities. When did "character" lose its importance, let alone relevance in defining modern leaderships? Did its descent start in the Kennedy era when, as an adored darling of the media, John Kennedy's tainted "character" was kept from public view by a willing coalition of advisors and a cohort of "liberal" media who conspired to keep the darker side of Kennedy's character hidden from public view until well after his assassination? Certainly, since the Kennedy era, and more notably since Clinton, "character" no longer plays a central role defining the modern political leader.

So, this book is a must-read for any Liberal, past or present, and for any observer interested in the human condition, the pathology of party politics and the deeper nature of public affairs in recent Canadian history. There are and have been various different narratives illuminating politics as a high calling culled from Canadian history. Perhaps the availability of the more revealing sources, the absence of personal restraint, the seeming need for each minor player to shamelessly illuminate his miniscule role, the advent of 24/7 news cycle, now brings a different deeper insight, and throws a brighter light on the history of party politics, and the primacy of party politics, a topic not fully explored and rarely understood by academics.

Prologue: The Pearson Era

"Mike" Pearson in his public persona did not exude charisma. Yet, in close quarters, he displayed a remarkable lively intellect and witty self-deprecation that endeared him to his Party followers, and charmed them. He wore this patent vulnerability coupled with a unique ability to bind diverse grouplets on principles rather than personalities. He was expert in smoothing the ruffled feathers of party peacocks. The so-called "left" wing led by Walter Gordon and Allan MacEachen, supported by Tom Kent, held strong policy views; yet these views did not destroy the unity of the party. The so-called "right" wing led by Robert Winters, Paul Hellyer, and Mitchell Sharp, to whom Jean Chrétien was an early acolyte, almost split over "Medicare" in the 1966 policy convention. Yet, loyalty to the Leader, to Mr. Pearson, his soothing, down-to-earth personality, his honesty and fairness was the glue that preserved Party unity. Pearson gave more than he got from politics, leaving public service, as he had entered, without even a home to call his own. Not unlike his predecessor, Louis St. Laurent, who for many years lived with his wife in one small room in the Elgin Hotel in Ottawa, and then left politics to return to his modest home in Quebec City. Those days were from an earlier era when public service was deemed a "calling", not a grasping occupation.

View From One Observation Post

One "mea culpa". My close party experience spanned the Pearson, Trudeau, Turner, Chrétien, Martin, Dion, and Ignatieff years. I was invited to Mr. Pearson's caucus from time to time, as a young Liberal activist, and participated in all the others as a full member. I served as John Turner's first Executive Assistant, policy advisor, and speech writer when, in 1966, he became a Minister without Portfolio in Mr. Pearson's cabinet, and later served as a Campaign Head in his 1968 bid for leadership, after urging him to run. *"The Politics of Purpose"*, a collection of John Turner's speeches delivered during that period from 1965 to 1968, was published to coincide with the leadership contest in that early era and has been recently republished. It might be read as a companion guide for that period. Having acted first as an advisor then as a volunteer during his period as Minister of Consumer and Corporate Affairs and then Minister of Justice, and episodically thereafter, I joined the throngs of fervent admirers who urged Turner to return to politics in the early '80s after he had resigned abruptly from the Trudeau Cabinet in 1975, having loyally participated in the disastrous "Land is Strong" Campaign of 1972 and the 1974 "Wages and Price Controls - 'Zap You're Frozen'" election that saw the Liberals return to majority government.

From the loss of leadership in 1968 until his return to public life in 1984, John Turner maintained contact with a loyal network of Liberal activists across the country based on the so-called "195 Club", a loose seemingly constantly expanding circle who claimed to have voted for him on the last ballot, until he was eliminated in the final rounds of voting.

I continued as a volunteer policy and communications advisor during John Turner's period as candidate for Leader-Prime Minister and then as Leader of the Opposition.

As Litt replays these colourful, turbulent events and sketches the major and minor players, what emerges, from the undulating sometimes blurred pictures encased in the morass of raw politics, is the riveting character of John Turner, who believed devoutly in public service as almost a sacred calling coupled with a Churchillian reverence for Parliament as the "vox populi" - the ultimate "voice of the people".

Turner's Preparation for Public Life

John Turner came well-prepared for public life, armed with an encyclopedic knowledge of Canadian history, and an especially retentive memory for people and striking anecdotes as well as a deep love for the expanses of Canadian geography. He was born in England where his mother, with humble Maritime roots, gained a post-graduate education and married an English journalist who died prematurely. Returning to Canada with two young children, his mother, tall and striking, served during WWII as the leading female bureaucrat in Ottawa where Turner received his primary education, and encountered leading civil servants and politicians of that era as a youth. Then it was on to the University of British Columbia where he excelled in academics, sports and sports writing, becoming a star athlete and then a Rhodes scholar at Oxford. He was called to the Bar in the U.K. but returned to start his practice of law in Montreal where he rose rapidly in the Quebec Bar to be elected head of the junior Bar. In Montreal, he cut a dashing larger-than-life figure as a handsome, ebullient bachelor in fine English tailored suits, exuded robust restless energy and a booming staccato-like voice that could reverberate in a small auditorium. A "bon vivant", he relished good music and food, fine wines and spirits, Cuban cigars, attractive company, and scintillating conversation. He had an interesting publicized turn with Princess Margaret. As a rising political star, he radiated an electric energy and a certain attractive charisma. His fiery blazing blue eyes riveted and captivated everyone who encountered him. He married an attractive bright woman, Geills Kilgour, from an established Winnipeg family.

He sought, fought for, and obtained the Liberal nomination in 1962 and gained a seat in the polyglot riding of St. Lawrence, St. George in the heart of downtown Montreal in a hotly competitive tough campaign.

During his swift rise in politics, John Turner was a witty, often gripping, "stump speaker" who had an excellent eye for the organizational detail of riding politics. He loved campaigning and was both a creative and inspiring "grass roots" team leader. His urban riding introduced cutting-edge political innovations at the time, for gathering lists, telephone numbers, and especially a keen talent for "blitz" canvassing in high-rise apartments and for soliciting votes among new "ethnic" voters.

Roots in all Regions of Canada

Uniquely, John Turner had lived, worked and vacationed, with vital family roots and relationships, in all regions of Canada, especially the Maritimes, Quebec, Ontario, Manitoba and British Columbia. Travelling with him across Canada was an exhilarating experience for he shared his exuberant love for the capacious Canadian landscape from East to West, his zest for the farthest reaches of the North, and the limitless Canadian wildernesses which he knew intimately from endless canoe trips, and where he relaxed, felt comfortable and at home. From childhood, he gained an early passion for conservation, and especially protection of our fresh water sources that he was to advocate throughout his career.

The Great Shift - Politics and Media

As depicted by Litt, John Turner was caught between two shifting political templates and periods: the first, during the hierarchal establishment mores of the Liberal Party under Louis St. Laurent and C. D. Howe in the late '50s, and the second which first enmeshed Mr. Pearson and his successors in the new explosive political scatter-gun environment that transformed politics in Canada, especially after the Kennedy/Nixon TV debates in 1960 in the USA.

The early '60s marked the great shift in the relationship between politics and the media. The American presidential media debates had a profound impact on politics in Canada and the way we conducted our day-to-day political discourse. Canadians were deeply influenced by American political techniques as American media reached all corners of Canada. The intrusive role of television replaced print as the primary source of "news" for the public. Electronic media extended and accelerated its pervasive presence into the '70s and '80s when Canada moved from the oligarchic new print agenda-making and combined with the then narrow prism of the national television network environment. Quickly, political news mixed with entertainment, flowed into the wider and wilder disparate world of cable television, and the even more capacious range of choices of the specialty channels universe to the current relentless 24x7 news cycle - all before the advent and even greater expansive and disparate reach of the "web". The line between "news", "politics" and "entertainment", began to overlap and dissolve. The tipping point between the "old' and the "new" politics had been reached. Canadians were confronted with a new political confusing concoction.

The velocity and diversity of electronic news gutted the old system of hierarchal patrician pundit columnists and print editorial influence that shaped and held sway over public opinion by its daily agenda setting. Now the public got their "news" from television and were more influenced by the political images and opinions fulminated by the electronic media. Now young untutored media voices, that knew or cared little for historic context and read less, focused all their competitive energy on the race for instant news clips without context - the 30-second "gotcha" soundbite of the moment.

Gifted in so many ways with a deep classical liberal education both in Canada and in England as a Rhodes scholar, well-read, well travelled in Europe and fluently bilingual, star athlete with his "hip" jargon in early professional life, John Turner, as Leader, never seemed quite able to make the shift, the transformation from the old, more personal, structured media hierarchy to the fractured factionalized horizontal electronic environment, until almost the end of his public career. The larger complex issues, he espoused, especially those that were process driven, were submerged in the waves of the new disjointed news, ripped from their historic context and swept away in the flotsam and jetsam of disparate news from everywhere. Larger political issues of substance were diluted or drowned in the noise of meaningless 24/7 chatter. The public was distractible and distracted.

Where once the nightly news first radio then television followed print front pages and editorials, thread to the public through the same information needle, now "news" from everywhere and everything clouded, confused and fragmented in the public mind.

The line between "politics" and "culture" and "identity" blurred. The "cultural" wars had overtaken traditional politics, especially in the United States with direct reverberations in Canada. The age of McLuhan had arrived: "perception" became "reality", and the "medium" became the "message".

McLuhan held a deeper insight into the interplay between politics and imagery. He wrote: "The Politician will only be too happy to abdicate in favour of his image, because the image will be so much more powerful than he will ever be". Once etched in public opinion, the public image becomes indelible, almost impossible to adjust or erase. Litt' s book goes a long way to refurbish the glistening aspects of Turner's public career that was forgotten, blemished by his surprisingly awkward, ungainly return to public life in 1984.

Hon. Jerry S. Grafstein. Q. C

Cabinet Minister - Consumer Affairs, Justice and Finance

Litt carefully recounts John Turner's earliest successful battles as a newly minted junior Minister in the Pearson Cabinet to skillfully overcome the reactionary bureaucracy and to establish a "liberal" Department of Consumer and Corporate Affairs, the first of its kind in the Western World, surfing the Ralph Nader consumer wave, and other issues which John Turner brilliantly steered a liberal path forward through the Cabinet, Parliament, and onto the public canvas. Litt reminds us that it was John Turner, as Minister of Justice, who drafted and piloted the wide-ranging legally contentious reforms of the "Just Society" through Parliament for which Trudeau has been given sole credit. It was John Turner, not Pierre Trudeau, who crafted, drafted and legislated the "criminal code" measures of the "Just Society", who was handed the divisive dossier on bilingualism by Trudeau when others in the Cabinet faltered, and failed, who muffled the renewed call for capital punishment and traversed abortion debates in Parliament, all of which are now seen, in retrospect, as conventional wisdom. Yet, a clearer story of the battle for bilingualism, or the October crisis, or other divisive issues will not emerge until future writers and scholars probe the Cabinet minutes of this era now opened to public scrutiny.

It is fair to ascribe to John Turner the accolade as Canada's greatest Minister of Justice and Attorney General to occupy that prestigious portfolio. As a Member of the Quebec Bar, he was an early advocate of legal aid, based on his passionate belief to rebalance state power in favour of the citizen. Invited to the Kingston Conference in 1961, he persuaded the Liberal party to adapt legal aid as a Liberal policy. In addition to legislating the contentious reforms of the "Just Society", he faced one of the greatest existential legal threats to Canada's existence during the FLQ crisis and, despite the visceral temper of those times, relied on the "rule of law". Despite resistance in the Cabinet, he insisted on amending the antiquated War Measures Act which he laid before Parliament to reduce its anti-civil liberties overreach.

His early experience as Counsel on the Quebec Bar persuaded him that the justice system had wrongfully put the onus for bail on the alleged criminal. He reversed this by amending the Criminal Code to place the onus on the Crown to prove why bail was necessary in the public's interest.

He renovated the judicial appointment process and was careful, fastidious, and fair in all the court appointments during his tenure, ranking merit over patronage, purging and transforming the judicial appointment process. Revamping the musty and reactionary Department of Justice, he gathered an outside circle of superb lawyers and academics to advise him on law reform. One concrete example was the establishment of the first Law Reform Commission as a template and replicated by some provinces to bring both the antiquated federal and provincial laws up to date. This was a radical departure from previous episodic law reform efforts, navigating past bureaucratic inertia, Cabinet objections and Parliamentary indifference. He followed my great law teacher, Cecil Augustus Wright's edict "not what the law is but what the law should be." He convened a conference on the law with leading social thinkers "outside the box", notably Ivan Illich, a radical Catholic theologian and author of such texts as *"Deschooling Society"*, to influence the Department, the Caucus, the Cabinet, and Parliament, and public opinion to make law reform a comprehensible public priority.

What is the central importance of the Ministry of Justice? The federal Department of Justice is the unsung Ministry of Government underlying all legislative initiatives. Law, lawmaking, and the administration of justice knit together the fabric of Canada's character. The criminal law power, which exclusively rested with the federal government, was never challenged by the Provinces. Equality before the law was and is an architectonic of Canadian history and part of Canada's DNA.

In the 1908, Rudyard Kipling, on a visit to Canada, wrote to his family his impressions of Canada and Canadians:

> *"The law in Canada exists and is administered, not as a surprise, a joke, a favour or a bribe ... but as an integral part of the national character - no more to be forgotten or talked about than trousers."*

Earlier, in 1861, John Anderson, a fugitive slave being discharged for murder by the Court of the Common Pleas in Upper Canada, said:

> *"I have never known that there was so much law in the world as I find in Canada."*

The late novelist, Robertson Davies, in his 1954 masterpiece, *Leaven of Malice,* wrote:

> *"Never go to the law for simple vengeance, that is not what the law is for. Redress, yes; vengeance, no."*

In 1960, Mr. Pearson, then Leader of the Opposition, spoke in the House of Commons Debate:

> *"Incorruptible and respected Courts, enforcing laws made by free men in parliament assembled and dealing with specific matters and, with specific sanctions to enforce their observance; these are the best guarantees of our rights and liberties. This is the tried and tested British way, and is the better course to follow than the mere pious affirmation of general principles to which some political societies are addicted.*
>
> *The paramount purpose of our working Parliament is no more and no less than to make laws. That is what Parliament does. Parliament transforms experience into principles, and these principles into explicit laws. We make laws and administer the execution of those laws, especially criminal laws. Parliament has exclusive oversight of the criminal law power, and this power is tied to the question of freedom, liberty and security, which are the organizing principles at the heart of federal governance. Criminal laws are Parliament's*

definition of our civilization's standards of conduct and care. To fall below these standards of care by unwanted conduct is to invite penalties, prompting state action and, more important, to provide a clear warning against unwanted conduct. Ultimately, criminal law seeks to prevent and ostracize egregious conduct and, hopefully, in the process, to transform the attitude and intentions of those who practice such conduct. It is to transform public opinion, public conduct and private conduct."

Both Turner and Trudeau understood this truism but it was Turner, as Minister of Justice, Attorney General and Chief Law Officer of the Crown who turned preferred principles into the sinews of our civic society, just as Trudeau did later with the Charter of Rights.

It was the advent of "culture" or "value" social warlike issues that John Turner was directed by Trudeau and his Cabinet to diffuse and he did. At the time when these explosive issues burst upon the public agenda, they were tempered, cooled and honed by John Turner's skills as an advocate, mediator and legislator morphing these emotive ideas into the comfort zone and quiet waters of conventional public wisdom.

Restored partially by Litt's account of Turner's forgotten abilities, much like the Lyndon Johnson gift (the so-called "Johnston treatment"), to persuade key decision-makers by personal contact to accept his viewpoint, this gift was on display by Turner with Provincial Premiers who opposed bilingualism when the Turner treatment persuaded them, one by one, to accept the advent of bilingualism, a triumph of the Trudeau era.

Turner and Trudeau on Economic Policy

When John Turner accepted Pierre Trudeau's calculated offer of the Finance Ministry, it represented a risk to Turner's leadership ambitions, for no previous Minister of Finance had ever acceded to the Prime Ministership. At that time, he was the youngest Member of Parliament to ever hold the prestigious Finance portfolio.

As Minister of Finance, John Turner early grasped that, to sustain the spiraling of public debts and deficits fed by inflation, irresponsible runaway spending, especially Medicare, would put unrelenting downward pressure on the entire social net. Unless redressed and rebalanced, the ballooning public cost would place an economic squeeze and undermine the entire social net. He early predicted that spiraling health costs, unless contained, would beggar other economic needs. This realistic view unfairly labeled him "Conservative" by the at times profligate so called "progressive" spenders in the Trudeau Cabinet who argued debt and deficits never were problems.

It is a shame that Litt did not explore more fully the roots of the deep philosophic differences between Trudeau and Turner on economic policy. Trudeau had studied economic theory at Harvard and the London School of Economics under the left leaning Harold Laski. Turner, while at Oxford, explored the ideas of Keynes then in vogue. Keynes was a lifelong Liberal and eschewed socialist prescriptions. Both had considered the thinking of Schumpeter and Hayek. Both agreed that "Keynesian" principles could not be blindly applied in Canada at times of inflationary prices and slow growth. Yet they had come to different economic nostrums. It was Trudeau who aggravated Turner when he assembled a group of economic advisors in the PMO/PCO, which Trudeau quickly disbanded when Turner properly argued that the Minister of Finance's duties to Cabinet as senior economic advisor could not be fragmented in this way. When, as Minister of Finance, he turned his attention to transparent fairness in the incomprehensible tax code, he gave taxpayers a simple cost-effective appeal process to address grievances with the prolix tax system.

The current debate in North America and Europe about relentless inflationary governance costs and unproductive entitlements continues to strip away the growth of the GDP. This endemic problem he spotted early and highlighted as a source of present and future malaise thus going against the grain of conventional thinking at the time when debt and deficit were spurting ahead of growth. The then current view in Ottawa was that deficits and debts were not even genuine problems. They were imaginary dangers imagined by some "right wing" nuts. Many in Ottawa held rigid and distorted "views" of "Keynesian" economics and failed to take account of the relative size of the government and the private sector when Keynes wrote his landmark texts. Many, not having carefully culled Keynes' theories which restricted public expenditures to public infrastructures not otherwise undertaken by the private sector and carelessly expanded and misapplied Keynes' limited strictures. Many simply forgot how Keynes had railed against socialist dogma.

Trudeau and Turner on Quebec in Confederation

Two titanic issues found John Turner opposed to Pierre Trudeau's vision of Quebec within Canada and Brian Mulroney's continental views of Canada in North America. These two visceral issues framed first by the Meech Lake Accords, cleverly instigated by Mulroney to upstage and trump Trudeau's brilliant constitutional victories of repatriation and the "Charter". Mulroney skillfully detected the fault lines running through the Liberal Party which, to a large measure, had accepted Trudeau's version of "One Canada" with a strong central government and ambitious provinces different but not "distinct", keeping the federal/provincial powers comfortably and constitutionally balanced against Quebec's incessant demand for more and more Quebec-only powers. This disruptive and incessant call by Quebec, breaking from the cocoon of "Duplessisism" into the "Quiet Revolution", demanding "more" powers, emerged again and again as the paramount cause of Federal-Provincial friction, then echoed by Alberta flexing its political muscles, feeling its new found-power in rich energy resources. The rise of separatism created a mood in the rest of Canada to mollify noisy Quebec, which Trudeau diagnosed as weakening the central governance while John Turner believed were historic cyclical ebbs and flows in power sharing between the provinces and the federal government.

During the great existential threat to Canada's unity, even existence, the FLQ crisis, John Turner as Minister of Justice modulated Trudeau 's more expansive reactions and worked in close harmony with Trudeau, carefully consistent with the "rule of law" to pull Canada through.

John Turner's beliefs about the nature of Quebec within Confederation clashed with Trudeau's long-held and carefully evolved ideas which now resonated within the bosom of the Liberal party. Both held deeply considered views about the relationship of Quebec in Confederation. Trudeau rejected the "compact theory" which led inevitably to the "two nations" theory that espoused the view that Canada was a "pact" between two founding nations, English Canada and French Quebec.

Trudeau agreed with St. Laurent that Quebec was a "province like the others." John Turner, unlike other more extravagant advocates of the "two nations" theory, took a different but less extreme, more moderate view than that held by academics in Quebec, taken by Federal and even Conservatives, some politicians like Robarts in Ontario, and Jean Luc Pepin in Ottawa. Turner was an early advocate of Quebec designating itself as a "distinct society" within Canada, as he believed it recognized a fact that would not legally alter the balance of powers within Confederation. Trudeau believed that the designation of Quebec as a "distinct society" would inevitably lead to new and unreasonable demands for more powers by Quebec. From his earliest days as a writer and dazzling pamphleteer, Trudeau argued that the "compact theory" was a false reading of the origins of Confederation.

The Canadian federation was "in law" and by "constitution" a balanced separation of powers between the federal government and the different provinces. As a result, Quebec had its different civil law, language, and education as available to other provinces had they chosen. Quebec was different as were the other provinces, but never "distinct." Quebec and, at times, others argued for greater powers from the Federal government - usurping some not occupied fully by the Federal government.

This fault line Mulroney essayed and exploited, splitting the Liberal Party asunder over the Meech Lake debate. As well, with a large restive Quebec "nationalist" contingent in his caucus, Mulroney was anxious to assuage and appease their concerns and expectations. Turner supported Meech Lake. Trudeau, then out of office, returned to the public forum only once, to advocate Meech Lake's defeat, which happened.

Trudeau and Turner - Remarkable Parallels

In many ways, John Turner and Pierre Trudeau had much in common. Both were raised without fathers, by strong independent mothers; both were highly schooled here and abroad, with a liberal arts education; both were avid rugged outdoorsmen who loved to vacation, canoeing and portaging, in quiet northern lakes and rushing waterways; both exuded a certain grace, practiced "old world" courtesy, animpeccable manners; both were effortlessly bilingual and facile with others; both had long held political ambitions and spent time preparing themselves for public office; both easily attracted and retained cadres of loyal friends; both had capacious recall for people and ideas; both were well-schooled skilled lawyers; both were impressively persuasive as counsel in Court; both were voracious readers with retentive memories; both were gifted speech-writers and, on occasion, could be incandescent speakers, especially in Parliament; both were "quick" studies who could deftly digest complex, fulsome briefing papers; both quickly cut to the heart of a political problem; both were impatient with the unprepared and with fools; both had an intense way of focusing on the issue at hand as if to wring the hidden essence of the subject matter; both diligently prepared for cabinet or public meetings; both were "conviction" politicians; both were men of high character, a somewhat debased or overlooked dimension of politics now rarely considered in the calculus of public opinion; both respected and even admired John Diefenbaker; both cut attractive debonair athletic figures; while both were devout practicing Roman Catholics who early had considered the priesthood as a vocation, Turner was influenced by the Basilians and Trudeau by the Jesuits; both regularly attended Mass and religious retreats; both shared ideas rooted in the social gospel; both regularly consulted and held close relationships within the church hierarchy, yet never allowed their Orthodox Catholicism to stand in the way of their liberal pluralistic principles. John Turner and Pierre Trudeau agreed that private religious beliefs should not trump secular or temporal considerations in a liberal society, yet each would nuance these principles in different ways with a markedly different temperament. Bereft of a father figure, the impact on sons is often left with tangled skeins of deep-seated complex ambitions more properly left to Freudian analyses.

While both shared almost a symbiotic relationship and mutual respect for each other's skills, both were puzzled by each other and could not grasp the wellspring of the other's drives, ambitions or goals.

Trudeau and Turner Differences

If there were marked differences, Trudeau as Leader, after false starts between 1968 and 1972, was able to put together a diverse, knowledgeable, and wide circle of capable political operatives and independent committed advisors who, for the most part, liked and respected each other that sustained him and each other in his ups and downs until his retirement.

When on the public stage, Trudeau was a superb actor who had an uncanny ability to observe himself and polish his techniques of public persuasion. Trudeau relished flamboyant theatrics. Turner, on the other hand, especially when he returned to public life in the early '80s to run for Leader, never seemed to meld his disparate groups of advisors or forge bonds among them as a coherent circle who liked or trusted each other and worked in concert in his best interests other than to carve out their own sphere of influence. On the public stage, it was only after his electoral defeat in 1984 that Turner was able slowly to adapt and hone his techniques to match the new public environment and to become comfortable, as he once was, and restore his undoubted skills as a public advocate. It was not that Turner was "rusty" as some observers alleged at the time; it was that the public arena itself was dramatically transformed during his decade of absence from public life, leaving him less certain and less confident in his public advocacy skills. His performance in 1988 election debates recouped his public reputation, tarnished by his earlier lack-lustre performance in the hastily called, ill-prepared 1984 election, and somewhat restored the Liberal Party membership in the Commons.

Turner and Mulroney on "Free Trade"

The other wrenching existential debate triggered by Mulroney that raged across Canada was about "Free Trade". Mulroney suddenly abandoned the age-old Conservative "protectionist" history and jumped into the shoes of liberal "free traders", who, like Laurier, had fought and lost an election campaign leading the Liberal Party in 1911, on the issue of North American trade reciprocity, and a more reluctant Mackenzie King who, after WW II, explored then withdrew from thoughts of "freer" trade with the USA. Louis St. Laurent's leadership on the building of the St. Lawrence Seaway with its bilateral implications was another tepid step towards "freer" North American trade. Diefenbaker veered to the anti-American "nationalist" protectionist perch of the classic Conservative. Mulroney had no electoral mandate on this issue. He did not campaign on "free trade"; rather, he took advantage of his close ties with the Reagan Administration, and surprised the country with his sudden lurch and leap to the FTA.

The Free Trade Agreement debate, the "FTA", deeply divided the Liberal Party between classic "Manchester" Liberals who were "free traders" and those gradualists who, like John Turner, believed the slower erosion and gradual reduction of GATT tariffs would ultimately result in "free trade." Gradualism, John Turner thought, was a more coherent route forward than a sudden advance to a fulsome Free Trade Agreement that was bereft of effective dispute mechanisms or shields from the inherent protectionism, dormant yet ever alive, in the bone marrow of the American Congress. John Turner railed against the fact that Mulroney had not sought or obtained a mandate for this major change and hence his use of his role as Leader of the Opposition on both principles and lack of mandate in resisting the enactment of the legislation needed to make the Free Trade Agreement effective.

Today, "free trade" remains a resonating issue which vindicates Turner's views to some extent. The untrammeled protectionist impulses of the United States Administration and the wayward Congress continue to produce unilateral protectionist measures, measures contrary to the spirit of the FTA. Yet the FTA has been, by any measure, a remarkable economic success of benefit to both Canada and the United States.

On both these issues, John Turner's careful "common law" lawyer-like approach failed to unite the bubbling diversities within the Liberal Party or the avalanche of boisterous "big" business support fomented by Mulroney, too cautious for the mostart to enter the competitive entrepreneurial American market place without the threat of protectionist measures nascent in Congress diminished.

Both issues were used unfairly by divisive ambitious players within the Liberal Party to bring John Turner down, by unscrupulous power hungry operatives, who exaggerated the chasms of division and engulfed the Liberal Party in destructive flames, the embers of which still glow dimly, rather than remaining united against an aggressive politically savvy Mulroney administration.

Litt carefully delineates John Turner's superbly honed advocacy and unparalleled legislative talents with clarity, accuracy, and balance. What emerges from this mosaic, yet still uncertain portrait, is a man of strong character, personal probity and relentlessly consistent principles that encased him in an aura of honesty, rarely seen in public life. As Winston Churchill once lamented of his father: "He sought to wrap himself in the mantle of Elijah". Any flaws, failures or foibles are far outweighed by the glowing honesty, probity and commitment to the Liberal Party, to public service, Parliament and to Canada that radiated from John Turner like a beacon to those who are interested in the good public life of Canada and in promoting Canada's vital interests.

When John Turner left politics to return a decade later to run as Leader, the tectonic shift in politics had accelerated. What was acceptable conduct in the past was now anathema. Now, "political correctness" magnified each gender comment or contact. A new sensibility was in place. Somehow Turner had lost his groove and it took a political loss to restore his political equilibrium.

"Confidence" - The Secret of the National Liberal Caucus

What is missing from Litt's book is the internal grammar of politics, a deeper parsing of political parties and how each Party plays a pivotal and virtual role in our political system. In that system, a Leader must immerse himself in the sinews of the Party corpus and emerge to claim political legitimacy the public's opinion of the viability and electability of the Leader. Once past the hurdle of Leadership approval in an open convention, the more opaque process of working of the National Caucus, the heart beat of the Party, takes over.

Unlike the United States, the executive branch in Canada is wholly made up of Members of Parliament, either House or Senate. The Ministries are responsible to Parliament. The House of Commons can refuse the money which the Governmen needs. This direct relationship of the Party leaders, government and opposition in Parliament and the necessity of preserving Caucus "Confidence" between elections, which distinguishes these two political systems, make the Leader's constant umbilical relationship to his caucus and its trust in the Leader especially important.

The heart of parliamentary democracy is the power of the members to give or deny their leaders their "confidence". As John Ralston Saul points out in his concise enchanting biography of Robert Baldwin, a father of responsible government

- "such a clear principle had not yet been established in Britain or anywhere else". Responsible government was forged in colonial Canada with "confidence" as its pivotal principle.

In the confines of caucus that meet in secret sessions, the ordinary member may speak freely and criticize Party positions and policies. The Leader, in turn, can advance his views, and how he expresses these views is regularly evaluated to gauge his knowledge and political skills. The Leader's comments in caucus have a far greater influence on members than the addresses to the public or Parliament.

The weekly National Caucus, a gathering composed only of members of both the Commons and the Senate holds the key to "confidence" - a paramount factor in our political system. The Leader must retain and renew "confidence" at each weekly meeting of the Party Caucus. Party unity depends on Caucus unity.

The Caucus meeting room vanes with status of Party in government or in opposition. For example, the high ceilinged Railway Committee Room, festooned with history, paintings and murals, lends an element of gravitas to each meeting of a large Caucus membership.

Mastery of the Caucus, on issues large and small, achieving and retaining the confidence of the Caucus, is the defining yet little known ingredient of political success and longevity. Pearson quit shortly after the accidental loss of a vote that shattered Caucus "confidence". Trudeau took his famed "walk in the snow" and suddenly announced his resignation as Leader when he felt he had lost Caucus "confidence". "Confidence" is the central, elusive, building block of our political system.

It is "confidence" that unites a party, and makes it powerful within and without.

By tradition, Caucus deliberations are kept confidential and secret. No written record is kept of its deliberations or conclusions. The rule of Caucus secrecy, like that of the Cabinet, is to allow free, open, and honest debate on the issues of the day, not ripped out of context to damage or enhance any advocate on a particular issue. A breach of secrecy in the Cabinet has its consequences as should have been the case with Caucus. The "right" to know what is decided and how issues were decided should, of necessity, have been more tightly proscribed. Of course, the national media, determined to get "news" and inflame and inflate Party division, attempts a weekly tussle to pry loose confidential Caucus information.

The National Liberal Caucus' weekly ritual, chaired by a member of the House, who is elected by secret ballot, convenes after meetings of the various Regional and Special Caucuses, to hear various reports. The House and Senate Leaders and the Whip report quickly on their responsibilities, followed by the Regional and other Chairs. Then the meeting is open for each member to give his "take" on the current public agenda, to promote issues of local concern, or housekeeping matters. Members seek to capture the Chair's attention to be recognized for several minutes to air and advocate his or her grievances and national or local concerns as each struts their political "smarts". Applause or negative reaction is heard immediately.

This review was written before the current Leader of the Liberal Party, Justin

Trudeau, eliminated Liberal Senators from the National Liberal Caucus. Humour, self-deprecating humour or clearly articulated passion on an issue vie for Caucus acceptance.

The Caucus is a dynamic platform for mutual preening. Members seek to attract the Leader's and colleagues' attention for preferment, while the Leader seeks to convince the Caucus of his competence as the Leader and his leadership qualities. Calls for the imperative of Caucus unity, especially on contentious or divisive issues, are always on the weekly agenda. Thus, the vortex of personal ambition and public policy is on weekly display in the confines of the Caucus. By tradition, the Leader as the final speaker and arbiter then summarizes the discussions and draws a consensus setting out the action plan for the week ahead, exhorting the Caucus to renewed dedication and commitment to the tasks at hand. The Leader uses the Caucus as a forum, almost a "focus" group, to pitch, practice and shape his public lines of advocacy. The Leader himself, or he designates a spokesperson if he chooses to, makes the public summary of Caucus' deliberations at the following "scrum". The best practice is to allow the elected Chair of the Caucus to address the media scrum awaiting tidbits after each Caucus meeting.

Leadership is on parade in these weekly meetings in words, demeanor, body language, dress, mannerisms, wit, and calls to action. Machinations of the Caucus members before, during and after Caucus in the parliamentary lobby are risible. Trudeau and Turner carefully refrained from manipulating the deliberations of Caucus by setting up sycophants to prepare their ground. Each allowed free discussion in Caucus and used their skills of advocacy to achieve coherence, enthusiasm, and team spirit if they could muster it, each week, not unlike a coach rallying his team at half time.

As a Caucus is a direct and candid exchange in the oral tradition, speaking notes or prepared statements are normally eschewed. Spontaneous reaction to individual Caucus concerns either in agreement or disagreement is spontaneously voiced by Members and then synthesized by the Leader. Whispered gossip, caustic critiques, and tart asides are parts of the normal fare.

Trudeau was skillful in startling original argumentation and analyses so as to weave together a Caucus consensus. Turner often seemed preoccupied, even episodic, at times ignoring hinted dissent and allowing unrest to fester. Both were plagued by Caucus "leaks" to the media, as was Mr. Pearson, by unnamed Members seeking to curry favour for themselves or their chosen colleagues, with the media, which always is anxious to exacerbate divisions within the Party.

Of course, performance in Parliament, especially the theatre of daily Question Period, like gladiators of old, demonstrated the public persona of nimble leadership again feeding the visceral instincts of the intently watching members of the Party in this relentless, demanding task of leadership.

To be fair, only anecdotal and biased views can be scoured to gain a fuller picture of Party life within the private precincts of Caucus and lobby rooms of Parliament unanswered questions

Turner was an avid policy "wonk", fascinated by political ideas. Before joining the Liberal Party, he was invited to attend, and actively participated in, the famed Kingston Conference. What would a Turner Prime Ministry have attempted? He was an early pre-political advocate of the abolition of the appointed Senate as being unrepresentative of the democratic will. The Turner-influenced 1988 Liberal Policy platform remained one unexplored avenue. Turner had distinct views on foreign policy, especially Canada's relationship with Commonwealth members, the United States, France and Germany where he maintained a network of political operatives. Could Turner's highly personalized style have made a difference on the international stage? Regretfully, the wider scope of Turner's thinking remains open and speculative.

Will the Liberal Party Survive and Thrive?

Litt begs the question: Will the Liberal Party survive to play a major role in the future of Canada? The answer is a resounding "Yes", provided that the Turner ethics of hard work, honesty, integrity, "grass roots" innovations, reformist ideas, commitment to principles are replayed in the Party and Parliament to once again chum the engines of the Liberal Party. What seems missing is the "politics of joy" that attracted so many young activists to the Liberal banner. As Litt says, perhaps John Turner's belief in the "Marquess of Queensberry Rules" applied to politics was outdated, but John Turner would not have it any other way. They formed a part of his basic convictions about the pursuit of politics - about the purpose of politics.

The Turner Legacy

In retrospect, Trudeau and Turner represented two vital strands of Liberalism, at times running together, at times colliding. It was the combination of these two resonating strands that kept the Liberal Party in power for the longest period in Canadian history .

Was John Turner, as said of Churchill who had a thirst for public office and power, determined to make history or is this too simplistic? The restless reach, at times even the frenzy, for reputation, celebrity, and renown abounds in all ambitious politicians. In the end, the still hidden keys of John Turner's persona, like those of most senior politicians, are mixed in the valorization of political life at the core of the Liberal Party. And, like all political parties, there resides a strange, largely unchartered, reservoir in each politician, self-aggrandizement of ambition, hopes, projections, redemption and escape. Hopes to make a difference, ambitions for personal preferment, Freudian projections, internal redemption, and, at times, even escape from the humdrum confines of private life. "Elusive," indeed.

John Turner, in his senior years, remains unbowed and ebullient about the future of the Liberal Party, the vital role of Parliament, encouraging youth into public service and optimistic about the future of Canada. In retrospect, despite all, he affirms that he was privileged to have played a role in the public life of the country. We shall not likely see that same unique public combination of intelligence, principles, energy, vivacity, drive and wholesome competitiveness come our way again. His life serves as a public primer in high public purpose, genuine reform, and principles characteristic of the classic Liberal. He remains in essence an "original" - an authentic Canadian. While institutional memory is a fading discipline, he and his special contributions to public service survive and will not be forgotten. Paul Litt is to be commended for his diligent pursuit of a scorchingly honest, balanced chronicle and portrait of the fascinating life and times of John Napier Turner.

For interested Liberals, let these two quotes suffice:

The less a man knows about the past and the present, the more insecure must prove to be his judgment of the future.
- Sigmund Freud, 1927

You cannot fight against the future.
Time is on our side.
William Ewart Gladstone, 1866

Index